THE COMFORT WOMEN HOAX

THE COMFORT WOMEN HOAX

A FAKE MEMOIR, NORTH KOREAN SPIES, AND HIT SQUADS IN THE ACADEMIC SWAMP

J. MARK RAMSEYER
&
JASON M. MORGAN

Encounter BOOKS
New York • London

First American edition published in 2023 by Encounter Books, an activity of Encounter for Culture and Education, Inc., a nonprofit, tax-exempt corporation.
Encounter Books website address: www.encounterbooks.com

Manufactured in the United States and printed on acid-free paper. The paper used in this publication meets the minimum requirements of ANSI/NISO Z39.48-1992 (R 1997) (*Permanence of Paper*).

FIRST AMERICAN EDITION

LIBRARY OF CONGRESS CATALOGING-IN-PUBLICATION DATA

Library of Congress Cataloging-in-Publication Data

Names: Ramseyer, J. Mark, 1954– author.
Morgan, Jason Michael, 1977– author.
Title: The Comfort Women Hoax: A Fake Memoir, North Korean Spies, and Hit Squads in the Academic Swamp / J. Mark Ramseyer & Jason M. Morgan.
Other titles: Fake memoir, North Korean spies, and hit squads in the academic swamp
Description: New York: Encounter Books, [2024]
Includes bibliographical references and index.
Identifiers: LCCN 2023046401 (print) | LCCN 2023046402 (ebook)
ISBN 9781641773454 (hardcover) | ISBN 9781641773461 (epub)
Subjects: LCSH: Comfort women—Korea—Historiography.
Comfort women—Japan—Historiography.
World War, 1939–1945—Women—Korea—Historiography.
Prostitution—Japan—History—20th century. | Ramseyer, J. Mark, 1954–
College teachers—United States. | Historians—United States—Biography.
Academic freedom—United States. | Education, Higher—Political aspects.
Classification: LCC D810.C698 R36 2024 (print) | LCC D810.C698 (ebook)
DDC 940.54/05082095—dc23/eng/20231005
LC record available at https://lccn.loc.gov/2023046401
LC ebook record available at https://lccn.loc.gov/2023046402

For my friends; you know who you are—you kept me sane.
—JMR

For my co-author, who bore it manfully,
and with charity and grace.
—JMM

"The glory which is built upon a lie soon becomes a most unpleasant incumbrance. [...] How easy it is to make people believe a lie, and how hard it is to undo that work again!"

—Mark Twain

CONTENTS

FOREWORD

Lew Seok-Choon
Retired Professor of Sociology, Yonsei University

I first came to know Professor Ramseyer through the "comfort women" controversy. On February 1, 2021, the Korean mass media were flooded with stories about a Harvard professor named Mark Ramseyer who published a paper alleging that the comfort women patronized by Japanese soldiers during the Second World War "were prostitutes, not sex slaves." Reports in the Korean media for the most part relied on an article in the *Sankei Shimbun*, a Japanese daily, which also reported that Professor Ramseyer's article would soon be published in the *International Review of Law and Economics*.

As an academic against whom criminal charges were brought and who was standing trial for having said almost the exact same thing during a university lecture, I immediately downloaded the article and read it on the spot. The article, titled "Contracting for Sex in the Pacific War," provided historical descriptions of the comfort women that largely dovetailed with my own understanding of the issue. However, the method of analysis was quite distinct from my own, and it was impressive.

The paper traced the rational choices that Japanese and Korean comfort women made under war conditions. By applying Oliver Williamson's "transaction cost economics" to the system of comfort women, the paper succinctly showed how licensed prostitution at "comfort stations" on the front lines of the Pacific War was typical of indentured servitude contracts that entailed high levels of risk but guaranteed high returns. For example, I learned that impoverished European immigrants signed similar contracts when they crossed the Atlantic to settle in the New World. I was familiar with Williamson's theory and taught it in courses on economic sociology, but it never occurred to me to apply it to the case of the comfort women.

In the meantime, the Korean media were busy viciously attacking Professor Ramseyer. They called him an apologist for Japanese imperialism, a "denialist" who dared to apply a contractual framework to women who (they said) were dragooned into sexual slavery. Using extreme feminist and nationalist rhetoric, the Korean media, especially on the left, accused Professor Ramseyer of being a worse racist than the neo-Nazis. They demanded the withdrawal or retraction of his paper.

Yet no matter how many times I read it, Professor Ramseyer's argument was unassailable. He had a clear analytical framework whose logic was flawless. To back up his findings, he made copious references to government and court documents, newspaper articles, and other primary as well as secondary sources. Far from being a "denialist," Professor Ramseyer was, if anything, a positivist. The only problem was that his findings, like my own, flew in the face of what Koreans were told to accept as facts.

During a lecture for the developmental sociology course that I was teaching at Yonsei University in 2019, I asked my students, "If you argue that President Syngman Rhee (in office: 1948–1960) and Park Chung-hee (in office: 1961–1979) were dictators who made no contributions to the modernization of the country as the leftists are wont to do, then when did the modernization of the Republic of Korea, a nation founded in 1948, actually start? If you agree that Korea is a developed nation, when exactly did modernization take place? Do you really believe that the Chosun dynasty, a decrepit monarchy that was on the verge of collapse by the mid-nineteenth century, laid the foundation for Korea's modernization a century later?"

I also asked, "Did thirty-five years of Japanese colonial rule (1910–1945) contribute nothing to Korea's modernization?" And, "Is it accurate to say that Japanese rule did nothing but exploit Korea's 'rice, land, labor, and women'?" I argued that the comfort women system was a form of wartime prostitution. For this statement, I was charged with the criminal offense of defaming former comfort women.

In the summer of 2022, I met two colleagues who also recognized the importance of Professor Ramseyer's work. They were Mr. Hwang Uiwon, CEO and chief editor of MediaWatch, and Dr. Lee Wooyoun, an independent scholar. Mr. Hwang recently won a civil suit against Yoon Mee-hyang, former head of the comfort women advocacy group called the Korean Council, and currently a member of the Korean National Assembly. Mr. Hwang had accused Yoon of being a North Korean sympathizer. Dr. Lee, for his part, is an economic historian who published papers arguing that there was no wage discrimination against Korean conscripted workers during the Japanese colonial era. For this, Dr. Lee has faced a severe backlash from the Korean media and the political Left.

The three of us agreed to translate several of Professor Ramseyer's papers on the comfort women into Korean and have them published in Korea. We selected five papers for a volume to be released in the summer of 2023:

1. "Indentured Prostitution in Imperial Japan: Credible Commitments in the Commercial Sex Industry," *Journal of Law, Economics, and Organization* 7, no. 1 (Spring 1991).
2. "Comfort Women and the Professors," The Harvard John M. Olin Discussion Paper No. 995 (2019).
3. "Contracting for Sex in the Pacific War," *International Review of Law and Economics* 65 (March 2021).
4. "Contracting for Sex in the Pacific War: A Response to My Critics," The Harvard John M. Olin Discussion Paper No. 1075 (2022).

5. Tetsuo Arima and J. Mark Ramseyer, "Comfort Women: the North Korean Connection," 2022.

We believe this volume will be a much-needed addition to the fledgling field of serious research on the topic of comfort women, a topic still dominated by ideologically motivated propaganda and hearsay.

Recently, two volumes on the topic of anti-Japanese sentiment in Korea, *Anti-Japan Tribalism* (2019) and *The Fight against Anti-Japan Tribalism* (2020), were published and became national bestsellers. Edited by Younghoon Rhee, a retired professor from Seoul National University and a respected economic historian, these two volumes have done much to expose the lies that underlie the vaunted anti-Japanese sentiment said to be deeply entrenched in the Korean psyche. We hope that Professor Ramseyer's work will further expose the lies that still undergird the anti-Japanese narrative so prevalent in Korea.

While putting the finishing touches on the translation of Professor Ramseyer's essays in March 2023, I received an email from him asking me to write a foreword for this book, which seeks to expose further the lies at the root of the comfort women issue. That Professors Ramseyer and Jason Morgan referred to "a communist hoax" showed that they clearly grasped the ideological motivation behind the issue. I gladly agreed to write the foreword.

The book vividly recounts the recrimination and discrimination that a tenured professor had to endure at Harvard University, a symbol of academic freedom and excellence. It also reveals the absurd nature of the job-market system in American colleges and describes how a young and intellectually honest scholar fell victim to it.

In September 2019, I delivered my last lecture before retiring from my alma mater, Yonsei University, where I had taught for thirty-three years. During the lecture, I argued that the modernization of Korea proceeded even during the Japanese colonial period. I suggested that the Japanese did not exploit the "rice, land, labor, and women," despite what the Korean history textbooks claimed. I showed that Japan traded, not looted, rice from Korea and that the infamous "land surveys" that nationalists and leftist historians claim were the main means by which the Japanese expropriated land from the Korean farmers were in fact undertaken to establish clear private ownership of land and to collect taxes. I also tried to show that Japanese companies paid conscripted Korean workers fair wages and that comfort women were professional workers in the wartime sex industry.

A heated discussion ensued. Feminist and leftist students, as well as those who advocate "political correctness," protested my views. In response to student queries, I made statements such as that the "comfort women [system] was a type of prostitution," that "the Korean Council is a pro–North Korean organization," and that "Korean Council members coached former comfort women to alter their testimonies."

My farewell lecture at my alma mater became the basis for my criminal prosecution. One of my students recorded and leaked the entire lecture to the left-wing media without prior consent. Thenceforth, I became the target of a relentless attack from the Left for being "pro-Japanese," or *chinil-pa*, a dirty word in Korean. In October 2020, a year after the lecture, I was charged with defamation, a criminal offense. Prosecutors argued that my alleged "false remarks" on comfort women, the Korean Council, and its leader Yoon Mee-hyang constituted a crime. To no one's surprise, all this transpired while Moon Jae-in, a left-wing president, was in office.

During the trial, I submitted countless records of communist lies, which are also detailed in this book. They include the fallacious stories of Yoshida Seiji that launched the controversy, the inaccuracies of the Kono Statement on the subject released by the Japanese government in 1993, Radhika Coomaraswamy's bogus United Nations report of 1996, records of the Korean Council and Yoon Mee-hyang's pro–North Korea activities, and irregularities associated with the Korean Council exposed during a conflict between Yoon, its former head, and Lee Yong-soo, a former comfort woman who had become the organization's most prominent public face.

In November 2022, two years after my indictment, the prosecution asked for an eighteen-month prison sentence. As of this writing (May 2023), my trial is ongoing, and the court has yet to render a verdict. At the most recent court hearing on March 22, 2023, the judge presiding over my case gave two reasons for having failed to render a verdict as of yet.

The first was that he was waiting for the Supreme Court's ruling on the case of Professor Park Yu-ha, a case that bears a striking resemblance to mine, because it too deals with the issue of academic freedom. The trial court had found Professor Park innocent. However, the intermediate court reversed and imposed a fine of 10,000 USD. The case has remained stuck in the Supreme Court for the past five years.

The second reason that the presiding judge gave for delaying a decision on my case was that the prosecution had so far failed to submit evidence to back up its claim that comfort women were forcefully abducted into sexual slavery. This is the evidence needed to refute my claim that the comfort women system was part of the wartime sex industry.

From what I understand, in a modern court of law, the defendant is to be acquitted if the prosecution fails to prove guilt beyond a reasonable doubt. It is astonishing that I have to wait while the prosecution finds critical evidence to convict me. I cannot help but think that Korea's legal system is dysfunctional and has failed me. Despite its glittering façade, Korea still seems feudal in many respects.

This book, therefore, is a godsend for me. So are Hwang Uiwon, Lee Wooyoun, Younghoon Rhee, and Park Yu-ha. It is not we who are making false claims; it is those who accuse us of doing so. The bizarre and toxic mixture of communism, nationalism, and feminism is suppressing the truth while perpetuating the myth of the "forced abduction" of comfort women. We are fighting for academic freedom against the communist hoax. Though some of us live and work oceans apart, we all believe that the truth will set us free.

Professor Nishioka Tsutomu in Japan, also fighting on the front lines of the struggle against communism and leftist hegemony, is likewise a crucial ally. So is the historian Hata Ikuhiko, whom I have yet to meet in person but know to be a scholar of integrity. Finally, I would like to recognize Kenji Yoshida, who helped translate this foreword. I look forward to the day that the Korea-U.S. and U.S.-Japan alliances tear down the wall of falsehood and historical distortion perpetuated by the leftist-feminist-nationalist alliance that has done so much to poison academic freedom in Korea and damage her relations with friends and neighbors.

May 17, 2023

AUTHORS' NOTE

In writing this book, both of us received support and advice from a wide variety of extraordinarily generous and long-suffering friends. You know who you are: thank you, thank you, thank you.

Parts of this book appeared earlier as J. Mark Ramseyer, "Contracting for Sex in the Pacific War," *International Review of Law and Economics* 65 (March 2021) ©Elsevier 2021; J. Mark Ramseyer, "Contracting for Sex in the Pacific War: A Response to My Critics," Harvard John M. Olin DP 1075, January 2022, SSRN WP 4000145; or as Tetsuo Arima & J. Mark Ramseyer, "Comfort Women: The North Korean Connection," August 2022, SSRN WP 4185081. We use the last of these with the gracious and generous permission of Professor Arima.

In both Japanese and Korean, a person's family name comes first and is followed by his or her given name. We follow this convention, except where other publications reverse the order or where the individuals themselves request otherwise, in which case we follow the original byline or request.

INTRODUCTION

If he tries to publish that comfort women article, he'll be sorry.

Ramseyer had been warned. A friend told him that someone on the Harvard campus (he never learned who it was) had vowed that Ramseyer would regret publishing his article on the subject. Some years earlier, Morgan had harbored his own apprehension about wading into the same waters. He suspected that his graduate adviser would not take kindly to his criticism of a joint statement about the comfort women that he knew she supported. Both of us expected to face opposition for expressing our views, but neither of us had any clue how virulent the attacks would be.

This is a book about the obscure historical dispute that upended both of our lives. It is also a book about our very contemporary world—about the hyperpartisan and brutally intolerant politics of the South Korean Left and of humanities departments in Western universities. Both of these groups have enshrined as fact a bizarre claim that literally began with a hoax—a fake memoir—and with the activities of North Korean spies in the South. Morgan approached the controversy from the discipline of history, and Ramseyer from law, but we reached the same conclusion: the claim was sheer fiction. For explaining why it was fiction, both of us found ourselves fending off academic hit squads that hurled endless accusations of "racism," "denialism," and "fraud," while they attempted to destroy our careers.

The comfort women were prostitutes who worked at the brothels near Japanese military bases during the Greater East Asian War. The war had begun with Japan's offensives on the Asian continent in 1931, and continued through August 1945.

The prostitutes came from several countries, but we focused on those from Japan and Korea, because this is where the contemporary dispute has been fiercest. Our transgression was to view the comfort women regime as a market phenomenon, and to treat comfort women history as empirically and archivally intelligible—not as an epiphenomenon of the evergreen identity politics that defaults to a formula of oppressors and victims. In the latter framing, the comfort women were sex slaves who had been forcibly conscripted by the Japanese military. But that is not what the documentary evidence told us.

The documentary evidence abounds, and points to one conclusion: prostitution was (and is, the world over) a job, one that some destitute women sometimes choose to contract to do for the money. Prostitution was a miserable job, and all the more miserable when the location was next to a godforsaken military outpost in a hostile foreign country. The Japanese military did some appalling things during the war, but it did not programmatically and forcibly conscript—or dragoon, if you will—either Korean or Japanese women into providing sex. Some of the comfort women had been sold into this prostitution by abusive parents. Some had been defrauded by dishonest private recruiters. But many—probably most—were desperately poor women who deliberately chose to sell sex for the money. They worked in a wretched job, but they were not "sex slaves." They were not "gang-raped." They were not conscripted into the job at bayonet-point. Instead, they chose prostitution as (in their minds) the least bad option available to them. We deceive ourselves and insult impoverished women if we deny that they could have made such a decision for themselves.

Both of us quickly discovered that this simple market-based explanation is not the account favored either by the left half of the electorate in South Korea or by humanities departments in the West. Understand that South Korea is a politically polarized society in which "left" has a specific and peculiar meaning, one that bears heavily on how this subject is viewed (more on this in Chapter 6). Intellectuals everywhere tend to view markets skeptically, of course, and we sometimes wonder whether professors in modern humanities departments even realize that markets exist. We knew all this in the abstract. But neither of us was prepared for the intensity of the hatred that hit us.

For Morgan, it happened in 2015 when he criticized a petition coordinated by American historians (specifically, Andrew Gordon, Jordan Sand, and Alexis Dudden) against the Japanese government for what the petitioners described as infringements of academic freedom. McGraw-Hill had published a world history textbook that contained wild historical inaccuracies about the comfort women; a low-ranking member of the Japanese consulate in Honolulu had met in private with one of the textbook authors to ask about his sources; academics erupted in fury, not at the fake history, but that the Japanese government had dared to ask a question.

For Ramseyer, it happened in early 2021 when Western historians (including the same Gordon and Dudden) and scholars with ethnic ties to South Korea (led by Michael Chwe and Jeannie Suk-Gersen) discovered a very short article—under eight pages—he had written about the comfort women and published in the *International Review of Law and Economics* (IRLE). Neither Chwe nor Suk-Gersen had shown any inclination to study Korean history before. But Suk-Gersen, as well as Dudden, did seem to enjoy talking about the comfort women, in English, on Korean TV news shows.

To both of us, the backlash against us seemed positively fanatical—but not just because we were the targets. Before we realized what had happened, we each found ourselves in the middle of an Amish *meidung*, a shunning, rebadged for the modern university as a "cancellation."

"I shouldn't have said that," remarked Hagrid to Harry and his friends. "I should not have said that." And so with us. In the circumstances, we took our humor where we could find it, even when it came from books that Ramseyer had read with his children. Apparently, the two of us had behaved like Hagrid. We should not have said what we did.

Both the South Korean Left and the Western humanities departments treat the comfort women as a morality play about imperialism and the hatred of women that professors like to call "misogyny." For both groups, the women embody what they posit to be the brutal legacy of the Imperial Japanese Army and the universal phenomenon of wartime violence against women. According to this morality play, some of the women were indeed defrauded by dishonest recruiters—but recruiters working as agents of the Japanese military. Some were sold by their fathers—but at the behest of the military. The rest, goes the story, had been kidnapped by the Japanese military at bayonet-point (never mind that very few women actually claimed to have been kidnapped). According to the morality play, none of the women had chosen the job voluntarily. All had been "sex slaves," and none were lying about it. The fact that the women themselves have told dramatically different stories about their lives, including their time as comfort women, does not intrude on the morality play. The complexity of lived history is banished in favor of the simplicity of foreordained conclusions.

The imperative to "believe all women" shapes the comfort women narrative for both the South Korean Left and the Western humanities departments. Mind you: we would avoid this issue if we could. We are not fools. We know the university landscape. Yet many people attacked us precisely because we did not simply take the comfort women at their word. "The oral status of [the] narrative" told by the comfort women ("narrative" being a favored word in these circles) was "the very element that makes it radically transnational and feminist," wrote one enthusiastic scholar.[1] To even consider checking the women's accounts, another had declared, would amount "to the trivialization of the women's testimony."[2]

In the midst of the ostracism campaign against us, the believe-all-women mandate struck us as a loyalty oath out of the 1950s: "Are you now or have you ever been a member of a group that asserted that some women might sometimes—however rarely—lie about sex?" We answered "yes." Of course people lie. Men lie and women lie. They lie about money, they lie about violence, they lie about sex, and they do all sorts of other unsavory things besides. It runs in the species. Study history or law honestly, and one faces these unfortunate truths early and often. We suspect that those who attacked us did so precisely because they worried that the most visible of the comfort women were lying. People rarely respond ferociously to someone who challenges their "firmly held beliefs," wrote the psychologist Christopher Chabris. They respond ferociously when challenged about "beliefs they wish were true but suspect at some level to be false."[3] Indeed, our attackers had reason to be defensive.

For there is more truth to tell. Much more. The controversy over the comfort women did not begin in Korea or elsewhere in mainland Asia, and it did not begin in the 1930s or 1940s. It began in 1983, when an obscure Japanese communist (he had run for office on a communist ticket) named Yoshida Seiji published a memoir in which he said he had led an army posse to Korea to kidnap young women at bayonet-point. The *Asahi Shimbun* daily newspaper in Japan played up his story to enormous fanfare. Yoshida published a Korean translation of his book in 1989, and the dispute exploded.

In 1991, several Korean women claiming to have been comfort women filed lawsuits against Japan. The Japanese and South Korean governments had already settled all claims relating to the war in 1965. The agreement covered any and all Korean claims against Japan—whether private or public, specified or unspecified—and

Japan paid massive reparations. The women sued anyway. These first claims led to more, and within a few years the lawsuits gave rise to a powerful social movement.

The South Korean government was nearly as blindsided by the movement as was the government of Japan. Almost immediately, a woman with close North Korean ties (her husband served prison time for passing documents to a North Korean spy) took control of this movement. Named Yoon Mee-hyang, she manipulated the comfort women themselves by controlling the nursing homes in which many of them lived. A few of the comfort women did tell variations on the sex-slave story that Yoon wanted; Lee Yong-soo alone provided twenty-something versions. They seem to have run through several very different stories before finding one that they and Yoon all liked. Those comfort women who dared to deviate from her preferred "narrative" Yoon punished ruthlessly. The comfort women played Yoon's game, or they stayed quiet. Most stayed quiet.

Under pressure from South Korea, the Japanese government officially apologized for the comfort women regime in the Kono Statement of 1993. Aside from the Yoshida memoir and the uncorroborated testimonies of several women, the Japanese government had found no evidence that its military had dragooned anyone in Korea into sex work. Neither had anyone else. The archival records amply contradicted the "sex slave" storyline. Nonetheless, the negotiators for the South Korean government, goaded by domestic extremists, demanded that Japan "admit" to dragooning Korean women. They assured their Japanese peers that they had no plans to demand more money, and the Japanese government responded by agreeing to state that its military had been involved in conscripting comfort women. The Japanese negotiators suspected it was not true—and maybe their Korean counterparts did too—but issuing the statement seemed politically expedient at the time. Most lies seem expedient at the time. The bill comes due later. The lie about the comfort women is one that the Japanese government has rued ever since.

A famously feral (yes, Yossarian declared death to all modifiers, but it describes the report so perfectly) United Nations attack on Japan over the issue followed in 1996. The rapporteur based it heavily on the Yoshida memoir and the testimonies of a small number of comfort women. "Testimonies" is putting it nicely, though. The best known of the accounts (one that Michael Chwe celebrated in his campaign against Ramseyer) is a hearsay report that activists who traveled to North Korea brought back for the rapporteur.

But no number of "testimonies" will ever amount to reality or create history. Yes, we understand that people everywhere bring their own perspectives to their accounts of the past, and that no account is whole. Trust us, we have seen *Rashomon*. But however many caveats one wishes to add, history is still an account of past reality, and one cannot make up reality retroactively. Yet make up history is precisely what Yoshida tried to do.

Scholars continued to search the archives and continued to find no evidence of forcible conscription. Before his death in 2000, Yoshida acknowledged that he had invented the whole story about dragooning women. It was a simple hoax, and by the late 1990s serious scholars in both Japan and South Korea had confirmed that it was a hoax. Then, in 2014, the *Asahi* newspaper finally acknowledged that it had fallen for a hoax and retracted its entire portfolio of Yoshida-based articles.

That was a watershed year. In 2014, at long last, the elaborate "sex slave" edifice collapsed. Other than a few on the activist fringe, virtually no Japanese scholars—left or right—anymore think the Japanese military conscripted Korean women into sex work. Many serious scholars in Korea also reject that claim. Unfortunately for scholarship, however, the South Korean government continues to bring criminal charges against professors who contest the officially favored conscripted-at-bayonet-point account. At least one such scholar has already served prison time.

Let us be clear: professors in South Korea face potential prison time for deviating from the "sex slave" narrative invented by Yoshida, embroidered by Yoon, and pushed relentlessly by Gordon, Dudden, Suk-Gersen, Chwe and so many others in Western humanities departments and among the South Korean Left. Professor Lew Seok-Choon, author of the foreword to this book, was on trial for precisely this speech crime as this book went to press. The Yoshida narrative presents the comfort women as abductees, chattel of the Japanese military. The story is demonstrably untrue, and South Korean scholars continue to defy it. One would never know it from reading the strident Korean American academics in the West, but prominent South Korean scholars like Professor Lew increasingly publish articles and books and give lectures that explicitly deny the government-enforced sex-slave account. They pay a heavy price for doing so, and their Korean American peers like Chwe and Suk-Gersen would apparently prefer to pretend that they did not even exist. The Korean scholars persist. They do it not for money, or promotions, or academic honors—for there is no money in honesty on this topic, no promotions or honors to be had. Only prison time. The scholars do it for simple reasons of conscience and professional integrity.

Only in the West, and only in the English-language literature, do writers present anything like a consensus that the Japanese military dragooned Korean women at bayonet-point into sexual slavery. Gordon wrote a general Japanese history textbook in which he completely missed the unraveling of the Yoshida hoax. In 2014—two decades after historians in Japan had dismissed Yoshida as a fraud—Gordon was still parroting the Yoshida tale in his textbook. (One of our critics called a fellow scholar a "useful idiot" when he expressed concerns about academic freedom in the midst of the attacks on us.[4] If only he knew.)

The Law of Holes comes to mind: when you find yourself in one, quit digging. Gordon dug in hard. In 2015, he teamed up with Dudden and Jordan Sand to attack Japanese historians and the Japanese government for trying to set the history straight in response to another textbook published that year. Morgan, a graduate student at the time, pointed out what the three were doing—namely, ignoring documentary history about the comfort women in favor of the politically correct grandstanding that brings professional gain in the American academy. He soon found himself canceled. In 2021, Ramseyer tried to move beyond the hoax, and Gordon set his former students upon him. History repeated itself—moving yet again from tragedy to farce, as Marx famously put it.

Such is the story we tell. We describe the comfort station system. We place the documented experiences of the comfort women themselves front and center. We recount the history of the later dispute and its origins in Yoshida's elaborate hoax. We detail the way that Yoon Mee-hyang and the rest of the North Korean network within the South exploited the hoax to the North's advantage. And we catalog the brutality—and the professional malpractice—by which Western scholars enforce that hoax.

We stress two caveats. First: we make no normative judgments about the arrangements involved. We are not here either to condemn or to justify the comfort women regime. We each have our beliefs about the propriety of prostitution, but this book does not concern those beliefs. Our project is descriptive, and only—only—descriptive: we explain what the comfort women system was, how it operated, and why it took the shape it did. We cannot stress this strongly enough: *we make no normative claims about prostitution.*

Second: we discuss only the comfort women from Japan and Korea. At the time, Korea was part of Japan, and Koreans were Japanese citizens. In some respects—perhaps in many respects—they were second-class citizens, but we explicitly table that question for another forum. Soldiers tend to treat women from their own country differently from foreign women in the war zone. There is evidence suggesting that some women from other countries experienced harsher treatment than did those from Japan or Korea. In this book, we focus only on Japanese citizens—women from either the Japanese islands or the Korean peninsula.

We begin by describing what happened to each of us when we stepped into this minefield (Chapter 1). They are separate stories. We were not acquainted when Morgan's own story began, but eventually we found each other through our common interests. Morgan works in modern history, particularly as it relates to legal scholarship. Ramseyer sometimes works in modern legal history. He noticed the ostracism that Morgan faced for contesting the orthodox account of the comfort women and admired him for risking his career to challenge the attack by Gordon, Dudden, and Sand against the Japanese government in 2015. Morgan had read some of Ramseyer's legal history. He liked it. We met over dinner in Tokyo in 2019, and kept in touch. When Ramseyer published his short article about the comfort women in late 2020, Morgan read it and was relieved to find someone finally telling the truth to the Anglophone audience.

And then, it all blew up. The South Korean press and American scholars in the humanities noticed Ramseyer's article on the subject, and marched into his life. It is not an easy day to forget. Think Richard Blaine's response to Ilsa: "the Germans wore gray, you wore blue." Or simply think Alexander's terrible, horrible, no good, very bad day. From that day forward and for months on end, gallows humor was usually all that Ramseyer could marshal. Almost immediately, he found himself swamped with hate mail. He faced attacks on his work from all quarters. There were petitions to force the journal to retract his article and for Harvard to fire him. One publisher canceled a manuscript that had been accepted and was in press. One journal dropped him from its editorial board. Thousands of people (in one case, thirty thousand) signed petitions or wrote letters to retract his article and punish him. Those thousands included some of the most prominent scholars on the globe—a dozen journal editors and three Nobel laureates. But the pain actually came from seeing the signatures of ordinary men and women he had thought were his friends.

When Morgan spoke out against the Gordon-Dudden-Sand attack on the Japanese government in 2015, he was still a graduate student. He found himself blacklisted by his dissertation advisers, the women who had promised to mentor him and guide him into the profession. He was bizarrely (and falsely, rest assured) accused of being an agent of the Japanese government, reprimanded by the Fulbright director in Japan, censored by his home department, and branded—like Ramseyer—a "racist" and "denialist."

Ramseyer was near the end of his career, Morgan at the beginning. People we knew—had known for years, had trusted, had considered our friends—appeared intent on destroying our careers. Others were blithely endorsing their plans, even (it seemed) wishing them well. And us? We were learning more about many of the people in our lives than we wanted to know, but Mephistopheles insisted on showing us still more. We would have preferred never to see what he showed us. Desperately, we did not want to know this. Some of the "best lack all conviction," we noticed (channeling Yeats), "while the worst are full of passionate intensity."

After telling our own stories, we turn to the history of the comfort station regime itself (Chapter 2). We describe how it simply represented the overseas extension of the licensed prostitution regime in prewar Japan and Korea. We explain how the dragooning myth began with the fraudulent Japanese memoir by Yoshida Seiji and became uncontestable "history" through the efforts of the North Korean network in South Korea (Chapters 3 through 5). We place the controversy within the hyperpartisan climate of South Korean politics and examine the activities of the North Korean–allied Korean Council, the group run by Yoon Mee-hyang that has ruthlessly manipulated the dispute and controlled the surviving comfort women (Chapter 6). We then return to our own experiences and their place within the world of the modern Western university (Chapters 7 and 8).

We did not know each other when Morgan was ostracized. By the time Ramseyer's show trial began in early 2021, we knew each other fairly well. We have now spent some two and a half years battling what feel like hit squads. But we are still standing, and for that reason we see our account as a story of hope. The ostracism that is "cancellation" is hell, but a hell that is sometimes survivable. We found inspiration in the tenacity of our subjects themselves—women who dealt with more difficult circumstances and survived. Sometimes, with enough determination and an enormous supply of luck, bad things can be overcome. Not always, but sometimes. As Winston Churchill put it, "if you're going through hell, keep going."

This book is both our story and the story of the comfort women. The comfort women deserve our sympathy, but they deserve much more: they deserve our respect. They deserve our respect for choosing a course through challenging circumstances. It is not a choice that many (if any) of us would make, but none of us face the challenges they did. It is not even the choice that many other destitute Korean and Japanese women made in the first half of the twentieth century. Many Korean and Japanese women came of age within the same economic constraints, but few of them chose to become prostitutes.

The women featured here are those who assessed their economic circumstances, weighed their options, gauged the costs and benefits, and did choose to become prostitutes. The "official narrative" would rob them of that past, and of the agency they exercised. We become who we are through our choices, wrote Sartre. To rob these women of the choices they made is to rob them of their humanity and of the lives they ever-so-painfully carved out for themselves. In offering comfort women sympathy rooted in a lie, their comfortably ensconced, self-appointed guardians—whether on the South Korean Left or in Western universities, whether Nobel laureates or postdocs—consign them to a life that is itself a living lie.

Park Yu-ha, a literature scholar who like Professor Lew is under criminal prosecution for flouting the sex-slave orthodoxy enforced by the South Korean government (see Chapter 5), put it best: high-gloss professors may use "gender theory" to "refine their critique," but through it all they merely project onto the comfort women the story they wanted to hear along. They pretend to give voice to colonial victims—the people they call "subalterns." But while purporting to "demand 'justice,'" they silence the very women they claim to support, and "create the 'subaltern who cannot speak.'"[5] Toward their own narrowly partisan and ideological ends, modern professors steal from the comfort women the very intelligence, courage, and resourcefulness that they brought to their lives.

The comfort women: this is their story more than ours.

CHAPTER 1

THE ANATOMY OF A CANCELING

In late 2020, I published "Contracting for Sex in the Pacific War," an article about the economic logic to the comfort women contracts, in the *International Review of Law and Economics* (IRLE).[1] The "comfort women" were the prostitutes—many of them from the Korean peninsula, which was then part of Japan—who worked at the brothels next to Japanese bases during the Second World War. An economics blog called *Marginal Revolution* gave my article a nice notice. Otherwise, it attracted no real attention. It was, as a friend in Japan would later put it, "the kind of article that only six specialists and your mother would read." That sounded right. Most of my articles are like that.

HOW IT STARTED FOR RAMSEYER

In late January 2021, another friend, Fukui Yoshitaka of Aoyama Gakuin University in Tokyo, summarized "Contracting for Sex in the Pacific War" for the *Sankei Shimbun* daily newspaper. The summary appeared on the newspaper's website on Thursday, January 28, and in the hard copy on Sunday.

I woke up on Monday, February 1, and checked my email. The hate mail had started. The Korean media had picked up the story about my article from the Japanese newspaper. I remember teaching my corporate law class over Zoom that day, and students wrote to complain afterward about the pinging sound from my computer every time an email came in. The pings were continuous for the entire two-hour session. By the end of the day, I had received seventy-seven pieces of hate mail, most of them obscene and virulently anti-Japanese. Every day for the next two months, I would receive more hate messages, often dozens in a day.

The hate mail came primarily from people with Korean family names. Given that the obscenity was in perfectly idiomatic English, the writers were probably either Korean students at American universities or second-generation Korean Americans. A nontrivial number of the emails included death threats. I notified the police of Harvard and of Lexington, where I live. A friendly twenty-something traced a couple of the threats back to the sender. In both cases, it was a young Korean American male located in the United States, most likely a college student.

Given all this hate mail, I checked my article on the IRLE website and noticed that the publisher (Elsevier) posts the number of times an article has been tweeted. My article had been tweeted 1,200 times. No one tweets articles by Ramseyer. No one.

I did not even know how to find a tweet. The friendly twenty-something helped me open a Twitter account and showed me how to do Twitter searches. I discovered that a group of American-educated scholars of Japan (mostly Japanese history) had read about the article in the Korean media (Korean newspapers often have English-language websites) and were livid. Hannah Shepherd, an assistant professor of Japanese history at Yale, seems to have been one of the first to respond to the article. Early Monday morning, she tweeted, "I don't really know where to start with this. A Mitsubishi endowed Professor of Law at Harvard is arguing that comfort women were all prostitutes." An hour later, she added: "We might want to ignore the article above, but given the front page reporting on it in Korea, which includes his institution in every report, I'm not sure we can, or should."[2] Amy Stanley (Northwestern), David Ambaras (North Carolina State), and Chelsea Szendi Schieder (Aoyama Gakuin in Tokyo) promptly chimed in. This early group tweeted back and forth all day.

Legions more joined the chorus. "Holy shit. I'm speechless," wrote Daniel Martin, a film studies professor at the Korea Advanced Institute of Science and Technology.[3] "The Sankei piece is horrific," exclaimed Mark Ravina, a tenured historian at the University of Texas, Austin.[4] Paul Kreitman, assistant professor at Columbia, described my article as a "batshit misogynistic commie-bashing screed[]."[5] (*Commie-bashing*?) Nick Kapur, associate professor at Rutgers, labeled me "a professional troll."[6] I had to Google "troll" to find out what he meant, but by May, Kapur would post at least seventeen Twitter notes about my academic perfidy. Jeremy Yellen, associate professor at the Chinese University of Hong Kong, added that I had "been trolling this issue for quite a while."[7] Gina Anne Tam, assistant professor of history at Trinity University in San Antonio, tweeted: "I was going to post some snarky version of wtffffff but I'm actually just too nauseated to mock this garbage."[8]

One writer wondered if I denied the Holocaust too.[9] Ambaras assured his Twitter followers that I "was like this even before the onset of white male privilege anxiety."[10] Paula Curtis, a UCLA post-doc with the Twitter identification of "Dr. Paula R. Curtis," swapped tweets about my dreaded article. A few days later, Maren Ehlers, assistant professor at the University of North Carolina, described my article as "an intentionally misleading provocation and flagrant violation of research ethics."[11]

By Tuesday, the tweeting scholars had convinced each other to organize a retraction campaign. In fact, Stanley and Shepherd had already sent their own individual retraction demands to the IRLE by the end of Monday. Shepherd proudly posted her letter to Twitter for others to use as a model. "All Ramseyer's article achieves," she asserted on the very day she noticed my article, "is the reiteration in an academic journal of talking points from the echo chambers of Japan's far right denialists...."[12]

The tweeting scholars seemed to be running a carnival. "Hey now that I've seen at least 5 women stating that they have already sent letters to the editor about that terrible JMR [my initials] piece (and most of them shared them publicly)," Curtis wondered, "how many of the male scholars have written?"[13] Declared Stanley (later in the month): "I am setting a personal record in the category of 'outraged letters.'" It was all, she explained, part of her "feminist activism."[14]

The IRLE editors wrote to me: "Boy, Mark —These people really hate you. I think we've gotten about 50 emails today." The editors asked several scholars (mostly Western scholars of Japanese history) to write responses to my article. They planned to organize a symposium. They would publish the responses and give me a chance to respond in turn.

The group invited to contribute responses caucused among each other. They harassed some of the people I had thanked in my first footnote. Rather than respond to the IRLE, however, they decided to demand that the article be retracted. And rather than publish their attacks in a forum where I would be able to respond, they decided to use the *Asia-Pacific Journal: Japan Focus* (APJJF), a (frankly) hard-left internet journal on Japanese studies—it calls itself "critical Japanese studies"—funded at least in part by Harvard's Japanese studies program, the Reischauer Institute. The journal is nominally peer-reviewed, but only nominally. When it decided to dedicate an issue to attacks on my eight-page article, the responses seemed to appear in the journal within a week or two of the time the authors first posted those responses elsewhere—suggesting a perfunctory review process at best.

Gordon

Among the senior professoriate, the attack arguably began at Harvard. And among the senior professors, it was apparently Andrew Gordon who first endorsed the crusade against me. Gordon is a modestly productive senior professor of Japanese history at Harvard. Very much an old-school labor historian, he has written several books on Japanese unions. His most recent book was a history of sewing machines in Japan. He and I have served together on the executive committee of the Reischauer Institute for over two decades. Relevant here, he was on the PhD committee of Amy Stanley and was the PhD adviser to Hannah Shepherd, Nick Kapur, Jeremy Yellen, and Hiromu Nagahara, an MIT associate professor who would also join the attacks. Stanley, Shepherd, Yellen, and Kapur were already caucusing on Twitter and harassing the IRLE editors. Within a week, Gordon posted his attack to the public.[15] The signal was obvious to the junior scholars: their professor had blessed their crusade.

Gordon wrote his attack together with Carter Eckert, a Harvard historian of Korea. They demanded that the journal retract my article. (We discuss their document at length in Chapter 5.) They sent the demand on February 7—the date is important. Gordon and Eckert accused me of violating the most basic "standard of academic integrity." That standard, they wrote, would "require that Ramseyer state in his article that he does not have access to actual contracts or sample contracts concluded with Korean women in Korea, acknowledge how few third-party statements he has seen about contracts, and note the limits to what one can learn from those references."

Gordon and Eckert's attack drew enormous attention. In part, it was the simple optics: senior Harvard professors trash longtime Harvard colleague. In part, it was the quotability of their claim: Ramseyer has no contracts. Over and over, month after month, critics, journalists, and activist groups quoted Gordon and Eckert's Ramseyer-has-no-contracts line.

In fact, I never claimed to have the actual contracts. To my knowledge, none have survived. The contracts were private documents between the brothels and the women. Neither were likely to have carried the paperwork home when they straggled back to Korea and Japan. Reporters around the world routinely cover conflicts and photograph the people fleeing attacks. How many photographs are there of fleeing people carrying file cabinets on their backs? When I challenged Gordon on the point, he quickly admitted (in private) that the contracts had once existed. I presume that he and Eckert knew this when they publicly accused me of having no actual contracts.

In writing my article, I relied on extensive documentation of the contracts in secondary and tertiary sources. The documentary evidence about the contracts is massive, and we detail it in the appendix to this book. Notwithstanding the enormous amount of material about the contracts, Gordon and Eckert apparently told my law-school colleague Jeannie Suk-Gersen (we discuss the *New Yorker* article that she wrote later in this chapter and in Chapter 5) that among my sources "there were no contracts involving Korean women at wartime comfort stations cited, nor secondary sources detailing those contracts, nor even any third-party accounts that confirm the relevant terms."[16]

Given the material in our appendix, Suk-Gersen's statement is clearly untrue. Whether Gordon or Eckert made an untrue statement to Suk-Gersen, or she falsely attributed the untrue statement to them, we do not know, and perhaps it does not matter to anyone else. Gordon may have made a similar claim to Stanley, though obviously we are not privy to this conversation either. On February 7, Stanley excitedly posted, "Historians have been going through [Ramseyer's article], and far as we can tell, they do not exist." Then, for emphasis: "you can't analyze contracts that do not exist."[17]

By February 15, however, Stanley seemed to have realized that her earlier claims were wrong. When asked "is there even any evidence such contracts ever existed?" she replied, "I think they did probably exist in some cases (not for all women in the system), bc there is indirect evidence."[18] Indeed, there certainly is indirect evidence, and it probably applies to all Japanese and Korean women in the comfort station system (for reasons we explain in the chapters that follow). For information about the contracts, we rely on many sources covering a lot of historical ground.

In any cancellation, Hanlon's razor is always a good place to start: never attribute to malice that which is explicable through stupidity—or, one could add, incompetence. Fairly obviously, Gordon does not know the field. To our knowledge, he has written about the comfort women only once, in a standard text on modern Japanese history (discussed in Chapter 5). For his first three editions he relied on two English-language sources,[19] one of which was based on the fraudulent Japanese memoir published by Yoshida Seiji in 1983.[20] Japanese scholars had already determined that the memoir was a hoax by the mid-1990s. Gordon was still relying on it in 2014.

A more troubling inference arises from the timing of the Gordon-Eckert attack. My article first attracted public attention outside Japan on Monday, February 1. Gordon sent me his and Eckert's completed retraction demand on Sunday, February 7. During this period, all Harvard libraries were closed because of Covid. More to the point, the Harvard copies of my source material—indeed, virtually all of Harvard's Japanese-language materials about the comfort women—were piled on the floor of my Harvard office. Yet this was the week during which Gordon claimed to have examined the sources on which I relied, and to have determined that there were no "secondary sources detailing those contracts, nor even any third-party accounts that confirm the relevant terms."

The Quintet

A couple of weeks after Gordon and Eckert posted their attack, five U.S.-educated historians of Japan announced that they had completed a cite check on my eight-page article. It was more than thirty pages long, and tendentious indeed. (We discuss the document more fully in Chapter 5.) The authors were Amy Stanley, senior historian at Northwestern; David Ambaras, senior historian at North Carolina State; Sayaka Chatani, assistant professor of history at the National University of Singapore; Chelsea Szendi Schieder, historian at Aoyama Gakuin in Tokyo; and Hannah Shepherd, assistant professor of history at Yale.[21] None of the five brought any background in comfort women history. Chatani actually admits this on Twitter—in Japanese.[22]

But they were having "fun." One of the oddest things about this group of five is how candidly they discussed everything on Twitter. They seemed oblivious to the possibility that anyone other than their friends would ever read what they posted. "I did not think—when I decided to be a historian of early modern Japan—that it would be so thrilling and high-stakes and full of heart-pounding adrenaline and panic," wrote Stanley in February 2021.[23] Less than two weeks later: "I always thought joining a woke cancel mob would be easy and fun. I didn't realize it would involve so much intense reading and analysis of historical sources...."[24]

Stanley would later insist that this was all in jest, but at the time neither she nor her friends took the "woke cancel mob" post as a joke. Ethan Mark, a University of Leiden historian, responded: "Yes, it's hard work—all the more so because there is so much pushback—but this is precisely why it's so important. Thank you so much for stepping up."[25] Replied Stanley, "Likewise!"[26] When Mark Ravina, a University of Texas historian, tweeted out, "Y'all are officially academic assassins," Stanley returned a smiley face wearing dark glasses.[27]

Reader, do pause for a moment and imagine that you were a law student: this is why you will want to stop your client from ever taking the stand. Stanley has long since deleted those comments from her Twitter feed, along with virtually everything else she posted in 2021–2022. Several of her collaborators have deleted most of their tweets as well. But law student or no, you should also realize that destroying evidence is never a great idea. Rest assured, the tweets are available for all to see on the Wayback Machine, and in any case we saved screenshots.

Whether producing their collective document was "easy and fun" or "hard work," the five triumphantly declared that my article "transgress[es] standards of scholarly integrity" and must never appear in print. The Reischauer Institute posted both the Stanley-Shepherd group's attack and the Gordon-Eckert attack on its website, and kept them there for about six months. Over the course of 2021–2022, Gordon would host Harvard lectures by both Chatani and his former student Stanley. In late 2022, the Institute would invite Stanley as the distinguished speaker for their annual dinner.

For the Quintet, this coordinated attack against me has formed part of a wider campaign to block public access to any English-language information on the subject that contests their favored account. In November 2021, for example, the five harassed the editors of *The Diplomat*, a Tokyo-based journal of Asian politics, into retracting an article by Lee Wooyoun, a prominent Korean economist (which we discuss more fully in Chapter 5). Like us, Lee had explained that the comfort women were prostitutes. They had not been dragooned by the Japanese army or been transformed into "sex slaves."

The Quintet also refuse to discuss the issue in public with those who disagree. In October 2021, a woman named Sachi Hirayama, who had argued at length on Twitter with several of the Quintet, suggested a joint forum:

> To you folks in "The Ramseyer article must not be allowed" army. Would you be willing to participate in an online debate? You could explain your perspective, and we could leave the decision to the audience. There are five of you. I could find five people too.[28]

Ambaras dismissed her invitation out of hand. Hirayama, he insisted, was a woman who "screeches out baseless denialist demagoguery." What is more, she "ignores the fact that the core problem with R's article is failure to meet standards of *academic integrity.* That's the baseline, and it's not up for debate."[29] Chatani reiterated the point: "Our report is not 'our perspective.' It's a fact check. There is no room for debate."[30]

The Quintet would soon expand their sanctions against me: not only must my article never appear in print, but I should be denied any "platform" to defend and explain my work (discussed further in Chapters 5 and 7). Ambaras heaped scorn on Joseph Yi, a University of Chicago–educated political scientist at Hanyang University, when Yi invited Ambaras to present his perspective at a symposium organized by the new Heterodox Academy in the spring of 2022. This group had been formed to encourage civil discussion among scholars and has also invited me and others who challenge the orthodoxy on the comfort women. As leader of the group's Asia branch, Yi coordinates symposia on politically sensitive issues. In reply to his invitation, Ambaras wrote:

> I have no interest in lending my professional credibility and reputation for assiduous archival research and academic integrity to any event that gives a platform to those who seek to obfuscate or deny Japanese military and state responsibility for the horrors of the Comfort Women system.... [Y]our premise that a critic of denialists must debate those denialists (let alone engage them in front of an audience sympathetic to

> them) in order to be credible is itself risible. To clarify: I am telling you that your mission is both deeply misguided and intellectually and morally flawed. The fact that you think your offer is reasonable speaks volumes about your own mentality, none of it good.[31]

We doubt that Yi wanted to borrow Ambaras's "reputation for... academic integrity." To our knowledge, Yi wanted a conversation.

Shaun O'Dwyer, an associate professor at Kyushu University, works with Yi to promote civil discussion. It can be a thankless job. After Ambaras brushed off Yi, O'Dwyer tried to persuade the Quintet to join a symposium. They refused. Chatani put it bluntly in an attack on O'Dwyer in 2023: "Our position, which is Ramseyer should not be platformed, has nothing to do with not 'confronting these issues.'"[32]

It is an odd group, this Quintet. The ringleader of the feminists appears to be Professor Ambaras, and if he ever modulates his opinions, we have not noticed. When the Heterodox Academy conducted a survey in June 2022 about whether conservative professors felt comfortable expressing their opinions, Ambaras dismissed it all as racist: "This Heterodox Academy survey on 'campus climate' is really something. This thread shows us the whole shitshow of motivated reasoning, flawed dichotomies, and dubious premises. And racism, did I mention racism?"[33] When Stanford held a conference on academic freedom in late 2022, Ambaras called it "a fcking shitshow" and exclaimed, "Jeezus H. Christ, what a monstrosity."[34]

One day in June 2022, Ambaras noticed an announcement for a Christian conference where Morgan would be one of the speakers (though he did nothing to promote the conference and made no mention of it to anyone but his family). The conference also featured Archbishop Carlo Maria Viganò, a prominent Catholic Traditionalist. It had nothing to do with East Asia, but that did not deter Professor Ambaras from ridiculing it. Paula Curtis concurred. Hiromu

Nagahara's response: "wtfffffffffffff."[35] Anti-Catholicism remains one of the last acceptable prejudices in some circles, and it apparently remains acceptable in theirs. Prejudice against conservative Protestants runs a close second, and Ambaras was not shy about this either. A couple of months earlier he had mocked John Chau, a young evangelist who was murdered in 2018 by the indigenous group he contacted on the North Sentinel Islands. Ambaras used the murder as the punchline of a joke featuring a video of Christians singing on an airplane, which he retweeted with the caption "John Chau Airlines."[36]

Twitter famously permits an enormous band of speech, but in the fall of 2021, even Twitter decided that Ambaras had crossed the line. To his account, it posted: "Our investigation found this account violated the Twitter Rules: David Ambaras @dambaras. Violating our rules against hateful conduct."

Amy Stanley describes herself as "possibly the most prominent of R's *critics*" (sorry, Andrew Gordon).[37] As she worked on the Quintet's attack, she complained that it just "is not right that my colleagues and I have to use our vast experience locating, reading, and interpreting Japanese documents" in order to "debunk fact-free pseudoscholarship."[38] Professor Stanley has won her share of awards. She was a finalist for the Pulitzer Prize for Biography, as her Twitter page prominently notes. She won the National Book Critics Circle Award, as her Twitter page also announces. She had the most Twitter followers of the Quintet, some four times as many as David Ambaras (who moved to Mastodon after Elon Musk bought Twitter). But apparently, she would be even more prominent if only she were male. "I don't know what it will take to convince the men of Twitter that women can have expertise in Japan, history, and/or World War II," she laments. "There is no level of knowledge or accomplishment that seems sufficient to the task."[39] And then: "Odd how when you make a feminist critique you are accused of 'throwing a temper tantrum' as if this shows that you are an over-sensitive overtired child and absolutely no misogyny could possibly be going on."[40] She blamed Covid for the publication of "misogynistic" scholarship: "Right now is an excellent time to publish misogynistic articles in journals because there's less competition from women academics, so you can get garbage published more easily, and a lot of qualified women are too busy to do peer review." Then she added: "I don't mean that as advice for misogynists; it's more just an observation of one of the subtler effects of a situation in which we force individual mothers to serve many of the proper functions of the state"[41]—raising children apparently being one of "the proper functions of the state."

When the *Asia Times* published an article on the comfort women dispute and described me as a "gently-mannered, grey-bearded academic,"[42] Stanley called it yet another example of bias. "This is always the line," she complained. "The gray bearded men are sober and rational. The young women are emotional and irrational. It has nothing to do with the words on the page." Instead, it shows "a reflexive skepticism of women's testimony and feminist scholarship." By Stanley's account, whenever she makes a "playfully sarcastic comment," she is called "a 'culture warrior' 'throwing a tantrum' who can't be engaged intellectually."[43] Women in the academy who "are enraged" about Ramseyer's article therefore "have had to maintain calmness in order to be believed."[44]

But reader, as Miss Brontë might have put it, we thank her. We are grateful, for in Stanley one has a gift that does not stop giving. In the surely-you-must-be-joking category, she posted a picture of a stack of books in June 2021. It was her "summer reading" project, she explained.[45] In the stack were the classic books on comfort women by Hata Ikuhiko (1999) and Yoshimi Yoshiaki (1995). As readers will discover in subsequent chapters, the works by these two professors (Hata is center-right, Yoshimi is center-left) constitute the core of modern scholarship on the comfort women. As hard as we find this to believe, Stanley apparently co-authored the thirty-plus-page attack on my article without reading even the two most basic studies in the field. Perhaps she had not read the original documents either. On July 16, 2022—nearly a year and a half into her attack—Stanley tweeted, "It's the Japanese Prisoner of War Interrogation Report #49!" This very well-known document (which we discuss in Chapter 7 and the epilogue) reports the interrogation of Korean comfort women. Stanley accented her tweet with a smiley face with bulging heart-shaped eyes. "Seriously," she followed up, dropping the heart-eyes emojis for scholarly effect, "you have no idea how fascinating this document is."

Unlike Ambaras and Stanley, Sayaka Chatani mostly studies the Korean community inside Japan. A large fraction of the Japan-resident Koreans marry Japanese and merge into the Japanese mainstream. The remainder disproportionately support the Japanese Communist Party (JCP), a political position that correlates with a propensity to join organized crime networks (a subject I have examined in academic works). Chatani sometimes retweets news from the JCP. She endorses the JCP newspaper *Red Flag*. She urges her followers to support her favored JCP political candidate.[46] She writes aggressive, hard-edged, in-your-face Japanese sentences that would be more at home in certain movie scripts or on certain street corners than in the groves of Japanese academe.

Chelsea Szendi Schieder is the only Japan-based member of the Quintet, but she may have the most caricatured view of Japan among the five. "Ramseyer's piece bolstered the ultranationalist Japanese worldview that rehabilitates Japan's history of militarism and colonialism," she wrote in *The Nation*. Indeed, she continued, it "denies the coercive and brutal nature of much of that era's violence."[47]

Violence intrigues Schieder. She speaks glowingly of Shigenobu Fusako, recently released from prison after serving time for her part in the Japanese Red Army's attack on the Lod (now Ben Gurion) Airport in 1972. Shigenobu and her group killed twenty-six people in that attack. But Schieder—so appalled by the "militarism" and "brutal" violence of Japan's past—describes "an elegant translation of [Shigenobu's] final newsletter from prison" and posts a picture of her holding a Kalashnikov and gazing (literally) into the sunset.[48] Schieder then refers her readers to an article by Shigenobu's daughter that discusses the Japanese Red Army's "revolutionary solidarity work in the fields of medicine, arts, culture, media, and literature," as she explains it.

Hannah Shepherd is one of the more junior members of the Quintet. In one of her tweets in Japanese, she boasts of her skill in verifying historical evidence, and then adds a symposium poster on which she has evidently promoted herself from assistant professor (*jokyo*) to associate professor (*jun kyoju*).[49] Like Stanley, she finds her Twitter audience insufficiently deferential: "I am begging people: please stop explaining Japanese history to me. I have a PhD in this history. I teach this history. I write this history."[50]

Shepherd reports that she liked seeing Ambaras and Stanley refuse invitations to civil dialogue from Yi and O'Dwyer. "I've enjoyed watching [O'Dwyer] be owned by my colleagues who actually Do the F-ing Work rather than standing at the sidelines bleating about procedural liberalism."[51] In Shepherd's mind, evidently, promoting civil and scholarly dialogue is "bleating about procedural liberalism," while doing "the F-ing Work" does not include reading the classic studies on the subject. We confess to being old-fashioned enough to find the junkyard prose off-putting. But in writing like this, Shepherd merely follows most of the others in this Twitter circle. O'Dwyer insisted on hosting people like Ramseyer at Heterodox Academy events, and Paula Curtis would have none of it: "take your suggestion and fuck all the way off."[52] Ambaras and Nagahara post in much the same prose.

But was the following a joke? When a white supremacist killed ten people in Buffalo in May 2022, Shepherd tied me to the attack. She retweeted an article about the killing and added: "There is a lot of work to be done by scholars of [East Asia] to tackle White Supremacy and its use of East Asia. We can make a start by debunking certain Law & Economics articles on Japan."

Institutional Responses

As soon as Gordon and Eckert wrote their attack on me, the Reischauer Institute at Harvard posted it prominently to its website. When the Quintet finished their cite check, the Institute posted it to the website as well. There the attacks stayed until the end of August.

Just to be clear: I have served on the executive committee of the Reischauer Institute since 1998. Quite who might be speaking for the organization was never obvious, but on its website "the Institute" offered this explanation:

> A recent publication by Harvard Law School Professor J. Mark Ramseyer has generated serious concerns among the Harvard Japanese studies community regarding the empirical foundations of the scholarship. Together with Professor Carter Eckert of the Korea Institute at Harvard, Professor Andrew Gordon of the Reischauer Institute submitted a formal statement in mid-February to the journal that published Professor Ramseyer's paper. An international group of scholars of Japan [i.e., the Quintet, two of whom were former Gordon students] reviewed the empirical evidence upon which its claims are based and issued a public response. Harvard Law School Professor Jeannie Suk-Gersen published an article outlining the international nature of the comfort women issue and responses by the academic community to Professor Ramseyer's paper [translated into Japanese by Gordon's former student Nagahara].... The Reischauer Institute reaffirms its call to the journal editors to fully address the concerns raised by scholars in the U.S. and abroad.[53]

No, they did not consult me in advance. They did not offer to post a response from me. They did not quote Chatani's statement that none of the Quintet brought any background in "the history or debates about the 'comfort women.'"[54] They did not even quote Stanley's euphoric "I always thought joining a woke cancel mob would be easy and fun."[55]

In the spring of 2021, Mary Brinton, a Harvard sociologist and chair of the Reischauer Institute, told me that other Japanese studies professors were receiving hate email and indicated that it was my fault. In just one day, she continued, they had each received three pieces of hate email. I tried not to laugh. After all, I was sometimes receiving several dozen a day. I also thought any hate email from Japan might have more to do with the decision to post the Gordon-Eckert and Stanley Quintet attacks on the Institute's website. For reasons we detail in this book, both attacks will strike most informed Japanese as fundamentally misleading and probably dishonest. A few days later, Brinton contacted me to report that Stanley was receiving hate email from Japan too. Apparently, Stanley was not having as much "fun" as she had hoped. My colleagues at the Institute, Brinton informed me, were outraged that I—the object of Stanley's attacks—had done nothing to stop it.

Shortly after the Reischauer Institute posted the attacks to its website, Harvard's Korea Institute posted the Gordon-Eckert statement to theirs as well, with this note:

> The Executive Committee of the Korea Institute endorses a formal statement written by Professors Carter Eckert and Andrew Gordon in response to the recent publication by Harvard Law School Professor J. Mark Ramseyer.[56]

And a little bit later, Harvard's Asia Center (on whose executive committee I have also spent several years) posted a long and sympathetic interview of one of my public critics, Jeannie Suk-Gersen (discussed below), by the center's director.[57] The Asia Center did not offer me a chance to respond either.

Perhaps it has no relevance, but Harvard being Harvard we note that the grandson of one of the founders of the prewar Korean government-in-exile immediately withdrew his offer to donate his family's historical material to the Harvard library. He had been negotiating with Harvard since 2015. Once my article appeared, he promptly canceled, giving this explanation: "Allowing employees to think they can hide behind academic freedom freely spewing such pointed false opinions about Comfort Women indicated Harvard is no place to deposit any of my archives."[58]

Like Hannah Shepherd, the Korean Studies committee of the Association for Asian Studies tied me to deadly violence. In this case, it was the murders of Korean women at an Atlanta spa in 2021. After expressing "grief" over the murders, the committee said:

> [The Committee on Korean Studies] stands against the waves of anti-Asian hatred and violence in the US, Canada, and Europe and the ideologies of white supremacy that have allowed for their recurrence over history and their contemporary intensification.... In this respect, the Ramseyer article affair is connected to what we face in terms of anti-Asian and anti-Korean hatred in North America. Harvard Law School professor J. Mark Ramseyer had an article accepted by a peer-reviewed journal claiming that the Japanese empire's system of forced military sexual labor was actually a system of volunteer, contracted prostitution.... The Ramseyer affair is an example of how racial and gendered violence in North America, Europe, and Asia, do not always express themselves in classifiable hate speech or hate crimes, but also in academic knowledge.[59]

Given the references to "anti-Asian hatred," we remind readers that Japan is part of Asia.

Chwe

Michael Chwe, a political scientist at UCLA, attracted attention in early 2021 for his own petition demanding that the IRLE retract my article. Chwe gives no reason other than ethnicity for anyone to think he has any particular knowledge about the comfort women, and seems to know nothing beyond the popular lore in South Korea. He does seem to be an inveterate activist. He organizes campaigns to rename buildings at Caltech. He encourages people to file "me-too" attacks. He campaigns for the UCLA graduate student labor union.[60] Like the other critics, Chwe claimed that I had committed fraud. He wrote that my article "goes well beyond mere academic failure or malpractice in its breach of academic standards, integrity, and ethics," and that I was "using economics . . . as a cover to legitimize horrific atrocities."[61]

In his petition, Chwe writes that "most" of the comfort women were girls "between eleven and twenty." They had been recruited through methods that "included abduction, deception, threats, and violence." They served as many as forty men per day. They "were subject to repeated rape, forced abortions, physical torture, and sexually transmitted diseases." If they complained, they were rolled over boards with nails and then beheaded. According to Chwe, "roughly 75 percent" of all the comfort women died from their experience at the comfort stations. We urge readers to keep these claims in mind as they read the rest of the book.

Chwe obtained support for his petition from prominent people. The twelve editors of the *American Political Science Review* unanimously declared that they "fully support" his demand for a retraction.[62] Two Nobel laureates, Al Roth and Paul Milgrom, wrote that my article "reminded [them] of Holocaust denial."[63] Another Nobel laureate, Eric Maskin, signed the petition himself. Roger Noll, a Stanford emeritus economist, said he was "saddened and dismayed" that the IRLE had published my article.[64] Roth, Milgrom, Maskin, and Noll are prominent economists. The twelve editors are prominent political scientists. Do remember, however, that none of them earned their prominence by being able to find Pyongyang on a map.

Dudden

The prize for the most imaginative responses to my article easily goes to Alexis Dudden, a historian of Korea and Japan at the University of Connecticut (and associate in research at the Reischauer Institute). During the spring of 2021, she seemed never to find a Korean television news camera she did not like. She appeared repeatedly on Korean programs, always speaking in English and usually accusing me of "fraud."

In February, Dudden told Korean viewers about her trauma upon reading my article:

> I actually thought I was misreading the opening sentences. That words were missing, to be very honest. And then I started shaking, because I couldn't understand why a professor would make such unfounded claims, when so much evidence proves the contrary. So it was really one of shock.... Many of us were just dumbfounded.... We are absolutely bewildered by his lack of evidence.... Or he's just simply making up sources.... The evidence doesn't exist, so it's academic fraud.... It's just fake news dressed up as fact.[65]

Dudden actually took a course from me in the 1990s at the University of Chicago, and she periodically appears at Reischauer Institute dinners. I cannot imagine her "shaking" at reading anything, much less a technical article in an economics journal.

By March, Dudden had moved on to assuring her Korean audience that there was no need to worry about hate mail sent to people like Jason Morgan and me. It was her like-minded "colleagues" in Tokyo who stood in danger: "Because those are the people that will get targeted with threats that are actionable. My colleagues in Tokyo, for example, I have three colleagues who have had their offices firebombed."[66] We have colleagues and friends in Tokyo too. Morgan lives in a Tokyo suburb. Our Tokyo friends and colleagues read the newspapers and watch TV news. Morgan does too. And no one—not one person—has said anything about any professor finding his or her office "firebombed." A serial phantom faculty-office firebomber is on the loose in Tokyo, apparently—but why was Dudden going on Korean television about it instead of calling the police in Japan?

My colleague Jeannie Suk-Gersen, in her *New Yorker* attack on my IRLE article (discussed below), reported lurid assertions by Dudden:

> Alexis Dudden... was one of the scholars invited to publish a reply to Ramseyer in the journal.... She told me of meeting Korean comfort women in Tokyo, in 2000, at the Women's International War Crimes Tribunal on Japan's Military Sexual Slavery. "One of them had her tongue cut out," she said. "Another woman literally lifted up her *hanbok* to show me where one of her breasts had been lopped off."[67]

And Ugarte died trying to escape. Given the bizarre claims that Dudden so routinely makes, we are less surprised that she said something like this than that Suk-Gersen seems to have believed it. Accounts of soldiers mutilating enemy women in such ways do occasionally appear in wartime atrocity reports, including the report of the postwar Tokyo trials. At least one comfort woman has made a similar claim.[68] Those wartime atrocity accounts, however, are about soldiers mutilating women as they killed them. Dudden claims to have met two comfort women who survived the mutilation and lived to the year 2000.

Dudden made this claim in print, in 2008 (though without corroborating evidence):

> Every now and then during the tribunal, when words failed one of the women, she would lift her shirt to reveal where a breast had been lopped off by an angry soldier.... One woman had no tongue; a Japanese man cut it out for trying to resist him.[69]

Unfortunately, at least one scholar has taken her at her word. Citing Dudden, Claudia Junghyun Kim writes that the tribunal in Tokyo "brought together 64 victims, including those from North Korea and East Timor—some of whom had their tongue, or a breast, cut off by Japanese soldiers (Dudden, 2008, 93)."[70]

Dudden's claim is implausible on its face. If a soldier had mutilated a comfort woman in the ways described, she would have been lucky to make it even to an army field hospital. She would have lost massive amounts of blood. If she somehow survived the blood loss, she would have died of the ensuing infection. And if she somehow miraculously survived it all, activists would have brought her front stage at the Women's International War Crimes Tribunal in 2000. They would have been telling her story in books and articles ever since.

Hwang Uiwon, a Korean journalist who has followed the comfort women debate for years, examined the report of the tribunal. He found many reports of sensational claims, but none about any surviving women having had a breast cut off. Hwang also contacted others involved in the comfort women controversy, and none of them had ever heard of any surviving comfort women who claimed to have had either her breast or her tongue severed by a member of the Japanese military. He contacted Dudden directly and asked her to provide corroborating evidence for the accounts she retailed. Dudden did not reply.

We have found no account prior to the 2000 tribunal of any surviving comfort woman who had a breast "lopped off" or her "tongue cut out." Neither have we found a firsthand account by anyone other than Dudden in the years since the tribunal. No one else—no one in Japan, no one in Korea—seems to have witnessed the gruesome injuries of either of these two women, displayed "every now and then during the tribunal" for all to see. What are the women's names? Where are they from? Where did they work as comfort women during the war? Apparently, Dudden alone knows.

Dudden also claims that "denialists" have been sending her death threats. On her University of Connecticut website, she proudly quotes a July 2022 *Nation* article:

> Alexis Dudden, a history professor at the University of Connecticut whose research specializes in Korea-Japan relations, helped organize a 2015 letter signed by a group of American academics condemning Japan's revisionist history regarding comfort women. Denialists retaliated by sending her 10 to 15 death threats every day; eventually, an FBI officer was assigned to her classroom.

We were able to test this claim as a consequence of a Freedom of Information Act request (FOI #20-091) that Morgan had submitted to the University of Connecticut in early March 2020 for all emails to or from Dudden, for a span of several years, having to do with her (unreported) work on a United Nations report attacking Japan.

The University of Connecticut was extraordinarily slow in responding to Morgan's FOIA request. Suspecting a stalling tactic, he filed a complaint with the Connecticut Freedom of Information Commission. On December 21, 2021, the university's interim president, Andrew Agwunobi, responded to the commission:

> To assist in your review, Dr. Dudden has provided a summary of relevant information and background (see Attachment 4). Since 2003, various right-wing individuals in Japan have openly targeted Dr. Dudden. These threats include, but are not limited to, death threats via landline telephone, cell phone, regular

> mail, and email.... There is a long history of violence against scholars whose research relates to the "comfort women" topic.

Attachment 4 includes three items. The closest thing to a death threat appears on the first page. It is an email dated May 25, 2015, sent to "Dudden, Alexis" by one "Wataru Takeuchi," signed in both English and Japanese. In addition to the signature, the email contains five Japanese characters, which read: *shi ne ya bo ke.* This means, "Drop dead, moron."

The next item in the attachment is a screenshot of a December 22, 2021 tweet by Kim Byungheon, author of a bestselling Korean book detailing the fraud behind the comfort women movement. The tweet includes a screenshot of Dudden from one of her many YouTube attacks against my IRLE article. As Dudden describes the tweet:

> Frame shot in Korean: screen capture from a Feb 2021 SBS TV interview with non-contextualized sentence of me referring to Ramseyer's Jan 2021 denialist essay; (link to TV clip at end with California Congresswoman Young Kim R-39):
>
> "If there is no evidence to support the claim, then the claim is not true."
>
> "Therefore, the history of the comfort women is false." (Professor Kim's words).

Needless to say, this is not remotely a death threat. It is not a threat of any kind, or even a message sent to Dudden in the first place.

A screenshot of three Japanese-language replies to Kim Byungheon's tweet about Dudden follows. The first: "I express my sentiments of respect for your activities in pursuit of the truth. Thank you." The second: "Thank you." The third begins by recapitulating Kim's comments (which were in Korean) in Japanese, then follows up with a sentence that Dudden translates as: "Thank you so much, Professor Kim. Let's 'protect' this American girl's bullshit."

Evidently, Dudden believes that this sentence evinces a threat against her. The Japanese is simple, but in fact Dudden mistranslates it. The sentence actually states: "Kim Byungheon-sensei, thank you as always. Let us protect the children of America from falsehoods (lies)." Obviously, this sentence does not threaten Dudden either. It threatens no one, and does not even mention Dudden. It does not use sneer quotes or vulgar language.

When 184 pages of emails were finally released, we found no death threats. We only found one claim to have received such threats, in a May 10, 2016 email to Jeffrey Wasserstrom, a China scholar, and David Kaye, a former UN rapporteur, under the subject line "another horrible piece by Sankei's Komori," referencing Komori Yoshihisa, a reporter for the *Sankei* newspaper. Komori had written about a talk by Dudden and Kaye at Kaye's institution, the University of California, Irvine, to be held on May 12, 2016. The talk concerned Kaye's UN report attacking Japan over journalistic freedom.[71] Dudden complains that "David [Kaye] is giving [*sic*] 'full frontal' absurd-land treatment in this Sankei essay," and says she got threats related to the article: "I've already received 2 death threats, and I'm second fiddle!" Rather than show distress, she closes with a yellow smiley-face emoticon.

Jinhee Lee

Curiously, the biggest source of problems for me may have been an obscure internet stalker. Jinhee Lee is a historian at Eastern Illinois University and yet another associate in research at Harvard's Reischauer Institute. I met her once over Zoom at a meeting for Christian faculty in the summer of 2020.

When the hate mail started in February 2021, I began to get cloying emails from Lee urging me to repent. They were all very long. One included lengthy Bible passages. On February 16, for example, Lee wrote:

> [We have] been praying over you continuously so that God will show you the WAY OUT as He accomplishes His good and perfect will orchestrating all things beautifully for His glory even through this mess.... I focused on my prayer for you, for your peace and wisdom.... I want you to know that we, the brothers and sisters in Christ Jesus you met through [the Christian faculty group], care for you as our brother in the Lord, as God Himself cares for you so deeply, unconditionally, and eternally. I think that's why He wants me to relay the following message to you which I will try to keep brief so you can rest a bit in the Lord in stillness and quietness before this evening....

Here is the message that God Himself wanted Lee to relay to me:

> Will your mother in heaven or daughter in Somerville be pleased with [your IRLE article] and in the future? Will our Lord Jesus who is in charge of our lives be pleased with what's going on right now?...
>
> In the end, we must choose whose we are, and that's more than enough. The rest will be taken care of by our God who is in all and above all.... Take heart, and have COURAGE to step out of this worldly mess. Declare who you are in Christ, and just walk away on the path the Holy Spirit wants you to be on.

Eleven days later, Lee wrote again:

> You still have the last minute chance to turn around and leave the legacies that will be respected for generations. Just reveal what has misguided you, make a simple but sincere apology for the mistakes, and get out of the pit.... Let them drown who choose the path to destruction, but not you, Mark. Your parents and grandparents must have prayed for you so much to live a life that is worthy of the name of Christ Jesus. It takes

> courage, but that courage will set you free for eternity. Love the truth, and be saved.

She continued in this vein, and additional similar letters followed.

The letters puzzled me, but only until I learned what else Lee had been doing. While she was assuring me of her deep and unconditional care for me as a "brother in the Lord," she was also scouring the web for any other recent or forthcoming articles or chapters of mine. Once she found a piece, she blanketed the editors and publishers with furious ad hominem attacks on me and demands that they stop publication or retract.

It was Lee's pride, her hatred of Japan, and her pride about her hatred, that did her in. I learned about her attacks because she was so proud of what she was doing. When she sabotaged an essay, she eagerly told the Korean news media about it. Korean outlets detailed her exploits, and then—this having become an international incident—the Japanese media reported what they learned from the Korean press.

On February 21, 2021, for example, *Yonhap News* reported how Lee had written Cambridge University Press to demand that they block a chapter in a forthcoming book in which I discussed the massacre of Koreans in the wake of the 1923 Tokyo earthquake.[72] She similarly harassed (it is hard to describe the letters any other way) the editors of the *European Journal of Law and Economics* over a recently published article of mine about the connection between criminal activity by Japan-resident Koreans and discrimination against them. Nevertheless, *Yonhap News* generously opined that Lee "is considered the most authoritative expert in this field."

In the course of scouring the web, Lee also found a copy of a talk I had given at an academic conference in 2019. She promptly contacted the officers of the organization in March 2021. At the same time that she was sending me her pleadingly devout letters, she wrote to the officers:

> The article reveals *not only* the distortion of a number of documented and proven historical facts regarding the history of these minority groups in Japan *but also* fraudulent use of historical evidence and the result of decades-long established scholarship on the topic. In particular, I am deeply concerned about the distortion of the history of Koreans in Japan in this paper, [and the way that it] promot[es] the on-going Japanese hate speech, hate crimes, and human rights violation against racial minorities in contemporary Japan.... I hope the blood will not be on your hands by delaying or ignoring this alarm concerning the deficiency and distortion of the historical facts....

Just as Shepherd tied me to the murders in Buffalo, and the Korean Studies committee tied me to murders in Atlanta, Lee wrote in her letter that I fomented racism and violence:

> The accuracy of facts matter in scholarly investigation, and making the best effort to stop spreading inaccurate, intentionally falsified information to promote racism and related violence—especially dealing with the cases of mass killing—matter greatly, and your action is required when they were known to you by other experts and your readers.[73]

More specifically, in a letter to the editors of the IRLE, Lee tied me to attacks on women in Afghanistan:

> I came to realize that there is no way for the journal and its editors to avoid its responsibility and culpability in this continuing crime against humanity by stabbing the survivors of sex slavery yet again. I clearly see the direct connection between the atrocity deniers' propaganda that the author and his fellow history falsifiers are spreading AND the rhetoric to justify the violence against women in Afghanistan right now.[74]

I was not the only scholar whom Lee tried to silence. She targeted Chizuko Allen, a historian at the University of Hawai'i, over a passage about the comfort women in her Korean history textbook saying they had not been dragooned by the Japanese military. Lee also attempted to stop a petition in support of Lew Seok-choon when he was hit with criminal defamation charges in South Korea for describing the comfort women as prostitutes in one of his sociology classes. (We discuss both efforts in Chapter 5.)

Suk-Gersen

Among the scholars who attacked me in 2021, my Harvard Law School colleague Jeannie Suk-Gersen probably reached the largest audience. She does not claim to know Japanese or Korean history, but she does write well, and she writes regularly for the *New Yorker*. Like Chwe, she apparently thought her ethnic background was sufficient qualification for evaluating a colleague's work about Korean history of the 1930s and early 1940s. After all, she pointedly tells her readers that she was "the first and only ethnic Korean to receive tenure at Harvard Law School." She has also cultivated a persona as champion of academic freedom and serves on the Legal Advisory Council of the Academic Freedom Alliance. The *New Yorker* chose to run her attack on me in its February 26 issue.[75] The Reischauer Institute endorsed it. Gordon's former student Hiromu Nagahara translated it into Japanese.

Perhaps Suk-Gersen approached her task as a journalist, because she did not approach it as a scholar. She did not even pretend to read any relevant documents. Instead, she contacted my critics: Chwe, Gordon, Stanley, Ambaras, Dudden, and the Australian historian Tessa Morris-Suzuki. A historian at Waseda University, Arima Tetsuo, ran a content analysis on Suk-Gersen's piece: 8.8 percent involved comments by other scholars about my comfort women articles; 32 percent concerned comments by other scholars on my other articles; 21.6 percent concerned American public opinion on

U.S.-Japan-Korea relations and the comfort women; and 8.8 percent concerned Suk-Gersen's own evaluation of my work. Arima commented that this was a bit as if Suk-Gersen had said that "xx says she doesn't like you" when what she really wanted to say was "I don't like you."[76]

Suk-Gersen contacted Ambaras and—surprise—found that he claimed I misused my sources. She contacted Gordon and found that he claimed I misused my sources. She contacted Stanley and found that "the established historical evidence that [I] omitted... 'destroy[ed]' [my] argument." She also contacted several editors whom Jinhee Lee had harassed and found that they were investigating my article. She did not contact Morgan or Arima or Hata Ikuhiko or, it seems, anyone else who knows the actual history of the comfort women.

I had given Suk-Gersen material summarizing the evidence that we discuss in Chapters 2 through 6. Let me stress this point: she had the broad outlines of the account we detail in this book. She had the evidence that the Japanese military did not dragoon Korean women, and that the women from Japan and Korea did not work as sex slaves. She had the evidence that they enlisted as prostitutes under indentured servant contracts, worked off their debt, and went home. She had this material—but managed to write a very long article in which none of it appears.

Suk-Gersen reports claims by scholars like Ambaras that I "misused historical sources." In the *Harvard Crimson*, she suggests that the peer-review process at the IRLE was inadequate to the task: "A peer-reviewed legal journal in this case was not equipped to catch the errors regarding Japanese-language sources that the historians of Japan have found and that led those historians to believe there was a problem of academic integrity here."[77]

It is true that editors of journals in law and economics will not know whether an author's claims about Japanese history are factual. They may also find it hard to identify a "problem of academic integrity" in such an article. In the current academy, however, it is at least as likely that any "problem of academic integrity" will involve the referees. If the editors of a law and economics journal were to ask a specialist like Ambaras or Gordon or Jinhee Lee to referee an article, they will find it just as hard to "catch the errors" or identify any "problem of academic integrity" in the review as in the article itself. After all, when Suk-Gersen contacted the people involved in the campaign to cancel me, she was—apparently—unable to see that they were dissembling.

What Suk-Gersen knew is that my article contradicted what she had been taught by her "ethnic Korean" community. That seems to be *all* she knew on the subject. The way a Japanese diplomat put it to me over dinner (paraphrased) is: "Look, second-generation immigrants in the U.S. haven't a clue what's going on in their parents' home country. But they're incredibly patriotic about that home country. A lot of Japanese Americans are the same. They don't read Japanese newspapers. They don't follow what's going on. But they're patriotic to the core. It's the same with the Korean Americans."

Recall that Suk-Gersen is a member of the Legal Advisory Council of the Academic Freedom Alliance. In that capacity, she purports to "defend the rights of academics to express unpopular opinions or views with which I strongly disagree." We should thank her for this commitment, I suppose. But it appears not to prevent her from burying information that does not support her preferred account, or from publishing nonacademic hit pieces on people whose "unpopular opinions" she does not like. Defend their right to hold unpopular opinions—and assassinate their character. There is a logic to this somewhere if we think about it long enough, I am sure.

A Cottage Industry

We are tempted to take a deep breath and sigh. The censorship and attacks could seem endless. Craig Freedman, an economist, and

Luke Nottage, a law professor, described a "virtual cottage industry of academic critiques" of my work. "Already in March 2021," they reported, "an editor of a Japanese studies journal (outside Japan) had recommended deleting all citations to Ramseyer's work despite the fact those works dealt with very different and general topics in Japanese law."[78]

My critics set up a panel on my article for the January 2022 meeting of the American Historical Association. Stanley excitedly tweeted the news on May 11, 2021:

> Happy to announce that our roundtable "It Can Happen Here: Confronting Denialism Through Interdisciplinary Collaboration" will be happening at [the American Historical Association meeting] in [New Orleans]! Join us to hear about our response to the Ramseyer debacle and what comes next!!![79]

Apparently, she thought others might find "joining a woke cancel mob... easy and fun" as well.

My critics set up a similar panel for the 2022 annual meeting of the Association for Asian Studies. Chatani worked with Sungyung Lim, a University of Colorado historian, to organize a session on comfort women. Chelsea Szendi Schieder was one of the panelists. Chatani promised that her panel would go "beyond 'ideological' fruitless discussions about the history of the comfort women." According to the panel abstract, the year 2021 had "brought to the fore many controversies concerning violence against Asian women, including the ongoing struggles around truth and justice regarding Japanese military sexual slavery during World War II." Stack a panel with people who assume one's desired conclusion, apparently, and one can go "beyond... fruitless discussions."[80]

My critics seem to enjoy conference panels. For the American Anthropological Association, they organized a panel expressly called "The Ramseyer Controversy":

> What are the problems in academia that led to Ramseyer's work getting a pass in multiple peer-review processes until this year? How could the power and influence of American academia, especially of elite institutions such as Harvard, hinder our pursuit for truth and our commitment to fight against bigotry and sexism as anthropologists? ... The controversy poses critical questions about racism and sexism in Japanese studies as well as the ongoing assault against critical race theory and feminist scholarship in and outside of the United States.... We will then discuss the larger issues that Japan Anthropology faces in difficult times in light of rising right-wing politics....

The panel organizers promised:

> The roundtable will provide an opportunity for Japan Studies and Japan Anthropology to engage in collective thinking and discussion for the possible strategies to fight against revisionism, racism, and sexism, and to commit to the social justice for the disadvantaged.[81]

Both of us instinctively think of "revisionism" as an intellectual advance. When earlier scholars get something wrong, later scholars revise it. But judgments on "revisionism" will depend in part on whose ideas are being revised. For the anthropologists now controlling the orthodoxy of Japanese studies, "revisionism" is something to "fight against." Paula Curtis made the point categorical: "Platforming racists and revisionists is bad and does harm."[82]

Pyong Gap Min, a Queens College sociologist, argued that the Harvard Internal Review Boards should have blocked my work from the outset.[83] IRBs are an institutional structure designed to oversee experiments involving human subjects, but some universities have been trying to censor controversial research through these boards. That is what happened to Laura Kipnis, a professor at Northwestern. (We describe her ordeal in Chapter 8.)[84] Her work did not involve "human subjects," but Northwestern's IRB bureaucrats came after her anyway. Mine did not involve human subjects either, but never mind.

In February 2022, Pyong Gap Min posted a call for articles for a special issue of the *Journal of International Women's Studies* about my IRLE article. Min wanted discussions of my article, but not just any discussion. He declared my article "unacceptable" and wrote that my response to my critics raised "no scientific evidence." Accordingly, he wanted only articles that would "effectively show how Ramseyer's arguments are empirically unsubstantiated and logically indefensible."[85]

Jinah Kim, a professor at Cal State Northridge, funds studies about the comfort women and writes about them. But as with Min's editorial work, she does not fund just any study. She directs a scholarship fund for "students and faculty... to support research and creative activity on women and girls forced into sexual slavery by the Imperial Japanese Army." Whether they actually were forced into sexual slavery is apparently not in question. Kim also disclosed that she wrote a response to my article for the IRLE, but pulled it after corresponding with the editorial board. "In addition to rebuttals," she explained, "the editorial board invited comments in favor of Ramseyer's article. I do not want to participate in a process that legitimates Ramseyer's support of a horrific history through a pro-con discussion."[86]

These efforts by scholars in Asian studies to block the dissemination of any material that contradicts the party line can turn nearly comical. In the dispute over my IRLE article, Y.S. Lee, a visiting professor at Georgia State University, might take the prize for sheer chutzpah. I had waited out the year of 2021, and then, in January 2022, I posted a long and detailed "response" to critics like Gordon and the Quintet in the "working paper" series of the John M. Olin Center for Law, Economics, and Business at the Harvard Law School.[87] Lee promptly contacted Steven Shavell, who is the Samuel R. Rosenthal Professor of Law and Economics and director of the Olin Center, and demanded (repeatedly) that Shavell retract my response. Shavell refused, but note the irony: critics accused me of fraud and demanded that the journal retract my article; I responded to the retraction demands and explained the evidence behind my position; and Lee wanted to block anyone from reading my response to the retraction demands or learning about the evidence.

The censorship campaign ranged far beyond the issue of the comfort women. In the spring of 2022, when a university press handling an unrelated book of mine announced its forthcoming publication, several of those who attacked my IRLE article on comfort women expressed their outrage on Twitter. For over a year, they had relentlessly accused me of fraud. To see a first-tier press now publish anything by Ramseyer apparently jeopardized their own credibility. Some of my critics surreptitiously contacted the press, as I would later discover. Exactly what they said, I never learned—but they ultimately succeeded in sabotaging the book's publication. (We discuss that book more fully in Chapter 7.)

Meanwhile, the petitions against me seemed endless. The largest petition drive came from Korea and claimed over 30,000 signatures. The petition demanded that Harvard "discipline" me and declared that my article:

> distorts Japanese war crimes, rationalizes the invasion of neighboring countries as the remarks by Goebbels, the propaganda minister during the Nazi era, and is being used as a megaphone by the Japanese government to take no responsibility for the war of aggression.

In tandem, another group demanded that Waseda University fire my friend and co-author, Arima Tetsuo. More than 10,000 people signed this petition. And Claremont-McKenna students targeted Eric Helland, a professor at the college and IRLE editor, for publishing my article.[88]

At least one petition urged Harvard to initiate a Title IX sexual assault case against me. Increasingly, university activists manipulate the Title IX rules to try to ban speech and writings with which they disagree. A 1972 statute designed to ban "discrimination on the basis of sex...has become a weapon," as one writer put it, with which the intolerant can "impose their views and punish dissenters, by means of an entrenched and destructive campus bureaucracy."[89] A petition against me styled a "Feminist Open Letter" collected 1,500 signatures and explicitly demanded that universities "Actively investigate hate speech and behaviors that perpetuate sexist, colonialist, and racist views under relevant university guidelines and Title IX regulations."[90] The petition was endorsed by Elisabeth Schuessler Fiorenza, a Harvard Divinity School theologian, and by Catherine Elgin, a Harvard Education School philosopher.

"White men"

Hannah Shepherd ties me to the white supremacist murders in Buffalo. The Korean Studies committee of the Association for Asian Studies ties me to the murders of Korean women in Atlanta. Jinhee Lee ties me to the attacks on women in Afghanistan. The critics call me a "racist." For good measure, they also call me a "white supremacist."

Sexual and racial essentialism lie barely below the surface of the attacks I faced. That anyone would publicly question the sex-slave narrative, Paula Curtis attributes to the "senior, white men at elite institutions," with their "right wing" connections:

> The toxic feedback loop of right wing social media was on full display when Ramseyer defended himself as part of a right wing video conference on Comfort Women hosted in Tokyo

> during late April 2021. Not only did he refer to his critics as Stalinists, but Ramseyer also alleged that the humanities in the United States harbors anti-Japanese bias. His comments played directly to the right wing's rejection of scholarship that does not affirm their views and served to fill a crucial gap that the historical denialist community needs to legitimize themselves within and outside of Japan....
>
> Privilege, institutions, and networks of enablers allow certain groups of people, most often senior, white men at elite institutions, to abuse their positions. These instances embody the "Ivory Tower" at its worst, the kind of academia that scholars have been struggling to reform and decolonize.[91]

Sonia Ryang, an anthropologist at Rice, complains in the *Journal of Asian Studies* that "white men" have long dominated Asian studies in the United States. Precisely because of that domination, I enjoyed the "systemic white male privilege" that enabled me to create such a "terribly abusive atmosphere":

> Asian studies in Western academe began with, and for a long time was led by, white men.... How did this affect the field of Asian studies? Very clearly and directly.... Recently, it was revealed acutely that we have been operating in a terribly abusive atmosphere in the wake of the Ramseyer affair, in which a Mitsubishi-endowed Harvard Law professor posted inaccurate and ideologically skewed articles that referred to "comfort women" as contracted sex workers.... Some publishing outlets, despite strong voices of protest from academics globally, refuse to pull Ramseyer's work.... The Ramseyer affair is not an isolated example of what might be called systemic white male privilege in Asian studies.[92]

We later return to the claim that white men dominate this field.

Mennonites

Ostracism campaigns against disfavored academics can reach far beyond the universities. They destroy friendships. They can destroy marriages. Sometimes they can destroy lives. In my case, they extended to the church into which I was born.

Raised in Japan by Mennonite missionaries, I attended the Cambridge Mennonite congregation for many years. Soon after the attacks on my IRLE article began, the church council demanded that I appear before them to justify the morality of my article. The pastor refused to have anything to do with this process, but the church council persisted. I offered to explain the relevant history, but the council declared itself uninterested. Like so many of the American scholars involved, it did not want to study history. It wanted to pronounce morality. This made no sense to me, and I refused. The council made it clear that I was no longer welcome at the church.

There is more than a little irony in watching nominally pacifist Mennonites endorse the hypernationalist hatred toward Japan that characterizes the South Korean Left. When a prominent Korean Mennonite wrote to a church website to complain about my article, the website coordinator directed readers to the Suk-Gersen attack for "additional background." Sara Wenger Shenk then wrote in to the website and identified herself as the former president of the Mennonite seminary in Indiana. She described her own visit to Korea and how "heartbreaking" she found it "to read the stories of many, many young women who at the age of 14–16 were forced into sex slavery." She repeated the claim that the Japanese government had never "offered an official apology," and praised the "Japanese guide" who showed her the comfort women museum—"a man clearly devoted to caring for and telling the stories of the victims his own government refuses to acknowledge."[93]

Bear these claims in mind as you read the chapters that follow. Where Chwe 's account was caustic, Shenk's was mawkish, but both are preposterous history. Like many Protestant denominations, the Mennonite Church is a highly fractured affair. A century ago, it was a largely conservative church for Swiss-German farmers in the Midwest and Canada. As socially and economically mobile members left the farm for urban professional jobs, they looked for more upscale church ties. When they formed urban Mennonite churches, they modeled them on the wealthier Quakers or the "mainline" denominations like the Episcopalians, the United Church of Christ, and the United Presbyterians. Several mainline groups explicitly endorse the comfort-women-as-sex-slaves story. By 2021, aspirationally mainline Mennonites apparently endorsed it as well.

MORGAN'S EXPERIENCES

The comfort women appear in many English-language textbooks, monographs, and scholarly articles in Asian studies. As an undergraduate in the 1990s and during my first stint in graduate school at the University of Hawai'i at Mānoa in the early 2000s, I saw the subject discussed briefly in any number of different works. I accepted what I read on the subject at face value.

The Western scholars had ample endnotes and testimonials all purporting to show that the Imperial Japanese Army had abducted 200,000 women and held them as sex slaves during the 1930s and 1940s. I had never (and still have not) been in a war zone or even remotely close to one, but I knew that war is a brutal thing, and so I concluded that anything is possible. I did not think much about the comfort women issue. I simply took what I was given in my class readings and outside study and filed that information away amid the growing constellation of facts and patterns that one must keep track of as a scholar-in-training.

As an undergraduate, I thought of myself as open-minded and fair, and I wanted to believe that the rest of the world was too. I had always been interested in other countries and followed the news intently, so I had a passing understanding of the events that shaped my time: the Israel-Palestine conflict, the Tiananmen Square massacre, the fall of the Berlin Wall, the collapse of the Soviet Union, the Bosnian civil war, the Rwanda genocide. The dark streaks in the global situation troubled me, and I spent long hours thinking about why such things happened. But for all this, I was an optimist. A globalist, even. I was sure that humanity was moving in a better direction.

I had played soccer in high school and college (mostly riding the bench, to be sure). Through soccer I met people from around the world—China, Sri Lanka, France, Venezuela, Switzerland, Germany, Sweden, and pretty much anywhere else on the planet where people go out and kick a soccer ball around in the afternoons. It was during intramural pickup games at the University of Tennessee in Chattanooga that I met someone from Japan, a person who would go on to be a lifelong friend. I visited that friend in the summer of 1999 at his home in Gifu, Japan. That visit changed my life. I decided to switch my major from the Greek and Latin classics to the history of East Asia. This has been my main focus since those first hours in Gifu nearly two and a half decades ago.

In my final undergraduate year, I went to study abroad in Nagoya, an industrial city located at a little below the middle of the Pacific Ocean side of Honshu, Japan's main island. Nagoya is not far from Gifu, and I spent most weekends with my friend's family. I didn't realize it at the time, but I was gradually coming to see things in a Japanese way. I found my cultural assumptions, as well as my assumptions about the past and the future, being challenged.

While in Nagoya I took a "deep dive" into big history, reading heavily in serious tomes by Herbert Bix, John Dower, and other senior scholars of Japan. In undergraduate classes I had read a variety of monographs and textbooks about Japanese history, but in Nagoya I began to read deeply about some of the more troubling episodes. The Second World War, the Rape of Nanking, the Bataan Death March, the war responsibility of the emperor, the atomic bombings of Hiroshima and Nagasaki, the American occupation. These were all things that anyone with even a passing interest in history will know of, but reading about them in detail while actually living in Japan made the past stand out, half-alive, from the printed page.

And then nineteen terrorists flew airplanes into the World Trade Center one September morning—nighttime in Japan. I watched the horror on a tiny television in a tiny apartment in suburban Nagoya, initially angered that a station would broadcast such a tasteless movie and then realizing that I was watching live news. The pages of *The Economist* that I had devoured while an undergraduate, the easy phrasings about a connected and peaceful world, began to seem almost naïve. Globalism, Fukuyama-ism, planetary managerial Hegelianism—whatever you wanted to call it, the rosy optimism that I was weaned on as a late-twentieth-century American was quickly overshadowed by suspicion and war. I grew skeptical of the academic milieu that had placed so much emphasis on liberal paradigms as answers to the horrors of the past. Something about the way history had been presented to me in my American years did not add up. Retrograde forces were in command of the present, and had not been confined in the dark corners of the past, a past that liberal democracy claimed to have overcome. I began to realize that if I wanted to understand either the past or the present, I would have to dig a lot deeper than liberal platitudes. I would have to spend a lifetime learning and thinking for myself.

Graduate School

It was in this frame of mind that I entered graduate school in Hawai'i after finishing my studies in Nagoya and doing a stint at Yunnan University, in what was then an underdeveloped corner of the People's Republic of China, and it made for heated discussions in many seminars. I quarreled with some of my fellow graduate students in the seminars, but I enjoyed many of the debates. After two years on Oahu, I earned my MA degree in Asian studies with a concentration on modern Chinese history, moved to South Korea to teach English and continue my Korean language studies, and then moved back to Japan.

Along the way, I began working as a full-time translator from Japanese. This period was transformative. I learned two skills: how to get words on paper quickly using panic as a muse (because translators work on tight deadlines and eating depends on typing), and how to read and understand Japanese until doing so became second nature. Getting words on paper and reading Japanese are both indispensable skills for writing a doctoral dissertation on the history of Japan. Being able to read Japanese and pick up on differences in how history is presented in different languages also led to a growing interest in the comfort women, both as history and as shibboleth in the humanities.

With about half a decade of work experience under my belt, I entered graduate school for the second time in 2011, this time at the University of Wisconsin. I knew that I would differ sharply with my professors and fellow graduate students on politics. But I was not there to learn about politics. I wanted to learn history.

The University of Wisconsin has a long-revered PhD program in history. Over the decades, it has produced a large corps of young scholars for top universities around the country. For me, it was a first look at how the academy made sausages. While the University of Hawai'i MA program in Asian studies was for people exploring academic careers or trying to win jobs or promotions in other fields, the Wisconsin PhD program was for people preparing for what academics call "the job market," as though only one kind of employment were even thinkable. This turns out to be a cutthroat world, tweed jackets on shoulders and ice water in veins. Graduate students jockeyed constantly for position. They went along with the shifting political winds and perjured themselves out of habit, just to stay one step ahead of the crowd and maybe secure the funding or the postdoc or the job that they coveted.

Seminars were mannerist routines. First of all, very few students read the assigned books. It was obvious even from the way their books opened on the table in front of them that they had gotten no farther than the introduction. When challenged, they simply changed the topic—or insinuated that the challenger was a racist. I remember one grad student with a fondness for Ultimate Frisbee tournaments. When I praised her for being able to travel to out-of-state frisbee events on the weekends while keeping up with the bone-crushing seminar workload, she smiled and admitted that she handled the challenge by simply not doing any of the assigned reading.

I saw a pattern emerge. When it came to contentious subjects, and particularly when it came to Japan, both faculty and students seemed to smuggle in politics and settle questions by a kind of secret fiat. In principle, my professors worked in "theory." In practice, they used whatever "theory" they needed to ferry them over the gaps in what they knew. Instead of going to the library and looking up the literature on a given subject, they created "narratives" and then spent their careers protecting that narrative. If they were very successful at it, their names would gain talismanic power that others could wield for the same purpose. Arguing from authority is surprisingly common in American academia. "Judith Butler locuta, causa finita est."

One of the main causes of this complicated exercise in applied ignorance is a refusal to read books in Japanese, or in any other languages besides English. At the University of Hawai'i, I broke my head open reading book after book in Japanese (and texts in classical and modern Chinese). Hard classic novels like those by Mishima Yukio, and bestselling modern paperbacks like *Baka no kabe* by Yoro Takeshi, a professor at Tokyo University. Reading Japanese is a difficult habit to foster, and it's easy to lose the taste for it unless one keeps at it constantly. But after my time in Hawai'i, and after working as a translator, I now prefer to read in Japanese: newspapers and books and scholarly articles. Given how many American scholars in Japanese studies stick primarily to English-language sources, this habit gives me a different perspective on the field. Things just look different when one is reading books in a completely different language and context.

History Wars

What put me firmly on a course radically different from my colleagues was going to study at Waseda University in Tokyo on a Fulbright fellowship in the fall of 2014. The divergence had largely to do with the comfort women. I hadn't gone to Waseda to study that subject. I was in Japan studying the history of Japanese law, and nothing in my research touched on the comfort women at all. Oddly enough, it was a chance encounter with the study of ancient Japan that would eventually bring me to the issue of the comfort women and set me on a collision course with the American professors.

At Waseda I met an engineering professor from another university in Japan who was a UW-Madison alumnus from decades earlier. He invited me to a Yamatai-koku study group that met on weekends. Yamatai-koku is the name for the proto-state that first established a discernible political dominion in Japan with something approaching a political center and radiating control. This subject was far from my specialty, but I enjoyed poring over the handouts distributed at the study sessions and listening to the lecturer discuss the various minutiae of the Yamatai-koku past.

What was striking about the Yamatai-koku study sessions was how meticulous the lecturer and the hundred or more students were in their use of evidence. There is archaeological, philological, iconographical, mythical, anthropological, and other kinds of evidence about the Yamatai-koku. There are mountains of texts, mounds of potsherds, fields and fields of farming implements and battle gear, village remnants, and human remains. All of this is weighed in the balance with great circumspection. There is no theory. When the professor did not know something, he did not paper over his ignorance with theoretical speculation. He said, "I don't know," not, "According to Bourdieu...." He then did his very best to find the answer by the next class. He went to the stacks to figure out what he could not understand.

What made this experience even more remarkable was the great intellectual dispute that divides the Yamatai-koku study group into two rival camps. One side holds that the original Yamatai-koku emerged in northern Kyushu. The other holds that it was near modern-day Osaka. Each position is passionately defended, yet I heard no cheap shots in the study sessions. No one belittled the other side or dismissed its views as unreasonable. No "fascist" or "revisionist" or "right-wing denialist" slurs were to be heard. The professor was not trying to win the argument for either side. He was interested in knowing where the original Yamatai-koku proto-state actually was. It did not matter to him who said what. What mattered to him was whether what was said was true.

To be sure, Yamatai-koku history is the stuff of people who have been dead for well over a thousand years. We are not talking about the ownership of islands in the South China Sea. We are not talking about the fall of the Soviet Union, or about the Dirty War in Chile. Yamatai-koku history has big ramifications for the later history of Japan, of course, and people who take Japanese history seriously may stake out a position about Yamatai-koku. But we are not likely to see mobs in streets over the Osaka vs. northern Kyushu dispute. This is not the fallout from the Sykes-Picot Treaty, not the Syrian civil war.

And yet, the meticulousness of the scholarship was striking, and eye-opening. How unlike American graduate seminars this seemed. The professor had clearly spent the time before his lecture digesting massive amounts of information. He had sifted through everything with the finest of fine-toothed combs. He took responsibility for what he said and absolutely did not lie, for his reputation would be ruined if he did. All of the hundred and more students in the lecture hall were looking at the same evidence he was. Were he to try to fake anything, they would discover it immediately, and his career would be in shambles. He would be a fool to stand in front of those conscientious and studious men and make things up. He would not last a minute if he did.

In early 2015, while still at Waseda, I began to hear rumblings of another "history war." This one concerned a short passage in a McGraw-Hill world history textbook by Herbert Ziegler and Jerry Bentley, both professors at the University of Hawai'i. The passage was about the comfort women: 200,000 sex slaves, it said, abducted at gunpoint, presented by the emperor as gifts to troops, then massacred wholesale when the war took a bad turn. It sounded much like what I had heard in Wisconsin. But then I saw that some Japanese scholars were taking exception to the passage. This was a first in my experience. I had never before noticed any objection to the standard American academic narrative.

At first there were nineteen Japanese scholars who objected, affixing their signatures to a letter of protest. Eventually there were fifty. I recognized a few of the names, which included Hata Ikuhiko, the doyen of modern Japanese historians in Japan, and Hirakawa Sukehiro, a comparative literature scholar who translated the *Divine Comedy* from middle Italian into Japanese and reads French, German, Chinese, and English besides. These were not stupid men. And they were not liars, either. The people who were rebutting the Americans' assertions about the comfort women were polyglots with top-tier educations—Princeton, Harvard, the University of Tokyo, and the best schools in Europe. They had had distinguished, decades-long careers in the highly competitive world of the Japanese academy. One couldn't simply dismiss them as cranks or buffoons.

And yet dismiss them as cranks and political hacks is exactly what the American scholars in Japanese studies tried to do. I had met some of those Japanese scholars. I knew from reading the Japanese newspapers and magazines that the fifty scholars held differing views on a variety of subjects, but they were united in believing that the passage on the comfort women in the Ziegler and Bentley textbook was flawed. My skepticism rose to the highest levels.

I knew from my Yamatai-koku study that it would be extremely strange if any reputable scholar in Japan were to be a bald-faced liar. I knew it would be almost impossible for fifty of them to be such.

I went to the Waseda library and began to read about the comfort women, in Japanese. I was astonished. There was a rich literature on the subject, and almost none of it comported with the sex-slaves-abducted-at-gunpoint narrative on which the Americans were insisting. I read works by Hata and Hirakawa, by Nishioka Tsutomu (fluent in Korean and an expert in modern Korean history and politics), by Yoshimi Yoshiaki (another well-known modern historian), and by feminists like Ueno Chizuko. I learned as well of the work of the South Korean professor Park Yu-ha. The comfort women had worked in a very complicated milieu, in the middle of a civilizational war for possession of the twentieth century. They worked also at the extremities of progressivism, on the coattails of a drive to regulate prostitution in the 1920s and 1930s in Europe, North America, and Japan. They wrote letters home, wired money to relatives, fell in love with soldiers (or did not requite the love that soldiers had for them), and survived famine and poverty by taking part in very old Korean and Japanese traditions—worldwide traditions, it must be said—of selling the body for money.

I also began doing my own research in English-language sources. I read the English book by C. Sarah Soh on the comfort women, a model of balanced scholarship. I read others, but found that the English-language literature by professional scholars was almost entirely one-sided. I contacted a veteran of the Korean War, Lt. Col. (ret.) Archie Miyamoto, who served in intelligence in Korea and later acted as a military liaison there. He was also a veteran helicopter pilot from the Vietnam War. He was raised partly in

Japan and speaks both English and Japanese as native languages. Miyamoto stressed several points.

First, the Korean peninsula had been Japanese territory from 1910. As such, it was obviously not a theater of war, and therefore no comfort stations had been established there—contrary to the assertions of some who later claimed to have been comfort women.

Second, the Americans had conducted interrogations of captured comfort women during World War II. These interrogations confirmed that the comfort women were prostitutes.

Third, the allegations about hunts for comfort women on the Korean peninsula were gravely insulting to Korean men. Had even one Japanese soldier tried such a thing, Miyamoto told me, Korean men would have risen up and there would have been a peninsula-wide rebellion. "Korean men are not cowards," Miyamoto said.

Fourth, kidnapping women and then taking them to the front lines was a notion that anyone with military experience would find absurd. Combat involves crouching in foxholes, running for cover, advancing over broken terrain, dragging shot-up comrades back behind concertina wire, throwing live grenades at the enemy closing in. Self-preservation is everything. Unarmed civilians, especially women with no combat experience whatsoever, are a severe liability. The war in the Pacific and in Asia was brutal, as anyone who has studied it—or lived it—will attest. Any platoon sergeant who ordered his men to risk their lives to protect a prostitute on the front lines would have been inviting insubordination, or fragging.

I began meeting with some of the Japanese professors and researchers to hear their side of the comfort women story. I met with Nishioka, Hata, Hirakawa, Yamashita Eiji (an economic history expert), Moteki Hiromichi (the director of the Society for the Dissemination of Historical Fact), magazine and newspaper editors and writers, and friends and colleagues. Nobody who could read Japanese and who knew the historical sources claimed that there were 200,000 sex slaves. The truth was much different and much more complicated than I had imagined.

Chizuko Allen, a UH-Mānoa professor (who happened by sheer coincidence to be my scholarship coordinator while I was at UH), accompanied someone from the Japanese consulate general in Honolulu to Herbert Ziegler's office hours to discuss the comfort women passage in the textbook.[94] An American scholar of Japan—who, it turns out, was almost completely unaware of the Japanese-language scholarship on the comfort women—denounced this visit as "an attempt to restrict academic freedom!" This other scholar then used a meeting of the Association for Asian Studies to marshal support for a petition that she was putting together along with another American scholar of Japan—who also had no discernible expertise in the history of the comfort women. (One of his most recent offerings is "People, Animals, and Island Encounters: A Pig's History of the Pacific.") Soon there were two petitions designed to defend the Ziegler and Bentley textbook from infringements of academic freedom. The newspapers picked up the story, and before long one of the petitions had more than five hundred signatures. It turned into international news.

But still there was no evidence, and the American petitions did not even specify the number of comfort women there had been. The American petitions were designed to defend the Ziegler and Bentley textbook from infringements of academic freedom, but presented nothing to substantiate any of the Ziegler and Bentley claims.

I wrote to the American Historical Association newsletter (*Perspectives on History*), where one of the petitions had been published, to point out its inconsistencies and to note that the Americans had much less convincing evidence than the Japanese scholars did. I also gave a private talk to a group of scholars and editors at the offices of the Japan Institute for National Fundamentals (JINF), a think tank founded and headed by Sakurai Yoshiko, a prominent journalist and telecaster and later a political analyst.

The Fallout

My venture into the comfort women issue did not go over well with my adviser at the University of Wisconsin, Louise Young. As I later discovered to my chagrin, Young had long been working behind the scenes to craft and maintain the American academic narrative on the subject. Before my letter to the AHA newsletter appeared in print, but at a time when it would probably have been circulating on social media, Young informed me that she would no longer be my adviser. She was passing me off to her junior colleague Sarah Thal (who also signed the petition). She gave no reason for the change—which had never been discussed or even mentioned in passing before—apart from vague comments about being busy.

Young had indeed been busy. I would eventually learn that she was tied up—and fit to be tied—all that spring investigating my activities relating to the comfort women. On April 28, 2015, Young wrote to Yukiko Hanawa, a New York University clinical associate professor, asking, in reference to information that Hanawa had sent her, "Did Jason's name come up in connection with Uemura Takashi? I surely hope not." Uemura Takashi, as readers will learn later in this book, is central to the comfort women controversy. Hanawa wrote back to Young on May 4:

> Hi Louise, He [Morgan] is speaking at the Central Washington University where there is a documentary being shown by one of the faculty there—a history denier film—and an event that is in response to that, which brings in various Japan studies folks (but not people who does [*sic*] work on comfort women either.) The whole thing is a nightmare of a mess. I know where I stand and none of the "Yoshida" controversy has swayed me, but the way that our side has constructed some of the argument is being picked off by the most rudimentary positivist methods. As if this is how "history" is done.

Hanawa is upset that people doing "rudimentary positivist" history—by which she seems to mean working with source documents—are ruining the argument "constructed" by her "side." According to Hanawa, it seems, working with source documents is not "how 'history' is done."

An email from Young to Sarah Thal could perhaps shed light on the reasons for her apprehension. On May 9, 2015, she wrote to ask Thal, "Did M[organ] write a letter to Perspectives [the AHA newsletter]? Or just rant about the statement here?" Young was referring to a May 2, 2015 story in the *Sankei Shimbun*, written by the same Komori Yoshihisa whom Dudden attacked in her messages to Jeffrey Wasserstrom and David Kaye. In the piece, Komori mentions me and my letter to the AHA about the comfort women controversy. He also details the response by nineteen Japanese historians to the American academics' defense of the error-riddled passage about the comfort women in the McGraw-Hill textbook.[95] Young had shared a link to that story with Thal and another UW-Madison history professor on May 7, and Thal had written in response: "Jim [probably Jim Sweet, UW-Madison historian and department chair at the time] was very interested in the chancellor's [Rebecca Blank] upcoming trip to Korea. I think a key point will be that it would be difficult to raise money from our wealthy Korean alumni if we've pissed them off by returning the Korea Foundation money...." In other words, "wealthy Korean alumni," and their money, were in the heads of those in the History Department who were making decisions related to Asia. The timing of my comfort women controversy may have meant—who knows?—that the Madison historians took steps to cancel me in consideration of what size checks "wealthy Korean alumni" would (or would not) write. But one hardly needs to be a weatherman to see which way the wind is blowing here.

I also learned that in May of 2015 Young had worked with the office at the University of Wisconsin that coordinated my Fulbright scholarship to reprimand me. I was called into the office of the

Fulbright Japan director, Matthew Sussman (not himself a scholar) and told not to mention in public that I was a Fulbright recipient when speaking to political groups. This talk was apparently a great relief to Young and the UW-Madison Fulbright coordinator, Erin Crawley. "I just read a response sent yesterday from IIE [the Fulbright agency] to me that the Japan [Fulbright] Commission was aware of his [i.e., Morgan's] activities," Crawley wrote to Young on May 22, 2015. "'The Fulbright Commission in Japan is aware of Mr. Morgan's activities and the Executive Director [i.e., Sussman] there has had a discussion with him regarding how he represents himself in public forums.' That's all they said, but it sounds like he at least heard that." This message was an attempt to reassure Young, who had written to Crawley the day before, May 21, with a link to a copy of my letter to the AHA, which the Japan Institute for National Fundamentals had reprinted with my permission and thanks on May 11. "See English text," Young wrote to Crawley, referring to the updated JINF page. "Morgan is no longer using his affiliations."

That was hardly the end of the panic. Or the beginning, for that matter. Young's behind-the-scenes maneuvering, and the enthusiastic cooperation her colleagues provided her in canceling me, brings my career at the UW into much sharper focus. I had never been shy about debating in seminar. And I had been outspoken on issues that the History Department and the University of Wisconsin as a whole saw as matters not open for debate, or even questioning. In 2013, a year or so before going to Waseda, I made the pages of the *Wall Street Journal* for protesting the "diversity training" that teaching assistants in the history PhD program were forced to undergo. Young had reprimanded me several times for speaking out.

Other grad students were vocal, even militant, about fringe-left causes. Some UW professors encouraged their students to take part in the demonstrations (which occasionally looked more like riots) at the state capitol against Governor Scott Walker, a Republican. To my knowledge, no left-wing student or professor was ever rebuked for activities like this. The internal list-servs at the History Department carried heavy doses of overtly partisan fringe-left sloganeering. Some of it was explicitly anti-Semitic, as in the TA union's April 2016 calls to support the Boycott-Divestment-Sanctions movement (which I reported to the Anti-Defamation League). Some of it was nakedly threatening, as when my fellow grad students told me not to "cross the line" in disagreeing about LGBT issues. History professors and department staff all received these list-serv emails. I am not aware that a single person reprimanded the people making threats against me.

While at Waseda, I decided to continue to speak out. This was higher education, after all, and open and honest debate was paramount. I pulled no punches and did not bite my tongue. As I studied the history of the comfort women, I grew increasingly convinced that the American narrative was not just wrong. It was, I began to suspect, deliberately wrong.

I returned to Madison, wrote my dissertation—"in record time," even Louise Young had to admit—and prepared to go on "the job market." I submitted perhaps two dozen applications for tenure-track positions, postdocs, and year-long research opportunities. I went to conferences, networked, wrote emails, made phone calls, went to colleges to speak with deans…and got nothing. Fortuitously, a friend in Japan contacted me about a possible position at Reitaku University, a small school in suburban Chiba, just outside of Tokyo. I applied, interviewed, and was hired.

Only later did I discover that my advisers had blacklisted me. After Young had dropped me, Sarah Thal took over as my adviser. She wrote letters of recommendation for all of my applications. She seemed very willing, even eager, to do so. I was grateful for her help. But by chance, when some application materials were later returned to me, the package contained, probably by mistake, a copy of Thal's letter. "Throughout 2015," she wrote, "Jason also became known on both sides of the Pacific for statements criticizing American historians of Japan and supporting Prime Minister [Shinzo] Abe's whitewashing of Japan's wartime past."

I was stunned. And hurt. I had trusted Thal. I believed that she was trying to help me get a job. As it turned out, she had another mission. I had dissented publicly from the prescribed narrative about the comfort women. Her task was to banish me from the guild. And Thal wasn't finished.

I had become very interested in the history of the comfort women during my time studying at Waseda University. So interested, in fact, that I translated Professor Hata's definitive history of the comfort women from Japanese into English. Hata supplied much new material that had surfaced over the decades since his book was first published. I learned a lot about Japanese history, and the histories of various places in East and Southeast Asia, by doing the translation and reading through the hundreds and hundreds of sources that Hata cites. When the book was finally published, I responded to a general call by the UW-Madison History Department for alumni news. A translation of a major Japanese scholar's book is certainly newsworthy, I thought. I sent the information about the book to the department email address as instructed. Soon enough, my news was posted to the department website and social media accounts. A cheerful letter from an undergraduate receptionist informed me that the news was live.

But then, just a few days later, the news was scrubbed. It had been posted across multiple pages and platforms. Then it disappeared, leaving no trace.

I later found out what happened. After receiving the copy of Thal's "recommendation letter" sabotaging my job applications, I used FOIA to get to the bottom of what was going on. I got hundreds of pages of emails from many at the History Department involved in my cases. Part of that FOIA trove included messages from Leslie Abadie, a History Department administrator at the University of Wisconsin. She wrote to Laird Boswell, the department chair; Joe

Dennis, a professor of Chinese history; and another administrator named Todd Anderson:

> Hi! Not copying [name of undergraduate receptionist who posted the Hata publication news] in until we all chat. [The undergraduate receptionist] doesn't know the back story, [and] unknowingly posted something on FB today about Jason Morgan's work on Japanese comfort women. Maybe it isn't problematic—I'm not qualified to judge—but someone should evaluate. And perhaps alert his advisors—Louise [Young] and Sarah [Thal].

Boswell forwarded the message to Young and Thal nineteen minutes later:

> See Leslie's message below. [...], our new undergraduate assistant and dept receptionist, who is in charge of posting on Facebook posted something today on our Facebook page about Jason Morgan's new book. Can you advise about what we should do (if anything)?

About an hour and a half later, Thal wrote back:

> I was shocked to see it on Facebook. Please take it down. Thanks, Sarah

About two hours later, Boswell replied:

> Once we remove the post (likely in the am when the office staff come back) should we post something to the effect that we disassociate ourselves from the book? Or will we merely compound the problem? Maybe the best solution is to remove the posts and move on.

Young replied about five minutes later:

> Just seeing this. I am not on facebook [*sic*] and need to get some help to evaluate the situation in order to responsibly weigh in. But I agree in principle with whatever Sarah suggests. In the past, giving him [Morgan] attention does seem to compound the problem.

Five minutes after that, Thal was back:

> I think just remove it and ignore it. If someone wants to find it again, they just won't be able to.... I don't think we should say anything. Thanks! Sarah

It took less than two minutes for Boswell to reply:

> Seems reasonable to me. Laird

Thal wrote back shortly thereafter:

> Exactly. Since you know Jason, you have a sense of Hata's stance on the issue, with which we don't want to be associated. But I also think the more we draw attention to it, the worse off we are. Thanks! Sarah

Boswell wrote to his administrative staff that same evening:

> Whoever sees this first should remove the posts about Jason Morgan's book from Twitter and Facebook immediately. He takes very controversial positions with which the department does not want to be associated.

At 8:02 the next morning, the undergraduate assistant wrote:

> Hi Laird, Sorry, I didn't know this when he reached out to me. The post was taken down from Facebook and Twitter.

After I discovered that I could no longer find the post online, I remonstrated with the History Department to put it back up. Joe Dennis replied:

> About your news item, it was posted prematurely. It has been taken down pending further consideration.

A week or so later, Colleen Dunlavy, a professor in American history and also the Web Committee chair, wrote to me:

> Thanks for getting in touch about your news and for your patience over Thanksgiving break and while we sort out our new processes for generating a flow of news.
>
> We removed the original post because the "voice" in which it was written—always an essential consideration for historians—was unclear (the department's, the publisher's, or yours). We have re-posted your news in a form that indicates the voice more clearly. (In the two news items you mention, you will notice that the authorial voice is clear, since both are excerpts from articles published by members of our faculty.)

This was very different from what Dunlavy was saying in private. Ten days before sending me the message just above, she had written to Boswell:

> I'm not sure what to think about pulling the Jason Morgan notice—that begins to feel like censorship. We're not routinely vetting the contents of publications that get notice, are we?

The post I sent in response to the call for alumni news had

been deleted from the department's website and social media accounts, and in its place was a post attacking the Hata book—something that Dunlavy doubted had been done for anyone else. The alumni and faculty news sections of the department website regularly featured op-eds and journal articles written by far-left professors, graduate students, and alumni with unabashed political viewpoints on full display. Shrill anti-Trumpism was all the rage in that shop. Professor Hata's book, by contrast, is apolitical. It is a history volume by perhaps the most esteemed living historian in Japan, and yet it was treated as something politically incendiary.

I later wrote to Susan Zaeske, dean of the College of Letters and Science at the UW-Madison. I shared my concerns about the censorship of my post, and also about Thal's recommendation letter torpedoing my career. I included a photo of the part of the letter where Thal leveled against me the unfounded and frankly bizarre accusation that I was acting as an agent for the prime minister of Japan. Dean Zaeske replied:

> I am confident that letters written by UW-Madison Department of History professors meet standards of professional conduct. The College of Letters & Science, the History Department, and the UW-Madison are committed to the full and free exchange of ideas from multiple perspectives. We remain steadfast in supporting that commitment.

I wrote back to Zaeske with a brief message of incredulity. I could not believe that anyone who had read Thal's letter would argue that it met "standards of professional conduct." It was a political hit job. Even more mind-boggling was the boilerplate assertion that the UW-Madison History Department was "committed to the full and free exchange of ideas from multiple perspectives," while one of its ranking professors suspected her employer of censorship. I had been canceled and sabotaged. Now I was being gaslighted too.

The story might have ended there. But I later learned that I was not the only person whom Louise Young had been censoring. Another was Miki Dezaki. The name may not be familiar, but Dezaki is a documentary filmmaker who made a film about the comfort women controversy as a graduate school project for Professor Nakano Koichi at Sophia University in Tokyo. The film, *Shusenjo* ("main battleground"), is narrated very clearly from an activist standpoint. To Dezaki's credit, it includes cameos by several people who are critical of the activist narrative and have been outspoken in calling for a reappraisal of the comfort women issue and history.

Dezaki wanted to screen *Shusenjo* at UW-Madison. In early August 2019, the Department of East Asian Studies, where the screening was to be held, sought advice from Louise Young and Charles Kim, another history professor. Young replied, "It sounds to me like Dezaki has done a 'both sidesism' version of the comfort women issue. One that provides a platform for deniers to speak basically unchallenged." She judged the film unworthy of being shown at Wisconsin.

Charles Kim opened by following Young's lead. "Seeing clips of the right-wing interviewees was quite jarring for me," Kim wrote. "My initial reaction was that I would not want to have these videos shown" at the UW. But Kim was persuaded to give an OK to *Shusenjo* once he confirmed that Dezaki shared his prejudices. (Indeed, several of the people in Dezaki's film, those whom Young had labeled "deniers," later unsuccessfully sued him over how unfairly they were portrayed.) "Based on the videos that we watched," Kim continued, speaking of *Shusenjo* clips, "I got the feeling that the documentary itself ultimately does steer viewers [to] the understanding that the conservative view is a form of fake history." Kim was "encouraged by the negative reaction by [Prime Minister] Abe [Shinzo] and the right-wing interviewees featured in the film."

Young was overruled. Dezaki was eventually able to screen his film. He evidently holds the "correct" views on the comfort women. I don't, so I was cast out.

By longstanding academic tradition, journals did not retract articles when critics alleged a misrepresentation of a publicly available source. Scholars have always objected (vehemently) to articles that misrepresented source material, but they did not demand retraction. Instead, they wrote critiques that proved their objections. Journals retracted articles primarily in the experimental sciences. There, the scientist holds the data privately, which means that other scholars cannot test his claims on the basis of those data. But if someone—say, a disaffected postdoc in a lab—shows that a scientist invented data or faked his results, the journal retracts his article.

We are not laboratory scientists. We do not have private data. Instead, we interpret widely available published material. No one has claimed that either of us invented data or faked results. Gordon, the Quintet, Dudden, and the others claim that we misread government memoranda. They say that we have information about too few contracts (Gordon implies zero contracts; Suk-Gersen explicitly states zero contracts) to warrant our generalizations. They claim that most young women lacked the agency we attribute to them. These are disputes of interpretation, not falsifying of evidence.

By longstanding academic tradition, when one scholar thought another scholar misread material or overclaimed—whether mistakenly, negligently, or intentionally—the dissatisfied scholar did not demand that the journal retract the article, or publish ad hominem attacks in the *New Yorker*. Rather, the critic wrote a rebuttal and submitted it to the same review process. If it was published, other scholars could then compare the two analyses. That is the method that honors the life of the mind and the free exchange of ideas that sustains it. This is the method to which we hope the university community returns.

CHAPTER 2

THE COMFORT STATIONS

Morgan's maternal grandfather worked in the Civilian Conservation Corps (CCC) in the 1930s. He had been born into a wealthy family in New Orleans, but his father lost everything in the stock market crash of 1929. Morgan's grandfather had been enjoying his days as a fraternity member at Tulane University. Then, one day, his family had no more money for tuition. He had to leave school (he was never able to go back) and find a job. The only work available was with the government, so off he went into the woods of the Southeast to build state parks and do other public works projects for the CCC. He had the two choices: work for the CCC, or beg on the street.

Imagine, if you can, that Morgan's grandfather had been born a daughter instead of a son. Imagine that she was born in a small farming village on the Korean peninsula in, say, 1922, instead of into a tony townhouse in uptown New Orleans in 1910. Poverty would have been a very different thing in that case. Many Koreans did not have the resources to send their children to school, where they could learn to read, write, and calculate, and perhaps learn the language of the colonizer—the skills needed to get the best work. Maybe there was no schoolhouse in the village or any of the surrounding villages. Maybe the family needed the children's labor on the farm.

Think back again to the Great Depression in America, to the famous photos taken by two employees of the Farm Security Administration, Dorothea Lange and Walker Evans. Think of the drawn, dirty, careworn faces, the tattered clothes, the calloused bare feet. Whether in Korea, Japan, or the United States, many farm families found themselves without resources. But in Japan and the United States, many children attended elementary school,[1] while in Korea many did not. People lived or died according to the weather. If the crop failed due to drought, flood, hail, or any other act of nature, people had no food. They had no money, no other skills, no way to eat.

Suppose a stranger comes to the village one day. He has an oily look about him, but he speaks Korean, maybe even the regional dialect. He approaches some of the men in the fields and makes an offer that in the United States might have gotten him run out of town on a rail, or shot. But in 1930s Korea, and in Japan too, the offer was within the Overton window of social plausibility. It was an offer made plausible by the crushing poverty of the people to whom it was made.

The oily stranger cuts to the chase. "I will give you ten thousand dollars for your daughter. She'll pay me back by working at a 'comfort station'—a brothel for the Japanese military. Room and board are free. She'll work for two years at most, and if she repays the debt before that she can quit early."

Most of the fathers would have refused. Whether in Korea or Japan, the vast majority would have had nothing to do with such an offer. For obvious evolutionary reasons, most fathers everywhere care for their children, and always have.

But every society has its exceptions. Parents do not necessarily love all their children equally. They do not face identical financial pressures. They do not have the same level of marketable talents. Suppose one father out of fifty leans on the handle of his hoe and mulls it over. He looks at the meager herbage sprouting in the field. It's going to be another lean year. His wife is already mixing grass in with the porridge to stretch it out for everyone. Ten thousand dollars, and one less mouth to feed, would make a difference.

In both Korea and Japan, some parents agreed to the offer. In many societies around the world—perhaps in most societies—some people have trafficked in children. It happened in Japan and Korea. It happened in Europe. Tragically, it still happens. Reporters write of orphans being trafficked out of eastern Europe, for example, or the "coyotes" smuggling children across the southern U.S. border.

But paying a parent was not the only way that brokers located the women who would work as prostitutes at the brothels called comfort stations. It probably was not even the most common way. Instead, brokers solicited young women directly. The women interacted with the brokers of their own accord and exercised what, in the universities, we call "agency."

In most societies around the world, some women have independently chosen to work as a prostitute. They choose it for the money. For some women in some situations, prostitution can pay extraordinarily well. Kimberly Kay Hoang, a sociologist at the University of Chicago, decided to study human trafficking in Vietnam and spent several years working as a barmaid in places where prostitutes sold their services. To her surprise, she found no human trafficking. Hoang writes:

> When I began my research in 2006, I also wanted, as a feminist researcher and scholar, to study "trafficked women," or "victims" of the sex trade. However, I found that few of the women in my study were forced, duped, or coerced into the sex trade. As far as I could tell, none of the workers I spoke with had been pressured by pimps or bar owners to have sex for money against their will.[2]

The women had not necessarily come from impoverished backgrounds:

> Women who catered to [overseas Vietnamese]... often claimed that they had entered into sex work because of poverty, but as I followed them to their homes and into shopping centers, I quickly learned that they came from families that were fairly wealthy by local standards and even in comparison to many people I knew in the United States.[3]

As prostitutes, they earned unambiguously high incomes:

> For the women I studied who catered to wealthy local and other Asian businessmen, the sex industry allowed them to escape rural life and move into some of the most lavish spaces in Vietnam. These women earned more than white-collar professionals with master's degrees who worked in local businesses.... Sex work provided these women with opportunities to advance economically and to escape exploitative working conditions. Critically, these women were not victims of trafficking. They were free agents who could quit working at any time.[4]

And they insisted on safe sex:

> [T]he vast majority of men and women... used protection. In fact, safe sex was part of the workers' negotiations with their clients because it enabled them to stay in the business longer. Male clients, moreover, often encouraged safe sexual practices in order to protect their wives and their other girlfriends and lovers....[5]

Return now to our hypothetical Korean family. If the daughter decided to accept a recruiter's offer, she would then have told her family. She did not do this out of filial respect. She did it because (if a minor) she needed their permission before she could obtain her exit visa. Otherwise, she could not get much farther than the local train station. On both the Korean peninsula and the Japanese islands, the government required people heading abroad to apply for an exit visa at the local police station. Young women were required to appear in person, bring their work contract, and (at least if a minor) have their parents' consent. The police officers checking the paperwork were required to ensure that the women understood the job for which they had contracted.

By the 1930s, many young women in Japan and on the Korean peninsula had already chosen to work as prostitutes abroad. Many would choose to work in the brothels, or "comfort stations," that were established for exclusive use by Imperial Japan's soldiers, sailors, and officers. Those choices may not fit the way we prefer to think about the world. But those choices were made. The comfort women chose what they thought—whether rightly or wrongly—was their least bad option.

The "king's shilling" is not out of place here as an analogy. In many ways, the Japanese and Korean soldiers, sailors, and officers who patronized the comfort women in the comfort stations had themselves faced a choice between poverty and a dangerous job. Over time, an increasing fraction were conscripted, to be sure. But many—both on the Japanese islands and on the Korean peninsula—chose the job of soldiering or of working on naval vessels as the least bad alternative to starving. We do not describe them as slaves. We also do not call the men who stormed the beaches of Normandy "slaves" or "victims," even though very few of them would have chosen to die in a hail of gunfire had they really had any say in the matter. Throughout history, many of the men who enlisted in armies knew the job was dangerous, but chose it because they lacked a better alternative. The comfort women did the same.

Morgan's maternal grandfather was far too young to fight in World War I, and too old for the front lines in World War II. He stayed in the United States, disassembling captured Japanese aircraft (including the much-envied Zero fighter) and trying to build an

American fighter plane that could match it. By the early 1940s, he was married and was supporting a family. He had recovered from his family's financial disaster, built a respectable lower-middle-class home for his wife and children, and would go to his grave giving thanks to God for Franklin Delano Roosevelt and the Civilian Conservation Corps.

By contrast, Morgan's paternal grandfather was born at just the right, or the wrong, time. He was seventeen and a half years old in December 1941, when news broke of the bombing of Pearl Harbor. It was obvious that there would be a war, and a draft. He joined the Navy, as his father before him had done.

This was probably not Morgan's grandfather's first choice. But he did not have many choices. He had dropped out of middle school, and his father—a merchant sailor—did not earn much, and was not around much of the time anyway. His family had no money. So, Morgan's grandfather left school to work as a delivery boy for a bread company and other firms in New Orleans—anything he could get. He lived with his mother in a neighborhood in the Ninth Ward, in the largely Black part of town. It was the same neighborhood where Louis Armstrong had lived, also in crushing poverty. The Navy was not a C-suite on Wall Street, but it probably seemed less dangerous than the Army or the Marines, both of which would soon be calling up draft numbers. He talked it over with some other young men in the neighborhood. The military was dangerous, they reasoned, but they would be paid and would be fed three times a day. So off they went.

Morgan's grandfather was sent to Connecticut for training and then sent on an aircraft carrier to the Pacific. His friends flew out on missions and did not come back. He saw kamikaze attacks. Death was very much a risk in this line of work, but promotion was possible and the pay was steady. The king's shilling is just a shilling, but it is more than nothing.

There is a world of difference between a poor young man in southern Louisiana and a poor young woman on the Korean peninsula. But they shared poverty and much that went with it. We respect them both, and we think that respecting people means honoring their agency, their ability to think and act for themselves and to navigate deep uncertainty with only their wits and their guts to guide them.

Some poor women in Japan and Korea chose to work as "comfort women" in the brothels next to the Japanese bases during World War II. The Japanese government had already regulated domestic prostitution with a licensing regime, and the "comfort women" regime merely extended it to the brothels overseas. Most of the prostitutes who worked there came from the Japanese islands and the Korean peninsula. Like domestic prostitutes, they demanded and received the bulk of their pay in advance. Prostitution is dangerous, harsh, and reputation-destroying anywhere. The war zone multiplied the risks manyfold. Before they left for the job, the women insisted on cash upfront.

The women agreed to work for a fixed period, typically two years. This period was a contractual maximum: they could leave at the end of that period regardless of how much revenue they had generated. Should they earn enough to repay their advance earlier, they could quit before the contractual maximum. Many (perhaps most) did exactly that. Typically, the women appear to have worked about one and a half years.

A Korean comfort woman named Hyun Byung-sook explained the process by which she became a prostitute working at a comfort station, in an interview first published in 2003 and recently reprinted by Lee Wooyoun, a prominent economic historian. For ease of reading, we identify the speakers and add our own comments in brackets:

Q: "How much did you get from [the first brothel you worked at]?"

Hyun: "500 won [Korean won and Japanese yen could be exchanged 1 for 1]. The term was for two years. I gave the 500 won to my father and mother. After the two years, I went home, but there was no point in just hanging around. I thought I'd go to another place, and make some more money to give to my father and mother. I didn't intend to stay in the village."...

Hyun: "So I went to Pakch'on to meet a person named 'Park Ka.' I went to an inn, and asked, 'I heard [someone came] to buy women. Where is he around here?' 'At that inn over there,' was the answer. 'He came from China to buy women. Why don't you go over there?' So I went...and a man was sitting there. 'Did you come to buy women?' I asked. 'What's this about, young lady?' he replied. 'I'd like to go to China too and earn money,' I said."

Q: "Grandma [questioner respectfully addressing Hyun]. Did you know at the time what you were going to be doing in China?"

Hyun: "I knew."

Q: "Did you also know you'd be dealing with lots of Japanese soldiers?"

Hyun: "Of course."...

Q: "Where did you hear that?"

Hyun: "I heard it through rumors. I heard lots of stories. I found [Park Ka] after wandering around. So I asked him if he'd buy me. He said sure, and asked how much I wanted. 'My father and mother would be bothered [if I were gone too long], so how much would you give me for a maximum 3 years?' I asked. 'I'll give you 2000 won,' he said. 'But 2000 won doesn't even come to 1000 won a year. I want 1000 won a year,' said I. 'Ok, I'll pay 3000 won. Go home and get your parents' consent.'"

[N.B.: Note that they expressly negotiated both price and term length.]...

Q: "Did you get [your parents'] seal?"

Hyun: "Of course. If you brought along your father or mother, you got the money. But I was told to get the seal of my grandfather and grandmother too. They were strict at the time."

Q: "How old were you?"

Hyun: "I think I'd turned 16.... I took my father down to the riverbank and talked with him. 'Dad, there's a man who came to buy women. He tells me how much he'll pay, so I want to go far away and make money.' I wanted to make a comfortable life for my father, and wanted him to be able to eat the food he liked. 'Dad, let me work.'"

[N.B.: In contemporaneous descriptions of the brothels, 16-year-olds are rare. Most of the women are in their 20s.]

Lee Wooyoun (editorial comment): The advance was not payable unless a parent was there in person. The consent of the parents and grandparents were also required. It's hard to understand why the consents and seals of the mother and the grandparents were also necessary. Probably they were joint guarantors....

Hyun: "'In that case, I'll let you go,' said my father, and wrote his and my mother's names and attached the seal.... We went to Pakch'on. My father said [to the man], 'I'm selling her to you, so don't sell her off to some other place.'...'My father demands this,' I said. 'Do as you like,' the man replied. 'Ok, let's go,' I said."...

Lee: She said that she was not able to obtain many customers at her first place. She attributed this to her appearance. So, she decided to move to Fengtian in China.

Hyun: "I didn't have a choice. I couldn't get a single customer at the place. I was not attractive. The customers all chose the pretty girls. Who's going to pick an unattractive one?...I said to the son of the man who had brought me there, 'If I stay here, I won't be able to pay off the principal, so let me go somewhere else.' 'But we wrote a contract promising your father that we wouldn't send you somewhere else,' he replied. 'You can do it if the person herself consents,' I said. 'OK, go to the Fengtian clearing office and if someone buys you, we'll take the money,' he answered. 'What about the interest?' I asked. 'Skip the interest,' he said. 'Work hard and go home.'" ...

[N.B.: Note that she cared about paying off the principal and returning home early before the expiration of the three-year term.]

Lee: Unfortunately, she was not able to earn money in Fengtian either. This time she decided to follow the military and move [to a comfort station in another location in China]. The owner there was Korean as well....

Lee: The amount of the advance was decided through negotiation. The length of the contract term was clear. There was a term

> dealing with transfers. The consent and seal of the household head was necessary. The comfort woman and her parents understood what work was involved with the Japanese soldiers, and that the advance would transfer to the new [brothel owner] in the case of a transfer. What else is necessary to prove that this was contractual?[6]

The comfort women were not, under any plausible definition, sex slaves. They were not slaves at all. Someone who is captured and sold into work for an indefinite period is a slave. But someone who agrees to work for a finite period of time and receives her wages in advance is an indentured servant. Most Africans who went to the New World went as slaves. But many Europeans paid for their transatlantic fare through indenture contracts. There is a universe of difference, recognized by precise legal categories, between someone who has no freedom—a slave—and someone who barters part of his or her freedom by the hour (a wage earner), by the month or year (a salary earner), or for a fixed period of time—an indentured servant, or, in some cases, someone who has enlisted in military or other government service. If the comfort women were slaves, then so is every soldier, a fortiori. So is everyone who is not financially independent and must work for a living. Constraints shape human life. But the human will works both within and against those constraints.

PROSTITUTION IN JAPAN AND KOREA

Since the comfort station program was an extension of the domestic licensing regime for prostitution that was already in place before the war, it is best understood in that context. In prewar Japan, elite bureaucrats were also intellectuals, and many of them shared the progressive reformist ideals of their peers in the United States and western Europe. The notion that prostitution should be legal only in licensed and regulated form reflected those ideals.[7] Progressive bureaucrats apparently hoped that the licensing framework would help to shield prostitutes from the worst of the depredations visited upon them by violent pimps and other criminals. Prostitutes would register with the police. They would submit to regular checkups (with licensed physicians) for disease. They would contract directly with an established business (the brothel) that had a public reputation. At least in theory, this framework gave women an institutional standing that kept them from being invisible to the authorities and at the mercy of a criminal underclass.

Licensing prostitutes, in other words, was about regulating prostitution. In principle, it was about ensuring that the women could leave the industry under the terms of their negotiated contract. It was not designed to lock prostitutes into the job. Rather, it was designed to provide them with a legal foothold from which to enforce the terms of their contract, and open the way to their eventually leaving that line of work.

In 1924, some 50,100 women worked as licensed prostitutes in Japan. Another 77,100 worked as licensed geisha (who sometimes sold sexual services), and an estimated 50,000 women worked as unlicensed prostitutes.[8] Women in the industry generally preferred to work at the licensed brothels rather than in the unlicensed sector. From 1920 to 1927, barely 62 percent of the women looking for jobs in Tokyo as licensed prostitutes found work.[9]

One reason that women preferred the licensed sector was because of the lower risk of disease. In 1932, for example, 3.2 percent of the licensed prostitutes in Tokyo had venereal or other infectious disease, while the rate was 9.7 percent among unlicensed prostitutes.[10] Other studies report a 1–3 percent infection rate among licensed prostitutes, but substantially over 10 percent among the unlicensed.[11]

The licensed sector also offered higher pay. The licensed brothel was an established business. It could invest in its reputation for high-quality service. For that reputation, it could charge a premium, and it could afford to pay high wages to the women that customers most preferred. During the 1920s, licensed prostitutes in Tokyo usually negotiated advance payments in the range of 1,000 to 1,200 yen.[12] They generally agreed to a maximum term of six years.[13] In fact, they typically repaid their advance early (often about three years) and then quit.

Earning 1,200 yen for about three years of work was a high income in the 1920s. Given that the licensed Japanese prostitutes apparently received revenue-based cash in addition, the actual income was higher still. Obviously, surveys of prostitute earnings are not likely to be precise anywhere. According to police and labor data, however, licensed prostitutes in Tokyo during the late 1920s and early 1930s earned incomes between 1.5 and 2.1 times the earnings of female factory workers. In 1926, for example, female factory workers earned 312 yen per year, often without room and board; licensed prostitutes earned 641 yen, usually with room and board besides.[14]

The Logic to the Indenture Contract

Licensed prostitutes in Tokyo generally worked under an indentured servitude contract. The economic logic was straightforward.[15] Young women understood that prostitution was dangerous and harsh, and that it imposed a large upfront hit to their reputation. What is more, they understood that they incurred the reputational hit even if they quit after a very short period. Recruiters promised them very high wages, but the women understood that recruiters had every incentive to exaggerate.

As a result, before a young woman agreed to work at a brothel she needed credible assurance that she would earn wages high enough to compensate her for all the dangers, risks, stigma, and other negative aspects of the job. Were there no reputational hit upon entering the industry, she might try the job for a few months to see how much she could earn. In the circumstances, however, she could not readily verify the recruiters' claims without incurring a serious reputational cost.

The women and the brothels solved this contractual problem through an arrangement in which the recruiters (a) paid the woman a large fraction of her future earnings upfront, and (b) capped the number of years she would have to work. If the brothel paid her 1,000 yen in advance and set the maximum term at six years, she knew the minimum she would earn. She also knew that if she repaid it earlier (as most prostitutes did), she would earn even higher effective monthly wages.

In turn, the brothel needed a way to create an incentive for its prostitutes to please their customers. The women performed harsh work in impossible-to-monitor environments. If brothels paid them a fixed wage (like an initial 1,000 yen payment on a fixed six-year term), they had little incentive to try to please their customers. If a prostitute were sufficiently unpleasant that guests seldom requested her by name, so much the better for the woman, as she would get paid regardless.

By coupling a maximum six-year term with the ability to quit early, the brothel gave a prostitute an incentive to please her customers. The more customers requested her, the more revenue she generated, and the sooner she could quit.

In practice, the prostitutes tended to repay their loans in about three years and quit. Historians sometimes insist that the brothels must surely have manipulated the charges for food and clothing to keep prostitutes mired in perpetual debt. But they did not do this, at least not on a large scale. The brothels—established institutions with a large capital investment—probably realized that cheating on their initial contract would raise their future recruitment costs. Not only did the brothels specifically promise a woman that she could quit debt-free at the end of six years regardless of the revenue she generated, they generally kept their promise.

If brothels manipulated charges or otherwise cheated on their terms to keep prostitutes locked in debt, the number of licensed prostitutes would have stayed reasonably constant across an age range at least up to 30. The minimum age for licensed prostitutes was 18. In 1925, of the 4,159 licensed prostitutes in Tokyo, 737 were age 21 and 632 age 22. There were only 515 age 24, however, 423 age 25, and 254 age 27.[16]

Similarly, if brothels were keeping prostitutes locked in "debt slavery," a substantial proportion of the women would have been in the industry for six or more years. Yet of 42,400 licensed prostitutes across Japan in the early 1920s, 38 percent were in their second or third year, 25 percent were in their fourth or fifth, and only 7 percent were in their sixth or seventh.[17] The data show comparable numbers entering and leaving the industry in a given year. Of a workforce of about 50,000 licensed prostitutes, 18,800 women registered as new licensed prostitutes in 1922 and 18,300 de-registered.[18] One-third of the workforce replaced itself every year, which is consistent with a typical tenure of about three years.[19]

Data on brothel revenues permit a calculation of the average length of time it would have taken for a prostitute to repay her initial loan. In 1925, customers made 3.74 million visits to the 4,159 licensed prostitutes in Tokyo. Aside from payments for drinks and food, they spent an additional 11.1 million yen. Of this amount, prostitutes retained 31 percent (3.4 million yen)—an average of 655 yen per prostitute. Under the standard contract terms, a prostitute would have applied 60 percent of this amount (393 yen) toward the repayment of her loan and kept the remainder of the money (262 yen). She would have repaid her initial loan of 1,200 yen in about three years.[20] By comparison, the average adult factory wage (for both sexes; room and board not provided) in 1925 was 1.75 yen per day, and in 1935 it was 1.88 yen per day.[21] To earn their income, the prostitutes in 1924 served an average (mean) 2.54 customers per night.[22] In a month, they typically worked about 28 nights.[23]

Korean Brothels

As Japanese emigrants began to move to Korea, they established in their communities structures akin to the licensed brothels at home.

Japan formally annexed Korea in 1910, and the new government imposed uniform licensing rules across all Korea in 1916. It set the minimum age for prostitution at 17 (not 18 as on the Japanese islands), and required regular medical examinations.[24]

Japanese women used the new licensing system more readily than the Koreans. The data about the Korean sex market are more haphazard than the data about Japan. But in 1929, there were 1,789 Japanese licensed prostitutes who worked in Korea and only 1,262 Koreans. That year, the Japanese prostitutes entertained 450,300 guests (252 for each prostitute), where the Koreans entertained 110,700 guests (88 for each). By 1935, the number of Japanese licensed prostitutes in Korea had fallen to 1,778, while the number of Koreans had risen, but only to 1,330.[25]

Plenty of Korean women worked as prostitutes, but most worked outside the licensing structure. In 1935 Korea, 414 Japanese women worked as barmaids and 4,320 as cabaret workers—both euphemisms for unlicensed prostitutes. At the same time, 1,290 Korean women worked as barmaids and 6,553 as cabaret workers.[26]

To recruit their licensed prostitutes, Korean brothels used indenture contracts much like those in Japan. Note, however, that Koreans—both potential prostitutes and potential customers—were poorer than Japanese. Over the economy as a whole, from 1910 to 1940, the ratio of Japanese to Korean wages varied from about 2.5 to 1.5.[27]

Prostitutes charged high prices, but Japanese women charged more than Koreans. By one account, in 1926, Korean prostitutes charged 3 yen for an assignation; Japanese prostitutes in Korea charged 6 to 7 yen. Customers spent an average 3.9 yen per visit to a Korean licensed prostitute; they spent an average of 8 yen per visit to a Japanese licensed prostitute in Korea.[28] In one (apparently poorer) Korean community in 1929, Japanese licensed prostitutes generated annual revenues of 1,052 yen; Korean licensed prostitutes generated 361 yen.[29]

The lower Korean revenues resulted in lower upfront cash payments to the Korean prostitutes than to the Japanese prostitutes working in Korea. One source described Korean licensed prostitutes receiving advances of 250–300 yen (and occasionally 400–500 yen) on three-year contracts; Japanese licensed prostitutes in Korea received 1,000–3,000 yen (which was more than Japanese licensed prostitutes earned in Japan).[30] Another source calculated the average upfront payment to Korean licensed prostitutes at 420 yen, while the Japanese licensed prostitutes received 1,730 yen.[31]

As in Japan, licensed prostitutes in Korea generally worked about three years. Younghoon Rhee, an economic historian, observes that over the course of 1924, about half to one-third of the prostitutes seem to have quit. Rhee estimates that the average prostitute worked two and a half years.[32]

Korean licensed prostitutes typically left the industry by their mid-20s, which is consistent with the experience of prostitutes in Japan quitting within five years. In one study, 61 percent of Korean licensed prostitutes were 20–25 years old; only 16 percent were over 25.[33] In another, 680 of the 1,101 licensed prostitutes in the Seoul area were age 20–24, while only 273 were 25–29. Among that group of 1,101 prostitutes, 294 were in their fifth year of service; 65 were in their sixth, and only 17 were in their seventh. Of the base population of 1,101 prostitutes, 317 entered the industry in 1924 and 407 quit.[34]

More detailed (if still haphazard) prefectural records confirm the general phenomenon.[35] Table 2.1 presents the statistics for two provinces in Korea (which was a part of Japan) in 1924. Most commonly, licensed prostitutes were in their early 20s. Relatively few continued working into their late 20s. Most worked for only a few years. In Gyeonggi, prostitutes seem to have worked four or five years and then quit. In South Gyeongsang, they worked two or three years before quitting.

TABLE 2.1: LICENSED PROSTITUTES IN KOREA, 1924, TWO PROVINCES

Age Distribution of Licensed Prostitutes, 1924 (Doke 1928, 787, 800)

	Gyeonggi province	%	South Gyeongsang province		%
18–19	104	9.45	18–19	176	19.22
20–24	680	61.76	20–24	415	45.30
25–29	273	24.80	25–29	230	25.11
30+	44	3.99	30+	95	10.37

Years' Experience of Licensed Prostitutes, 1924 (Doke 1928, 788, 801)

	Gyeonggi province	%	South Gyeongsang province		%
0+	134	11.17	0+	328	35.81
1	154	13.99	1	198	21.61
2	186	16.89	2	158	17.25
3	222	21.16	3	99	10.81
4	294	26.70	4	65	7.10
5	65	5.90	5	44	4.80
6	17	1.55	6	20	2.18
7+	29	2.64	7+	4	0.44

Sources: Doke Saiichiro, *Baishunfu ronko* [Studies in Prostitution] (Shishi shuppan, 1928), reproduced in Suzuki Yuko et al., eds., *Nihon gun "ianfu" kankei shiryo shusei* [Collection of Documents Relating to the "Comfort Women" of the Japanese Military] (Tokyo: Akashi shoten, 2006), 1:787–88, 800–801.

THE COMFORT STATION REGIME

Japanese and Korean women were already traveling abroad to work as unlicensed prostitutes during the first decades of the twentieth century. In Manchukuo in 1940, writes the economist Lee Dong-Jin, 19,059 Chinese women worked as prostitutes (*shakufu*, the standard euphemism), alongside 2,264 Japanese and 3,586 Koreans.[36] In Shanghai in 1930, notes Hata Ikuhiko, 712 Japanese women and 1,173 Korean women worked as prostitutes.[37]

The Japanese military command hoped to identify a corps of disease-free and spy-free prostitutes, either from the Japanese islands or from the Korean peninsula, who would agree to follow health standards as a way of keeping the risk of venereal disease in check at its overseas bases. Toward that end—and not because of any shortage of prostitutes—it created the comfort station regime, extending the domestic regulatory framework over prostitution into its occupied territories.[38]

As the military moved into East and Southeast Asia and the Pacific, it encouraged entrepreneurs to establish comfort stations for the exclusive use of officers and enlisted men. Those entrepreneurs set up brothels that varied greatly in size and scope, but the military command wanted the establishments for three basic reasons.

First and foremost, the military command wanted to lower the incidence of rape in the war zone. Rape in war zones has been frighteningly common. The invading Soviets raped German women en masse in 1945. They raped Japanese, Korean, and Chinese women too as they overran Manchuria and the Korean peninsula.[39] Few actions turn a local population against an invader more quickly than rape. Military strategists with a war to win cannot afford to antagonize locals and risk insurrections at the tail end of their tenuous supply lines. Japanese troops did rape local women. Japanese military commanders recorded in their diaries about meting out harsh and swift sentences for rapists, but rapes continued all the same. The military wanted brothels as a way to stem the rapine of local women.

Second, the military command wanted to minimize losses from venereal disease. Had it only cared about lowering the incidence of rape, the command could have made do with local brothels. It had no reason to import the Japanese licensing regime. But the command did not just want prostitutes; it wanted disease-free prostitutes. It was paying soldiers to fight, but risked those very soldiers' sitting out the battle because of syphilis and gonorrhea. During Japan's 1918 Siberian expedition, the military had not designated brothels for its troops. Instead, individual soldiers had frequented local establishments as they chose. Many of them contracted venereal disease. Senda Kako located the medical records for one set of battalions. From August 1918 to October 1920, the units suffered 1,387 deaths and 2,066 injuries in battle. During the same period, these battalions suffered 2,012 reported cases of venereal disease. Senda estimates that they suffered many more cases that went unreported.[40] As it expanded its reach over the continent during the 1930s, the military command wanted badly to avoid a reprise of that Siberian disaster.

Prostitutes follow armies everywhere, and they followed the Japanese armies across Asia. What the military needed were prostitutes who would not give their soldiers debilitating diseases, and toward that end it extended the domestic licensing regime overseas.

Third, the command wanted to protect military secrets. Men fighting wars live under enormous strain. They bivouac in primitive tents in deserts and jungles. They eat bad food, get lice and dysentery, and run the risk, every moment, of being machine-gunned or hit with a mortar round. When they arrive at a place with liquor and women, they often unwind and talk. They drink and talk, and reveal military plans. Enemy commanders know this, and so they send agents to pose as prostitutes and learn about those battle plans. To reduce this risk, the military (at least during the early years of the war) tried to staff its comfort stations with women from the Japanese islands or the Korean peninsula. These women tended not to speak the language used outside the garrison. Monitor them, and the military could monitor who interacted with which soldiers at which times.

The Health Effects

By most accounts, the Japanese military command did indeed keep venereal disease generally in check. As at domestic licensed brothels, it required customers to use condoms. It prohibited women from having sex with a man who refused. It required both a prostitute and her customer to wash with disinfectant after each sexual encounter. It required prostitutes to submit to weekly health inspections. If a woman contracted a venereal disease, it banned her from taking customers until a physician certified her health. It barred soldiers from patronizing any brothels other than the licensed comfort stations. And in many cases it barred the stations from accepting any nonmilitary customers.[41]

By most accounts, the comfort stations enforced these rules strictly—probably more strictly than the Tokyo brothels did. In

Tokyo, the licensed brothels operated in a competitive market, and the police did not station officers at the brothels to monitor compliance with health regulations. Prostitutes and brothels had incentives to be lax about the rules. A licensed Tokyo prostitute in 1924 saw an average of 2.5 customers per day, but by 1931 it was only 1.8.[42] Both she and the brothel would want to attract more customers, and one can imagine neither objecting if a customer complained about the condom requirement.

The comfort stations operated in a much more closely monitored environment. The military command was physically present, both as customers and as military police. The command wanted the health standards enforced, not out of charity but to maintain fighting capacity. The comfort stations typically had few (if any) licensed competitors. Operating at close to full capacity already—and with regulatorily set prices—they had little reason to try to attract more customers.

The regulatory strategy may largely have worked as intended. At least one Allied report from late 1945 noted that "the venereal rate among Japanese troops in South West PACIFIC is exceedingly low."[43]

Incomes

A woman who agreed to work at a comfort station incurred substantially higher risks than a woman who worked at a licensed Tokyo brothel. Most obviously, she sometimes worked in the war zone, where she could face the risk of violent death along with the men she served. Working in a foreign place, she could not as easily walk out and fade into the urban landscape if the brothel owner tried to cheat her, as she could in Tokyo. Abroad, she would find survival more complicated. She had fewer potential allies. In Tokyo, she could complain about a cheating brothel owner to friends, family, reformist organizations, and sometimes even a sympathetic police officer. Abroad, she would find fewer allies.

Given these higher risks, the comfort women obtained shorter maximum terms and (probably) higher annual wages. About Tokyo prostitutes, we have data collected by the metropolitan police. About the comfort stations, we have only haphazard observations (detailed in the appendix). Necessarily, any numbers are merely estimates. During the 1930s and early 1940s, the comfort women seem to have received upfront payments in the range of 500 to 1,000 yen—a large sum of money. Note, for example, that in 1945 a sergeant made 23–30 yen per month, and a lieutenant general made 5,800 yen per year.[44] By 1943–45, the comfort women seem to have received higher upfront payments than in the 1930s, but the economic turmoil makes the amounts hard to gauge. The women seem usually to have negotiated maximum terms of two years.[45]

We would not expect brokers to advance sums this large without demanding documentary proof of receipt. Accounts about these contracts survive in abundance (see appendix). Take the form contract reproduced in a 1938 memorandum from the Ibaraki prefecture governor's office. The memorandum discusses the recruitment efforts of a Kobe brothel owner. It includes the contract solely for informational purposes, and neither praises nor criticizes its terms (see Table 2.2). Note the following: (a) the contract is for a maximum two-year term; (b) the advance payment would range between 500 and 1,000 yen; (c) the recruits would serve at a Shanghai army comfort station; and (d) the recruits would be from 16 to 30 years old (although most comfort women in practice appear to have been in their late teens or 20s). The contract specifies that the brothel would pay for food and clothing, and for the woman's return trip. Although the contract does not detail the accounting by which a woman would pay down her advance, comfort stations typically seem to have applied 40–60 percent of a woman's earnings toward the advance.[46] The contract further provides—specifically—that a woman could quit even before she had either completed her two-year term or repaid her advance.

TABLE 2.2: SAMPLE FORM CONTRACT

Contract

Item: Working term [stated below to be two years].

Item: Contractual amount [stated below to be 500 to 1,000 yen].

Item: To work as a prostitute (*shakufu*) at the comfort station (*ianjo*) of the Fourth Army stationed in Shanghai.

Item: Bonus shall equal 10 percent of revenue (half to be saved).

Item: Food, clothing, and supplies shall be the obligation of the [brothel] owner.

Item: Should this contract be dissolved during the contractual period, the remaining principal, the penalty [defined below as 10 percent of the principal per year], and costs incurred at the time of hiring shall become due and payable.

Conditions

Item: Contractual term: Two full years.

Item: Advance loan: 500 to 1,000 yen; provided, however, that 20 percent of the advance shall be deducted and applied toward incidental and startup expenses.

Item: Age—16 to 30 years old.

Item: [Consent of parent required.]

Item: The advance and the repayment formula expire upon the completion of the term of years. In other words, should the contracting party be unable to work because of illness, the advance shall be considered paid in full upon the end of the term.

Item: Interest shall not be charged during the term of the contract. Should the contracting party quit during the term of the contract, interest shall be charged at the rate of 1 percent per month.

Item: The penalty shall equal 10 percent of the contractual advance per year.

Item: Should the contracting party quit during the term of the contract, calculations shall be made on a per-day basis.

Item: Upon completion of the term of years, the cost of returning to the home country shall be borne by the [brothel] owner.

Item: 10 percent of the calculated earnings [presumably net] shall be paid to the contracting party [i.e., the woman] as income on a monthly basis.

Item: Upon completion of the term of years, a reasonable payment of gratitude shall be paid in proportion to the contracting party's earnings.

Source: Ibaraki ken chiji, "Shanhai haken gun nai rikugun ianjo ni okeru shakufu boshu ni kansuru ken" [Case Regarding the Recruitment of Barmaids for the Comfort Station Attached to the Army Stationed in Shanghai], February 14, 1938, in Josei no tameno Ajia heiwa kokumin kikin, ed., *Seifu chosa: "Jugun ianfu" kankei shiryo shusei* [Government Investigation: Documents Relating to the "Military Comfort Women"] (Tokyo: Ryukei shosha, 1997), 1:50, 52.

Should she choose to do so, the contract provided that she would owe the brothel the unpaid portion of the advance and a specified penalty. This is an unusual provision.

In Table 2.3, we detail the charges at several wartime comfort stations.

TABLE 2.3: ASSIGNATION CHARGES FOR COMFORT STATIONS

	Privates	NCO	Officers
Manila	1.5 yen	2.5 yen	
Shanghai	1.5	1.5	3.0
Tacloban	1.5	2.0	3.0
Burauen	1.5	2.5	5.0
Rabaul	2.0	2.5	2.5
Myitkyina	1.5	2.0	5.0

Note: The figures are from an Allied military report, for 1 hour for the officers in Manila and Shanghai, for 40 minutes in Burauen, and in all other cases for 30 minutes. Privates include sailors.

Source: SCAP, Research Report, "Amenities in the Japanese Armed Forces," November 15, 1945, in Josei no tameno Ajia heiwa kokumin kikin, ed., *Seifu chosa: "Jugun ianfu" kankei shiryo shusei* [Government Investigation: Documents Relating to the "Military Comfort Women"] (Tokyo: Ryukei shosha, 1998), 5:137–66.

An upfront payment of 500 to 1,000 yen for a maximum two-year term was a large amount, even by comparison with the already high incomes (for uneducated lower-class women) that prostitutes earned in the domestic Tokyo market: 1,200 yen for a maximum six years. Younghoon Rhee makes exactly this point: "Compared to licensed domestic prostitution, the military comfort system was 'hard work, high income, and high risk.'"[47] The comfort women saw more men per day and faced all the risks of working on the front lines, but "from the perspective of the comfort women, the comfort station was a market where demand was guaranteed and income was high."[48] Hata Ikuhiko estimates that comfort women made five times the income of domestic Japanese prostitutes and ten times the income of prostitutes in Pyongyang.[49] Lee Wooyoun observes that comfort women were involved in "high-risk, high-return" work and that some "earned enormous sums."[50]

Crucially, many comfort station owners paid their prostitutes (and let them earn tips) beyond the large up-front advance. One Korean publisher recently reprinted a diary kept by a receptionist at comfort stations in Burma and Singapore. Several times, the receptionist noted that the comfort women kept postal savings accounts and that he deposited money in them on the women's behalf.[51] Indeed, some comfort women earned and saved enough to establish comfort stations of their own.[52]

Of all the Korean comfort women who left records, Mun Ok-ju (Mun Ok-chu) seems to have done well for herself the most flamboyantly. She writes in her memoir:

> I saved a considerable amount of money from tips.... I knew that all the soldiers put their earnings in the saving accounts in the field post office, so I decided to put my money in the saving account. I asked a soldier to make a personal seal and put 500 yen in the account.... I became the owner of the savings passbook for the first time in my life. I worked in Daegu as a nanny and a street seller from the childhood but I remained poor no matter how hard I worked. I could not believe that I could have so much money in my saving account. A house in Daegu cost 1,000 yen at the time. I could let my mother have an easy life. I felt very happy and proud. The savings passbook became my treasure....
>
> It was fun to go shopping by rickshaw. I can't forget the experience of shopping in a market in Rangoon. There were lots of jewelry shops because many jewels were produced in Burma, and ruby and jade were not expensive. One of my friends collected many jewels. I thought I should have a jewel myself, so I went and bought a diamond.
>
> I became a popular woman in Rangoon. There were a lot more officers in Rangoon than near the frontlines, so I was invited to many parties. I sang songs at parties and received lots of tips.[53]

Quitting

Comfort women could and did quit at the end of their terms. They finished the maximum length of their contracted term, or generated revenue sufficient to repay their contracted amount, and then left. They could leave—subject to the obvious caveat that there was a war on and they faced the same travel restrictions as everyone else.[54]

Quitting early by generating sufficient revenue was not uncommon. The absence of comprehensive statistics makes these observations hard to gauge. But the sources available (see appendix) suggest that the women typically worked only one or two years. Yamada Seikichi worked for the Japanese military monitoring the comfort stations in Wuhan. He reported that the 280 comfort women in the area (130 Japanese, 150 Korean) in 1943–44 tended to pay off their debt in about a year and a half.[55]

The comfort station "was an extremely fluid place," as Younghoon Rhee puts it. "It was a place that many comfort women left—they left when they had completed the contractual term, or when they had earned the money they hoped to make, or when they had paid off their advance."[56] Similarly, Lee Wooyoun writes that "there would have been far more comfort women who returned home before the end of the war" than there were still working at the comfort stations in August 1945.[57]

The anthropologist C. Sarah Soh observes that the "lived experience of some Korean comfort women has corroborated Ramseyer's research findings" about Japanese prostitution as set forth in a 1991 essay:

> Ramseyer notes that the women who became licensed prostitutes were "not women with many attractive alternatives" and that "prostitution did pay well." His study concludes that women in prewar Japan became licensed prostitutes by signing six-year indenture contracts, and "most prostitutes did *not* become slaves" (emphasis in original). Instead, most of them quit when their contracts expired, and some were able to quit earlier by repaying their debts in three or four years.[58]

But this has not been the preferred view of the comfort women, Soh writes. Instead, "The lived experience of some Korean comfort women has corroborated Ramseyer's research findings, but their personal histories have remained a part of strategically 'subjugated knowledge' in contemporary politics."[59] In this context, "subjugated" means that comfort women who speak out about their actual experiences find themselves brutally harassed by the organization that nominally works on their behalf, as we will see.

Compassion

Park Yu-ha, a professor of literature, is the most prominent of the scholars who have faced criminal prosecution in South Korea for deviating from the "sex slave" narrative. (We discuss her case and others in Chapter 5.) The most incendiary passages of the book on the subject that she published in 2014 were probably those where she describes the compassion that the comfort women and the men showed for each other.[60] Sometimes, Park found, the women—whether from the Japanese islands or from the Korean peninsula—saw their job as part of the national war effort. Sometimes they treated the men with compassion and tenderness, sometimes they even offered love, and sometimes the men reciprocated. The observation obviously violates the hypernationalistic and aggressively anti-Japanese line pushed by the South Korean Left. It just as obviously violates Western academic orthodoxies about "sex slavery" and "wartime violence against women." But the accounts of the war include too many references to the phenomenon to ignore. At root, they remind us that we are speaking about human beings, and not about abstractions.

The comfort stations were brothels. Work at the comfort stations entailed having sex with soldiers. But at least some of the time, the comfort stations were more than this. The comfort women were not simple sex slaves, deprived of all ability to structure their lives; neither were they simple cash registers, maximizing nothing but their financial return. And the men were not ruthless machines of imperialist brutality; neither were they vestibules of misogynistic contempt.

In their rooms, the comfort women encountered very young men who lived on the precipice of death. Most of these young men would have been very afraid. Many seem to have wanted more than a physical encounter. They wanted a sympathetic ear, a soft presence otherwise absent from their hard and harrowing world. As the comfort women themselves told it, sometimes a young man wanted the compassion and peace that came from talking with a woman from home. Talking with a caring woman who understood that he was scared. Who let him talk about how badly he missed his home, his friends, his family. Who understood that he did not want to die. And who offered him caring and compassion.

Although the comfort women in the political limelight routinely recount the "sex slave" orthodoxy, others have given radically different accounts in private. Could these others have been lying? They could, of course, though it is hard to see what benefit they would gain by it. The female writers to whom they told their stories—Park Yu-ha, C. Sara Soh, Hirota Kazuko—are not partisans in this debate.

By the words of these other comfort women, some of the women and soldiers sometimes found sympathy and compassion in each other. The prostitutes worked a degrading and dangerous job, but so did privates second class. Some of the prostitutes may have been sold by abusive parents, but most of the privates had been equally unwillingly drafted. They were roughly the same age. Call it false consciousness if you will, but some of the comfort women and soldiers found love. Some soldiers even proposed marriage.[61]

Mun Ok-ju, for example, recalled her love for a Japanese soldier named Yamada Ichiro:

> [I]f he did not show up on his once a week holiday, I became so worried wondering if he was killed by the enemy that I could not work properly. He made me worry so much.... I prayed

> for [the] safety of Ichiro Yamada. After two or three…months, the troop unit to which Yamada belonged returned from the front. Yamada returned in good health. He immediately came to the comfort station. He said "I, private first class soldier Yamada, have just come back from the front." Yamada gave a salute to me. We hugged…full of joy. Such a day was so special that the comfort station owner Matsumoto (a Korean from Daegu) closed business for the day. The comfort station was full of excitement, and we, comfort women, contributed 1 yen per woman to hold a big party for them.

They—comfort women and soldiers—were in it for the same reason, recalled Mun:

> The soldiers and we had the same thoughts, that is, we must work hard for our emperor. The soldiers gave up their wives, children and their own lives. Knowing how they felt, I did my best to solace them by having conversation with them.[62]

Another comfort woman described it this way:

> Some of the men said they were scared, and would cry before going into battle. Those times, I always tried to comfort them, and to tell them to "be sure to come home alive." And when they really did come home alive, I was happy.[63]

For the soldiers, their time with the comfort women provided what Park Yu-ha called "private space."[64] It was a place where they could express emotions and say things not allowed in the military environment. One comfort woman recalled:

> Some men came because they wanted to talk together.… They wanted to tell me their hearts.… They'd remember their wives

> back home, and then sit there and cry.... They'd think about their wives...and wouldn't want to have a relationship with other women like us. Some would leave without doing anything, but they'd still come.... They wanted to talk while they had a drink. Lots of men came without having sex.[65]

A Japanese comfort woman spoke fondly of meeting men from her home island, some of whom wanted only to chat:

> What were the happy times? Well, for me it was probably when I met soldiers from Shikoku. The closer they had been to my home (like Ehime or Matsuyama), the happier I was. The soldiers, too, felt like they had met a relative. Some didn't even have sex. They just chatted with me about the festivals at home, or the mountains and the rivers. The soldiers seemed satisfied with that.[66]

Hirota Kazuko, a journalist, interviewed several veterans in the 1970s and heard similar stories about the comfort women. "On the front where they did not even know whether they would survive another day, holding a woman [and having sex] had been proof that they were alive," wrote Hirota.[67] One veteran recalled: "At the comfort station in Manila, I held women [and had sex] frantically. As long as my money held up, I went to [the comfort station].... Only when I held a woman could I finally think to myself, 'ahhh, I'm alive.'"[68]

Hirota also quoted a former comfort woman about the effort to provide real comfort to men facing the risk—or the certainty—of imminent death:

> The ones who served on planes or submarines really spent money. Because they didn't know when they were going to die. We tried to comfort them as much as we could. Especially the men who were going to be flying planes the next day, we

> wanted to treat as well as we could. After all, they absolutely were not coming back.[69]

To some of the comfort women, as to many of the soldiers, they were there to serve the country, Park notes. They each had a hard job, but—as one comfort woman put it—"we were both doing this under the emperor's command, so it couldn't be helped."[70] In some posts—perhaps in many—the result was a curious sort of domesticity. Life in the army was not relentless battle. It could include weeks of waiting. During those long periods of calm, the men and women found solace in each other. Park quotes one lieutenant on the relationships that developed between the women and the soldiers:

> If you're stationed at a post for a long time with the same comfort women, they start to feel like wives.... The soldiers took good care of them, and the comfort women responded in kind. On their days off, sometimes they'd bring over some local produce, or do the laundry for the soldiers. Sometimes the comfort women would sit and watch the soldiers fix their machine guns.... The soldiers would sometimes share their lunch with them. The relationship between soldiers and comfort women in these posts was like this everywhere.[71]

In 1975, Hirota reported the lonely suicide of a middle-aged woman named Yamauchi Keiko who had lived in a one-room apartment and killed herself by running the city gas. Hirota had talked with her and another woman several times about their work as comfort women on the Truk (Chuuk) Islands. Both women recalled their time at the comfort station as the high point of their lives. Both seemed melancholic when Hirota interviewed them, for a surprising reason: "because they had been comfort women, their lives thereafter had seemed dark" by comparison. "Every 30 minutes, they'd receive a different man. Each time, they would go to the toilet and wash. It's not as though that had been fun. But it had been not necessarily harsh and sad either, and it was not embarrassing."[72]

In relating their lives to Hirota, the women described their stints in the comfort stations as the time in their lives when they had had purpose. They had served the country by providing comfort to men who were giving their lives in battle. After the war, they were simply uneducated women whom a rapidly modernizing Japan had left behind.

By insisting on an account of universal victimization and rape, writes Park Yu-ha, the modern hypernationalists in Korea have robbed many surviving comfort women of their past. Quite self-consciously, the nationalists set out to construct an edifying national history. Toward that end, they imposed onto the past a patriotism born of zealous opposition to the occupying Japanese. But in doing so, they have denied the comfort women the chance to relive their memories in peace.

Koreans had been Japanese citizens. To be sure, the Japanese government treated them in many ways as second-class citizens. It had conquered the peninsula and annexed it in 1910, and not out of kindness. Some Koreans had launched a violent independence campaign in 1919. Yet not all Koreans were hostile to Japan. Where the indigenous dynasty had been both corrupt and ineffective, the Japanese government imposed a stable order. Many Koreans responded by embracing this new regime. From 1938 to 1943, at least several hundred thousand Koreans volunteered for the Japanese army. Among those who joined, some served in the officer corps and some climbed to the rank of general.[73]

Within this world of conflicting allegiances, many of the Korean comfort women felt a common national identity with the soldiers. The love and compassion between them flowed from that identity. These memories, writes Park, the nationalists have forced the women to "discard."[74] In the decades since the war, "Korea itself has lived by erasing—in the same way as these women—these memories."

In the newly invented collective history, the only identity allowed the comfort women is that of "victims abused by Japan."[75] A history in which comfort women "loved Japanese soldiers" and in which they accepted "the apology of Japan" is a history for which there is no place. A history in which a destitute young woman "sacrificed herself for the good of the family" is similarly one for which there is no place.[76]

The Numbers

How many women worked at the comfort stations? We do not know the exact number; no one does. Given that the comfort stations were small, mostly privately owned and operated businesses, no one has located any record of the total number of comfort women. Like so much else about this field, however, activists and Western scholars insist on the number with a dogmatism inversely related to the plausibility of the claim.

Although no one knows the number for sure, there are good guesses...and less good ones. North Korea insists on 200,000 Korean comfort women.[77] Just because North Korea insists on a number need not make it untrue, of course. Tessa Morris-Suzuki, a retired historian of Japan at the Australian National University, and Qiu Peipei, a literature scholar from the People's Republic of China, add in comfort women from other places and note that some estimates reach as high as 400,000.[78] But one can probably consider 200,000 the most aggressive upper bound possible.

Serious scholars begin with the number of Japanese military personnel abroad. They posit a soldier-to-prostitute ratio. They posit a prostitute length-of-service term, and from it estimate a turnover ratio to cover replacements.

Among the most prominent scholars in the field, Hata Ikuhiko provides several complex calculations.[79] A simplified version of his account would go like this: Start with 3 million overseas soldiers. Most men apparently hoped to visit a comfort station once a month, and comfort women probably averaged five customers per day. This yields a soldier-to-prostitute ratio of 150:1, which in turn points to a total of 20,000 comfort women. Hata also suggests, however, that only about 2.5 million soldiers were within range of a comfort station—a number that implies a total of around 17,000 comfort women at any one time. He estimates a replacement ratio of 1.5 for some areas, but writes that replacements did not necessarily arrive. From this, he suggests an aggregate wartime figure somewhere in the area of 20,000. From other material, he concludes that the comfort women were 40 percent Japanese, 30 percent local, 20 percent Korean, and 10 percent of other nationalities.[80]

Yoshimi Yoshiaki observes that the Japanese military had 2.32 million soldiers overseas in 1942, and 3.51 million in August 1945.[81] Nevertheless, he follows Hata in working from a 3 million figure. Yoshimi suggests a soldier-to-prostitute ratio of between 100:1 and 30:1. The figures imply a comfort women total (at any one time) in the range of 30,000 to 100,000. Yoshimi then suggests that the replacement ratio was between 1.5 and 2.0—yielding an aggregate wartime total somewhere between 45,000 and 200,000. Yoshimi argues that the comfort stations would have hired local women for short terms when the army was on the move. If true, this would imply a relatively high aggregate number. By contrast, if no one set up comfort stations in response to armies on the move, the aggregate number would remain low.

Consistent with Hata, Younghoon Rhee reports that the Japanese military command used a 150:1 soldier-to-prostitute ratio when they planned the system in 1937.[82] On a population of 2.8 million Japanese soldiers (his number), this would require 18,000 comfort women at any one time. Rhee further observes (as does Hata) that in 1942 the Japanese military supplied 32.1 million condoms. Suppose five customers per prostitute per day, and the figures imply a total population at any one time of about 18,000 comfort women. Rhee suggests a replacement ratio of 2.0. He follows Hata in writing that the comfort women were 40 percent Japanese, 30 percent local, 20 percent Korean, and 10 percent from other areas.

Recruiting

The Japanese government regulated recruiting activities strictly. In structuring the comfort station regime, it understood the political risk entailed. It was drafting its young men into war (from Japan; Korean men were not subject to conscription), and many were not returning. Now, it was about to invite brothel owners to hire young women to work in the war zone as well.

The government also understood that Korea (less so Japan) faced a longstanding problem of fraud in the recruiting industry. Recruiters arrived at isolated farming villages. They promised attractive factory jobs in the cities. And then they assigned the men and women to far worse jobs, and the women sometimes to the urban brothels.[83]

To limit the bad press, the Japanese government encouraged recruiters for the comfort stations to focus on women already working as prostitutes. And to monitor the recruiting, officials required exit interviews of all women going abroad to work in the comfort stations.[84] As noted earlier, a young woman seeking an exit permit needed to obtain the consent of a parent, come to the police station, and bring her contract. The officers conducting the interviews were required to ensure that each woman was choosing this course voluntarily.[85]

Importantly, the Japanese government enforced exit interviews in Korea as well as in Japan. On their face, the surviving documents detailing these requirements applied only to the Japanese islands. For reasons explained in detail by Arima Tetsuo and confirmed by Lee Wooyoun, however, they also applied to the Korean peninsula.[86] What is more, when the new hires arrived at the comfort station, they were required to produce these documents once again. Park Yu-ha writes that those most closely involved in the comfort women dispute have known this all along, even as they have kept the information from the public.[87]

The exit interviews obviously did not stop all fraud. A recruiter could hire an imposter to stand in for the interview. If a woman had been tricked and—upon discovering at the interview what she had contracted to do—wanted to quit, she would need to return the money. If (as was probably sometimes the case) her parents now held the money, she would need to convince them to return it. The requirements do not show that the Japanese government stopped all fraud. They do indicate that it put in place measures apparently designed to limit the extent of any fraud.

The Economics of the Contracts

We close this chapter with two basic economic observations. The first goes to the determination of contractual efficiency: in competitive markets, competition among market professionals for customers will lead them to offer relatively efficient (i.e., cost-reducing for both parties) contractual terms even if no one negotiates contracts explicitly. The second observation goes to the importance of what economists call the "margin": in a world where professionals use form contracts, they will offer to all their customers the contractual terms most attractive to the people most reluctant to accept the contract.

Consider each point in turn. First, recall that the comfort woman named Hyun Byung-sook explicitly negotiated the terms of her contract. She negotiated price. She negotiated the term length. And she negotiated the brothel's right to assign her contract. Most recruits probably did not negotiate specific terms—and some misunderstandings of the comfort station arrangements seem to reflect misunderstanding of the role that explicit negotiations play in the determination of contractual structure.

Economically inclined readers will understand that market competition drives buyers and sellers toward relatively efficient contractual terms regardless of whether anyone explicitly negotiates anything. For example, posit a labor market with many employers, many workers, and free competition. Suppose that employers by custom supply the contracts that the parties will use. In this world, employers will compete with each other to attract workers. Obviously, they will compete on the basis of wage. But if other aspects of the contractual structure matter to workers as well, they will also experiment with alternative contractual terms. The employers who succeed in the competition will be those who offer the combination of price and contractual terms that maximizes the joint returns to the employers and workers.

The second observation is that contractual terms, as well as price, turn on what is needed to attract the people on the "margin." Posit again a labor market with many employers, many workers, and free competition. Suppose that the wage is the only variable at issue. The equilibrium wage will be the wage that equalizes marginal revenue and marginal cost. Now posit that the employers cannot price discriminate. Workers who would happily have worked at a lower wage will receive the higher wage necessary to coax the marginal worker—i.e., the most reluctant worker—to accept the employment contract. If workers care about other aspects of the employment contract besides their wage, this equilibrating process will cause employers to compete for the marginal worker on those other terms as well.

This marginal analysis is crucial to understanding the role that fraudulent recruiters and exploitative parents played in the labor market for prostitutes. As we have noted multiple times, some of the comfort women were recruited through fraud. Some of them were sold by their parents (who may or may not have fully internalized the costs that their daughters incurred). In both cases, the women may have received lower advance payments. After all, the recruiters set prices individually, and hence they could price-discriminate.

Although recruiters could price-discriminate, however, they seem to have used standard form contracts. They discriminated in price, but they generally did not discriminate in contractual terms. If this is true, then the contractual terms that emerged would have been those that most cost-effectively induced the marginal worker to take the job. On this dimension, the defrauded women and the women sold by their parents were "infra-marginal." Provided that the brothels needed to recruit a nontrivial number of women who actually knew what they were doing, the brothels would have used a form contract that promoted the combined welfare of the brothel and the worker both.

None of this minimizes the plight of the women involved. We make these observations simply to explain why we focus on women who knew generally what they were doing. They were the workers "on the margin." For purposes of determining contract structure, they were the women who mattered.

The history of the comfort women is a story about poor but resourceful young women who made the best—or what they thought was the best—of a very bad situation by agreeing to undertake dangerous and harsh work in exchange for extraordinarily high pay. Nearly a century later, a wide variety of documents reflect the world in which they worked. There are advertisements for comfort women work from Korean newspapers. There are government regulations, form employment contracts, diaries of comfort station employees. There are detailed comfort station rules for how to divide the revenue from sex work between the brothel and the prostitute. There are rules specifying working hours, days off, terms of employment, and conditions of travel to and from the comfort station.

The comfort women regime was an industry, and it operated by the standard principles of economics. It was not sexual slavery, institutionalized rape, or any of the other bizarre descriptions used by the modern South Korean Left and Western university professors. These crass characterizations do not date from the war and they do not come from the Korean peninsula. Instead, they come from Japan—more specifically, from a Japanese memoir. In 1983, an obscure writer named Yoshida Seiji published a book in which he claimed to have led a platoon of soldiers to the Korean island of Jeju to dragoon young women into comfort station work at bayonet-point.

Before he died, Yoshida in effect admitted that he had fabricated the entire account. As we see in the following chapter, he created a hoax—and the hoax lives on today.

CHAPTER 3

THE HOAX BUILDS

Take an American university course on Japanese history and you might hear that Japanese soldiers in the 1930s and early 1940s captured Korean women at gunpoint and forced them to work as their "sex slaves." Follow the *New York Times* and you might read the same. You might even learn that any Japanese who disputed this was a "right-wing denialist." What you will not learn is that this "sex slave" account of the comfort women began with a Japanese book published in 1983.

The account did not start in South Korea, or on the Korean peninsula, or in continental Asia at all. It started in Japan. Not until a Korean translation of the Japanese book appeared in 1989 did Korean women begin to claim that Japanese soldiers had forced them into working as comfort women. In 1991, several of these women sued the Japanese government. Under pressure from Korea, the Japanese government stated in 1993 that it had indeed drafted women by force. In 1996 and 1998, the UN followed with scathing attacks on Japan. In 2000, activists organized a show trial of World War II–vintage leaders (like the Showa emperor, dead since 1989) for orchestrating the sexual slavery. And in 2005, Amnesty International added its own diatribe.

"Churnalism," we call it today—one document following another, each repeating the earlier story, and none adding any real independent evidence. No one bothers to investigate the original claims. It made for something of an evidentiary Ponzi scheme: A cited B, who cited C, who cited D. At the base, under all the documents and reports and kangaroo courts, lay the 1983 book.

1983: The Yoshida Story

Yoshida Seiji ran for local office on a communist ticket in the early postwar years. But "Yoshida Seiji" was almost certainly not his real name.[1] He was a compulsive liar. In 1982, he began talking about "comfort women hunts" he had led. He gave lectures, and soon he incorporated his stories into what he styled a memoir, *My War Crimes*.[2]

Starting in 1942, said Yoshida, he had worked in a labor office in Shimonoseki, where he supervised the work of mobilizing Korean workers. In May 1943, he continued, his office received an order to recruit two thousand Korean workers. More to the point, it received an order to acquire two hundred Koreans to work as "comfort women." With nine soldiers, Yoshida said, he went to the island of Jeju off the southern coast of the Korean peninsula and "hunted" for comfort women. Yoshida said that he rounded up the women in the name of the Women's Volunteer Corps (*Joshi teishintai*). The *Asahi* newspaper played up the story to great fanfare.[3]

In a typical account, Yoshida recalled finding a compound where twenty or thirty women worked.[4] He and his team went in with guns. When the women started screaming, Korean men came running from nearby. He and his team grabbed the women by their arms and dragged them off. The mob of Korean men soon grew to over a hundred, but Yoshida's soldiers drew their bayonets and held them at bay. They loaded the women into the truck, drove five or six kilometers, and then stopped for a half hour to rape them. The military transported the women to the harbor and loaded them onto its ships—hands tied and each woman bound to the next.

Hata Ikuhiko doubted the story from the start. The leading modern historian in Japan, Hata has spent his life examining documents from the Japanese military and other bureaucracies. Given how the military command structure functioned during the war, he knew that someone working at a labor office in Shimonoseki would not have received an order to command a detachment and kidnap people. He would not have been sent to the Korean peninsula at all.

Hata reached Yoshida by telephone in 1992 and asked him about this order. He and his men "procured comfort women... under the name of the Women's Volunteer Corps," Yoshida explained. "As I recall, it was about 950 women in total. But my subordinates say the number was two thousand. Prostitution operators were also scrambling for women, so there was a woman shortage. We went to Jeju Island to hunt them, because there were plenty of women there."[5] (We quote this conversation more fully in Chapter 4.)

The Asahi *Newspaper*

The left-leaning *Asahi Shimbun*, as close to a "newspaper of record" as any in Japan, gave extravagant coverage to Yoshida's story.[6] His claim fit its editorial slant perfectly (think "1619 Project" at the *New York Times* and you have the general idea). In September 1982, the *Asahi* covered a lecture that Yoshida gave in Osaka. He told his audience that he had made multiple trips to Korea between 1942 and 1945. In his official capacity, he had directly supervised the forcible conscription (*kyosei renko*) of about 6,000 Koreans, including 650 comfort women. "Hunts," he called them. In one week on Jeju Island in 1943, he and his team had captured 200 young Korean women in their comfort women hunts (*kari*), he said.[7]

In the years after 1982, the *Asahi* covered Yoshida's sensational accounts in over a dozen articles. Evidently, no one in the newsroom or the editorial office bothered to check any of his claims about capturing teenage Korean girls and making them "sex slaves." The *Asahi* newspaper is the institution that made Yoshida and his tale famous, and gave birth to the modern comfort women dispute.

In 1984, the *Asahi* also ran a story about a Korean comfort woman living in Thailand.[8] The author was one Matsui Yayori, daughter of a mainline Protestant minister and board member to an antinuclear group affiliated with the Japanese Communist Party. She had gone to a small village in Thailand in 1984 to interview a woman who claimed to have been dragooned (*kyosei renko*) by three or four Japanese patrolmen in Korea. After working as a comfort woman, she had settled in Thailand. Matsui made no attempt to check her story; she simply printed the woman's claims as straight-up journalism. In time, Matsui would quit the *Asahi* to lead the comfort women movement within Japan.

1989: The Dispute Moves to Korea

The comfort women dispute arrived in Korea in 1989 when a Korean publisher brought out a translation of Yoshida's book. In 1990, activists organized what would eventually be called the Korean Council, a group tied to North Korea, which we explore in Chapter 6. In January 1991, North Korea demanded that Japan pay compensation for the comfort women regime.[9]

In July 1991, Matsui published a fluff piece on the Korean Council in the *Asahi*.[10] The organization had just begun its work and was helping to coordinate litigation against Japan. It needed women who would claim to have been dragooned. Yoshida's book and Matsui's story gave them cover.

1991: Uemura and Kim Hak-sun

The *Asahi* soon compounded its failure to check its comfort women stories with what some observers still call deliberate misreporting. The paper's lead reporter on several of the comfort women articles was Uemura Takashi. His supervisor was Matsui Yayori. Uemura was also son-in-law to a South Korean activist who was organizing litigation against Japan over war-related claims. These family ties presented an obvious conflict of interest, but Uemura did not disclose them.[11]

In August 1991, Uemura announced that he had found a woman in Seoul who had been forced to work as a comfort woman. "It has become clear that a woman exists within Seoul" who was "taken [*renko*] to the battlefield and forced [*shiirareta*] to engage in prostitution with Japanese military men," he wrote.[12] Japanese lawyers were in Korea recruiting plaintiffs to sue the Japanese government over World War II claims, and the woman had volunteered. The Korean Council had recorded the woman's statement and let Uemura listen to it.

The woman was Kim Hak-sun. Uemura reported that Kim had been dragooned as part of the Women's Volunteer Corps (*Joshi teishintai*). In fact, Kim had said nothing about the Volunteer Corps. Uemura simply added it in writing the story. The detail matters, because the Japanese government had indeed used the term in the waning months of the war, but in reference to the men and women (and boys and girls) it sent to factories in 1944–45, both on the Japanese islands and on the Korean peninsula, to replace the men sent to the front. The government had not used the term to refer to the comfort women. Yet Yoshida had claimed to recruit the women in the name of the Volunteer Corps.[13] Were Kim to have testified that she was dragooned into the Women's Volunteer Corps as a comfort woman—employing Yoshida's otherwise idiosyncratic use of the term—she would have corroborated his story in a particularly credible fashion.[14]

The misuse of the name "Women's Volunteer Corps" by Yoshida and by Uemura to refer to prostitution also created confusion within Korea. Given that the government had in fact conscripted boys and girls to work in the Volunteer Corps, the misuse probably contributed to the popular impressions both that the military had forced the comfort women into the work and that the dragooning had included young girls.[15] In 2014, the *Asahi* would finally acknowledge that the Volunteers Corps in fact had nothing to do with the comfort women.[16] But by then it was too late. The confusion started by Yoshida and fanned by Uemura and the *Asahi* had taken on a life of its own.

Two other comfort women soon joined Kim Hak-sun in her lawsuit.[17] The lower courts rejected their claims. They appealed to the Japanese Supreme Court, and the court dismissed the appeal. In 1965, the South Korean government had waived all claims that it or its citizens might have against Japan and Japanese citizens for acts arising out of the war and Japanese annexation. In exchange, Japan had paid South Korea a large sum in reparations (amounting to about 10 percent of the Japanese national budget). The treaty bound, and the courts dismissed the claims.[18]

According to Uemura's account in the *Asahi*, Kim said that she boarded the train that would take her to her comfort station after cryptically being told, "If you go there, you can make money."[19] No one explained what her work would involve. In fact, Kim had told the Korean press that her mother had sold her at age 14 to a kisaeng house in Pyongyang for 40 yen.[20] The Korean equivalent of the Japanese geisha, the kisaeng provided private customers with song, dance, and—occasionally—sexual services. There, Kim had studied for three years.

Elsewhere, Kim had given a fuller account of her kisaeng training. The dates do not quite match, but the story is roughly consistent. What is more, it adds a level of detail that suggests authenticity:

> My mother sent me as a foster daughter to a house that trained kisaeng. I was 15 at the time. I went to the house with my mother, and passed [the entrance requirement when I] sang a song. I remember that my mother took 40 won from the foster parents and sent me to live there under a multiyear contract....

> There was also a foster daughter who had arrived earlier than me in that house. The two of us commuted together to the kisaeng exchange. The exchange was a two-storey building with a big sign at the gate, and had about 300 students. I attended for about two years, and studied dance, song, and poetry very hard.
>
> When you obtain your diploma from the kisaeng exchange, you can go into business as a proper kisaeng. You could obtain your license as a kisaeng from the office at age 19, but I had graduated at age 17. Even though I'd graduated, I couldn't work. My foster father took me to several places in an effort to get a license. I looked older than my age, and my foster father lied about it. But given that the office had recorded my age as 17, his schemes didn't work.
>
> My foster father wasn't able to find work for us within the country, so he said, "if we go to China, you can probably make some money." And so it was that I and the older [foster] sister with whom I had been studying kisaeng work at the exchange went to China with our foster father. It was 1941, and I was 17 at the time.
>
> Before leaving for China, my foster father contacted my mother and obtained her permission. On the day I left, my mother bought a yellow sweater and came to see me off at Pyongyang station.[21]

Rather than disclose that Kim had trained as a kisaeng, Uemura wrote that she had been "taken" and "forced" to engage in sex.[22] Kim had indeed recounted being taken to the comfort station—but not by the Japanese military. Instead, she told the Korean press that she had been taken there by her adoptive father (her kisaeng manager). At the end of her training as a kisaeng, the manager had taken her to a comfort station in China.[23]

At the Tokyo District Court in December 1991, Kim still blamed her kisaeng manager for taking her to the comfort station. Professor Arima Tetsuo of Waseda University writes that she brought the lawsuit against the Japanese government because she had been paid in military scrip, which had become worthless at the end of the war.[24] In her complaint—in which she refers to herself in the third person—Kim wrote:

> Although Kim Hak-sun's mother took various jobs like housekeeper, their family was poor. In order to work as babysitter or home helper, Kim Hak-sun dropped out of regular school. At age 14, she was adopted [as a foster child] by Kim Tae-won, and attended a school for kisaeng for three years. In 1939 (now age 17 by Asian reckoning), she was assured that "if you go there you can make money." Her foster father took her and her colleague Emiko (one year older than she) to China. They rode a truck to Pyongyang, and boarded a military train. The only other passengers were soldiers. They changed trains several times, and passed through Andong [present-day Dandong] and Beijing. Eventually, they reached a small village in North China called [not identifiable]. They arrived at night. She parted with her adoptive father, and was taken by an officer to a Chinese house where she and her colleague were locked in rooms. For the first time, she thought "I've been tricked." ...
>
> One autumn night that year, a Korean man sneaked into Kim's room. The soldiers were off at war, so not many were nearby. When he told her he was Korean as well, she asked him to help her run away. That night, they quietly escaped. The man was a silver-coin trader named Cho Gen-san. Kim Hak-sun went with him to Nanking, Suzhou, and then Shanghai. They were married in Shanghai, and hid until liberation in the French quarters where they ran a pawn shop for Chinese customers. She gave birth to a daughter in 1942 and a son in 1945. In the summer of 1946, she returned to Korea on the last boat from China with her countrymen in the liberation army.[25]

Kim would tell a different story in 1992 for the Korean Council's book on the comfort women (discussed below). There she would claim that Japanese soldiers had detained the kisaeng house owner and sent her to the comfort station.

1992: The Yoshimi Discovery

The *Asahi*, continuing its comfort women campaign, declared in 1992 that the historian Yoshimi Yoshiaki had found proof of the Japanese government's involvement in the comfort station regime. In fact, what Yoshimi had found was proof that the government had been worried about deceptive recruiters.[26] The key memorandum on which he relied came from 1938. It provided:

> Several matters requiring close attention have arisen with respect to the recruitment of women from Japan for comfort stations in the vicinity of the China incident. Some recruiters claim to have received the acknowledgment of the military. They threaten to damage the good name of the military, and to create misunderstanding among the general public. Some recruiters risk creating social problems by recruiting unsystematically through the intervention of military journalists or sympathetic outsiders. Some people have dealt with inappropriately chosen recruiters, and they in turn have transformed recruitment into something close to kidnapping, and found themselves the subject of arrests and police investigation. In the future, recruitment should be coordinated through the local military, and recruiters should be selected carefully. In carrying out their activities, recruiters should keep any ties to the local police and military police confidential in order to maintain the good name of the military and minimize social problems.[27]

There was nothing especially revelatory in this document. No scholar had ever seriously suggested that the Japanese government had not been involved in the comfort women regime. The government had wanted its soldiers to have access to prostitutes who required their customers to use condoms and who received regular medical examinations. Toward that end, it had extended its domestic prostitution licensing regime overseas. No one seriously questioned that much. The question was whether the government conscripted the women and ran the brothels. That question Yoshimi's memoranda did not address.

Nevertheless, for asserting that he had proved the government's involvement, Yoshimi became the darling of the Japanese studies crowd in the United States. Columbia University Press published a translation of his 1995 book on the comfort women in 2001. Yoshimi had said nothing new in his book, but—as the historian Bob Tadashi Wakabayashi put it— "the Western media lionize progressives such as the late Ienaga Saburo... and Yoshimi Yoshiaki...."[28] When claiming to follow established scholarship, American historians routinely cite Yoshimi. And when the time came to attack Ramseyer in 2021, they duly brought Yoshimi to the battle.[29]

1993: The Kono Statement

The time was 1993. Yoshida's 1983 book was still in the news. Yoshimi had claimed to have proved that the government had operated the comfort stations. The *Asahi* had given sensational coverage both to the book and to Yoshimi's "discoveries." It was in this context that the Japanese government issued its "Kono Statement" (named after Kono Yohei, the chief cabinet secretary).

The Japanese government had done its own research into whether the military had coerced Korean women into prostitution. It found nothing to support the claim.[30] But the South Korean government insisted that the Japanese military had indeed coerced Korean women: "From 1943, comfort women were rounded up using methods similar to those employed during the slave raids in black Africa in the nineteenth century."[31] In truth, other than the late-in-life statements of several comfort women, the Korean government had no evidence of any coercion. According to Hata, all it proffered in support of its accusation was Yoshida's memoir.[32] Yoshida was standing by his story, and so was the *Asahi*.

Seoul and Tokyo exchanged accusations, and in August 1993 the Japanese government caved. Its official statement said:

> As a result of the study which indicates that comfort stations were operated in extensive areas for long periods, it is apparent that there existed a great number of comfort women. Comfort stations were operated in response to the request of the military authorities of the day. The then Japanese military was, directly or indirectly, involved in the establishment and management of the comfort stations and the transfer of comfort women. The recruitment of the comfort women was conducted mainly by private recruiters who acted in response to the request of the military. The Government study has revealed that in many cases they were recruited against their own will, through coaxing, coercion, etc., and that, at times, administrative/military personnel directly took part in the recruitments. They lived in misery at comfort stations under a coercive atmosphere.
>
> As to the origin of those comfort women who were transferred to the war areas, excluding those from Japan, those from the Korean Peninsula accounted for a large part. The Korean Peninsula was under Japanese rule in those days, and their recruitment, transfer, control, etc., were conducted generally against their will, through coaxing, coercion, etc.
>
> Undeniably, this was an act, with the involvement of the military authorities of the day, that severely injured the honor and dignity of many women. The Government of Japan would like to take this opportunity once again to extend its sincere apologies and remorse to all those, irrespective of place of origin, who suffered immeasurable pain and incurable physical and psychological wounds as comfort women.[33]

This Kono Statement would haunt the government for years. Despite finding no evidence that its military had ever recruited (much less coerced) Korean women into sex work, the Japanese government had announced the contrary. It said that the military had been "involved in the establishment and management of the comfort stations and the transfer of comfort women." What is more, "in many cases they were recruited against their own will through coaxing, coercion, etc.," and sometimes "administrative/military personnel directly took part in the recruitments." Faced with an angry neighbor, crowds of activists and attorneys, and reporters from the *Asahi*, the Japanese government chose expedient capitulation. Yoshida's account now had the imprimatur of the government of Japan.

1993: The Korean Council Interviews

The movement was acquiring its own momentum by the time the Korean Council (the group praised by Matsui in the *Asahi*) published the testimonials of nineteen surviving comfort women in 1993. Founded in 1990, the Council played a part in the 1991 litigation against Japan. It quickly took center stage in the comfort women dispute, and soon in South Korean politics more broadly. In 1992, the group claimed to have interviewed forty former comfort women. It chose to publish nineteen of the testimonials, assuring readers that they were the most important (see Table 3.1).[34]

None of these women claimed to have been forcibly conscripted by the military in any Yoshida-style "comfort woman hunt." Those hunts would soon become central to the Korean Council's campaign, but as of 1993 none of the nineteen had yet mentioned any hunt. Three of the women—Kim Hak-sun (No. 1), Mun Ok-ju (No. 10), and Kan Dok-kyon (No. 18)—claimed to have been forcibly abducted. Yet remember that Kim Hak-sun, just two years earlier, had told the Tokyo District Court that the owner of her kisaeng shop had tricked her into going to a comfort station. Kan Dok-kyon did not work at a comfort station at all. We discuss Mun Ok-ju's claim in Chapter 5.

TABLE 3.1: COMFORT WOMEN TESTIMONIALS

In 1992, the Korean Council interviewed forty surviving self-identified comfort women. In 1993, they published summaries of the testimonials of nineteen of these comfort women. They described these as the women whose interviews they were able to complete.

1. (p. 41) Kim Hak-sun. She hated her parents. They put her up for adoption as a kisaeng entertainer (singing, dancing, sex). Her adoptive father (owner of the kisaeng house) then took her to China to find work, but en route she was abducted by the Japanese military and taken to a comfort station. (N.B.: discussed earlier in this chapter.)
2. (p. 57) Kim Dok-chin. She was tricked by a Korean recruiter who claimed that she would be doing factory work, and was taken to a comfort station near Shanghai.
3. (p. 71) Lee Yon-suk. She followed a Korean recruiter who promised a job in Japan, and was taken to a comfort station in Guangdong.
4. (p. 84) Ha Sun-nyo. When she was 20 or 21, she followed a Korean man and a Japanese man, both wearing business suits. They promised her a well-paying job in Osaka, but she was taken to a comfort station in Shanghai.
5. (p. 95) O O-mok. A Korean man promised her a job in a cotton-spinning factory, but she was taken to a Manchurian comfort station.
6. (p. 103) Fan (Hwang) Kum-ju. Her village head (who was Japanese) promised her high wages in a Japanese factory, but she was taken to a comfort station.
7. (p. 117) Mun Bil-gi. A local Korean man and the Japanese patrolman promised her a position where she could both earn high wages and study, but she was taken to a Manchurian comfort station.
8. (p. 131) Lee Yong-soo. Early one morning, her friend came to her window and urged her to come out. She discovered her friend with a Japanese man, who handed her a bag with a dress and a pair of shoes. She followed them and was taken to a comfort station in Taiwan. (N.B.: Lee is notorious for later changing her testimony in a wide variety of ways; discussed in Chapter 5.)
9. (p. 144) Lee Ok-pun. She was told by a Japanese man (in riding pants) and a Korean man that her father was looking for her. She followed them and was eventually sent with several other captured Korean adolescent girls to a comfort station in Taiwan. In 1942, she was sent to a comfort station for the suicide squads. (N.B.: The suicide squads were not formed until 1944.)
10. (p. 159) Mun Ok-ju. She was captured by Japanese in military uniform and sent to a Manchurian comfort station. (N.B.: Discussed more fully in Chapter 2.)
11. (p. 180) Lee Su-nok. She was recruited by a Chinese man for a Japanese silk-weaving factory, but sent to a comfort station in China.
12. (p. 195) Lee San-ok. She was recruited by a Japanese civilian (affiliated with the military) to work at a factory in Japan, but sent to a comfort station in Palau.
13. (p. 212) Lee Tok-nam. While she was working at a cafe in Manchuria, a Japanese civilian offered to introduce her to a better-paying cafe. Instead, she was taken to a comfort station in Hankou.
14. (p. 227) Lee Yon-nyo. She was first sent by her father (who received an advance loan) to work at a bar in Seoul. The owner (a woman) promised to introduce her to a good-paying place in Japan. When she agreed, the owner paid her a large sum. She boarded a ship and was taken to a comfort station in Burma.
15. (p. 241) Kim Te-son. A Japanese man (who may or may not have been wearing a military uniform) and a Korean man recruited her by promising a high-paying job at a Japanese factory. She boarded a ship and was taken to a comfort station in Burma.

16. (p. 253) Park Su-ne. At age 16, she married an impoverished man. She ran away, and at age 18 remarried as the second wife to a rich Korean. She bore a child, but her husband (who received an advance loan) transferred her (now age 23) to a recruiting station in Seoul. At the recruiting station she learned of a job as a nurse and laundress for the Japanese military, and enlisted. She was taken to a comfort station in Papua New Guinea.
17. (p. 269) Che Myon-sun (also known as Kim Kyon-sun). A town leader recruited her for a high-paying job in Japan. Upon arrival in Japan, she was made a mistress to a Japanese military officer. When she asked to go home, she was taken to Osaka, where she was regularly raped by many military men.
18. (p. 286) Kan Dok-kyon. In 1944, she was drafted to work in Japan at an aircraft factory. She escaped one night, but was caught. She was taken to a military installation where she was regularly raped.
19. (p. 301) Yun Do-ri. While walking past a Pusan train station, she was stopped by a police officer, who promised her a good job. She was taken by military truck to the harbor, and from there to Japan. From Japan, she was taken by boat to a comfort station on an island off the coast of Korea. (N.B.: there were no comfort stations in Korea.)

Source: Kankoku teishintai mondai taisaku kyogikai, ed., *Shogen—kyosei renko sareta Chosenjin gun ianfu tachi* [Testimonials—the Dragooned Korean Comfort Women of the Military] (Tokyo: Akashi shoten, 1993).

Almost uniformly, the women in the Korean Council's anthology claimed to have been defrauded. Some claimed that Korean recruiters fooled them, some that Japanese fooled them, and some that a pair of recruiters from each country fooled them. However, none argued that the Japanese government had caught her in a programmatic campaign to dragoon women for sexual slavery. Instead, most simply said that their recruiters (typically private recruiters) had lied.

Prewar Korea had a large corps of professional labor recruiters. In 1935, Korean police records counted 247 Japanese and 2,720 Korean recruiters. They included both men and women, and they recruited workers for factories as well as brothels.[35] As noted in Chapter 2, those recruiters had a history of using deceptive tactics. Throughout the prewar decades, newspapers reported recruiter fraud specifically related to the sex industry.

Already in 1918, the Japanese-language daily in Seoul complained of "a massive increase in the number of cases where a delinquent entices a woman to Seoul and, after playing all sorts of tricks on her, sells her off to one of the 'dubious restaurants.'"[36] In the late 1930s, Korean newspapers reported a ring of eleven recruiters who attracted over fifty young women into prostitution.[37] They reported one astonishingly skillful couple who had deceived over a hundred women. Apparently, the couple promised the parents of these young women that they would find a job for their daughters in Seoul factories, paid the parents 10 or 20 yen, and then forwarded the daughters to overseas brothels for 100 to 1,300 yen each.[38]

The Japanese government realized that this deception posed a problem for its comfort station regime. This is why it circulated the 1938 memorandum that Yoshimi found. It wanted to eliminate deceptive recruiting. This is why, at roughly the same time, the Home Ministry issued the following order:

> (a) For women traveling for the purpose of prostitution, approval shall be granted only to those women heading to North and Central China who are currently working as licensed or effective prostitutes, who are 21 years old or older, and who are free of venereal and other infectious diseases....
>
> (b) When receiving the identification documents detailed in the preceding section, the women should understand that they should immediately return to Japan upon the conclusion of their provisional contract or when that completion is no longer necessary.
>
> (c) Women intending to travel for the purpose of prostitution must apply to the police office for their identification documents in person.
>
> (d) In issuing identification documents regarding women traveling for the purpose of prostitution, special care should be taken in investigating the labor contract and other matters in order to ensure that the transaction is not a sale of the woman or a case of kidnapping.[39]

For the comfort stations, the government wanted only women who understood exactly what job they were accepting. It realized that some of the recruiters were cheating, and stepped in to address the problem. Yoshimi had not found evidence that the government dragooned women. He had found evidence that the government was trying to stop private recruiters from tricking women into sex work.

1995: Compensation

Despite having waived all war-related claims in 1965 in exchange for massive reparations, South Korea refused to let the matter die. The Japanese Diet, aiming to improve relations, passed a resolution in 1995 ordering the government to make things right. The government solicited private donations beyond the budgeted amount and organized a compensation fund that would top 5 billion yen. To each comfort women, it offered to pay a flat 2 million yen (around 15,400 USD at the May 1995 exchange rate) plus up to 3 million yen (around 23,100 USD) toward medical care.[40]

Almost immediately, the Korean Council sabotaged the compensation plan. It claimed that the Japanese government was denying responsibility by routing the compensation through a private entity created for that purpose, the Asian Women's Fund. The Council urged the comfort women to refuse the compensation and attacked those who accepted the money.

1996: The First UN Report (Coomaraswamy)

Radhika Coomaraswamy, a Sri Lankan human rights activist, wrote a virulently anti-Japanese diatribe about the comfort women for the UN in 1996.[41] Coomaraswamy explicitly cited four sources: Yoshida's 1983 book, a book on the comfort women by George Hicks published in 1995,[42] a 1994 report by the International Commission of Jurists (ICJ),[43] and unspecified documents provided by Yoshimi Yoshiaki (which she apparently used to claim that the Japanese government controlled the comfort stations). Yoshida's book is cited only once. It is in Japanese, and Coomaraswamy does not know Japanese. George Hicks is cited repeatedly. He was an Australian. He did not read Japanese either, but relied for his research on a Japan-resident Korean activist named Lee Yumi.[44] In turn, Lee had relied heavily on Yoshida's book.

It was like the telephone game: the original book, reconstituted by an activist, dramatized by an Australian (who did not know Japanese), and transformed into a UN report by a Sri Lankan (who also did not know Japanese). The game of telephone had other players too. Coomaraswamy twice cited the ICJ report, which cited both Yoshida and Hicks. Again, the game began with Yoshida's 1983 book and ended with the Coomaraswamy report. As Sarah Soh observed, "Yoshida's work served as a crucial resource for international human rights activists and the United Nations as they constructed the paradigmatic comfort women story."[45] Ultimately, it lies at the heart of the 1996 UN report.

Coomaraswamy relates the testimonies of three comfort women. Hwang So Gyun stated that in 1936, when she was 17 years old, the head of her village promised her a job in a factory.[46] After truck and train rides, she found herself in a military brothel in China. Observe that she claimed to have been defrauded by her village head (and probably a recruiter). She did not claim to have been conscripted by the Japanese army.

Hwang Kum Ju stated that in 1940, at age 17, she was drafted as part of the general wartime Japanese mobilization into work at a military factory.[47] After three years, she was raped by a Japanese soldier and then forced to provide sex to military personnel on a regular basis. Crucially, the basic premise of her conscription claim is false: the Japanese government did not draft either Japanese or Korean civilians into factory work until the fall of 1944.[48] Like Uemura and Matsui, Coomaraswamy seems not to have troubled with corroboration.

The woman with the strangest statement by far was one Chong Ok Sun. Because its very extravagance causes it to be quoted frequently by activist scholars like Michael Chwe and Y.S. Lee (a law professor), we reproduce it at length:

> One day in June, at the age of 13, I... went to the village well to fetch water. A Japanese garrison soldier surprised me there and took me away.... I was taken to the police station in a truck, where I was raped by several policemen. When I shouted, they put socks in my mouth and continued to rape me....
>
> After 10 days or so, I was taken to the Japanese army garrison barracks in Hyesan City. There were around 400 other Korean young girls with me and we had to serve over 5,000 Japanese soldiers as sex slaves every day—up to 40 men per day....
>
> One Korean girl who was with us once demanded why we had to serve so many, up to 40, men per day. To punish her for her questioning, the Japanese company commander Yamamoto ordered her to be beaten with a sword. While we were watching, they took off her clothes, tied her legs and hands and rolled her over a board with nails until the nails were covered with blood and pieces of her flesh. In the end, they cut off her head. Another Japanese, Yamamoto, told us that "it's easy to kill you all, easier than killing dogs". He also said "since those Korean girls are crying because they have not eaten, boil the human flesh and make them eat it."....
>
> Once they took 40 of us on a truck far away to a pool filled with water and snakes. The soldiers beat several of the girls, shoved them into the water, heaped earth into the pool and buried them alive.
>
> I think over half of the girls who were at the garrison barracks were killed....[49]

Thirteen-year-old girls as comfort women; 400 comfort women having sex 40 times a day to serve 5,000 men; troublemakers rolled over boards with nails and then beheaded; women forced to eat the flesh of their compatriots; women buried alive; half the women killed—these are the stories "Chong" told.

Hata Ikuhiko sardonically notes that the "scenario writer" might have done a bit more research.[50] The woman claimed to have been abducted in 1933, but Hyesan, where "Chong" said she worked as a comfort woman, is a city in the current North Korea, and Japan had not established comfort stations in Korea in 1933.

What's more, Coomaraswamy never met any "Chong Ok Sun." The woman styled "Chong" lived in North Korea, and Coomaraswamy never went there. Instead, members of an activist group called the Center for Human Rights went on her behalf. The statement quoted here is the document they brought back when they returned.[51] More generally, as Park Yu-ha noted, the testimonies of the North Korea–based comfort women have been overwhelmingly the most bizarre—and it is precisely those testimonies on which Western observers have relied.[52]

1998: The Second UN Report (McDougall)

The UN issued a second attack in 1998. The author of this report was Gay McDougall, an activist lawyer who took a position even more aggressive than Coomaraswamy's. The comfort stations did not just involve "sex slavery," said she. They constituted "rape centers":

> It is now clear that both the Japanese Government and military were directly involved in the establishment of rape centres throughout Asia during the Second World War. The women who were enslaved by the Japanese military in these centres—many of whom were between the ages of 11 and 20—...were forcibly raped multiple times on a daily basis and subjected to severe physical abuse....[53]

By McDougall's account, it would appear that none of the women took the job for the high pay. Instead, she writes, to "obtain these 'comfort women,' the Japanese military employed physical violence, kidnapping, coercion and deception."[54]

McDougall herself is nothing if not a star in the field of human rights. She worked extensively in South Africa. She received a MacArthur Foundation "genius grant" in 1999. She received an award for her "lifetime advocacy for civil and human rights" from the American Society of International Law in 2011. The American Association of Law Schools bestowed on her the inaugural Nelson Mandela Award in 2023, citing her "groundbreaking study on the issue of systematic rape and sexual slavery practices in armed conflict."[55]

Acknowledged star that she is, McDougall claimed to rely "exclusively on the facts established in the Japanese Government's own review of the involvement of Japanese officials in establishing, supervising and maintaining rape centres during the Second World War." In fact, she does nothing of the sort. She does cite the Kono Statement repeatedly. But for her preposterous claims (of which there are many), she instead turns to a law review article written by an activist, Karen Parker, with the help of a student.[56] The two follow the Yoshida-school line, apparently embroidered with abandon:

> As many as two hundred thousand women were tricked or abducted into slavery for sexual services for the Japanese Imperial Army during World War II. Women and girls as young as twelve were taken from their homes in Korea, China, the Dutch East Indies, Taiwan, Malaysia, Burma, and the Philippines. They were sent to locations throughout Japanese-occupied Asia where they were imprisoned in facilities known as "comfort houses," raped daily by soldiers, and forced to endure torture and abuse. Only about 25 percent survived this treatment.[57]

1991–2000: The Lawsuits

During the 1990s, self-identified comfort women would file several lawsuits against Japan. Nishino Rumiko, a journalist and activist, identifies ten such suits in Japanese courts, three by Korean comfort women. All ten were unsuccessful. In 2000, fifteen comfort women filed a class action suit against Japan in the United States. In the course of several opinions, the federal district and appellate courts variously dismissed the suit on grounds of sovereign immunity and the "political question" doctrine (by which federal courts avoid questions that are fundamentally political rather than legal).[58] In truth, all of the cases—whether in Japan or in the United States—were massively overdetermined. The 1965 treaty between Korea and Japan, sovereign immunity, the statute of limitations, and the basic absence of any corroborating witnesses or documentary evidence—any one of these reasons would have been enough to doom the litigation.

Yoshida-school writers claim to rely on the court cases. According to the Columbia historian Carol Gluck, the Japanese judges "recognized the truthfulness, the 'irrefutable historical evidence,' of the plaintiffs' accounts of abduction, brutality, and violence."[59] According to Y.S. Lee, a legal scholar, one of the cases "affirmed the illegal nature of military sexual slavery."[60] Nishino writes that a "total of 93 victims testified before Japanese courts, and judges have accepted most of their depositions as factual.... Both Tokyo and Yamaguchi district courts...acknowledged the plaintiffs' personal accounts of sexual violence and direct Japanese military involvement to be trustworthy."[61]

The best known of the Japanese judicial opinions on the comfort women is probably the one mentioned by both Lee and Nishino—the decision by the Shimonoseki branch office of the Yamaguchi District Court. In 1994, several Korean comfort women sued Japan in the Shimonoseki court for damages from their dragooning. The court awarded them each 300,000 yen plus interest in 1998. On appeal, the Hiroshima High Court reversed on the grounds of sovereign immunity.[62]

If Gluck, Lee, Nishino, or anyone else relies on these cases for "the truthfulness...of the plaintiffs' accounts of abduction, brutality, and violence," they miss a basic legal principle: judges decide only the questions that the parties contest. Having just issued the Kono Statement, the Japanese government deliberately chose not to contest the plaintiffs' factual claims. It had no reason to contest them. Regardless of what the facts might be, the plaintiffs had no legal claim—most obviously because the Korean government had waived all Korean claims in the 1965 treaty. The Shimonoseki court cited the Kono Statement and explicitly noted that the government had not challenged the plaintiffs' factual assertions. On appeal, the Hiroshima High Court again noted that the government had not contested the factual claims, but reversed for several legal reasons, including the 1965 treaty. Again, the point is basic: judges do not decide questions that the parties do not contest. Whether the military forcibly conscripted women into the comfort stations was not at issue in the Shimonoseki case.

Besides the Shimonoseki decision, Nishino lists two other court cases—both filed in the Tokyo District Court—where, she asserts, the judges accepted the factual claims of Korean comfort women. As in the Shimonoseki case, the courts in both of these Tokyo cases expressly noted that the government chose not to contest the claim that the Japanese government forcibly conscripted Korean comfort women. Whether the military dragooned the comfort women was simply not at issue. Instead, in both, the courts straightforwardly paraphrased the statement to that effect in the Kono Statement.[63]

In 2000, Gay McDougall published an "update" to her 1998 UN report. The Shimonoseki branch of the Yamaguchi District Court had issued its judgment in the interim, and McDougall—as a lawyer—surely understood that the government had not contested the plaintiffs' factual assertions. Nevertheless, she described the opinion as "establishing as fact that the 'comfort women' were confined and forced to have sex with Japanese soldiers," and claimed the court had found that "the women essentially were held in sexual slavery for which the Government of Japan is responsible."[64]

2000: The Women's International War Crimes Tribunal

In late 2000, several activist groups joined together to try Japan's wartime leaders for their role in "sexual slavery." All of those leaders were dead, but the show trial went on anyway. The event was held in Tokyo. The activists called it a "people's tribunal," enthused Alexis Dudden. It gave the former prostitutes "an opportunity to testify about their enslavement."[65]

Predictably, the show trial convicted the Showa emperor (Hirohito), the wartime prime minister Tojo Hideki, and several others. The guilty verdict against the Showa emperor was an "outstanding" moment, explained Norma Field, a University of Chicago literature scholar (and one of Dudden's former professors). It was a moment when "the audience rose to its feet in response to the utterance of words that few who know Japan would have thought likely to hear in public...."[66]

Hata Ikuhiko attended the last day of the trial. He remembered it a bit differently. A "kangaroo court," he called it. There was only one hearing, and "no attorneys spoke for the defense." The court found twenty-five military leaders guilty. All were dead, and many had already been tried in the Tokyo war crimes trials. But "when the judgment was read," the audience "burst into a wave of applause and endless screaming. The scene thereafter was fanatical.... It was as though the audience members were in a new religious cult and were heralding the arrival of their foundress."[67]

The tribunal took both the original postwar Tokyo trials and Yoshida's dragooning claims at face value. It stated that "the Japanese presence in Korea was one of long and brutal economic and social exploitation of the Korean land and society." It asserted that "[t]ens of thousands of Korean women and girls were forced into the sexual slavery system through such means as deception and force, after which they were subjected to rape and other forms of sexual violence and confined in 'comfort' facilities under inhumane conditions."[68] The comfort stations "were not brothels staffed with voluntary workers," according to the tribunal's report. "They were places...of unspeakable horror, facilities where women were enslaved against their will and repeatedly raped and otherwise brutalised for months or years on end...."[69]

Matsui Yayori served as one of the key members of the organizing committee. Recall that Matsui, as the senior staff member at the *Asahi* newspaper, had supervised Uemura Takashi as he transformed Yoshida's memoir into international outrage against Japan. Yun Chung-ok served as a second organizer. She had founded the Korean Council—the group behind the 1991 litigation and the 1993 collection of testimonies, and the pivotal group we will examine in Chapter 6.[70]

2005: The Amnesty International Report

Amnesty International published its own report on the comfort women in 2005. Like others, it obtained its evidence from the telephone game that started with Yoshida's memoir. Amnesty International explained the comfort station regime as a variation on wartime rape: "Sexual violence, including rape, is used as a weapon of war—it is used deliberately to demoralize and destroy the opposition...."[71] Where Japanese military planners had described the regime as a way to reduce the incidence of rape, Amnesty declared it a form of rape itself. Recall that the plurality of comfort women were Japanese. Amnesty nonetheless characterized the regime as "the legalized military rape of subject women on a scale—and over a period of time—previously unknown in history."[72] This was a quotation from George Hicks, who of course relied on Yoshida.

For Amnesty International, any notion that the comfort stations involved voluntary prostitution was simply fiction. Citing the report from the 2000 show trial, it wrote that "Apologists for Japan's military sexual slavery system claim that the 'comfort women' were voluntary prostitutes, however, testimonies and other evidence reveal that women were enslaved, repeatedly raped, tortured...exclusively for the benefit of the Japanese military."[73] Amnesty claimed that the military "often used extreme violence to obtain women and girls," and cited the reference in the Coomaraswamy report to "large-scale coercion and violence amounting to 'slave raids.'"[74] The Coomaraswamy report did indeed make this claim. Coomaraswamy cited Hicks, and Hicks cited Yoshida.

By now, readers will guess the people involved. For help from Japan, Amnesty gratefully acknowledged the assistance of VAWW-NET, the Violence Against Women in War Network. Matsui had helped found this group after retiring from the *Asahi*. For help from Korea, Amnesty thanked the Korean Council.

2015: The McGraw-Hill Textbook

Until 2015, it was hard to find a single account of the comfort women that captured the academic consensus in the West. That year (as we discuss in Chapter 1), a now-well-known (or perhaps "infamous") textbook published by McGraw-Hill solved that problem. It was written by Herbert Ziegler and Jerry Bentley, and the relevant passage read:

> The Japanese army forcibly recruited, conscripted, and dragooned as many as two hundred thousand women age fourteen to twenty to serve in military brothels, called "comfort houses" or "consolation centers." The army presented the women to the troops as a gift from the emperor.... The majority of the women came from Korea and China.
>
> Once forced into this imperial prostitution service, the "comfort women" catered to between twenty and thirty men each day. Stationed in war zones, the women often confronted the same risks as soldiers, and many became casualties of war. Others were killed by Japanese soldiers, especially if they tried to escape or contracted venereal diseases. At the end of the

> war, soldiers massacred large numbers of comfort women to cover up the operations.[75]

When the passage hit the news, Japanese observers noted the arithmetic with amusement. Japan had at most 3 million military personnel overseas. If each of the 200,000 comfort women "catered to" 30 men a day, the 3 million soldiers would each have had sex twice a day. This did not, observers mused, leave much time for fighting.

The Japanese government complained and declared the book preposterous. Twenty prominent U.S. historians of Japan, apparently lacking any arithmetic sense of humor, rushed to defend the textbook in the newsletter of the American Historical Association, called *Perspectives on History*.[76] The lead author on the defense was Alexis Dudden, the University of Connecticut historian and associate in research at Harvard's Reischauer Institute. Jordan Sand, historian at Georgetown, joined Dudden in spearheading the defense. Other signatories included Andrew Gordon (Harvard) and Carol Gluck (Columbia). The twenty historians wanted to "express [their] dismay" at the Japanese government's reaction to the textbook, they explained.

> Historians continue to debate whether the numbers of women exploited were in the tens of thousands or the hundreds of thousands and what precise role the military played in their procurement. Yet the careful research of historian Yoshimi Yoshiaki in Japanese government archives and the testimonials of survivors throughout Asia have rendered beyond dispute the essential features of a system that amounted to state-sponsored sexual slavery. Many of the women were conscripted against their will and taken to stations at the front where they had no freedom of movement. Survivors have described being raped by officers and beaten for attempting to escape.[77]

Elsewhere, Dudden further explained why the group had chosen to speak out in defense of the textbook. Apparently, they believed that everyone deserves academic freedom—so long as that person does not "deny" what they consider to be "proven international history":

> Our concern was and remains with two basic features of historical research in an open society such as Japan. First, academic freedom; and second, the repression and denial of a proven international history—the brutal mid-20th century system of state-sponsored sexual slavery throughout the Empire of Japan.[78]

Note that Dudden purports to speak on behalf of the group here. To our knowledge, no one among the twenty has challenged this explanation. (Dudden and Gordon both, of course, would try to block the publication of Ramseyer's IRLE article in 2021.)

Dudden then draws a straight line from the comfort women regime to Boko Haram's treatment of women:

> I think of Boko Haram and (the Islamic State group's) current use of sexual slavery as a weapon of war critical to why denying away historical evidence is so deeply retrograde.... Will it become possible in today's Japan to declare that this history did not happen, when many of us in Japan and around the world possess historical materials that prove it took place.[79]

As far as we know, Dudden has never disclosed to the world quite what these probative "historical materials" that she "possess[es]" might be. Yet she would later assert that questioning the Yoshida-school assumptions about the comfort women is a form of "hate speech" as it is defined in some countries, and even comparable to what in Germany "would bring criminal charges of Holocaust denial."[80]

To our knowledge, none of the nineteen other scholars so eager to defend the McGraw-Hill textbook has ever complained about their lead author's comparison of the Japanese army to Boko Haram and the Islamic State. Morgan did object, in print, and Dudden replied, in print, doubling down on the comparison and also reiterating her charge that those who disagree with her are engaging in "denialism."[81]

Instead of the scholars' distancing themselves from this choice of analogies, a classic pile-on ensued. After the twenty scholars published their letter in early 2015, some 180 others (primarily from the United States and Europe) signed another letter in support of the McGraw-Hill textbook. By some accounts, the number of signatories eventually soared past 450.[82] Kumagai Naoko, a Japanese scholar, soon contacted the AHA newsletter, where the group of twenty had posted their proclamation. As she put it, the "statement that as many as 200,000 women age 14 to 20 were forcibly recruited, conscripted, or dragooned by the Japanese army... is unrealistic in view of the Japanese military's quite limited material capabilities and strategic purposes."[83] Fourteen of the twenty summarily replied, "This is not true." Arithmetic or no arithmetic, they said that Kumagai was advancing a "denialist thesis."[84] Another signatory to one of the letters was Jason Morgan's adviser. Morgan too had written to the AHA newsletter to protest the proclamation by the group of twenty. His adviser dropped him as his advisee (discussed in Chapter 1). Her colleague in the department who became Morgan's pinch-hitter adviser (and who also signed one of the protest letters) would later write in a "recommendation letter" that Morgan had "whitewashed" history for the prime minister of Japan.

At root, only two types of evidence back the claim that the Japanese military dragooned Korean comfort women by force: the accounts of several comfort women, and Yoshida's 1983 book. For their testimony, none of the women produced any corroborating witnesses or documentary evidence. They told stories that contradict the wide range of evidence. And many of the women maintained close ties to the Korean Council.

As the years passed, historians began to investigate Yoshida's book, and journalists began to investigate the Korean Council. In neither case did the results support the claims of the activists.

CHAPTER 4

THE HOAX COLLAPSES

Yoshida

It took some time, but Yoshida Seiji's account of "hunts" for comfort women began to attract skeptics. Shortly after the Korean translation of *My War Crimes* appeared in 1989, a local newspaper on the island of Jeju published a review:

> [A] book has been published recording the impressment of 205 women from Jeju Island to work as comfort women during the Japanese imperial period. This book is having an enormous impact. However, there are no testimonies that corroborate the author's claims....
>
> The people of Jeju have dismissed this tale as "nonsense,".... Cheong Ok-tan, an eighty-five-year-old female resident of [a Jeju village where Yoshida claimed to have abducted women], says, "This village has only slightly more than 250 households, so if fifteen people had been pressed into service it would have been a major incident. Nothing like that happened here."[1]

Hata Ikuhiko could confirm that Yoshida had worked in Shimonoseki, but not much else. Military history was his field, and the story about receiving an army order at a labor office to dragoon people from Korea—men or women—did not fit what he knew about the military bureaucracy. Not only that, but Korea was not a theater of the Second World War, and it had been part of Japan since 1910. Dispatching a contingent of troops to Jeju under the command of a labor office to attack a factory in broad daylight would have been akin to PACCOM's ordering the New Jersey National Guard to go slave raiding in Puerto Rico under the command of the National Labor Relations Board.

In fact, Yoshida had told a different story in an earlier book, published in 1977. There he wrote that he had worked in a government labor office in Shimonoseki and had received an order to recruit a hundred Korean women to work as comfort women. He recruited them, he said, by lying to them and promising them other kinds of work.[2] That book seems not to have sold. A few years later, Yoshida wrote the book in which he claimed to have led a posse of soldiers to Jeju Island and dragooned two hundred women at bayonet-point, raped them, bound them together by rope, and sent them to the comfort stations. That book did sell.

Hata tried to meet Yoshida in person, but Yoshida refused. Finally, Hata managed to talk with him by telephone in 1992. His notes record this exchange:

> *Hata:*...What kind of work did you do in Shimonoseki?
>
> *Yoshida:* It was the association's duty to procure day laborers...under contract from the police. About ten thousand free laborers lived in Shimonoseki, so they were the main ones we would procure. However, even these laborers were not enough during the second half of the war, so we gathered them from the Korean Peninsula.

Hata: Did you also procure comfort women?

Yoshida: We procured comfort women in the same way, under the name of the Women's Volunteer Corps. As I recall, it was about 950 women in total. But my subordinates say the number was two thousand. Prostitution operators were also scrambling for women, so there was a woman shortage. We went to Jeju Island to hunt them, because there were plenty of women there. . . .

Hata: You say that your wife copied down in her diary the text of the mobilization order from the Western District Army given in May 1943 [in which you were ordered to obtain comfort women]. However, in your previous book, you write that you did not get married until February 1944. . . .

Yoshida: At that time, it was common knowledge that a de facto marriage did not take place at the same time that one submitted the marriage registration.

Hata: So when did your de facto marriage take place?

Yoshida: Before the war, so I suppose in 1941.

Hata: You wrote that you went to prison in 1940, and were released in June 1942. Did you get married while you were in prison?

Yoshida: My wife is dead, so I have no way of finding that out.

Hata: I'd like to corroborate your story, so please tell me the names of some of your subordinates.

> *Yoshida:* When I was writing this book, I invited about ten former subordinates to be my coauthors, but they were afraid and so they refused.... I absolutely cannot tell you anything about them.[3]

The conversation left Hata unhappy. Others looked into Yoshida's account, and they too lost confidence. When a public TV network tried to assemble a program about Yoshida's book, they contacted his publisher. They were "told Yoshida's book was a novel."[4]

Hata reached Yoshida again in 1996. This time Yoshida straightforwardly admitted to having invented facts. As Hata summarized the conversation:

> *Yoshida*: The comfort women hunt on Jeju Island is mixed in with fiction. To avoid causing trouble for the women, I took care to intentionally change the place-names and also my descriptions, but some of what I wrote is true.... The Jeju Island comfort-women-hunting scene actually took place in Cheollanamdo.[5]

Obviously, "some of what I wrote is true" will not leave historians happy. Hata then asked Yoshida about Cheollanamdo, the coastal area next to Jeju Island:

> *Hata*: Well, then, the whole story from Cheollanamdo is true?

> *Yoshida*: No. It wouldn't have been right to cause trouble for the victims in Cheollanamdo, so I weaved in stories from other places.[6]

Speaking to a magazine a short time later, Yoshida suggested that his fabrications were like what newspaper reporters do:

> Well, there's nothing to be gained by writing the truth in books. Isn't it the case that even newspapers conceal the truth and mix in what the reporters themselves want to say? If some parts don't fit with the rest, then what's to be done about it?[7]

Hata called Yoshida again in 1998 to ask whether he would issue a statement describing his book as a novel. He replied, "I have my pride. I'm eighty-five years old, so to change it now... Let's just leave things as they are."[8]

After interviewing Yoshida several times and raising several questions that he could not answer, Hata hired a Korean interpreter and traveled to Jeju himself. There he interviewed local reporters and elderly people. No one remembered any kidnappings of young women during the war, whether by Japanese or anyone else. An article in the local newspaper quoted a local historian, Kim Pon-ok:

> I have been searching for traces of this event for years, ever since the Japanese version [of *My War Crimes*] came out in 1983. The result of this search is that I have found [Yoshida's claims] have no basis in fact. This book is a superficial commercial product that shows the villainy of the Japanese.[9]

A Korean War veteran, Lt. Col. (ret.) Archie Miyamoto, made the realistic point that any attempt by anyone, and especially by the Japanese, to kidnap women in Korea would have provoked immediate and fierce resistance. Imagine, Miyamoto writes, if a foreign occupier tried to kidnap young women in Texas. There would be hell to pay, no matter what the consequences.[10]

Yoshimi

By 1997, even Yoshimi Yoshiaki, ever the icon of Western academics, had abandoned Yoshida. He and his colleagues had visited Yoshida, he said. They urged him to respond to his critics. In the end, Yoshimi concluded that "it would be impossible to use Yoshida's memoirs as testimonial." He had "no choice."[11]

Western historians cite Yoshimi, but they apparently do not read him. Yoshimi implies that the Japanese army did not forcibly dragoon Korean women. In an interview for the *Mainichi* newspaper in 2019, he said:

> So, how were the comfort women gathered? There were three general methods. First, an industry member [recruiter] selected by the military lent money to a woman's family (the advance loan), and she in exchange worked at a comfort station (the purchase of a human). Second, a member of the industry [recruiter] fooled a woman into thinking that she would be working in a job like bar hostess or nurse (kidnapping). Third, government officials or a member of the industry used threats or violence forcibly to impress the woman (capture).
>
> On the Korean peninsula, which was a colony, the first and second were common. There is testimony and court material indicating that forcible impressment by government officials occurred in occupied territories like China and Southeast Asia.[12]

The military may have dragooned women in China and Southeast Asia. It did not, Yoshimi writes, dragoon women in Korea. In late 2021 one could still locate the interview on the internet. Curiously, either the newspaper or Yoshimi himself (it is not clear which) has apparently chosen to try to make it disappear. The interview no longer appears in the official *Mainichi* internet repository.

Uemura

In 1991, Uemura Takashi had fueled the Yoshida narrative when he wrote about a woman named Kim Hak-sun who said she had been forcibly conscripted into comfort woman work by the Japanese military as part of the wartime Women's Volunteer Corps. The *Asahi* newspaper published his story, but Nishioka Tsutomu thought Uemura's *Asahi* articles were intentionally false, and said so in an April 1992 article in the highly respected culture and politics journal *Bungei Shunju*. Around the same time and in multiple outlets, the journalist Sakurai Yoshiko also publicly criticized Uemura's assertions about the comfort women in the *Asahi*. Uemura sued both of them and their publications for defamation. By 2019 he had lost both cases at trial, and in 2021 he lost his appeals all the way to the Supreme Court.[13]

The Tokyo District Court was particularly brutal. Nishioka claimed that Uemura had deliberately written his article to convey the impression that the Japanese military had dragooned Kim, even though Uemura knew that she had actually not said that. Wrote the court:

> We find it reasonable to hold that [Uemura] deliberately wrote his [December *Asahi* article] in a way that introduces [Kim] as a military comfort woman who was dragooned [*kyosei renko*] to the front. In other words, we find that he deliberately wrote [his December *Asahi* article] in a way that differed from the facts....[14]

Sakurai recalled that the judge in the case pushed Uemura on the issue of whether he had known that the comfort women were not part of the Women's Volunteer Corps. The point mattered, because Yoshida claimed to have dragooned women as part of the Volunteer Corps. If Kim Hak-sun had used that term, her statement would have added credibility to the Yoshida memoir. Under questioning, Uemura replied that he had indeed known that the two groups were distinct. He had known this even when he described Kim as stating that she was conscripted as part of the Volunteer Corps, although she herself had not said so.[15]

Nishioka also claimed that Uemura had deliberately misstated the facts of Kim's recruitment in order to benefit his mother-in-law's litigation campaign against Japan. The court concluded simply: "[T]here was a reasonable basis for [Nishioka] to believe this."[16]

The U.S. House Resolution

While scholars were exposing serious problems of credibility in the Yoshida sex-slave narrative, Western institutions were doubling down on it. In 2007, for example, the U.S. House of Representatives passed a resolution alleging that the comfort women regime had been "unprecedented in its cruelty and magnitude, [and] included gang rape, forced abortions, humiliation, and sexual violence resulting in mutilation, death, or eventual suicide...." All told, it was "one of the largest cases of human trafficking in the 20th century."[17]

The House resolution was introduced by Rep. Mike Honda, a Democrat from the 15th Congressional District in California. Honda would lose his seat to a challenger in 2016, in the wake of an ethics probe into misuse of official resources.[18]

In March 2014, Rep. Honda was one of several people who met with Fang Fang (Christine Fang) at the embassy of the PRC in Washington, D.C.[19] Fang was later outed as a Chinese operative who had been running an extensive influence and espionage campaign targeting Democratic politicians in the United States. In 2017, Honda visited the offices of the left-leaning *Hankyoreh* newspaper in Seoul along with Russell Lowe, the man who would later be revealed as a PRC spy who for twenty years had been running espionage operations against his employer, Senator Dianne Feinstein, as a "staff liaison to the Asian-American community."[20] Lowe has a direct connection to the comfort women issue: after leaving Senator Feinstein's employ, he went to work as "a leader of the Comfort Women Justice Coalition (CWJC)."[21] The CWJC helped broker the deal that brought a comfort woman statue to San Francisco in 2015. That effort was led by Judith Mirkinson, a member of the Prairie Fire Organizing Committee (founded by the Weather Underground Organization), and Eric Mar, who was affiliated with the Chinese government organization formerly known as Hanban.[22] Here, Honda himself reenters the picture. Among the publications listed in Mar's faculty profile is this:

> "RIP Halmoni Kim Bok Don on the 3rd Anniversary of the SF 'Comfort Women' Memorial," with Congressman Mike Honda and Meehyang Yoon of the Korean Council, Chinatown, SF, September 2019.[23]

Members of Congress can quite properly visit embassies. They can visit foreign newspaper offices. Some of the people who approach them will be spies. We would not detail Honda's visits but for the bizarre House resolution he introduced. It was bizarre not just in its savagely anti-Japanese character, though it certainly was that. It was anti-Japanese in a way that tracked the Chinese and North Korean sympathies of the South Korean organization masterminding the comfort women campaign. We return to this subject in Chapter 6.

The Asahi *Reassessment*

It was the *Asahi Shimbun* newspaper that had made Yoshida a phenomenon. It had taken the unknown author and showered him with coverage, publishing more than a dozen articles on his sensational stories. Before Yoshida, the world had not known a comfort woman dispute. After Yoshida—after the *Asahi*'s coverage of Yoshida—the dispute left the South Korea–Japan relationship in tatters.

Journalists and scholars continued trying to check Yoshida's story. As the evidence of fraud mounted, even the *Asahi* could not ignore it. In 1997, the newspaper acknowledged: "There were soon people who questioned his testimony. From the people on Jeju Island, as well, there were no testimonies to corroborate his writings. The truth of these writings cannot be confirmed."[24]

The *Asahi* waited nearly two more decades before coming entirely clean, but it finally did. In 2014, it pronounced its articles based on the Yoshida account unambiguously "false" and retracted the entire portfolio.[25] "From April to May of this year," explained the *Asahi*, "we interviewed approximately 40 residents of Jeju Island in their mid-70s to 90s. We were not able to obtain any testimony corroborating the forced recruitment claims of Mr. Yoshida." Accordingly, "we have concluded that Mr. Yoshida's claims that he forcibly recruited comfort women from Jeju Island are fraudulent. We retract the articles."[26]

The response to the *Asahi* retraction varied by continent. Western intellectuals refused to let Yoshida's memoir die. Writing for the *New York Times*, Martin Fackler stressed not that Yoshida had fabricated his story but that the *Asahi* had caved to politics. As he framed the story, "influential conservatives" in Japan were trying to "question the internationally accepted view that the women . . . were forced to provide sex to Japanese soldiers."[27] The *Asahi* had retracted the articles, Fackler claimed, because of "a broad, vitriolic assault by the right-wing news media and politicians" on the newspaper.[28]

Radhika Coomaraswamy was likewise unmoved. She had based her 1996 report for the UN on Yoshida's account (generally filtered through George Hicks) and on the uncorroborated statements of a few comfort women. Once the *Asahi* had confirmed that the Yoshida book was false, only those testimonials remained. The Japanese government contacted Coomaraswamy and asked her to retract the report.[29] She refused.

Revisiting Diplomatic Expediency

In 2014, the Japanese government decided to retrace its diplomatic history and determine what had induced it to state in 1993 that the military had participated in coercing women into the comfort station regime. The government had not itself found evidence of any such dragooning. Uemura had clearly lied about Kim Hak-sun. Some of the most insistent comfort women were obviously lying. Even the

Asahi would soon declare that Yoshida's story about "hunts" for comfort women was false. Momentum was building to tend to this open wound in Japan–South Korea relations.

The diplomatic records made clear that the Japanese government had issued the Kono Statement only after long and elaborate negotiations with its counterparts in South Korea.[30] The negotiations began in October 1992 and continued until Japan issued its declaration in August 1993. Throughout, the South Korean government stressed that the Japanese government must state that the military had taken women forcibly. Any claim that some of the women had chosen the job voluntarily, it insisted, would be flatly unacceptable.[31] Simultaneously, it assured Japan that it had no plans to demand compensation for the comfort women.[32]

The Japanese government asked to speak with some of the comfort women. The Korean Council replied that it would let Japanese representatives talk to women under its control only if it agreed in advance to conclude that the military had dragooned the comfort women.[33] The Japanese government refused this condition, of course. Eventually, another group did introduce some women to be interviewed.

According to its own records, then, the Japanese government had not found any evidence of dragooning by the military. It had agreed to issue the Kono Statement only after negotiating with the South Korean government for nearly a year. Those negotiations had included the Korean Council. And in the course of the negotiations, the Korean government had assured the Japanese government that it would not demand compensation.

Postwar Media Accounts

With Yoshida's memoir exposed as a fraud, the oral testimonials of several of the comfort women constitute virtually the only evidence that the Japanese army ever dragooned Korean women. Had the Japanese military kidnapped young women in Korea at gunpoint, one would expect to find contemporaneous corroboration. One would expect to read stories in newspapers, police reports, personal diaries. But almost no accounts of dragooning exist, and those that do mostly appear only in the wake of the 1989 Korean translation of Yoshida's book.

C. Sarah Soh explored the postwar media accounts in Korea at great length.[34] She found no mention of comfort women before 1964. That year, the *Han'guk Ilbo* newspaper ran an article about a comfort woman who "was forcibly taken, during the period of imperial Japan, to the Southeast Asia," as the paper described it.[35] The woman had died in 1963. Soh does not give more information about how she came to be a comfort woman. Soh continues:

> Almost all Korean publications concerning the comfort women issue surfaced after the 1965 bilateral agreement was signed between South Korea and Japan. Nearly all have presented postcolonial nationalist perspectives, denouncing Japan for the forced mobilization of "virgins"... who, many Koreans have continued to assert, were abused as comfort women.[36]

Soh identifies the beginning of "public discourse" in Korea on comfort women with an article published in 1970.[37] She does not say much about the content of the article, but instead moves on to list the occasional publication on the subject.[38] She then writes, "Nevertheless, it was not until 1981 that the first Korean-authored volume devoted to the topic of the Korean comfort women was released to the general public."[39] Soh does not say much about this volume either, but proceeds to describe a novella featuring a comfort woman named Sun-i. The story says that she earned 2,000 won in the job, and Soh observes:

> It is also remarkable that the author gives the amount of money saved by Sun-i as 2,000 won because, after the redress movement began, it has become socially unacceptable and politically

> embarrassing to state that the women had been paid for their sexual service....[40]

Finally, Soh turns to the lavish attention given by the Korean media in 1984 to an unnamed Korean comfort woman who had been living in Thailand. This woman reported: "I was forcibly recruited by Japanese policemen in 1942 and sent to Singapore, where I labored as a comfort woman for three years."[41] In Soh's chronology, this is the first reference after the 1963 article where the woman clearly asserts that she was recruited "forcibly." Recall that Yoshida published his book in 1983 and that the *Asahi Shimbun* promoted it aggressively. The Japanese newspaper that first published this woman's story was the *Asahi*, and the reporter involved was Matsui Yayori (discussed in Chapter 3).[42]

The two Korean newspapers with the largest circulation are the *Dong-A Ilbo* and the *Chosun Ilbo* (both dating from 1920). From 1945 until after the Korean translation of Yoshida's fraudulent memoir appeared in 1989, neither of these newspapers gave any significant coverage to the comfort women.

At Ramseyer's request, Joo Ikjong (an economic historian) very generously agreed to search two newspapers, the *Dong-A Ilbo* and the *Kyunghyang*, for references to the comfort woman. The *Dong-A Ilbo* is sometimes described as currently right-of-center, while the *Kyunghyang*, a smaller-circulation newspaper founded in 1946, is considered left-of-center. In Figure 4.1, there are three shadings. The darkest shading counts the number of times the term "comfort women" is used in reference to prostitutes working at the U.S. bases. Note that this is the largest group prior to 1990. The medium shading (very rare) is used for general references to "comfort women." The lightest shading counts the number of times "comfort women" is used for prostitutes next to the Japanese bases. Note that this lightest shading is common after 1990, but almost entirely absent before 1980. The obvious conclusion: prior to 1980, the Korean newspapers included virtually no mention of the comfort women who had worked next to Japanese bases.

FIGURE 4.1: NUMBER OF ARTICLES ON THE COMFORT WOMEN, *DONG-A ILBO* AND *KYUNGHYANG* DAILY NEWSPAPERS

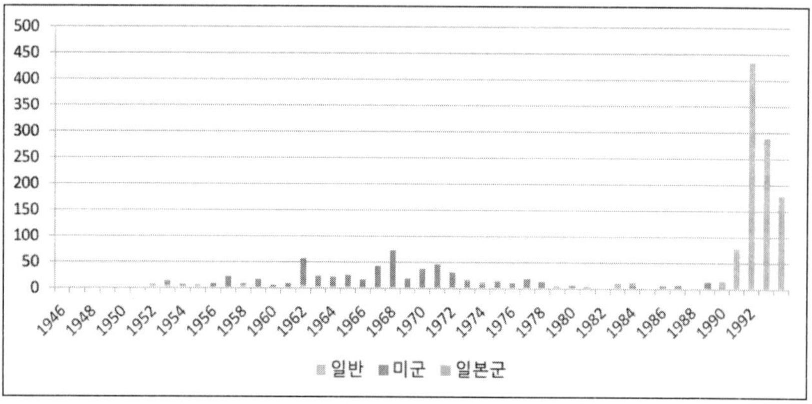

Note: ■: Unspecified (general); ■: American military; ■: Japanese military

Source: Personal correspondence with Joo Ikjong.

In 1982, 1984, and 1989, the papers did include at least ten references to the so-called "Teishintai" (*chongsindae*). These were the Volunteer Corps by which the Japanese government mobilized Koreans for industrial jobs under the emergency mobilization program of late 1944 and 1945 (when it also mobilized Japanese). For a brief period (as we discuss in Chapter 3), these corps were confused with the comfort women.[43] Note that the term *teishintai* also occurs several times (albeit never more than six times per year) during the 1970s, but most of these articles appear to discuss one of two movies: a Japanese documentary about prostitutes (not coerced) in Okinawa, or a pornographic movie by the name *Joshi teishintai* ("Women's Volunteer Corps").[44]

Choi Sok-yong ran a similar search in the *Dong-A Ilbo* newspaper alone. We give the results in Table 4.1. Choi's results track those of Joo: the newspaper did not include more than a trivial number of articles on comfort women serving the Japanese military until after the Korean translation of Yoshida's memoir appeared in 1989.

Kimura Kan, a law professor at Kobe University, searched for the appearance of the phrases "comfort women" and "transported labor"

TABLE 4.1: NUMBER OF ARTICLES ON THE COMFORT WOMEN *DONG-A ILBO* DAILY NEWSPAPER

	Comfort women for the Japanese military	Comfort women for the U.S. (UN) military
1951–55	1	17
1956–60	0	36
1961–65	0	56
1966–70	1	118
1971–75	5	39
1976–80	0	20
1981–85	4	9
1986–90	5	8
1991–95	616	3

Source: Choi Sok-yong, *The Real Reason behind "Anti-Japanese Nation" Written by a South Korean* (Saizusha, 2012), 100, as reported in Hata Ikuhiko, *Three-point Suite: The Facts about South Korea's Comfort Women, 1945–2015* (August 2015) (translated from *Seiron* by Jason Morgan).

in the pages of the *Chosun Ilbo*—the principal rival to the *Dong-A Ilbo*. From 1945 to 1990, he found a small number of articles on the forced transport of Korean laborers (a second controversial historical issue between South Korea and Japan), but none at all on the comfort women (Table 4.2).

TABLE 4.2: NUMBER OF ARTICLES USING GIVEN WORD IN HEADLINE OR BODY, *CHOSUN ILBO* DAILY NEWSPAPER

	Japan	Reparations	Forced transport	Comfort women
1945–49	1,236	47	0	0
1950–54	936	13	0	0
1955–59	3,250	24	0	0
1960–64	4,534	22	2	0
1965–69	3,535	7	3	0
1970–74	5,620	8	2	0
1975–79	4,643	5	0	0
1980–84	5,133	4	2	0
1985–89	4748	4	11	0
1990–94	17,539	344	150	3
1995–99	28,121	357	186	459
2000–04	34,943	286	44	349
2005–09	35,867	215	27	366

Source: Kan Kimura, *The Burden of the Past: Problems of Historical Perception in Japan-Korea Relations*, trans. Marie Speed (Ann Arbor: University of Michigan Press, 2019), 6, Fig. 1.1.

Kimura similarly searched for the phrases "comfort women" and "transported labor" in the *Asahi Shimbun*, the Japanese daily that first gave Yoshida's story so much exposure (Table 4.3). Here, Kimura searched only in the headlines. Before 1980, he found only one reference to the comfort women.

The point is simple: prior to the publication of the Korean version of Yoshida's fabricated memoir, the Korean newspapers rarely discussed World War II–era comfort women. To the extent that they did discuss the sex industry, they discussed the prostitutes and brothels that catered to American military personnel.

On the Legendary Massacre

Western writers routinely report that the Japanese military massacred comfort women at the end of the war. Gay McDougall repeated the story in her 1998 UN report. Michael Chwe repeated it in his 2021 petition. Herbert Ziegler and Jerry Bentley repeated it in the McGraw-Hill textbook. When Morgan and several other dissenters pointed out that the McGraw-Hill passage about the massacre had no basis in documentary history, the Yoshida-school academics in the United States cried "denialism." (Ziegler, the surviving McGraw-Hill author, has been asked directly by at least one scholar to provide his sources for the comfort women passage. Morgan has also called, in print, for Ziegler to reveal his sources. As of this writing, Ziegler has offered no sources for his and Bentley's claims.) We suggest that a massacre across vast swaths of the Asian continent and the Pacific Ocean would have left a trail of documentary and other evidence, as well as countless witnesses. Apparently, to do so is "denialist."

Scholars have traced the massacre story back to Arafune Seijuro, a conservative Japanese politician. Arafune wanted to justify the enormous transfer of funds that the Japanese government committed to in 1965 when, to normalize relations, it paid the South Korean government 300 million USD and lent another 500 million

TABLE 4.3: NUMBER OF ARTICLES USING GIVEN WORD IN HEADLINE, *ASAHI SHIMBUN* DAILY NEWSPAPER

	Comfort women	Forced transport
1945–49	0	0
1950–54	0	0
1955–59	0	0
1960–64	0	1
1965–69	0	0
1970–74	0	5
1975–79	1	15
1980–84	1	8
1985–89	6	14
1990–94	600	275
1995–99	822	222
2000–04	126	169
2005–09	225	142
2010–14	413	57

Source: Kan Kimura, *The Burden of the Past: Problems of Historical Perception in Japan-Korea Relations*, trans. Marie Speed (Ann Arbor: University of Michigan Press, 2019), 26, Fig. 2.1.

besides. In this context, he asserted that the Japanese military had killed three-quarters of the Korean comfort women at the end of the war. In fact, Arafune invented the story out of whole cloth. He was famous for making up stories as he pleased, and he made up this one as well. No one has ever found any evidence that the military massacred comfort women.[45]

According to Park Yu-ha, "one cannot exclude the possibility" that there was a massacre of comfort women, but "we should recognize that it was not a general phenomenon. In the accounts of the comfort women . . . there is no mention of massacres. Instead, there are many stories about 'pulling up roots' = returning home."[46]

Yoshida invented the story about forced conscription. Arafune invented the story about a massacre. In both cases, professional historians realized within a few years that the stories were not true. Inside Japan, the stories died.

Internationally, the stories did not die. Instead, scholars like Gordon, Eckert, Suk-Gersen, Stanley, and Chwe have worked ruthlessly to bury all references to Yoshida and keep the forced-conscription hoax alive.

CHAPTER 5

THE ATTACKS REDUX

Given the collapse of the Yoshida account in the mid-1990s and the absence of any evidence of dragooning besides uncorroborated testimony, the attacks on us by Western professors continue to puzzle us. When the assault on Ramseyer began in early 2021, Harvard's Reischauer Institute declared on its website that his IRLE article on the comfort women had "generated serious concerns among the Harvard Japanese studies community regarding the empirical foundations of the scholarship." It kept this declaration on its website for nearly half a year, together with three principal documents: the short attack by Andrew Gordon and Carter Eckert (both Harvard historians) claiming that Ramseyer had no evidence for his statements about the contracts; the long, tendentious cite check by Amy Stanley (Northwestern) and her four co-authors accusing him of deliberate fraud; and the *New Yorker* article by Jeannie Suk-Gersen (Harvard Law).

In Chapter 1, we described the attacks in the context of the cancellation campaign generally. In the chapters that followed, we turned to the history of the comfort women and of the dispute over the comfort women. We return now to the principal attacks, especially to the three posted on the Reischauer website.[1]

Gordon

Andrew Gordon, the first of the U.S. historians of Japan to attack Ramseyer publicly, issued a statement to the public together with Carter Eckert, a historian of Korea. Their central objection was this:

> Any reasonable standard of academic integrity would require that Ramseyer state in his article that he does not have access to actual contracts or sample contracts concluded with Korean women in Korea, acknowledge how few third-party statements he has seen about contracts, and note the limits to what one can learn from those references.

Ramseyer never claimed to use actual contracts, and neither do we make that claim here. Instead, he used data *about* the contractual arrangements. His citations make clear the extent of that data. In the article, he then used the data to reconstruct the nature of the contracts. In a private email to Ramseyer, Gordon actually admitted that the comfort stations and comfort women used contracts: "Nowhere in our letter to the editors did we say no contracts existed or were concluded. Certainly they did (and perhaps do)."[2] Gordon and Eckert now acknowledge this in their publicly posted statement. This caveat was not in the retraction demand they sent to the IRLE.

There is a question of candor here. Gordon's statement goes to the material in (or more specifically, purportedly not in) the sources listed in Ramseyer's article. As we have noted, "Contracting for Sex in the Pacific War" first attracted public attention on February 1. Gordon sent Ramseyer the completed Gordon-Eckert statement on February 7. During this period, all Harvard libraries were closed because of Covid, and the Harvard copies of the source material were in Ramseyer's Harvard office.

The reason we do not have the actual contracts is simple. The brothels—not the government—held the contracts. Only the brothels and the women (and sometimes their parents) were party, and only they would have kept copies. As the comfort station owners straggled home to Korea and Japan during the last months of 1945, very few, if any, would have bothered to carry the contracts they had concluded with their prostitutes. The war was over. The comfort stations were gone forever. The contracts were as worthless as the military scrip that the Japanese army had issued as currency in occupied territories. Losers in wars don't keep souvenirs. They try to get home alive. Remember too that Tokyo burned to the ground during the wartime carpet bombing. The Korean peninsula was ravaged by the Korean War.

In her *New Yorker* article on the controversy, Jeannie Suk-Gersen reported that Gordon and Eckert assured her that among Ramseyer's sources "there were no contracts involving Korean women at wartime comfort stations cited, nor secondary sources detailing those contracts, nor even any third-party accounts that confirm the relevant terms."[3] Only Gordon and Suk-Gersen know exactly what he told her, but on South Korean news shows Suk-Gersen doubled down on her statement:

> Professor Ramseyer can make this claim only if he does not believe the accounts of force and coercion, and that's why it was important that the historians actually look into the sources to see if there were in fact sources that would indicate that any of these arrangements were voluntary…and they found that there were no such sources at least that he had found.

Then she flatly declared: "There are no sources that can show the terms of the contracts."[4]

In fact, Ramseyer had—and we have—many sources for the information about comfort women contracts for both Japanese and Korean women. We detail our sources in the appendix. In Ramseyer's 2021 article, he cited the form contract that we reproduced in Table 2.1. He also cited a U.S. Army interrogation report that details (in

English) the nature of the contracts between a group of Korean comfort women and their brothel. We discuss this report more fully in Chapter 7 and the epilogue. Hyun Byung-sook, the Korean comfort woman quoted in Chapter 2, talked at length about how she negotiated the terms of her employment contract (the Japanese translation of the interview appeared after Ramseyer's article). Do consult the appendix; we have detailed sources of information about the contracts—memories of the prostitutes, along with accounts from officers who supervised comfort stations, from other people who worked there, from soldiers who patronized the women, and from Americans who interviewed POWs.

Suk-Gersen relied on Gordon, but Gordon does not seem to know the field. Consider how he treated the topic of the comfort women in his history of modern Japan, third edition, published in 2014. After discussing various war victims, he wrote:

> Another group of war victims received much less public attention at the time or immediately after the war. These were the many thousands of young girls or women who were forced to work in euphemistically named "comfort stations" near the front lines of battle. About 80 percent were Koreans, and the remainder included Chinese, Japanese, and a small number of European women. Recruiters told some women they were hired as waitresses or servants. They simply captured others at gunpoint. Once at the front, all the women were forced to serve as prostitutes for Japanese troops. The soldiers were typically required to pay for the services of these women. From their perspective, the comfort stations appeared little different from the licensed brothels throughout Japan proper. But many of the women received no pay. Others received "pay" in the form of military tickets whose only use was to purchase daily necessities such as soap or food. The women thus worked in conditions closer to slavery than to prostitution.... Estimates

> [of the numbers of women involved] range from one hundred thousand to two hundred thousand.[5]

For this entire paragraph, Gordon supplies only one footnote, citing two English-language sources. One is to a far-left journal; the other is to George Hicks, the man who could not read Japanese but through a translator spread the Yoshida story across the English-speaking world and into the 1996 UN report. Gordon cites him with respect to the number of comfort women. Note that Gordon cited this Yoshida-based source in 2014—seventeen years after both the *Asahi* and Yoshimi announced that they could not rely on Yoshida.

Virtually nothing in Gordon's account is true. The plurality of the women were Japanese, not Korean. Two hundred thousand is the number claimed by the North Korean government; the probable number is closer to twenty thousand. Like the licensed prostitutes in Korea and Japan, the women received massive upfront payments (in hard cash) for their services and generous amounts throughout the course of their work. Some women may or may not have received additional pay as "tickets," but their earnings went to pay down their original hard-cash loan, and many women sent money home. And none—none—of the women from either Japan or Korea were "captured ... at gunpoint."

It bears repeating that almost nothing in Gordon's account is true—and yet evidently that never bothered the faculty at the Reischauer Institute. As embarrassing as this account would be to anyone who cared about historical accuracy, the Reischauer Institute faculty never complained. What matters most in some segments of the academy is not scholarship. By our experience, it is politics.

The Stanley Quintet

The second attack that the Harvard professors at the Reischauer Institute posted to their website was the thirty-plus-page document by Amy Stanley, Hannah Shepherd, Sayaka Chatani, David Ambaras, and Chelsea Szendi Schieder. This Quintet, whose most prominent public liaison is most definitely Amy Stanley, claimed to have compiled a list of mistakes in Ramseyer's eight-page article. It is a tendentious list indeed. The authors' purpose seems to have been to bury Ramseyer with innuendo. Certainly, they do not produce evidence to the contrary of what he contends.

To their credit, the Quintet did find three substantive errors, though none that mattered.[6] First, they correctly noted that a very young prostitute—not a comfort woman—was surprised when first required to have sex. (The incident in question occurred long before the Japanese government ever considered establishing a system of military brothels.) Second, they noted that Ramseyer had incorrectly tabulated the amount of the advances listed in a Home Ministry document. Third, they noted that Ramseyer had incorrectly read a government document about travel petitions. Ramseyer has responded at length and in detail to their other accusations. Our favorite: that Ramseyer cited to page 451 of Park Yu-ha's 2014 study. The Quintet correctly note that "Page 451 does not exist as the book is 336 pages long." Mea culpa: the correct page number was 41. Ramseyer's detailed response to all of their attacks (as well as an overlapping attack by Yoshimi)[7] is freely available on the internet. We spare our readers the tedium here, but encourage anyone interested to consult that response.[8]

As with Gordon, it is unclear how much comfort women history the Quintet actually knew. On Twitter, Chatani forthrightly admitted (but only in Japanese) that none of the five had studied the subject.[9] Suk-Gersen tells her readers in the *New Yorker* that Stanley assured her that Ramseyer had omitted "established historical evidence" that "destroy[ed]" his argument. But recall that when Stanley tweeted her planned "summer reading" in June 2021, her list included the basic histories of the comfort women regime by Hata and Yoshimi, along with Mun Ok-ju's memoir.[10]

In this light, we should probably not be surprised that the Quintet fail to tell readers much about the comfort women regime. They do not tell the reader that the comfort women only started to claim that they were dragooned after the Korean translation of Yoshida's memoir appeared. They do not tell the reader that Yoshida fabricated the entire account. They do not mention the Yoshida scandal at all. They do not tell the reader about the *Asahi*'s retracting its articles, or about Uemura's losing his defamation suits when he challenged two people who asserted publicly that he had mispresented a comfort woman's testimony. They do not tell the reader that several of the women claiming to have been dragooned live in nursing homes connected to the Korean Council, or that several of these women had earlier told dramatically different stories.

The attack by this Quintet—"a model of academic integrity," Paula Curtis assures us[11]—flagrantly misstates some sources. The critics focus on Mun Ok-ju, who had been very popular among the soldiers and accumulated an enormous amount of wealth through her work (though she was never able to withdraw the portion deposited in a Japanese savings account). The Quintet stress that she claimed to have been forced into the job by the military. Had they read the literature in the field, they would have realized that even their idol Yoshimi Yoshiaki explicitly states that he doubts her claim.[12]

The Quintet fail to tell the reader the crucial ending of the story. Maybe they did not know the end of the story. By 1944, Mun had been in Burma for two years and had repaid her advance. She obtained permission to return home, and traveled to Saigon to catch the boat to Korea. At the last minute, Mun decided not to board the ship, and instead returned to comfort station work in Rangoon.[13] This fact appears in the very memoir that the Quintet cite. But then, judging from her Twitter account, Stanley had not read it yet.

Note the point: Mun had a boat ticket to return home, yet she chose deliberately—of her own volition—to go back to her comfort station. Mun recalls: "When I arrived at [the comfort station]

Rangoon Hall, everyone was surprised. 'Why didn't you go home to Korea? How did you get back here?' they asked. Since everyone was joyful, I was happy."[14] Hata gives a hint as to what might have persuaded Mun to return to her old job: "In less than three years, she managed to save up 26,000 yen, and sent 5,000 yen home to her family. At that time, the average salary of a Japanese Army sergeant was 30 yen per month."[15] Assume that Mun had spent nothing in three years and had earned no more than the 31,000 yen she had either saved or sent home. That works out to a little over 861 yen a month in earnings, which is more than twenty-eight times what a high-ranking enlisted man was making.

In his article, Ramseyer noted that three women who disliked their brothel in Borneo simply walked to the harbor and left town. They had previously worked in the town of Sandakan on Borneo, but were transferred when the brothel owner died. They disliked their new employer, so they returned to Sandakan. Ramseyer noted that "even overseas, women who disliked their jobs at a brothel could—and did—disappear." To this, the Stanley Quintet reply that the three "knew that their new employer would come after them. They threw themselves on the mercy of a woman brothel keeper in Borneo," but the woman would hire only two of them. "They drew straws, and one of the women had to return. In other words, the women could not—and did not—'disappear.'"

The three women did indeed walk to the harbor and leave for Sandakan. But it was a small town at the time, with a population of about 10,000. On board the boat, one of the three women noted that "once they discover that we're gone, the brothel owner will figure that we must be bound for Sandakan. He's bound to come find us. In Singapore, there are way more Japanese than in Borneo. And prostitution is said to be a booming business. Why don't we stay on the boat beyond Sandakan, and go to Singapore?" A second woman preferred to work in Sandakan, however, so the three decided to plead with the woman they knew there to take them under her wing.[16]

No, if prostitutes had come from a very small town, they could not "disappear" by returning to that small town, as the three women knew well. But nothing required them to return to that town. They could stay on the boat, go on to Singapore, and there fade into the metropolis. Nonetheless, they decided to return to Sandakan and hoped that the friendly brothel owner would assume their debts. She did agree to assume the debts of two, but not the third. They had the option to disappear in Singapore rather than gamble on their friend in Sandakan, but they chose not to take it.[17] The Quintet tell the reader nothing about this very deliberate choice.

In a May 2021 post to her website (styled an attack on Ramseyer's article), Stanley describes at length an infamous rogue Japanese POW camp in Indonesia.[18] The guards in this camp had built for themselves a "brothel" in which they routinely raped young female prisoners. This episode is well known and is covered in Hata's definitive history. It is covered in many other histories and scholarly treatments besides. Ramseyer explicitly limited his article to "comfort stations" and to comfort women from Japan and Korea (which was part of Japan). The Indonesian camp obviously violated fundamental army rules for comfort stations and for POW camps. The Japanese army command insisted on strict discipline. When it learned about the rogue "brothel," the army shut it down immediately.

Stanley fails to disclose this crucial information to her readers. When serious historians point out that the Japanese army command ordered the "brothel" closed for its egregious violations, she savages them as "denialist." More troubling still, she fails to tell her readers the brutal end to the story. She knows it; she acknowledged it on Twitter.[19] But she does not include it in her essay. When one guard tried to continue the earlier practice of raping young women prisoners, the new commanding officer assembled the camp and called the guard to the front of the group. He handed him a pistol and stood there until the guard dutifully blew his own brains out.[20] Contrary to the narrative that Stanley and her colleagues so desperately want to perpetuate, the Japanese army command did not turn a blind eye to violence against women.

Another member of the Quintet trained his attention on Morgan when the first installment of his interview with Arima Tetsuo, the Waseda historian and author of a recent book on the comfort women, appeared at *JAPAN Forward*. David Ambaras, one of the most energetic of Arima's and Ramseyer's attackers, used the same "cite check" method against Morgan that the Quintet had used against Ramseyer. Here's how it worked this time.

In a tweet on October 16, 2021, Ambaras highlighted an endnote from one of Morgan's recent essays in Japanese, cropping the screenshot so that his Twitter audience would see just this one endnote.[21] Morgan had cited an American pundit named David Horowitz, a reformed Marxist who often writes from a conservative or countercultural standpoint.[22] What Ambaras was signaling is that Morgan reads books by authors whom Ambaras does not like (and surely has not read himself), so Morgan must be treated as a pariah. Horowitz, like Ramseyer and Arima, is on Ambaras's Forbidden List. It was a cue to dogpile Morgan, just as Ambaras and his friends dogpiled Ramseyer and then Arima.

Morgan's whole essay is available as a free download.[23] Readers will notice that there are forty-nine endnotes (most in English). Immediately above the one that Ambaras posted is a reference to a collection from *Radical America*, a hard-left magazine in the holdings of Brown University. And immediately after it is a reference to an essay by Tomomi Yamaguchi, a copartisan of Ambaras. The views that Yamaguchi expresses there are the opposite of Morgan's—which is precisely why he cited her, so readers can get a fuller picture of the background to his arguments.

Morgan also cites the perennial comfort women gadfly Alexis Dudden. He cites the Italian Marxist revolutionary Antonio Gramsci and an essay from Marxists.org. He cites Nakano Koichi, the putative adviser to Miki Dezaki, whose documentary on the comfort women is a favorite of Ambaras and his friends. But Ambaras ignored all of this. The point is not to debate, but to shut down debate by giving readers keyhole distortions of a much bigger picture.

More Blocking Maneuvers

Readers might already have known the comfort women history if so many of the self-styled Japan specialists in the American academy were not so determined to ensure that their critics never appear in print. They ambush anyone who mentions facts inconvenient to their narrative. They refuse to discuss the issue in an open forum.

A few years ago, before the brouhaha erupted over the Ramseyer IRLE paper but shortly after the donnybrook over the Ziegler-Bentley textbook, Morgan tried to convince the Association for Asian Studies to run a business-card-sized ad inviting scholars to visit a website and exchange views on historical topics, including the dispute over the comfort women. The answer: No. Morgan remonstrated: Why not? It's an advertisement, can't anyone buy one? We're not even stating any views. We're just inviting people to have a conversation. The journal sent Morgan's request up the chain of command to Lucien Ellington, by coincidence an acquaintance from the University of Tennessee-Chattanooga who runs one of the AAS publications. Ellington reluctantly sent the request out for review (which Morgan found absurd). The reviewer returned with the answer the AAS had been looking for: No. The reason the anonymous reviewer gave: Carol Gluck would not approve. Gluck is a historian of Japan at Columbia and the most senior and most prominent of the Western scholars writing about the comfort women. The beginning and end of all discussion in American academia is "Ipse dixit, QED." Ellington closed the case and told Morgan not to contact him anymore about the comfort women.

On November 23, 2021, Morgan asked to post his three-part interview with Arima Tetsuo on the H-Japan website, a section of

H-Net Humanities and Social Sciences Online.[24] H-Japan promises to "provide[] scholars, graduate students and professionals a free daily forum to discuss Japanese history, culture, religion, and society...." The website's editor, Janet Goodwin, refused Morgan's request. "I gather that this post is a response to the article by Paula Curtis," she wrote, referring to a vicious ad hominem attack against Ramseyer that Curtis had posted to H-Japan three days earlier.[25] Morgan had mentioned nothing about Curtis or any other H-Net posting when filing his request. But Goodwin, evidently untroubled by the error of her assumptions, simply rejected the submission on the grounds that it did not devote enough space to "addressing any concrete issues or providing any evidence that the comfort women had contracts."

Also in November 2021, the Stanley Quintet set out to block an article that the economist Lee Wooyoun published in *The Diplomat*, a journal of Asian politics based in Tokyo. The comfort women were prostitutes, Lee explained. The Japanese army did not forcibly conscript them. Neither did it turn them into "sex slaves."

> "Comfort women" were engaged in a "high-risk, high-return" occupation. Some occasionally earned enormous sums, and a great many returned to Korea or re-entered the workforce after their contracted term of employment ended. Restrictions on daily freedoms applied equally to military personnel, civilian employees, nurses, and anyone else in the battlefield environment. In conclusion, comfort women were not sex slaves, but sex workers who were fundamentally no different from today's sex industry workers.[26]

Once Ambaras noticed Lee's article, he posted a screenshot on Twitter: "Comfort Women denialists are despicable," he fumed. "Why is @Diplomat_APAC publishing this garbage?"[27] Amy Stanley and Paula Curtis retweeted the article. Sayaka Chatani chimed in.

Within hours, Mitch Shin, a correspondent for *The Diplomat*, tweeted a reply: "I am working on it. Sorry."[28] As if that were not sufficient: "It's down now. I am truly sorry that we made such a horrible and unacceptable mistake."[29] And in case that were still not penitent enough, he posted yet another apology: "I sincerely apologize that we published this story on our website. It's down now."[30]

A bystander expressed approval: "Good to hear! This is a better retraction than many."[31] Ethan Mark, a University of Leiden historian, thanked Ambaras for policing the magazine: "And thanks to you David for keeping after this, it's really not acceptable."[32]

Ambaras was not done, though. "The editors still owe it to the public to explain why they allowed it to appear in the first place and what steps they will take to avoid such mistakes moving forward," he tweeted.[33]

Shin replied: "The statement will be coming up in our official account, David. Again, there is no excuse I can make. As a Chief Correspondent on the two Koreas, I will do my best to work more closely with our editors to review the articles from contributors outside of the organization." Lee Wooyoun's article was "an awful and biased story by a comfort woman denialist," Shin declared, adding, "I really don't want to make any excuses as there was no reason for us to publish such a terrible story."[34]

Ambaras again: "Thank you, Mitch. We all have our work cut out for us when it comes to dealing with denialism."

Shin still had more atoning to do: "Lastly, I would like to express my deepest gratitude to those who brought up this issue and directly asked me and our organization to take action in a timely manner. Please keep checking our contents and deliver your perceptive thoughts whenever you are available. Thank you."[35]

Another of the "denialist" scholars targeted for cancellation is Chizuko Allen, a University of Hawai'i historian. In her Korean history textbook published in 2021, she discussed the prevalence of Korean prostitutes across East Asia.

> By the 1930s...brokers sent many Korean women to Korean proprietors in Manchuria, Japan, and China for greater profit. While some women were simply deceived or even kidnapped by the brokers, other women "sold" themselves or signed contracts for two or three years of prostitution in exchange for advance payments....

On the subject of the comfort women in particular, Allen wrote:

> When the Japanese military required "comfort women," or prostitutes who serviced Japanese troops in war zones...the same recruitment methods were used....[36]

Allen states the history exactly as it was, but it was intolerable to Jinhee Lee (Ramseyer's internet stalker). Lee began to pester the publisher, Cognella, claiming that the passages were "straight out of such wartime atrocity denialist groups' propaganda journals."[37] She described Allen as having been "active in propagating the denialists' claims not only on the c.w. issues but also on the forced labor and on other topics in recent years." Indeed, Allen's articles "appear in the far right wing denialist groups' publications regularly."[38] In a follow-up message, Lee began with some rather pointed small talk—"I hope this message finds you and your loved ones safe and well"—before getting down to brass tacks and demanding that Cognella recall Allen's textbook.[39] Over the course of many emails, she harassed Cognella into compliance.

The censors often couch their attacks in boilerplate about freedom of academic inquiry. For example, the Reischauer Institute faculty began their attack on Ramseyer with the usual platitudes: "We honor the pursuit of truth, a commitment that includes supporting the highest standards of academic integrity." We "reiterate the Institute's goal to promote intellectual exchange and discussion." On those grounds, they explained, they posted the Stanley

Quintet's attack to their website and kept it there nearly half a year. But when Stanley revealed a few months later that she had not yet read the basic studies by either Hata or Yoshimi at the time she wrote her attack, the Institute faculty said nothing. When Stanley, Ambaras, and Chatani savaged Lee Wooyoun and intimidated *The Diplomat* into blocking his article, the Institute faculty again said nothing. When Jinhee Lee—associate in research at the Reischauer Institute—badgered Cognella into recalling Allen's textbook, the Institute faculty said nothing. Quite possibly the Institute scholars were not paying any attention to this. What matters most to some segments of the academy is simply not intellectual exchange. It is blanket conformity.

Comic Relief

Ramseyer's cancellation made for a tension-filled time for his family. Those were grim days for everyone in the house, try as they might to put on a smile. To his children, the mob was trying to destroy their father's career. How would he handle this crisis?

One morning, one of the children provided some comic relief: "Hey, Dad. You've got one critic out there who says that the comfort women couldn't possibly have made contracts, because no one could contract before the war. Honest. She really says this. They were all subjects of the emperor rather than citizens, so they couldn't have made any contracts."

Everyone laughed. Ramseyer did not bother looking for the statement on the web. Who would take anything that crazy seriously, anyway? Several weeks later, however, he discovered that the writer was Alexis Dudden, of the University of Connecticut and longtime associate in research at the Reischauer Institute. This is the Dudden who acted as lead author to the group of twenty who attacked the Japanese government for complaining about the nearly comical account of the comfort women in the McGraw-Hill textbook. This is the Dudden who compared the Japanese army to Boko Haram.

This is the Dudden who attended the 2000 show trial for the dead emperor and his dead associates, and later claimed that one of the former comfort women at the trial periodically raised her blouse to show where a Japanese soldier had sliced off her breast (something no one else seems to remember). This is the Dudden who claimed to have been so traumatized on reading Ramseyer's article that she "started shaking."[40] This is the Dudden who reported on Korean television that three of her colleagues' academic offices in Tokyo had been "firebombed" (still a mysteriously unreported string of crimes).

This Alexis Dudden now described Ramseyer's article on the comfort women as "race baiting." *Race baiting*? And this in the *Asia-Pacific Journal: Japan Focus*, which claims to be peer-reviewed and is subsidized by the Reischauer Institute. But there is more. Dudden writes that Ramseyer's "worldview is racially essentialist, revanchist, and history-denying, resonant with similar movements around the world such as Trumpism, LePenism, Modi-ism, and so on." Take a breath. She continues:

> [A contract is] a legal, economic, and social agreement that in this article's usage presupposes equal bodies freely negotiating.... It is nothing less than shameful, however, to deploy this term to a history that the United Nations and Amnesty International have determined a "crime against humanity." Moreover, its meaning is moot during the era of Imperial Japan (1868–1945) because there were no "citizens" freely acting as such. *All* individuals—Japanese nationals and colonials alike—were "subjects" of the emperor....[41]

Never mind the troubling way that a professional historian of Japan relies on three reports written by people with no knowledge of the Japanese language. Never mind that all three reports in turn relied on the Yoshida memoir. (We apologize to readers who are dizzy. In our business we are always circling back to Yoshida.) Dudden's claim that there were no contracts in Imperial Japan would have come as a shock to the prewar bank that had lent money to a firm on the strength of the borrower's promise to repay. It would have come as a shock to the farmer who thought he had a deal with an urban buyer to sell his rice at a given price on a given day. It would have come as a shock to the judges who handled the litigation over the arrangements. Citizens or subjects, they thought the parties had a contract. But not so, apparently. It fell upon Alexis Dudden in 2021 unilaterally to declare them incapable of making those contractual agreements.

Suk-Gersen

In her *New Yorker* article on the comfort women dispute, Ramseyer's Harvard colleague Jeannie Suk-Gersen does not mention the roots of the dispute in the Yoshida fraud, though Ramseyer discussed it at length in the material he gave her while she was writing the piece. Neither does she discuss the often obviously unreliable and always uncorroborated nature of the testimonies by the comfort women. She instead begins by assuring her readers that the Yoshida-school sex-slave narrative is "the historical consensus" on the subject:

> [The] "comfort women" [were] women and girls who were transported to war-front "comfort stations" to provide sexual services to soldiers in the Imperial Japanese Army. The women were taken by force or entrapped in many countries in and beyond Asia, but a large number came from Korea.... Estimates of the number of victims have ranged widely, from tens of thousands to hundreds of thousands.... [Since that time, these] crimes against humanity...have been mired in waves of conflict and denial about the truth of what happened.[42]

Suk-Gersen does not mention that the Korean comfort women began to claim that they had been dragooned by the Japanese military only after the Korean translation of the Yoshida memoir appeared in 1989. She does not discuss the way that the *Asahi* newspaper famously amplified the story. Neither does she mention that Yoshida was shown to have fabricated the entire account, or that the UN based its scathing 1996 report on his hoax, or that the *Asahi* finally announced in 2014, after an extensive investigation, that it had no choice but to conclude that Yoshida had lied and to retract its entire portfolio of his stories. All this was in the material that Ramseyer had provided her.

None of those facts appear in Suk-Gersen's long essay. Instead, she presents a virulently anti-Japanese account of the comfort women regime as the "historical consensus." She interviewed (primarily) Japanese studies scholars in the humanities, whom she describes as assiduously nonpartisan:

> My conversations with scholars who spent the past three weeks investigating Ramseyer's claims have been remarkable to me because of the strength of their commitment to upholding professional standards and procedures. While his claims are provocative and distressing to many, the scholars' concern was not that, but only the claims' truth.

Suk-Gersen contacted Gordon and Eckert, and learned from them that Ramseyer discussed contracts he had not seen. They claimed to have reviewed his footnotes and found "no contracts involving Korean women at wartime comfort stations cited, nor secondary sources detailing those contracts, nor even any third-party accounts that confirm the relevant terms" in his sources. But do recall that they made this comment when the Harvard libraries were closed. Recall too that Gordon's own published account of the comfort women cited only two English-language sources in support, one of them being George Hicks, who did not himself read Japanese and depended heavily on a Japan-resident Korean activist's account of Yoshida's fabricated story.

Suk-Gersen contacted the Stanley Quintet, who together drafted a thirty-plus-page list of errors in Ramseyer's article but identified only three substantive mistakes, none of any importance. She does not mention that some of these five scholars so committed to "upholding professional standards" spent time on Twitter calling Ramseyer a "white supremacist."[43] A *white supremacist?* Suk-Gersen quotes Ambaras's attacks on Ramseyer. She might have mentioned his Twitter handle at the time: "David Ambaras is anti-fascist." Obviously, he can call himself anything he wants, but that someone adopts the sloganeering of Antifa in early 2021 might suggest a motive other than scholarly commitment for saying what he does about an article by an old-school Chicago law and economics professor.

Suk-Gersen closes her article with an account of Lee Yong-soo. Fondly calling her "Grandma Lee," she writes that Lee had been "conscripted as a comfort woman at fifteen." She mentions that Lee recently spoke at Harvard Law School.

In fact, Suk-Gersen could not have chosen a more appropriate way to end her story about the comfort women. Several of the most vocal of the comfort women have changed their stories, and of them Lee is the most notorious. She has variously claimed to have been abducted at age 14, 15, 16, and 17. She originally told historians that she left home in the middle of the night with a friend who urged her to "come out quickly," so she "tiptoed out" and followed her friend to meet a Japanese man who gave her "a red dress and a pair of leather shoes in a packet." So excited was Lee that she followed him "readily" and "without any further thought."[44]

A decade later, when Lee had become the public face of the Korean Council, she was telling a different story. In 2002, she visited the Japanese Diet and claimed that she had been "taken away at age 14 at bayonet-point."[45] Later, she told the U.S. House of Representatives that she had been "kidnapped by Japanese soldiers." At a Tokyo news conference shortly afterward, she added that "Japanese soldiers had dragged her from her home, covering her mouth so that she could not call to her mother."[46]

ACADEMIC FREEDOM IN KOREA

At this point, the story takes on a more troubling cast. Shortly before Lee Yong-soo's Harvard lecture, Suk-Gersen reports, she herself received an email describing Lee as a "fake comfort woman." She assures her readers that it came from "a small far-right fringe group in Korea." The "fringe group" that contacted her was MediaWatch. It may be small, but it is "far-right" only if favoring a collective security arrangement with Japan and the United States over being dominated by North Korea and China is "far-right," and only if a commitment to documentary fact and historical accuracy is "far-right."

The man who wrote that email was Hwang Uiwon, the CEO and chief editor of MediaWatch and the whistleblower who first reported the rampant fraud by Lee Yong-soo and the Korean Council that we detail in Chapter 6. For writing an article raising the suspicion that the Korean Council and its leader Yoon Mee-hyang had North Korean ties, the Council and Yoon brought civil and criminal cases against Hwang. He won both cases, but he had to fight the civil suit up to the Korean Supreme Court.[47]

In 2014, Hwang began to report the wild variations in the stories that Lee Yong-soo had told. In 2018, he published a table detailing twenty public statements that Lee had made since 1993 (see Table 5.1). Originally, she stated that she left home voluntarily, but later she claimed to have been forcibly conscripted—at the point of a sword in one account. She gave various ages for when she was conscripted. She gave differing years for when she became a comfort woman—1942, 1943, 1944. She claimed to have worked as a comfort woman for ten months, for two years, and for three years. On at least one occasion, she claimed to have been dragooned into work as a comfort woman in 1944 and then forced to stay in that job for three years.[48]

In an interview about his findings, Hwang talked about how "completely incoherent" Lee Yong-soo's changing statements were, and concluded that she was likely a "fake comfort woman":

TABLE 5.1: TESTIMONIAL BY LEE YONG-SOO ("GRANDMA LEE"), LONGTIME PRINCIPAL SPOKESWOMAN FOR THE KOREAN COUNCIL

A. *Time, age, and tenure*

Year of testimonial	Year became CW	Age upon becoming CW	Length of CW tenure
1993	1944	16	10 months
1997	1944		
1998	1942	14	3 years
1999	1942	14	3 years
2002		14	
2004	1944	16	3 years
2006	1942	15	3 years
2007 Feb.	1944	16	3 years
2007 June	1944		10 months
2009		15	
2012		17	2 years
2014		15	
2014		16	
2015 Mar.	1943	16	2 years
2015 Apr.	1943	14	2 years
2015 Apr.		15	
2015 June	1943	16	2 years
2016		16	
2018		15	

B. *Circumstances by which she became a comfort woman*:

1993: Followed a friend out of the house; received a red dress and shoes from Japanese man; was delighted.

2002: Captured at point of bayonet, beaten, and subjected to electric shock.

2004: Captured by a man in military costume, repeatedly raped while on boat, and subjected to electric shock.

2006: Captured by Japanese military while asleep at home.

2012: Captured by Japanese military in home garden.

2014: Called by a Japanese soldier, ran away, was caught and placed on train bound for Taiwan.

2015: Captured by Japanese military while asleep at home, and prodded by something sharp in the back.

2016: Captured by military while asleep, and subjected to electric shock.

2017: Told she would be sent to a factory, but made a sex slave instead.

2018: Was in the house when a girl she knew motioned for her to come out; the girl then put her hand over Lee's mouth, and a soldier prodded her with a sharp object in the back.

Sources: Nishioka Tsutomu, "Kankoku no ianfu undo no 'naifun'" [The "Internal Dispute" of the Comfort Women Movement], *Rekishi ninshiki mondai kenkyu* 7 (2020): 103–5 (based on work by Hwang Uiwon); Oh Sonfa, *Kankoku "Han-nichi minzoku shugi" no naraku* [The hell of Korean "Anti-Japan Tribalism"] (Tokyo: Bungei shunju, 2021), 30–34.

> Nowhere do her earlier and later statements match. Let me give you some representative statements. At first she claimed to be led away by a Japanese. Later it was by a Japanese soldier. At first she said she was enticed away by a red dress and leather shoes. Later she was dragooned with a sword in her back. In terms of length, [at one point] she said that she was taken away in 1944 and worked as a comfort woman for three years. But that's completely incoherent, [of course]. In August of 1945, Korea was liberated from being a colony, so the numbers didn't work. Then the year changed to 1942—but then changed again, this time to 1944 with an 8-month length. It's all this kind of stuff....
>
> We think she's a fake comfort woman. Unless she confesses, we can't know the truth. But there's no corroborating evidence for her comfort woman testimony. There are no third-party witnesses. There are not even eyewitnesses. It's just the statement of one person. At the very least, there should be a consistency to her testimony. But among Lee Yong-soo's public statements, there's not a shred of that consistency.[49]

More than anyone else, Hwang is responsible for breaking the media silence on the Korean Council (detailed in Chapter 6) and Lee. Over the course of the last decade, the South Korean government has ruthlessly attacked those who would publicly question the Yoshida-school sex-slave story. Suk-Gersen describes it as a "consensus." It most assuredly is not a "consensus" in South Korea. It is a party line. There is a difference. In modern South Korea, scholars who question the story risk their jobs and their freedom. Those who keep silent do not "consent" to the narrative. Some of them are just too afraid to speak out.

But some speak out anyway. In the West, the best known of the South Korean scholars to question the sex-slave thesis is probably Park Yu-ha. Park published a book about the comfort women in

2014, followed by another in 2022.[50] She did not just examine the statements from well-known comfort women like Lee Yong-soo. She also interviewed women who had deliberately avoided the limelight. Park found that private recruiters had hired Korean women for privately owned comfort stations.[51] The Japanese military did not hire them, and certainly did not dragoon them. Some of the women may have been fooled by the private recruiters, but many chose the job knowingly and deliberately. They were not slaves, except in the metaphorical sense of being part of a society that had lost its independence as part of the colonization effort.[52]

Although Suk-Gersen mentions the case against Park, she badly misdescribes Park's 2014 book. But then, the book is available in full only in Japanese. It is not available in English. In Korean, it is available only in censored form. The summary of the book in English-language Wikipedia bears virtually no resemblance to the actual book (but if you need to be warned of this, you do not deserve a place in the academy).

Jun Bong-Gwan of the Korea Advanced Institute of Science and Technology reviewed Park's monograph and found nothing especially controversial in it:

> After reading the book, I was a little bit disappointed because there was nothing in the book that I didn't know. We all knew that Korean comfort women were not coercively taken away by the Japanese military. Korean comfort station owners recruited women in the Korean Peninsula and operated comfort stations in the battlefields.

Jun added a commonsense observation: "The Japanese military was busy fighting all over Asia, and it certainly didn't have time to be in Korea recruiting women."[53]

Nevertheless, Seoul prosecutors filed criminal defamation charges against Park for writing the book that she did. She was acquitted, but in October 2017, after leftist Moon Jae-in was elected president, a court of appeal overturned the acquittal and imposed a fine of 10 million won (8,848 USD).[54] The case is currently on appeal to the Supreme Court, as prosecutors again seek a prison term of three years for Park.

In July 2020, Lee Yong-soo and several other people—nine descendants of comfort women, wartime laborers, and military personnel—filed criminal complaints against four scholars whose accounts of the comfort women regime they did not like.[55] Do let this sink in a bit: Suk-Gersen, a member of the Legal Advisory Council of the Academic Freedom Alliance, celebrates as beloved "Grandma Lee" a woman who files criminal complaints against scholars who contest her account of history. Lee and her allies claimed that their lectures and scholarship violated the National Security Act and constituted criminal defamation. The charges carry potential prison sentences. The four scholars against whom Lee Yong-soo launched her criminal complaints were Younghoon Rhee, Lew Seok-choon, Lee Wooyoun, and Joo Ikjong.[56]

Rhee, an emeritus professor of economics at Seoul National University (SNU), had described the comfort stations as "regulated houses of prostitution for the army." More specifically:

> The comfort woman system was a licensed prostitution system under the control of the military.... The comfort women were not sex slaves.... Korean comfort women were recruited by pimps by means of advance payments and outright fraud.... There is no evidence that there were 200,000 Korean comfort women. The number is somewhere around 5,000.[57]

In 2004, Rhee explained the history on television. No Korean scholar, he implied, thinks the Japanese government forcibly conscripted comfort women.

Almost immediately, the Korean Council attacked. It demanded that Rhee resign, and that the university fire him if he refused. Rhee went to visit the surviving comfort women in their nursing home and tried to explain himself, but the women went livid. For forty minutes, according to reporters, they berated him. "It's inconceivable that he would compare us to the women who are selling their bodies at Tondochon," one woman later declared. Another exclaimed, "I'd like to slug him if I could. We were forcibly taken away." After the berating, Rhee went down on his hands and knees, literally, and apologized.[58]

More recently, Rhee and a group of his Korean scholar-colleagues discussed the comfort women dispute in great detail in two best-selling books that examine the anti-Japanese sentiment among segments of modern South Korea: *Anti-Japan Tribalism* (2019) and *The Fight against Anti-Japan Tribalism* (2020).[59] The gist of their account: the comfort-women system was an overseas extension of the domestic Japanese and Korean licensed prostitution regime. Some of the women from Korea were deceived by private recruiters into taking the job. Some of the women took the job under pressure from their families. And the rest took the job because they wanted the high pay. Most of them did indeed earn extremely high incomes. They worked one or two years and then returned home.

The first of the two "Anti-Japan Tribalism" books sold 110,000 copies in South Korea and was briefly the best-selling book in the country.[60] When the Japanese translation appeared later in the year, it sold 200,000 copies and hit the number 1 bestseller spot in Japan.[61]

We find it hard to believe that any self-respecting scholar with ties to Korea would encourage massive attacks on a fellow scholar without first reading these two extremely well-known books by an SNU economist on exactly the topic at issue. Suk-Gersen had indeed heard about them. She referred to them in her *New Yorker* attack. But we doubt that she read them. We would find it even harder to believe that anyone could have read either of the two books and still have written what Suk-Gersen and Chwe did. But so be it.

The think tank for then-president Moon Jae-in's leftist ruling party in South Korea responded to the publication of the "Anti-Japan Tribalism" books by urging the government to criminalize books like them. The proposed law, as the political scientist Meredith Shaw explained it, would have "included criminal penalties for anyone who 'praises, incites, or sympathizes with Japanese organizations that seek to justify colonial rule.'"[62]

In 2020, Lee Yong-soo filed criminal charges against Younghoon Rhee. She did not need Moon's proposed statute. For his scholarship, this retired SNU professor faces potential criminal prosecution.

The second of the four scholars targeted by Lee Yong-soo and her allies was Lew Seok-choon, the sociologist (now retired from Yonsei University) who contributed the foreword to this book. Lew was already facing other charges initiated by the Korean Council. He had suggested in class that the comfort women had not been forced into the work by the Japanese military. Instead, he said, the work was "a form of prostitution."[63] Lew went on to explain the Korean Council's ties to North Korea. Prosecutors filed charges in 2020, and the case is ongoing.

Although the *Wall Street Journal* reported on Lew's case, it buried the crucial historical and political context. It failed to report the roots of the dispute in Yoshida's fraud and its amplification by the Korean Council. About that context, according to Lew, the *Journal*'s Seoul bureau (Timothy Martin and Dasl Yoon) omitted everything he said:

> The *Wall Street Journal* gave my problem big notice. With comments from both sides, it presents the appearance of being even-handed. Yet when I agreed to the interview, I explained at great length the way that the comfort women had changed their stories, the way that the U.N. Coomaraswamy report relied on Yoshida Seiji's book (*My War Crimes*) that was shown to be a fabrication, and the way that the Chong Dae Hyup [i.e.,

> the Korean Council] and Yoon Mee-hyang are being tried for suspicions of embezzlement, etc. Unfortunately, the *Journal* left out all of this.[64]

In truth, Lew was being kind. The *Journal* reporters did not just omit what he had said. They framed his prosecution within a bizarre account that took the fraudulent Yoshida-school narrative as fact. "Decades of research clash with Mr. Lew's interpretations of history," they wrote, asserting that the comfort women "were forced into sex slavery by the Japanese military." They described the North Korean–allied Korean Council as simply "a Seoul-based advocacy group for the survivors," and said that the principal remaining disagreement between Tokyo and Seoul "largely revolves around whether the government bears any legal liability."

For what the *Journal* reporters apparently thought conclusive proof, they cited Jinhee Lee, the Eastern Illinois University professor and associate in research at the Reischauer Institute who stalked Ramseyer relentlessly on the internet through 2021: "The body of evidence totals hundreds of survivor testimonies and historical documents that point to Japanese coercion...." This claim is absurd in the extreme. Recall that of the nineteen comfort women whose testimonials the Korean Council chose to publish, only three claimed to have been abducted. If there are any documents that point to abduction by the Japanese military, we have yet to see them.

Several of Lew's supporters organized a petition drive among Western scholars. Regardless of one's position on the controversy, they declared, a professor who dissents from the sex-slave narrative should surely not face prison time for discussing the issue in class. By mid-August 2021, sixty-three people had signed the petition.[65] Jinhee Lee stepped in and tried to stop the petition by writing to people who had signed it. To one person, she described the people from Japan and Korea who had signed as "the leading history denialist organization core members." Because Western signatories were unaware of this, Lee told them, "many well-intended scholars' names were misused." At least one prominent scholar removed his name from the petition after corresponding with Lee.[66]

The third target of Lee Yong-soo's criminal complaints was Lee Wooyoun.[67] This is the economist who tried to publish an article about the comfort women in *The Diplomat*, only to have Stanley, Ambaras, and Chatani gleefully intimidate the editors into censoring it. He has studied as a visiting scholar at Harvard and has taught at Kyushu University. He was one of the contributors to the two "Anti-Japan Tribalism" books edited by Rhee.

The last of the four scholars targeted by Lee Yong-soo for criminal prosecution was Joo Ikjong.[68] Joo provided the data about the newspaper coverage of the comfort women during the postwar years that appears in Chapter 4. He too has studied as a visiting scholar at Harvard, and he too contributed to Rhee's two "Anti-Japan Tribalism" books.

Other scholars have also been punished for stating unapproved views. The economist Yoon So-young said to his class: "If you start fabricating history at your disposal, you're doomed. Comfort women grandma, there is no basis.... In a way, we are constantly fabricating history. This may work in Korea, but not abroad." For these comments, Yoon was asked to apologize to the university's student council and the Korean Council.[69]

Ji (Jee, Chi) Man-won, a social critic and management PhD, suggested that many of the self-identified former comfort women had not in fact worked as comfort women at all. Of those who had indeed been comfort women, he said, most "were people [who] wanted to enter the sex trade because of the terrible economic situation." He further observed (as we confirm in Chapter 6) that the Korean Council is "pro–North Korea." The Korean Council declared this to be criminal defamation and petitioned the local prosecutor's office to initiate criminal prosecution. The court imposed a six-month prison sentence, subject to a one-year probation.[70]

Subsequently, Ji received another prison sentence for a speech crime related to a different issue. He asserted—plausibly, to our minds—that North Korean agents had participated in riots against the military government in the city of Gwangju on May 18, 1980. The Gwangju riots hold sacred significance for the South Korean Left. For claiming North Korean involvement, Ji was sentenced to two years in prison. In January 2023, the Supreme Court confirmed the sentence.[71] Ji was eighty-one years old.

In April 2017, Song Dae-yup, a physics professor at the Sunchon National University, suggested in class (in passing) that the comfort women "probably had a clear idea what they had to do." Prosecutors launched criminal defamation proceedings. For this and other comments, Sunchon National University fired Song, and the district court sentenced him to six months in prison. The appellate court declared that he had "committed a serious crime of spreading false information and defaming the comfort women," and the Supreme Court affirmed.[72]

This is what it can mean to study history in South Korea. The comfort women dispute in South Korea is a story about brutal censorship. It is a story about attacks on scholars and journalists who contest the Yoshida hoax that scholars in the West continue so blindly and passionately to follow. It is a story about their harassment by the South Korean Left who control the universities. And it is a story about their suppression by the South Korean politicians who control criminal prosecutions.

There is a moral here for people who might be tempted to emulate scholars like Suk-Gersen, Gordon, Stanley or Chwe. It is not a good idea to try to destroy other people's careers. It is especially not a good idea when you are in way over your head and winging it. You just might be wrong—and God help you when you are.

It was March 12, 2021, the second session of Lew Seok-choon's trial for disputing the permitted account.[73] A representative from the Korean Council testified as witness for the prosecution. With the court's permission, Lew asked him, "Name even one example of a woman who was forcibly conscripted through the power of the state."

Rather than give an example, the Korean Council representative contested the meaning of "forcibly conscripted," saying there was no reason to limit it "so narrowly to physical force." After all, the women were working at the comfort stations under the reign of Japanese imperialism. All of them were working under "structural coercion."[74]

The Korean Council lies at the center of the continuing controversy over the comfort women. It is the Korean Council that controls the comfort women who speak, that launches criminal complaints against scholars like Lew who question the dragooning line, and that has relentlessly sabotaged rapprochement between Korea and Japan. In the next chapter, we examine this organization in detail.

CHAPTER 6

THE KOREAN COUNCIL

Consider one timeline:

1983: Yoshida Seiji published a fraudulent memoir. He claimed to have gone to Korea with a team of soldiers and dragooned two hundred women at bayonet-point into working as comfort women.

1989: Yoshida published a Korean translation of his memoir.

1991: The *Asahi* newspaper reported that Kim Hak-sun claimed that the Japanese military had forcibly conscripted her into comfort station work, and that she was suing Japan.

1993: The Japanese government issued its Kono Statement in response to Korean government pressure. It apologized and stated that it had participated in the conscription of comfort women, and that some of the conscription had involved force.

1995: Japan offered compensation to the comfort women. As it did, though, activists pressured the comfort women to refuse the money. When some of them took the money anyway, the activists denounced the women as traitors and prostitutes.

2015: The Japanese government made another offer of compensation. The Korean government accepted the offer and promised not to raise the issue again. This was to be "final and irreversible." Activists protested strenuously.

2018: The Korean government repealed the agreement.

Now consider a second timeline:

1991: This was a bad year for North Korea. The regime had long pegged its security on a loose balance of power. The South counted on U.S. and Japanese support. The North relied on China and the Soviet Union. The Soviets had been especially generous.[1] But in 1991, the Soviet Union collapsed and the balance of power on the peninsula shifted dramatically against the North. To offset that shift, the North Korean regime escalated its nuclear weapons program. It had developed chemical weapons in the 1950s and had begun work toward nuclear weapons in the 1960s. Neither the Soviet Union nor China had helped it build bombs, but the Soviets had at least provided nominally nonmilitary technology. With the Soviet Union gone and China appearing to move toward market-oriented reforms, North Korea needed to ensure that Japan and South Korea did not coordinate their opposition to its nuclear program. All the while, it continued to play cat-and-mouse with the UN and the International Atomic Energy Commission, buy technology from Pakistan, detonate its first underground nuclear explosion, conduct more tests at steadily higher power, and develop increasingly sophisticated missiles to carry nuclear warheads.

1991: This was also the year that the Japanese government determined unambiguously that North Korea had been kidnapping its citizens and forcing them to coach its spies in the Japanese language. The government had suspected this since the 1970s. After North Korean agents blew up Korean Air Flight 858 en route to Bangkok in 1987, the one surviving bomber, on death row, explained that she had learned Japanese from a certain Lee Un-hae, who had regularly wept because she missed her children so much. In 1991, the Saitama police determined that Lee Un-hae was actually Taguchi Yaeko, who had disappeared in 1978.[2] The discovery had profound implications. It confirmed that the rumors of North Korean abductions had been true. Over the years, North Korea had abducted at least several hundred South Koreans. Some observers suspect that it may have abducted just as many Japanese. (As of November 2021, the Japanese Ministry of Foreign Affairs confirmed seventeen North Korean abductions, but stated that it could not rule out North Korean abduction in another 873 cases.)[3] With the Saitama police determination in 1991 that Lee was Taguchi, the North could anticipate that Japan and South Korea might begin to work together to pressure it to return the men and women it had kidnapped.

1991: North Korea was also negotiating with Japan over the establishment of diplomatic relations. A Japanese government delegation had gone to Pyongyang in September 1990. By pressing comfort women claims against Japan in 1991, the North Korean regime hoped "to acquire moral leverage over Japan and thereby secure an advantage in the normalization of diplomatic relations between the two countries," suggests Bak Sunjong, a South Korean journalist.[4]

It was the North Korean government that first demanded compensation for the comfort women, in January 1991.[5] In other words, the idea that Japan should pay "compensation" for these "war crimes" was one raised first by the North. Indeed, the very notion that "200,000 girls were forcibly conscripted" was an idea that originated in North Korea, as Park Yu-ha notes.[6] And the group that has zealously driven the comfort women campaign itself brings deep and strong ties to the North.

The Power of the Korean Council

Within South Korea, the comfort women dispute is a bitterly partisan matter. More than a little like the modern United States, the South Korean electorate stands fiercely and almost evenly divided. Those on the right support a continued alliance with the U.S., and the cooperative relationship with Japan that the alliance entails. Those on the left support a shift toward North

Korea and China. The comfort women issue is a convenient shibboleth for determining political allegiance, as well as a powerful tool for keeping South Korean governments from straying too far from the North and into a closer embrace with Japan, America's staunch ally.

Attacks in South Korea alleging pro-Japanese sentiments carry economic consequences. By law, the government can confiscate property if it shows that the owner has historical Japanese ties. Statutes dating from 2004 and 2005 define "'pro-Japanese and anti-national' actions committed during the colonial period," as Meredith Shaw explains, and "allow for assets to be confiscated from collaborators' descendants and redistributed to the descendants of independence fighters."[7]

Attacks on Japan also have rhetorical consequences in South Korean politics. The activists who attack Japan over the issue of the comfort women indirectly attack the political Right itself. The modern Korean conservative party traces its antecedents to the Park Chung-hee regime in the 1960s, and one of that regime's key achievements was the 1965 treaty with Japan. Within the world of modern South Korean politics, to press comfort women claims is to attack the treaty that did not address the issue. It is "to attack one of the core legacies of the [Park] regime and, by proxy, its successors in today's conservative party," as Shaw put it.[8] The 2015 attack by American academics on Japan over the Ziegler-Bentley history textbook was perceived by many, rightly, as a proxy attack on the Japanese prime minister, Abe Shinzo, a conservative who also favored a strong anti-North relationship with South Korea and the United States. But it was also a proxy attack on the South Korean president at the time, Park Geun-hye. She is the daughter of Park Chung-hee.

One organization lies at the heart of the comfort women dispute, and it is an organization that has relentlessly manipulated the dispute to block rapprochement between South Korea and Japan. It is the Korean Council for Women Drafted for Military Sexual Slavery (recently renamed the Korean Council for Justice and Remembrance). As the comfort women issue has taken an ever more contentious part in the tension between South Korea and Japan, this group has become an increasingly central player in South Korean politics more generally. The Korean Council systematically pressured the former comfort women to reject any Japanese compensation.[9] It organizes weekly protests in front of the Japanese embassy in Seoul. It installs (and sometimes funds) comfort women statues wherever it can around the world. And it instigates many of the attacks on Korean scholars who challenge the sex-slave orthodoxy.

The Korean Council controls most of the statements by the comfort women who appear in public. It maintains its ability to do this by collaborating in the operation of nursing homes for the women who recount the stories it wants told. As the political scientist Joseph Yi put it, the "prevailing narrative of abductions is based on the oral testimonies of a small number of women (16 of 238 registered survivors in 1990s), associated with activist organizations (e.g., House of Sharing; Korean Council)."[10] By controlling the nursing homes, the Council controls which women will be seen by scholars and reporters and what those women will say.

Park Yu-ha, a harsh critic of the Korean Council, confesses herself puzzled that the group ever let her interview the comfort women:

> I regained my interest in [the comfort women] issue in the early 2000s when I heard that [the Korean Council] was confining surviving women in a nursing home called House of Nanumu. The only time these women were allowed to talk to outsiders was when [the Council] needed them to testify for the UN Special Rapporteur or the U.S. politicians. But for some reason I was allowed to talk to them one day in 2003.[11]

Park found the Nanumu women deeply unhappy with the Korean Council:

> I could sense that women were not happy being confined in this place. One of the women (Bae Chun-hee) told me she reminisced the romance she had with a Japanese soldier. She said she hated her father who sold her. She also told me that women there didn't appreciate being coached by [the Korean Council] to give false testimonies but had to obey [the Council's] order.[12]

In 2004, several of the comfort women sued the Korean Council to try to retake control of their own movement.[13] The Council retained its power, however, and successfully intimidated most of the surviving comfort women into submission.

Sabotaging Reconciliation

Thwarting reconciliation between Japan and South Korea seems to have been the Korean Council's goal from the start. An Byeong-jik, an economic historian at Seoul National University, worked with the Council when it first began interviewing the comfort women, but eventually he left the project. "They were doing this as an anti-Japanese effort," he complained. They were not doing it to help the comfort women. "If the result of the research led one to join an anti-Japanese movement, that might be unavoidable. But to make the deliberate aim of the project be anti-Japanese? That's just not right."[14]

When comfort women seemed inclined to make peace with Japan, the Council threatened them. It made those threats credible when Japan offered compensation to the women in 1995. Nominally, the Council fought the compensation program because the Japanese government routed it through a private fund. The government took the position that South Korea had waived all claims against Japan in 1965 in exchange for reparations. To preserve that position, it contributed its funds to a newly organized private entity, the Asian Women's Fund, which it expected to raise additional contributions from the public and then pay the total to the comfort women. Japan promised the comfort women 5 million yen each (a little less than 59,000 USD at the exchange rate on June 30, 1995).[15]

The Korean Council objected that the Japanese government was denying responsibility by going through the private fund, and it ordered all comfort women to refuse the compensation. Many of the elderly women disagreed with the Council's view. They were old, they were poor, and they wanted the money. When Japanese officials set out to interview the potential recipients, the Council contacted the women and told them, "Come to the office. We have money to pay you." The Council then promised them 2.5 million won in exchange for a pledge not to cooperate with the Japanese program (about 1,400 USD at the exchange rate as of the late 1990s).[16]

Many of the women accepted the money from Japan, and the Korean Council was ruthless. According to Park Yu-ha, "When Japan offered compensation through Asian Women's Fund in 1995, 61 former Korean comfort women defied [the Korean Council's] order and accepted compensation. Those 61 women were vilified as traitors."[17] Their names had been a confidential part of the government's records, but the Council obtained the names and published them.[18] Park continues: "Their names and addresses were published in newspapers as prostitutes, and they had to live the rest of their lives in disgrace."[19] The South Korean government added that the women who cooperated with Japan would lose their government pension, and lose their right to stay in public housing besides.[20]

Sarah Soh confirms Park's account. Many former comfort women "have firmly refused to be further interviewed after the initial investigation for the government certification process." They have "kept their silence," Soh explains, "out of fear of making 'speech errors' that might lead to the cancellation of their registration and hence the cessation of their welfare support money."[21]

In late 2015, in part under pressure from the international campaign nominally fronted by American academics over the Ziegler-Bentley textbook, the Japanese and Korean governments cut yet another deal over the comfort women. Prime Minister Abe Shinzo issued another apology. The government added another 1 billion yen in compensation (approximately 8.1 million USD at the exchange rate on December 1, 2015), and the South Korean government agreed not to make further demands. The deal, they promised each other, was "final and irreversible."[22] At least 34 of the remaining 46 comfort women accepted the compensation.[23]

"Final" it was not to be. A panel appointed by the South Korean government soon pronounced the 2015 deal unsatisfactory.[24] President Moon Jae-in stated that the agreement ignored justice and the victims' perspectives. Effectively, he killed the agreement.

In truth, the Korean Council had done its best to guarantee that the agreement would fail. In May 2020, Lee Yong-soo (Jeannie Suk-Gersen's "Grandma Lee") accused Yoon Mee-hyang, the head of the Korean Council, of deliberately ensuring that the deal did not reflect the views of the comfort women. Yoon had known the details of the negotiations, Lee explained, but had purposely not told the comfort women. She had intended to sabotage the agreement all along.[25] The point was never to arrange a better deal for the surviving elderly women. The point all along was to prevent reconciliation between South Korea and Japan. Insofar as the deal represented a possible end to the comfort women issue as a political tool for North Korea–friendly elements in South Korea (and elsewhere), it was essential that those elements destroy it. The terms were irrelevant. It was the deal itself that had to go.

The North Korean Connection

By sabotaging reconciliation between South Korea and Japan, the Korean Council directly promotes a key North Korean political goal—and that seems to be the point. The Korean Council works assiduously on behalf of North Korea. Lew Seok-choon (author of the foreword to this book) describes the Council as "working in collaboration with North Korea" on the comfort women issue (as of early 2023, Lew is under criminal prosecution for his statements).[26] The Council "has used the comfort women issue for its political purpose, which is to drive a wedge into U.S.-Japan-South Korea security partnership," writes Park Yu-ha. "Formed by South Korean communists," according to Park, the Council is fundamentally a North Korean–allied organization that works deliberately to sabotage reconciliation between Japan and South Korea, and to do so precisely because it serves the North Korean agenda (Park is also under criminal prosecution).[27]

The origins of the Korean Council lie in an international antinuclear conference held in Hiroshima and Nagasaki in August 1987. Shimizu Sumiko of the Japanese Socialist Party later recounted the history in the official publication of Soren (Chongryon), a Japanese group allied with North Korea. Shimizu secretly met with Lee Wu-jong, the chair of a South Korean church group, on a boat in Nagasaki harbor to avoid observation by the Korean Central Intelligence Agency.[28] "She held my hand tightly and said, Tell me about Chairman Kim Il-sung. Tell me about our brothers and sisters in the North!" Shimizu recalled. "Make it possible for me to meet our Northern sister Lyuh Yeon-gu [Ryo Yon-gu, a prominent member of the North Korean ruling elite]. You could do it."[29]

Aboard the boat, Shimizu and Lee Wu-jong discussed how best to start their collaboration with the North. More specifically, they began to plan a joint project that would involve the North Korean group known as the Democratic Front for the Unification of Our Country.[30] In time, their project would become the Korean Council.

Shimizu and Lee's teamwork led to the Symposium on Peace and the Place of Women in Asia. Held in May 1991 in Tokyo, the symposium included a representative of the newly formed Korean Council. Lyuh Yeon-gu arrived from North Korea. In 1992, the symposium was held in Pyongyang.[31] There, the first chair of the Korean Council, Yun Chung-ok, met with Kim Il-sung.

Yoon Mee-hyang joined the Korean Council in 1991. The Council had its roots among the Korean Christian elite, and Yoon brought that background. Born in 1964, she attended Hanshin University (tied to the Presbyterian Church) and Ewha Womans University, and she worked for the South Korean Presbyterian Church. Lee Wu-jong (who met with Shimizu on the boat) had been a professor at Hanshin. Yun Chung-ok (who met with Kim Il-sung) had been a professor at Ewha.

Ewha Womans University is a school for women from what New Yorkers of the mid-twentieth century might have called "good families." Think of it as the Korean Wellesley. Recruiters in 1930s and 1940s Korea did not hire their comfort women from families that would eventually send their daughters to Ewha. They hired their comfort women from among the most destitute of the rural poor. The social distance between Ewha and the comfort women probably resembles the distance between a dinner for Wellesley alumnae at the New York Yacht Club and lunch at a diner in the fentanyl-wracked hills of Appalachia. Not surprisingly, class tension has inhered in the Korean Council from the start.

Although Yoon came from the South Korean church bureaucracy, she simultaneously brought deep ties to North Korea's network within the South. The very year that she joined the Council leadership, South Korean police arrested her husband, Kim Sam-seok (Kim Sam-suk), and his younger sister for spying for the North.[32] The two had gone to Japan, met with a North Korean agent, passed documents, and received money. The courts convicted both, and sentenced Yoon's husband to four years in prison and his sister to two years. The Korean Supreme Court affirmed.[33]

Kim demanded a retrial, and upon a new trial the court vacated his conviction for spying. The court confirmed that he had indeed passed documents to a North Korean agent, however, and upheld his conviction for violating the National Security Act (albeit with a two-year suspended sentence). It vacated the specific "spying" charge on the ground that prosecutors had not shown the elements of the crime in South Korea—that he had passed "state secrets" under orders from the North.[34] Do note that judicial independence has a tattered history in South Korea. Starting in the 2000s, the judiciary in Korea has steadily turned leftward. The Korean Council capitalized on this to silence many scholars who held unapproved views on the comfort women. The Council maintained close ties to the leftist Moon Jae-in administration, and the Supreme Court vacated Kim's spying conviction in May 2017, immediately after Moon became president.[35]

North Korean ties seemed to run in Yoon's family. In 2007, police arrested the husband (Choi Ki-young) of Yoon's sister-in-law (the woman convicted along with Kim Sam-seok of passing documents to a North Korean agent). The arrest was made in connection with another spying case. The court convicted Yoon's sister-in-law's husband and sentenced him to three and a half years in prison.[36]

In fact, Yoon's sister-in-law's husband (Choi Ki-young) had also been part of the senior leadership of the pro-North, now banned Unified Progressive Party (UPP). In 2013, police caught UPP leaders planning a massive sabotage operation. As Meredith Shaw told it, "secret recordings revealed that members [of the UPP] had plotted to assist a North Korean takeover."[37] Or maybe not so secret. Joshua Stanton, a U.S. JAG Corps officer in Korea and a longtime Korea observer, writes that the UPP members had been "plotting attacks against South Korean infrastructure targets in support of a North Korean invasion... *over an open conference line*" (italics in the original). When the Korean courts cut the sentence for one of the defendants from twelve years to nine, Stanton suggested that perhaps "South Korean law has a sentencing guideline for aggravated stupidity."[38]

In 2014, the Constitutional Court of Korea ordered the UPP disbanded—and, according to Lew Seok-choon, the party leadership promptly moved over to the Korean Council.[39] Lew can point to specific people in support of this claim. Yet he currently faces criminal prosecution in part because of this statement to his college class: "Do you really think the Council is a group that straightforwardly serves only the comfort women grandmothers?... The Council is simply using them. It plays on the heartstrings of well-meaning people like you.... The central management of the UPP now works through the Korean Council."[40]

The Ningpo 12

In April 2016, the manager of a North Korean–owned restaurant in Ningpo, China, defected to South Korea with twelve of its nineteen waitresses. The restaurant had been among the hundred or so that Pyongyang ran in foreign locations, mostly in Asia. The waitresses at these establishments entertained patrons by singing, playing the accordion, and dancing in special costumes.[41]

These waitresses had been trained for the North Korean regime's performing arts programs. Participants were chosen to be groomed for the programs while they were still children.[42] Inevitably, some of them would turn out to be not quite talented enough for the best positions in the arts, and the women who didn't make the cut were sent to sing and dance in the network of restaurants abroad.[43] These restaurants helped Pyongyang raise the foreign exchange it needed, and they provided an additional benefit. As a cash business, they were an avenue through which to launder the money gained by selling drugs and military equipment in the illicit market.[44]

For the Pyongyang regime, the Ningpo defection was a public relations disaster. The recruits for its arts programs were primarily children from elite families. Now, "a dozen vetted daughters of the Pyongyang elite," in Joshua Stanton's words, had chosen to defect as a group. The defection posed "a threat to the very stability of the regime."[45] Pyongyang immediately declared that the South Korean National Intelligence Service (NIS) had tricked or kidnapped the young women.

Here the bizarre politics of the modern South Korean Left resurfaces. For at this point, an elite group of leftist South Korean lawyers adopted the North Korean cause. Named Minbyun (Lawyers for a Democratic Society), the group embodies the leftist upper crust. "No organization is as identifiable with the elite of South Korea's political left as Minbyun," observes Stanton. Two recent presidents, Roh Moo-hyun and Moon Jae-in, had both been members.[46]

Minbyun announced that it represented the parents of the twelve waitresses. Quite how it obtained a power of attorney from the parents is not clear. Given that North Korea is North Korea, Minbyun obviously worked on behalf of the regime itself.[47]

Minbyun now filed a "habeas corpus petition" to call the twelve into court. It wanted to question them, it explained, to determine whether they had come voluntarily or had been kidnapped by South Korea's National Intelligence Service.[48] The petition was a flagrant breach of loyalty to Minbyun's nominal clients. The group purported to represent the families of the waitresses. By calling the women to court, the lawyers jeopardized the lives of their family members, as Stanton explained:

> If [the Ningpo 12 are] forced to reaffirm their asylum claims in public, Minbyun will have succeeded in winning its "clients" a slow death in the gulag. If, knowing and fearing this, the 12 publicly renounce their asylum claims, they'll be sent back to North Korea and a dark, uncertain fate. And if Minbyun establishes a precedent that it has a right to interrogate refugees every time Pyongyang trots out a terrified family member as a cat's-paw plaintiff, no North Korean refugee would ever dare to enter South Korea again.[49]

None of the waitresses wanted to return to North Korea, but the manager stayed in the limelight for some time. Multiple times he changed his story. Sometimes, he insisted that they defected on their own volition; sometimes, he told people that the defection had been a South Korean plot. Stanton observed, "There is no question that Heo [the manager] lied; the only question is when."[50] Eventually, he and several of the waitresses decamped to a third country—apparently out of concern for their personal safety.[51]

In 2018, several Minbyun attorneys contacted the manager and introduced him to Yoon Mee-hyang and her husband, Kim Sam-seok. They met regularly in a suburban Seoul house that the Korean Council had bought in 2012. The Council had apparently bought it from a left-activist acquaintance of Yoon's husband for treble the market value. No one lived in the house, but Yoon's father worked as the paid caretaker.[52]

Yoon, her husband Kim, and the Minbyun lawyers then met with the manager and three of the waitresses multiple times, insistently urging them to return to the North. Kim apparently belted out a famous North Korean revolutionary anthem.[53] Several times, the attorneys paid the manager cash that they explained had come from the Korean Council.[54]

THAAD

Recent investigations into Yoon's financial decisions at the Korean Council (instigated by Lee Yong-soo; see below) have disclosed the places to which the Council sends its funds. Some of those funds it has sent to an organization devoted to returning defectors to North Korea. Some, however, it has sent to two groups devoted to blocking the deployment of the THAAD (Terminal High Altitude Area Defense) missile system in South Korea.[55]

The United States has committed itself to helping defend South Korea. The military threats to the South come in part from North Korea and in part from China. Should the South Korean government refuse to install necessary defensive equipment, it would obviously reduce the willingness of the United States to defend South Korea in the face of threats from either of those two countries. This is exactly what North Korea and China want—and it is what the Korean Council, as part of the North Korean network within the South, has aimed for.

A Rift in the Korean Council

By the 2010s, Lee Yong-soo (Suk-Gersen's beloved "Grandma Lee") had become the public face of the Korean Council's virulently anti-Japanese crusade. Recall that Lee originally recounted leaving home with a friend in the middle of the night to meet a Japanese man, who gave her "a red dress and a pair of leather shoes in a packet," and then following him "readily" and "without any further thought."[56] After joining the Korean Council's campaign, she changed her story (or stories). In 2002, she told the Japanese Diet that "she had been taken away at age 14 at the point of a sword."[57] Subsequently, she told the U.S. House of Representatives that "she had been kidnapped by Japanese soldiers at age 16." At a Tokyo news conference, she added that "Japanese soldiers had dragged her from her home, covering her mouth so that she could not call to her mother."[58]

Recently, however, Lee Yong-soo has split the comfort women campaign down the middle. Publicly, the dispute has concerned money. Although the Korean Council received large amounts of government subsidies and private donations, it paid very little to the comfort women themselves. Instead, massive sums went to dubious use—like opposing THAAD or inducing defectors to return to North Korea.[59] Much the same thing happened at an affiliated nursing home.[60] Lee complained publicly in May 2020 and triggered an investigation into the Korean Council's finances.

According to tax returns, from 2014 to 2019 the Korean Council raised donations of 4.9 billion won (about 4 million USD) in its own organizational name (nominally on behalf of the comfort women). It raised another 3.1 billion won (2.5 million USD) in the name of its predecessor organization.[61] Of the 4.9 billion won, the Council paid 920 million (about 750,000 USD) to the comfort women. Of this sum, it paid 100 million (about 81,000 USD) each to eight comfort women who (following its instructions) had refused to take the money offered by Japan in 2015.

Other than the 100 million given to those who refused the Japanese money, from 2014 to 2019 the Korean Council had paid the comfort women a total of 120 million won (about 98,000 USD), 2.4 percent of the 4.9 billion raised. Despite the criticism about not using the donations for the comfort women, the Council has not disclosed how it spent the 3.1 billion it raised in the name of its predecessor organization. Given this nondisclosure, the historian Nishioka Tsutomu plausibly argues that it probably did not pay any of this money to the women.[62]

Korean media continued to investigate Yoon and her husband's finances. They found bank deposits of 321 million won (about 262,000 USD), a condominium worth 186 million won (about 152,000 USD; paid for in cash), a vacation house worth 47 million won (about 38,000 USD), and two cars. They found that Yoon had solicited some donations to her personal bank account. And they found that she and her husband had declared to the tax office a combined annual income of 50 million won (about 40,000 USD).[63]

The conflict between Lee and Yoon brought out some (perhaps unplanned) candor. Once Lee had publicly accused her of graft, Yoon responded by accusing Lee of fraud. In doing so, she articulated what many observers (and most scholars in the field) had long since concluded: that Lee was not telling the truth about her life. Yoon posted on Facebook her memory of her first encounter with Lee. She said that Lee had telephoned her and introduced herself by saying, "I'm not a victim myself, but my friend. . . ." Note the import: the leader of the aggressive and long-running campaign to extract money and apologies from Japan was publicly accusing her own star victim of having fabricated the life history she had been telling.[64]

Lee responded: "I was used for thirty years. I was deceived." Yoon had called her and her colleagues "sex slaves," but Lee recoiled. "Why would I have been a sex slave? That's absolutely preposterous."[65]

Nishioka attributes the break between Lee and Yoon not to money, but to Yoon's failure to stand behind Lee when she came under attack.[66] For years, the Korean media had hesitated to criticize the comfort women—even in the face of the obvious dishonesty of several of them. Then Hwang Uiwon, the young CEO and chief editor of MediaWatch (which Suk-Gersen dismissed as "a small far-right fringe group in Korea"), finally broke the press embargo in 2014. He began reporting to the Korean public both the ties between the Korean Council and North Korea, and the wild variations in the stories that Lee had told. The Council claimed criminal defamation, and made Hwang suffer. Prosecutors filed charges, but Hwang fought all the way to the Supreme Court. His was a patently costly battle, but one that ultimately he won.[67]

In 2018, Hwang published the table (discussed in Chapter 5) in which he set out twenty public statements that Lee had made since 1993. She had started with an account of leaving home voluntarily, then proceeded to tell various stories of forcible conscription—at the point of a sword in one account. She made contradictory claims about her age and the year when she was purportedly abducted, and about her length of service as a comfort woman.[68] Lee had no corroborating evidence, said Hwang. There were no eyewitnesses, no third-party witnesses. There was "not a shred of... consistency" in her public statements. For all these reasons, Hwang concluded that Lee Yong-soo was "a fake comfort woman."[69]

Nishioka traces the Yoon/Lee split back to Hwang's investigation. Faced with his disclosures, Yoon and the Council chose not to defend Lee. Instead, they sidelined her and substituted another comfort woman as the movement's face. In response, Lee complained publicly. "I've been giving exactly the testimony that they told me to give," she said. "How come they aren't protecting me?"[70] But once Hwang began to report the radical inconsistencies in Lee's accounts, her credibility crumbled. Realizing that they could not use her anymore, Yoon and the Council abandoned her, and she retaliated. And as she did, the façade of the comfort women movement collapsed.

When Yoon Mee-hyang sabotages rapprochement between South Korea and Japan, she promotes a key North Korean goal: prevent a collaborative response to its nuclear program. North Korea presents a fanatical threat to both South Korea and Japan—a next-door nuclear-armed regime headed by a mentally unstable sociopath. The two countries desperately need to work together to shut down the North's nuclear program. North Korea wants them so distracted by mutual hostility that they cannot coordinate their responses.

South Korea and Japan almost settled their dispute in 1995 and again in 2015. Both times, Yoon and the Korean Council derailed the rapprochement. Yoon did not help the women themselves. They were old, they were poor, and they needed the money that Japan offered. Neither did Yoon advance the interests of South Korea, which needs pressure on the North, not 1940s-vintage quarrels with Japan. She did, however, raise comfortable amounts of money for herself.

Explicit instructions from North Korea or no, Yoon stands near the center of a deeply entrenched network of pro-North activists in South Korea. From that position, she has kept South Korea and Japan at odds for thirty years, while the North has aggressively advanced its nuclear weapons program. More than anyone else, Yoon has inflamed the ethnonationalism that drives anti-Japanese hostility in South Korea and effectively blocks any reconciliation. In this, she has done exactly what the North Korean regime needed done.

CHAPTER 7

MAKING SENSE OF THE CANCELING

Last night I dreamt I went to Manderley again. It seemed to me I stood by the iron gate leading to the drive, but I could not enter, for the way was barred to me. There was a padlock and a chain upon the gate. The beeches with white, naked limbs leaned close to one another and leaned over the path. The squat oaks and tortured elms straggled cheek by jowl with the beeches, and thrust themselves out of the quiet earth.[1]

The past haunted Manderley, and it blocked the second Mrs. DeWinter as she approached it in her dream. The past has not blocked us. We have both retained our academic posts. But the past haunts us, for that is what ostracism does. *Meidung* to the Amish, canceling to the academic—ostracism haunts everyone it touches. It haunts because it divulges character. It reveals the nature of the people who inhabit our lives. One of our critics smugly insisted that a canceling was no more than a "dog whistle" used by "conservative hacks."[2] Another described it as a "shibboleth promoted by comfortable elites and rightists."[3] Neither is true.

In the course of an ostracism, you learn about the spine, courage, compassion, and integrity among the people in your life—or about their absence. You learn about the people you touch as you work, as you play, and as you walk the streets. You learn facets of these people that they have spent their entire lives trying to hide. Some of what you learn comforts. Some of it damns.

The dispute over the Korean comfort women is a dispute over history: over what happened on the peninsula in the 1930s and early 1940s. It is also a dispute over current international relations: over whether Japan and South Korea will strengthen their ties in the face of a mad North Korean tyrant and a brutal and expansionist Chinese Communist Party, or remain at odds. And it is a dispute over partisan politics within South Korea today: whether the Left will shift the country toward North Korea and China, or the Right will maintain and enhance the country's relations with Japan and the United States.

Within the Western academy, the dispute over the comfort women has become a fight over how scholars should respond to a colleague who says what they did not want said. In late 2020, Ramseyer published an article that described many comfort women as prostitutes who chose the job for the money. That is what the evidence straightforwardly shows. But scholars either in the humanities or with ties to South Korea (and in at least one case with a long career's worth of accumulated slights, grudges, and resentments) tried to force the journal to retract his article and to punish him severely enough to deter anyone from ever trying to make the point again. When Morgan deviated from the party line, his supervising professors retaliated. The very women who had promised to assist his entry into the profession instead circulated letters to the field that destroyed his chances of finding a job.

Nights are long during an ostracism. You read tweets from your adversaries. You read "I always thought joining a woke cancel mob would be easy and fun," and you think "I'll meet you in hell." You make plans to meet lots of people in hell during an ostracism. Then you try to forgive. You desperately try to forgive. But you rarely get beyond Jack Kennedy's "forgive your enemies, but never forget their names." You used to know how to pray. So you try to relearn how to pray. Ostracism is about sorrow, and sorrow takes us back to faith. Sorrow—as Dante put it—marries us again to God.[4] Many victims pray a lot during an ostracism. We did.

We will not parrot fake history. But for refusing to do so, both of us found ourselves canceled. Like the shadow of Rebecca hanging over Manderley, a canceling is a haunting presence. It is real. It is brutal. It is lonely. And it is profoundly, morally wrong. Canceling is wrong in society at large, and it is wrong in the university—and there it directly threatens the academic freedom and integrity upon which the entire scholarly enterprise depends.

The Conflagration—Morgan's Account

In late 2020, I invited Ramseyer to contribute a short piece to *JAPAN Forward*, where I do some editing work, as part of a year-end retrospective. The South Korean courts had recently been handling cases involving wartime claims by South Korean citizens against Japan. Both of us have an interest in these cases, and some of them involve comfort women. In fact, the history surrounding the comfort women is a big part of the South Korean claims against Japan. Ramseyer's "Contracting for Sex in the Pacific War" was slated for publication in the *International Review of Law and Economics* later that year, so he summed up his findings from that paper for *JAPAN Forward*. He concluded that much of the academic and popular narrative about the comfort women in the West was "simply untrue." It was "pure fiction."[5]

Shortly after Ramseyer's piece appeared at *JAPAN Forward* in January 2021, the Japanese-language *Sankei Shimbun* daily newspaper published a summary of his IRLE article. *JAPAN Forward* works closely with the *Sankei*, a stolid industry-and-economics publication that is probably closest in the American context to the *Wall Street Journal*. For obvious reasons, people who follow

memoir by Yoshida Seiji, a Japanese communist. Under orders from the army, wrote Yoshida, he had led a posse of soldiers to the Korean island of Jeju. There, they had conscripted young women at random, raped them, and then sent them on to the comfort stations abroad.

Once the Korean translation of the memoir appeared, Yoon Mee-hyang took over the organization that would in time become the Korean Council. Yoon maintained close ties to North Korea. Her husband had served prison time for passing documents to a North Korean spy, and his sister's husband had served time for his role in another spying scandal. Through a series of draconian tactics, Yoon—and the Korean Council—tightened their control over the actual comfort women (even as they defrauded them of their money). They decided which of the women would speak to the press and what each would say.

Yoon used the elderly women to push the Yoshida account and sabotage rapprochement with Japan. The North was pursuing its nuclear weapons program, and the last thing it wanted was a united front from Japan and South Korea. By endlessly repeating Yoshida's claim that the Japanese army had forcibly conscripted Korean women, Yoon helped to block that rapprochement.

In fact, Yoshida had fabricated the entire account. Historians had doubted his story from the start, and by the mid-1990s had concluded that virtually nothing in the memoir was true. Before he died, Yoshida admitted he had made up the story.

Japanese historians are not the only ones to contest the Yoshida-based account that the Korean Left and Western scholars try so hard to enforce. In 2019, a group of economic historians under Younghoon Rhee (Naksungdae Institute of Economic research president and emeritus Seoul National University economics professor) put out a book titled *Anti-Japan Tribalism: The Roots of the Korea-Japan Crisis*. In this book, the South Korean scholars diagnosed the obsession with anti-Japanism as unhealthy for, and ultimately destructive of, their home country. The book became a runaway bestseller in Korea and then in translation in Japan as well.

Beyond the comfort women hoax, Rhee and his team dismantle a wide variety of historical fictions on which the South Korean Left has staked its legitimacy. No, Koreans were not kidnapped to work in Japanese mines during the war. No, Mt. Baekdu in North Korea—where Kim Jong-un and his vampish sister like to ride through the snow on white horses for photo ops—is not the spiritual home of the Korean people. No, there were no evil plots by the Japanese occupiers to fiddle with the peninsular feng shui of Korea and doom the Korean people to generations of bad luck (a notion that is seriously alleged by the Korean Left). Yes, the 1965 treaty normalizing diplomatic relations between Japan and South Korea settled all claims for reparations.[7]

But historical fictions die hard. For their troubles, Rhee and his colleagues were assaulted, attacked, and ostracized. Another South Korean scholar, the brilliant literature professor Park Yu-ha, has also been denounced and criminally prosecuted for refusing to describe Japan as absolute oppressor and Korea as absolute victim during the first half of the twentieth century. Cancel culture is not an invention of American campus snowflakes. It has run rampant in South Korea for decades. The Korean peninsula is a rough political neighborhood and the Korean Left tolerates freethinkers about as well as they would be received in a revival tent. Ramseyer's paper, once sketched by the Korean media in the Korean language and branded as heterodox, was bound to provoke an uproar, and that is exactly what happened.

Anti-Japan tribalism may be the Left-Korean brand, but it is clearly unsustainable and getting worse by the day. That is deeply worrying to Rhee and his co-authors, to the two of us, and to others who care about the peninsula and about scholarship and academic freedom. The trajectory of South Korea under Moon Jae-in, the former president, was a sharp sprint to tribalist pan-Korean socialism. It remains to be seen whether the putatively conservative administration of Yoon Suk Yeol can turn things around.

As if to underscore the shared vision for the peninsula they had with the Moon administration, the North Koreans chimed in to denounce Ramseyer. They drew from what is surely the most fecund reservoir of putdowns in all of geopolitics. Ramseyer, they declared, was a "repulsive money grubber."

Lost in all this are the comfort women themselves. Yoon Mee-hyang and the Korean Council have ensured that none of them talk to the press, aside from a few staged performers like Lee Yong-soo. Yoon blocked compensation from Japan and prevented the comfort women from telling their own stories. Only through interviews with Park Yu-ha and the occasional memoir do their lives start to take shape.

Theirs is a story that the West has not heard. More specifically, theirs is a story that the South Korean Left and U.S.-educated historians of Japan have worked hard to prevent the West from hearing. The comfort women were poor, tough, filial (many took the job to help provide for their families), and above all survivors. Most of them knew what they were doing and chose it as the best alternative available. They sold sex to soldiers in battle zones, and for it they incurred a massive physical, emotional, and psychological toll. But many of the women were able to send money back to their families. Some bought houses. Others made Japanese nurses jealous with their outlandish purchases in occupied towns. Some earned more money than senior officers in the Japanese army. They lived almost impossibly hard lives, but they made the best of what they had. They deserve better than what the Korean Left and the Western academic mob have given them. They deserve deep respect.

"Orientalist" Arrogance

Trust us, we gag at the word "Orientalism" too. But we remain puzzled by the "contempt"—a strong word, to be sure, though it fits better than any other we know—that our Western colleagues show toward Japan and their fellow scholars in Japanese universities. Back in the 1980s, the high-zoot literary theorist Edward Said called it "Orientalism" when his colleagues treated people in the Middle East with what he thought was disdain. His "Orientalist" colleagues assumed that the West was thoughtful and rational, he said, while they called Arabs brutal and impulsive.

What Said claimed about Middle Eastern studies applies in spades to Western studies of Japan. According to our Western colleagues, the mindless brutality of the Japanese army knew no bounds. To our knowledge, no military anywhere has ever lacked for impoverished young women eager to sell sex for money. Yet according to our colleagues, the Japanese army dragooned Korean girls and women at gunpoint, locked them in their quarters, raped them multiple times a day, tortured them, killed them if they tried to escape, and then, for good measure, massacred three-quarters of those still alive at the end of the war.

More troubling still, our colleagues refuse to treat Japanese scholars as their peers. Do step back here and review the lay of the land. On the one hand, we have several hundred Americans and other Westerners with varying degrees (ranging down to zero) of Japanese-language ability and varying degrees (ranging down to zero) of knowledge about Japanese history—let alone the specialist field of the comfort women. On the other hand, we have Japanese scholars, including esteemed historians, many of whom are multilingual and have shown a demonstrated ability to work in archives in several different countries. Yet the Americans in this picture—Dudden, Gordon, the Quintet, most of the others who have written about the comfort women—insist that the Japanese scholars are wrong about their own history.

For many of these Western scholars, their Japanese colleagues are simply invisible. Paula Curtis complains about "senior, white men at elite institutions" with their "right wing" connections. Sonia

Ryang claims that "Asian studies in Western academe began with, and for a long time was led by, white men.... The Ramseyer affair is not an isolated example of what might be called systemic white male privilege in Asian studies."

Curtis and Ryang complain that white men dominate their field. What field? Ryang specifies "Asian studies in Western academe," but why? White men do not dominate the study of Japan, and never did. Japanese scholars, many of them women, dominate it overwhelmingly. Go to the National Diet Library in Tokyo and browse through the catalog. The vast majority of scholarly work on Japan—and virtually all of the highest-quality work—is done by Japanese scholars teaching in Japanese universities. We scholars in and from the West are a mostly irrelevant sideshow.

Andrew Gordon has not studied the comfort women. He does not know the literature. As of 2014, he was still relying on a source based on Yoshida's long-since-debunked memoir. As of 2021, he obviously had not read the two classic studies in the field, Hata (1999) and Yoshimi (1995), both cited by Ramseyer in an earlier and longer draft (freely available on the internet)[8] of the article he eventually published in the IRLE. Hata and Yoshimi both explain in detail the terms of the contracts under which women worked at the comfort stations. If reading the originals involved too much work, Gordon could have read one of the English translations (e.g., Morgan's translation of Hata). Apparently, Gordon did not care about what he might learn from his Japanese colleagues—from the scholars whom Ramseyer had followed when Gordon accused him of academic fraud.

As of 2021, when she and the rest of the Quintet publicly accused Ramseyer of fraud, Amy Stanley seemingly had not yet bothered to read Hata or Yoshimi either. Instead, she announced her plan to read them over that summer.[9] She continued this astonishing standup routine in the summer of 2022. In early June, while Shaun O'Dwyer was encouraging her to join a discussion about the comfort women, Stanley instead sent a long string of tweets and then informed him of the great favor she had done him. By reading her tweets, he had "had a more robust exchange, and learned more" than he ever could have in a year of talking to Ramseyer. "This is because I read the sources, I am a historian of women (and 'sex work'), and I have thought deeply about the concept of agency," she explained. "In other words, I have done the work, and am doing the work, with these sources."[10]

At the end of June 2022, Stanley told her Twitter audience that she had decided to study comfort women history herself. She delivered herself of yet another rambling soliloquy on Twitter—this time one in which she marveled at how well that history was documented. "The thing that had surprised me the most has been the abundance of evidence about the lives of 'comfort women,'" Stanley wrote. "The comfort woman system is extremely well-documented. It is all over military records, Allied soldiers' memoirs, Japanese soldiers' memoirs, diaries, etc., many before the 1990s."[11] Predictably enough, she later added a few ad hominem attacks against Hata—duly "liked" by Hiromu Nagahara, the MIT associate professor (and former student of Gordon) who had joined the early attacks on Ramseyer.[12]

Stanley seems to have discovered the extensive literature on comfort women for the first time a year and a half after launching a no-holds-barred attack against Ramseyer for his paper on the subject. The comfort women history is well documented, she reports. It is complex. It is a product of its time.

Welcome, Professor Stanley, to the library. She could have learned about the abundance of Japanese-language sources two decades earlier by reading Hata's 1999 treatise. After 2018, she could have read it in Morgan's English translation. Had she read Ramseyer's response to her own cite check, she would have known about the many Japanese sources in January 2022.

Stanley closed her routine by bemoaning the fact that there were so few high-quality histories of the comfort women in English.

Fancy that. Ramseyer could suggest one reason for that shortage. Lee Wooyoun (of *The Diplomat* censorship fiasco; Chapters 1 and 5) would probably offer the same explanation. So would Chizuko Allen (of the Cognella publishing company censorship fiasco; Chapters 1 and 5).

One writer replied to Stanley from the Philippines. He was puzzled that she expressed surprise at the wealth of material available in Japanese: "This is very surprising to hear for someone like me from the Philippines. Comfort women victimization is well documented in our side of the world.... Maybe it's just lazy researchers in the past?"[13]

Come mid-August, Stanley reported on Twitter how she had spent her summer vacation: she had worked on the U.S. Army's POW Interrogation Report No. 49.[14] People kept posting the report to Twitter, she explained, so they must find it important. Report No. 49 describes how the army in August 1944 had captured "20 Korean Comfort Girls" in Burma. According to the report, filed in October, "A 'comfort girl' is nothing more than a prostitute or 'professional camp follower' attached to the Japanese Army for the benefit of the soldiers."[15] The Korean women told the interrogator that they had "assumed" they would be doing "work connected with visiting the wounded in hospitals, rolling bandages, and generally making the soldiers happy." The report continued:

> On the basis of these false representations many girls enlisted for overseas duty and were rewarded with an advance of a few hundred yen.... The majority of the girls were ignorant and uneducated, although a few had been connected with "oldest profession on earth" before. The contract they signed bound them to Army regulations and to work for the "house master" for a period of from six months to a year depending on the family debt for which they were advanced.... The interrogations show the average Korean "comfort girl" to be about twenty-

> five years old, uneducated, childish, whimsical, and selfish.... Her attitude in front of strangers is quiet and demure, but she "knows the wiles of a woman." She claims to dislike her "profession" and would rather not talk either about it or her family.... They lived in near-luxury in Burma in comparison to other places.... They lived well because their food and material was not heavily rationed and they had plenty of money with which to purchase desired articles. They were able to buy cloth, shoes, cigarettes, and cosmetics to supplement the many gifts given to them by soldiers who had received "comfort bags" from home. While in Burma, they amused themselves by participating in sports events with both officers and men, and attended picnics, entertainments, and social dinners. They had a phonograph, and in the towns they were allowed to go shopping.... The girls were allowed the prerogative of refusing a customer. This was often done if the person were too drunk.

Although we include the report in our appendix (item C), we did not discuss it in the preceding chapters. The report does broadly confirm the account we give: the recruitment involved some fraud, but the women explicitly served under indentured servitude contracts with an upfront payment and a finite length, and some of them had already been prostitutes. We do not focus on the report for a simple reason: it is only one piece of evidence. Rather than rely on a document here and a document there, we discuss a wide range of government and private-sector evidence. Our many sources for the terms of the contracts appear in the appendix. For government documents about the comfort station regime, we have two full compilations. One set is two volumes long. The other runs to five volumes.

Stanley implies that people were posting Report No. 49 to Twitter because they found it important. We suggest a simpler reason: it is in English. Japanese scholars and intellectuals have been flummoxed by the way that Western scholars consistently refuse to read and take seriously the enormous amount of documentary evidence and careful historical scholarship on the comfort station regime. This material is in Japanese. Rather than read and discuss it, Western scholars simply trumpet the Yoshida hoax and blithely move on. Perhaps Japanese users are posting Report No. 49 to Twitter in a desperate hope that maybe—just maybe—if a document is in English then Western scholars might read it.

A still more egregious example of "Orientalist" contempt for the work of Japanese scholars is provided by Louise Young, Morgan's onetime adviser at the University of Wisconsin. "US institutions have dominated the global circulation of scholarship on Japan," writes Young. Indeed, "the intellectual production of Japan knowledge remains overwhelmingly anglophone (German and Japanese scholars need to publish in English to get international visibility) and is still centered in the US."[16] Young, like Stanley, might consider starting to read the Japanese-language scholarship.

Again: Japanese scholars dominate the "global circulation of scholarship on Japan." Overwhelmingly. And they mostly publish in Japanese.

On a South Korean YouTube news show in February 2021, Alexis Dudden assured her audience (in English) that anyone can study comfort women history without reading Japanese. "Korean scholars, Japanese scholars have worked together for decades now to put out much of this evidence in English, in Japanese, so that the local audience can read it," she asserted. "At this stage, it almost doesn't matter what languages one knows because so much has been published as a factual resource."[17]

We list the sources detailing comfort women contracts in the appendix. There is Morgan's translation of Hata's treatise. One of Yoshimi's books is available in translation. POW Interrogation Report No. 49, being an American military document, is in English. Otherwise, readers will not find much in English. But we are not surprised that scholars who read mostly what they find in English might think that most "scholarship on Japan" is in English. After all, most of the other scholars who write in English mostly read English material too. Dudden will not discover what is available in other languages until she starts reading other languages. And as long as Young stays in the anglophone world, "the intellectual production of Japan knowledge" will indeed seem "overwhelmingly anglophone." This is what the self-replication of mediocrity is all about.

A final example of "Orientalist" contempt comes from Harvard's Japanese studies center, the Reischauer Institute. Recall that this Institute kept the Gordon and Stanley Quintet attacks on its website for nearly half a year. The Institute faculty knew that Gordon did not follow the comfort women literature, and knew that he claimed to have checked Ramseyer's sources during a week when the Harvard libraries were closed. If they had read a few pages into the Quintet's attack, they would have seen that Stanley & Co. did not know the Japanese scholarship either. The Institute faculty did not care—and by November 2022 they had invited Stanley to be the guest speaker at their annual dinner.

Disciplinary Arrogance

Our western colleagues in "Japanese studies" match their contempt for Japanese scholars with their contempt—again, a strong word, but it fits better than anything milder—for other disciplines. Consider the response to Ramseyer's use of concepts that are familiar to economists. He had written a series of articles on ethnic discrimination in Japan, which he then compiled into a book. He suggested that the discrimination observed in Japan better fit the economic theory of "statistical discrimination" than the "animus-based" theories so popular in the humanities. The concept of "statistical discrimination" was first advanced by Kenneth Arrow and Edmund Phelps (both Nobel laureates). It is standard in economics but not well known outside the field (Ramseyer had to explain it to Morgan).

Some observed discrimination, Arrow and Phelps suggested, reflects information failure. Suppose a member of group A wants to hire an employee. About members of his own group A, he has substantial information and can estimate how productive each applicant will likely be. Suppose, however, that he lacks equivalent information about applicants from group B. If he cannot judge the relative productivity of each group B applicant, he will treat them all according to the group average (mean). Group B members who are more productive than the B group average will find themselves treated worse than they deserve; those less productive than the mean will be treated better than they deserve.

In his articles, Ramseyer explored several cases of group discrimination in Japan. For purposes of the discussion here, we focus on the discrimination against Koreans living in Japan. Many Koreans came to work in Japan during the first half of the twentieth century. Most were young, single men. Many were straight off the farm, had no education, and could not speak Japanese. They planned to stay in Japan for a few years, save some money, and go home.

An employer faced with a Japanese applicant could chat with him. He could ask about work experience. He could test whether the applicant could read, calculate, speak politely. If the applicant were local, he could contact references. Spend a little time, and he could acquire a good sense of how productive the applicant would likely be.

With a Korean applicant, the employer had no comparable information. Many applicants could not speak Japanese. They had no local references. But the employer knew that while virtually all Japanese applicants had attended school for six years, many of the Korean applicants had not. He knew that many had no outside work experience.

The employer also knew that the Korean applicants came from a high-crime group. That was not because they were Korean, but because Koreans living in Japan were mostly young, single, transient, and male. Young single men are a high-crime group everywhere, including prewar Japan. In traditional societies, older men and women try to cabin this criminal proclivity through the dense and overlapping networks of social and family ties they maintain within the community—what social scientists call "social capital." They monitor each other and try to stop people before they deviate too far from accepted norms of good behavior. The young Korean men had left those social networks at home.

One result was tensions between ethnic Japanese and the Japan-resident Koreans, and these tensions continued after the war. The Koreans in Japan now lived as families and no longer planned to return to Korea, yet curiously this population remained a high-crime group. It also maintained a fierce and bizarre loyalty to the North Korean regime rather than the South.

These features of the postwar Korean population in Japan reflected what economists call "selective outmigration." The Japan-resident Koreans who were best able to thrive in Japanese society married Japanese and stopped identifying as Korean. From 1950 to 2015, the population of Japan-resident Koreans fell from 535,000 to 412,000. It did not fall because this group had no children. Instead it fell because many had left the Korean community and joined Japanese society.

As a whole, the descendants of the original Korean migrants were not high-crime. They were not badly educated. They were not loyal to the Pyongyang regime. But the people who remained in the observably Korean communities were the men and women left over after the most low-crime, educated, and industrious members of the group had integrated into Japanese society. Hence the continuing tension between the Japan-resident Korean community and indigenous Japanese.

We tell this story because of what it discloses about our Japanese studies colleagues. In the spring of 2022, the university press handling Ramseyer's discrimination book announced its publication. Immediately, several of his critics surreptitiously contacted the press. Exactly what they said, Ramseyer was never told—but they did what they needed to do to sabotage its publication.

They also made their opinions known on Twitter. On June 30, 2022, one academic tweeted a notice about the book from Amazon. Several of Ramseyer's critics—think "usual suspects"—were livid. They seem to have staked their own careers on running him out of the academy. Hiromu Nagahara frantically tweeted to the publisher,

> Are you for real...??? Why are you publishing the already discredited arguments of a WWII-atrocity-denialist-turned-darling-of-Japanese-far-right???[18]

Sayaka Chatani sounded equally furious in a tweet apparently alluding to the attacks already sent to the publisher:

> Seriously...? We know prominent scholars informed you of the distortion of basic information in his work. We demand explanation on your decision making process. What made you think this racist view based on many outright lies has academic value?[19]

Paula Curtis repeated Chatani's allusion to the stealth attacks:

> This, after so many credible scholars have effectively criticized Ramseyer's "research" & proven that it has no basis in academic integrity. [The press] should be ashamed for letting this through AFTER the racist and incorrect content of this book was brought to their attention.[20]

Curtis was not done. She continued her harangue for fourteen posts.

Observe the basic point: two youngish professors in history and a postdoc claim the authority to tell a university press what books it can publish in law and economics. These writers showed no sign of understanding the economic theories of "statistical discrimination" and "selective out-migration" used in Ramseyer's book. But they did claim the right to ban them.

The principal article by "prominent scholars" (Chatani's words) to which the attackers directed the press was one co-authored by David Ambaras. It appeared in the online "critical Japanese studies" journal subsidized by the Reischauer Institute, the *Asia-Pacific Journal: Japan Focus*. Ambaras and his co-authors explicitly call Ramseyer "racist." They describe this work as "game theory," which it is not. The logic is microeconomic. Any economist could tell you that not all microeconomics is game theory.

In one chapter of the book, Ramseyer uses very basic econometric methods to explore his hypotheses. He co-authored the study on which it is based with a professional economist, and the econometrics are not peripheral. They are central to the study. About those empirics—the very heart of the study—Ambaras and his co-authors write only:

> Ramseyer also employs a statistical strategy that might be called the "mego" approach to statistics, namely "my eyes glaze over" when I attempt to work my way through the volume of statistical tests presented within one paper. The sheer volume of data and statistical tests cause [*sic*] any but the most determined reader to relinquish concerted attempts to examine the empirical work closely. This approach extends generally to all of Ramseyer's work.[21]

This is the attack apparently endorsed by Nagahara—an associate professor at MIT, of all places. Ramseyer wrote his study for specialists in economics and in law and economics. It is in the nature of disciplinary specialization that a reader will need more than high school algebra to understand it. Nagahara, Ambaras, and his co-authors did not even pretend to understand it. All the same, they did claim the right to ban it.

Ramseyer's enraged critics added the usual threats to the university press. Ambaras wrote that he hoped other scholars would "think long and hard before submitting manuscripts to you, refereeing manuscripts for you, or assigning your publications to students."[22] Curtis reported that people had contacted her to say that they would "never publish[] with [the] Press again or in the future."[23] One alumnus of the school wrote that it was "not getting a dime from me if this is what we're investing in now."[24]

Still—we confess that one librarian delighted us with her response to the dispute: "Faculty could use [Ramseyer's book] in seminars to help students engage in critical thinking, but *it is so damn dangerous to be out in the wild.*"[25]

OSTRACISM

A canceling is a Stephen King haunting. It brings a harrowing sense of exile. To be canceled is to be abandoned, to lose social ties, colleagues, friends, sources of compassion and emotional warmth. Think spiritual void, existential dread, Kafka's K, Edvard Munch's *Scream*, Becket's Godot.

Canceling is an old phenomenon, of course. It is merely the synonym for ostracism among the blue-state professional class. Ostracism itself dates from prehistory, and even from prehumanity. Nonhuman primates practice ostracism. For hunter-gatherer humans, ostracism was a death sentence. Hunter-gatherers collected food in groups. They guarded each other from predators by living in groups. They raised their children in groups. We apologize for the melodrama—but those exiled from the group in fact starved, found themselves attacked, and saw their children left to die.

In a canceling, people you do not know try to destroy your career. People you do know sign their petitions. And throughout, you know only that you know nothing about the future. You have no sense of how far it will go or when it will end. You wake up in the morning (or sometimes in the middle of the night) and check your cell phone. You wonder how many—how many dozen—hate emails have arrived. You wonder which article of yours is next on the kill list, which publisher will drop a manuscript of yours, which students will petition the dean about what malapropism you spoke in class, which organizations will dump you from their boards, which website will publish what defamation. You have no idea what will come next, but you do know that things will never be the same again.

Why do attackers lie? Why do victims apologize?

In the course of a canceling, people lie cavalierly. Others may not quite lie, but they mislead in ways we would never allow our six-year-old children to do. Our close friends did not do this, but people we knew well did. People with whom we thought we were on good terms did. They said things that we knew were misleading (or even flat-out false), that they knew were misleading, and that the surrounding audience knew were misleading. What could they be thinking, we wondered? Did they not expect to face any penalties for doing this? But of course they did not expect any penalties, and in fact did not suffer any penalties. During a canceling, the group suspends its moral rules. The world is never fair, of course, but during a canceling what is wrong becomes an iron law with a life of its own. Almost everyone plays along.

Why do people do this? A dozen people will have two dozen different reasons. One of Ramseyer's attackers was obviously exacting revenge for a long career's worth of slights, grudges, envy, and God knows what else. Other attackers seemed to be using Ramseyer as a cardboard cutout for target practice. He was (still is) old, white, male, politically conservative, and a Harvard professor. He was not a person; he was a symbol. And in many circles, that symbolism is apparently reason enough. By contrast, Morgan was a graduate student at the time of his canceling. Whether on the left or on the right, some faculty (too many faculty) treat graduate students as expendable. Morgan's advisers wanted to send a lesson to would-be dissidents. For that purpose, graduate student Morgan worked just fine. And Morgan had certainly made his enemies by bucking the party line in the past. Settling scores with him was a nice byproduct of falling in with a galloping "herd of independent minds."

To be canceled is to go through the day clueless about who will decide to sabotage what part of your life next. You do not know who will attack, when they will attack, what they will attack. You may go through the occasional day without an attack. But on most days you will be hit, the hit will be dishonest, and you will not know where it will come from until after it has destroyed another facet of your life.

By now, most of us in the academy have seen a canceling. Often, in the middle of the turmoil, the canceled victim says something unhinged. There is a reason for this: in a canceling, the attacks are ubiquitous, profoundly dishonest, and utterly unpredictable. All too often, that combination of dishonesty and unpredictability will eviscerate a person's judgment. The victim will then desperately reach out, flailing in the whirlwind, grasping for support. He will say something weirdly inappropriate. And the critics will pounce: we told you he has no business in the academy.

When canceled, you lose the ability to gauge what is happening around you. You lose your ability to sense how others perceive you. You lose this, because the people around you are being deliberately dishonest. They are lying. They are—as we used to say over beers—"messing with your mind." They are "gaslighting" you. Remember how irritating it could be in college when someone "messed with your mind" to throw you off-kilter. In a canceling, everyone around you is messing with your mind.

All too many victims of a canceling respond to the gaslighting by groveling. We saw an example while we were writing this book over the summer of 2022, when the intolerant fringe of the historical community decided to cancel the president of the American Historical Association (AHA). James Sweet was a chaired professor at the University of Wisconsin and a specialist in African history. Morgan knew him slightly from Wisconsin. Sweet was an honest scholar with a reputation for being a wonderful dissertation adviser and someone who was generous with his time and talents in the local community. As president of the AHA, he wrote an essay for the association newsletter that gently criticized the 1619 Project. For good measure, he added equally critical comments about the Supreme Court's historical discussion in the *Dobbs* abortion decision. Historians, he cautioned, need to avoid letting current political controversies shape the substance of their work.[26]

The activist fringe attacked Sweet and the AHA en masse. Ever on Twitter, Ambaras, Stanley, Shepherd, and Nagahara joined the attacks. The critics seem not to have raised any questions of substance. Instead, they launched dead ahead into political attacks.

Within two days, Sweet caved. On the AHA website, he posted a confession straight out of the Soviet show trials of 1936–38:

> I sincerely regret the way I have alienated some of my Black colleagues and friends. I am deeply sorry. In my clumsy efforts to draw attention to methodological flaws in teleological presentism, I left the impression that questions posed from absence, grief, memory, and resilience somehow matter less than those posed from positions of power....
>
> Once again, I apologize for the damage I have caused to my fellow historians, the discipline, and the AHA. I hope to redeem myself in future conversations with you all.

Perhaps Sweet posted this apology out of personal fear. Fear would have been a perfectly reasonable response. But then again, it is hard to say why anyone does anything in the midst of a canceling.

A canceling is a totalizing attack that hits from all directions. Most victims will find their internal stress soaring to levels far beyond anything they ever experienced before. They will not be able to sleep. They will feel profoundly disoriented. How someone lashes out in the middle of all this is almost entirely random. The canceling experience disorients profoundly, and does so precisely because the attacks are so flagrantly dishonest.

Sweet's attackers claimed to be standing against harmful words and ideas, but if perchance someone somewhere was actually offended by his article, the obvious response would have been to quote the University of Chicago's 2014 report on academic freedom: "it is not the proper role of the University to attempt to shield individuals from ideas and opinions they find unwelcome, disagreeable, or even deeply offensive."[27] Working in a research university takes a thick skin. Anyone offended by a scholarly discussion as gentle as what Sweet posted to the AHA newsletter should find another line of work.

If Sweet hoped that groveling would stop the attacks, he hoped in vain. An honest friend, if he had one, could have told him that apologies never stop a mob. Blood in the water does not make sharks swim away. Bukharin confessed, and Stalin shot him anyway. As soon as Sweet apologized, writers on Twitter began demanding his resignation. Priya Satia, a Stanford historian, demanded his article's "retraction."[28]

Apologies like Sweet's have two overwhelming effects, one personal and one public. Sweet will have discovered the personal effect almost immediately: an apology does nothing to mitigate a scholar's internal stress. Instead, apologizing makes it worse, much worse. Sweet faced attacks that he knew were disingenuous, and that everyone involved knew were disingenuous. He responded by parroting a public apology that was itself disingenuous. A confession like this will not leave a speaker comforted; it will leave him with a profound sense of moral failure.

For the community of historians itself, the apology was a disaster. Sweet had taken a question of scholarly importance and discussed it as a scholar should. By then caving to the fringe, he set a precedent. On the one hand, many (if not most) scholars who work in areas adjacent to what Sweet discussed will be more likely to self-censor. If even the AHA president cannot say certain things, they will think hard before they say anything similar.

On the other hand, the best undergraduates will increasingly avoid history as a profession. Applications to history PhD programs will not disappear entirely. Some good students decide they love history at age ten. They will not let yet another disaster turn them away. And the weakest students (the students with the fewest alternatives) will not turn away. But most top students have multiple interests and multiple career options. They do not have to become academics, and within the academy they do not have to study history. Post-Sweet, if they do become historians they enter a world where even the discipline's president cannot or will not stare down the Maoist enforcers. To anyone with a shred of intellectual self-respect, a career in history is now profoundly less attractive.

Why do people sign petitions against their peers?

In Chapter 1, we mentioned the petition circulated by Michael Chwe, a UCLA political scientist, attacking Ramseyer as a fraud and demanding that the IRLE retract his article. The petition described the comfort stations as a set of brothels in which "most" of the prostitutes were girls "between eleven and twenty." The Japanese military had assembled them through "abduction, deception, threats, and violence." These preteen and teenage girls served as many as forty men per day. They "were subject to repeated rape, forced abortions, physical torture, and sexually transmitted diseases." Those who complained were rolled over boards with nails and then beheaded. "Roughly 75 percent" of the comfort women overall did not survive their experience at these military brothels.

Chwe's account is preposterous in the extreme. As we noted earlier, armies stationed at a base never find themselves short of young women willing—eager, actually—to sell sexual services for money. If an army cares about venereal disease, it can require the women at designated brothels to undergo regular medical examinations. The U.S. Army did exactly that in South Korea in the 1950s (with the blessing and encouragement of the South Korean government).[29] Given that a willing corps of women would have assembled themselves voluntarily, the Japanese army had no reason to enslave and imprison unwilling teenage and preteen Korean girls. Given that Korea was part of Japan, they would have been imprisoning their own child citizens.

Japan was fighting a war. Enslaving unwilling children to do tasks that grown women regularly choose to do willingly would have been a pure case of gratuitous make-work. The army had no time or resources for a project so bizarre. And, at the legal level, Japan has long had a complex skein of laws and regulations governing conduct at home and (sometimes) abroad. Kidnapping is and was illegal. Kidnappers would have faced the full force of legal penalties for their crimes. The entire story made no sense.

So why were people signing Chwe's petition? Day in, day out, during the first half of 2021, Ramseyer kept asking himself that question. These were bright men and women. Some of them he knew personally, and some of them he had considered friends. Some of them held Nobel prizes. Yet here they were, supporting a petition slamming his article as fraudulent and immoral, and endorsing a historical claim, and by extension a legal claim, that was obviously ridiculous. What could they be thinking?

Mind you, most of these people could not find Pyongyang or Pusan on a map. But that just moved the question up a notch. Why would anyone savage a fellow scholar over a topic he knew nothing about? Why endorse a preposterous account in a field about which one is clueless?

"The awful thing about life is this: everyone has his reasons," as Jean Renoir put it in *La regle du jeu*. But part of the answer probably lies in seventh grade. Think "mean girls." As any study of ostracism in traditional societies (or even among primates) will explain, a group that decides to ostracize someone will not just ostracize the designated victim. It will also ostracize everyone who tries to sit out the ritual, and most people (as Luke Burgis put it) "would rather be wrong than alone."[30]

A second part of the answer, suggests Mark Bauerlein, a professor of English at Emory, lies in the way that we select for instinctual conformity in the university. Bauerlein notes that the chaired professors at the top schools (a category that includes not just those who signed the petitions but also Ramseyer himself) hold the positions they do because of what others think of them, and are who they are (in their own minds) because of those positions they hold. Successful scholars acquired their positions and became who they are by nourishing, cultivating, and grooming that reputation. At "every crucial state of his career from his time as an undergraduate forward, our professor has moved ahead, prospered and shined, because of *what others have said of him*," writes Bauerlein.[31] "The high grades he got as a junior and senior, admission to a top graduate program, acceptance of his thesis, a job offer, publication of his manuscript as a book, tenure review, and onward"—all these accomplishments "depended on the judgment of others." For all too many senior professors, success has been something earned by worrying about the reaction of others until it became "a reflex, an instinct of self-preservation." We select, in short, for Rosencrantz and Guildenstern.

A third part of the reason why brilliant professors would sign preposterous petitions brings us back to the essential—fundamentally Orientalist—arrogance of the Western academy: the assumption that any fact that matters will appear in the English-language literature. Recall Curtis and Ryang's accusations that white men dominate the study of Japan. Recall Gordon's cavalier reliance on English-language sources that had long since been rejected as fraudulent by Japanese scholars. Recall Stanley's eagerness to accuse Ramseyer of fraud (apparently) without bothering to read the basic Japanese-language literature. Recall Louise Young's claim that American universities "have dominated the global circulation of scholarship on Japan." Or recall Dudden's assurances that everything one needs to know about the comfort women is available in English. What could these people (in the language of those of us who came of age in the wake of the 1960s) have been smoking?

When area specialists assure their peers that everything of consequence in the academy occurs in English, people who are stars in other fields have no reason to hesitate in asserting their opinions. They hold chaired appointments in elite schools. They edit high-gloss journals. Some of them have Nobel prizes. Gay McDougall—author of the preposterous second UN report on the comfort women—holds a MacArthur "genius grant." The nonspecialist men and women knew nothing about Japanese or Korean history beyond what they could read in English, but even the specialists assured them that it did not matter. Everything significant was available in a language they could understand.

HOW BAD HISTORY HAPPENS

When everyone feels pressure to toe the party line regardless of the evidence, dissenters personally suffer. But the damage from the pressure goes much deeper and broader, for it goes to the cause of truth itself. When everyone fears to say a story makes no sense, fabrications gain credence and become accepted as fact. The simple seventh-grade mean-girl dynamic wreaks a disaster that goes to the soul of the university.

"Jackie"

In 2014, a reporter named Sabrina Rubin Erdely published a story in *Rolling Stone* about a "Jackie" being gang-raped at a University of Virginia fraternity.[32] In fact, none of it had happened. The story was a fraud. The *Christian Science Monitor* explored the reporting and editing at the *Rolling Stone* to understand "How Bad Journalism Happens."[33]

According to the *Monitor*, "Notwithstanding the allegations made by 'Jackie' in the article, there was simply no evidence that there had ever been an event at the fraternity in question during the time period that she claimed that the assault had occurred."[34] In other words, the reporter had trusted the statements of the self-described victim, and made no effort to corroborate them. The parallels to the comfort women dispute are straightforward.

The Columbia School of Journalism conducted its own after-the-fact investigation. According to the Columbia account:

> Erdely said she was searching for a single, emblematic college rape case that would show "what it's like to be on campus now...where not only is rape so prevalent but also that there's this pervasive culture of sexual harassment/rape culture," ....[35]

Erdely had set out to find what Jackie claimed to offer. As a result, confirmation bias (people finding what they want and expect to find) "seems to have been a factor here," as the Columbia report put it. Likewise, the standard comfort women story confirmed what the wartime-violence-against-women industry in humanities divisions already held to be true.

At root, politics drove the "Jackie" disaster. Confirmation bias was a strong tide running in a political sea. "*Rolling Stone*'s fundamental mistake, [managing editor Will] Dana said, was in suspending any skepticism about Jackie's account because of the sensitivity of the issue," reported the *New York Times*.[36]

Rape is a politically charged topic, and so the editors took "Jackie" at her word, just as Erdely did. The *Times* also quoted Jann S. Wenner, the publisher of *Rolling Stone*, admitting that Erdely "was willing to go too far in her effort to try and protect a victim of apparently a horrible crime. She dropped her journalistic training, scruples and rules and convinced Sean [Woods, articles editor] to do the same."

Bad journalism happened because everyone was scared. The party line on rape claims is clear, and questioning a self-described victim violated that party line. Jackie claimed to speak as a victim, and the party line did not permit doubt.

One commentator described how a "sense of danger" at *Rolling Stone* kept too many people silent even when they knew the gang-rape story was dubious:

> [T]he *Rolling Stone*–University of Virginia rape hoax[] disaster could have been avoided... [if] many people—progressive people, feminist people, progressive feminist women—said from the jump "this isn't right, something's not adding up, this isn't how it works." The whole story was so unconvincingly operatic; a gang rape, with dozens of witnesses, as fraternity initiation ritual? That's not remotely typical of campus sexual assault and so cinematic it seems obviously made up. A lot of people knew something didn't add up, right from the start.
>
> But because they were operating in an environment of omnipresent, existential personal threat, because they knew people might attempt to destroy them if they said the wrong thing, they said this *privately.* Publicly, they dutifully golf clapped and retweeted the story on Twitter and were good soldiers. And then of course it turned out to be a fraud, its narrative so strange and unrepresentative because it had been entirely invented by a young woman who appeared to have been suffering serious instability.... Perhaps if the people at *Rolling Stone* hadn't lived under the shadow of professional destruction for violating progressive mores, some of them would have spoken up. But no. I remember when that story came out; the sense of danger was palpable. Those are the wages of living under the constant fear of people who want to divest you of your job, your friends, your reputation, and your future....[37]

Bad history happens because people are scared. A writer—think Michael Chwe or Jeannie Suk-Gersen—tells an inherently implausible story, but it fits the political narrative of the moment. People know that "this isn't right, something's not adding up, this isn't how it works," but no one speaks up. They know that others "might attempt to destroy them if they [say] the wrong thing." So they look left and look right, swallow hard, and say nothing.

Rigoberta Menchú

Consider another parallel. In 1983, a book appeared in French that would be published the next year in English as *I, Rigoberta Menchú: An Indian Woman in Guatemala*. In due course, it would appear in twelve languages and sell over a half million copies. It was her story, a woman named Rigoberta Menchú announced: the autobiography of a young Mayan woman caught with her family on the target list of a brutal Guatemalan military junta and victimized by the combined depredations of international capitalism and U.S. imperialism. Her book became an immediate hit among humanities faculties determined to let "indigenous" and "marginalized" groups speak in their own voices. Professors assigned it in hundreds of classes. Rigoberta Menchú became the face that launched a thousand reading lists.

As the *New York Times* put it, Menchú claimed that her father had spent his life fighting "a battle against wealthy landowners of European descent who manipulated Government agencies into trying to drive [him] and other Indian peasants off unclaimed land that they had cleared and farmed."[38] He never succeeded, and she and her family had no choice but to toil on a plantation. Working day in, day out, Menchú herself never attended school. Two of her younger brothers starved to death. In time, the Guatemalan army captured another of her brothers. They brought him to the town center, doused him with gasoline, and forced her family to watch as they burned him alive.

Menchú was a talented speaker and she had an engrossing tale to tell. Besides publishing her book, she traveled the western European and North American lecture circuits telling her story. She had joined one of the Guatemalan revolutionary groups, and through her book and her lectures she built a powerful international network of support for the guerrillas. In 1992, she won the Nobel Peace Prize.

If only her story had been true. David Stoll, an anthropologist, visited Menchú's home village. When he related Menchú's account of her brother's immolation, residents were perplexed. Burned alive in the town center? No, that didn't happen. What is more, others informed Stoll that Menchú, having been identified early as a precocious child, went "as a scholarship student [to] two prestigious private boarding schools operated by Roman Catholic nuns."[39] No younger brother died of starvation, because none ever existed. Nicolas, the "younger brother" whom Menchú names as suffering that fate, turned out to be healthy and prosperous—and "a full decade older than his famous sister."[40] Nicolas had never heard of any other younger brother. One of Menchú's brothers, Petrocinio, was killed by the army—shot after being kidnapped, Nicolas said.[41] And Menchú's father did not fight over land with European elites. Instead, he spent his life fighting over land with his relatives and in-laws. As Stoll put it, the in-laws had "felt he was using the national land-titling system to steal their land."[42]

The Guatemalan army had indeed been brutal. But according to Stoll, "the guerrillas often deliberately provoked army atrocities as a tactic for galvanizing popular support. Nonpartisan villagers—a group mostly overlooked by other academics—were the war's most tragic victims...."[43] The farmers had increasingly gained power in local governments through electoral channels.[44] They did not support the army, but neither did they support the guerrillas.

But for Western scholars in the humanities, it was confirmation bias all over again. They embraced the book passionately because they "knew [it] was true," as Stoll put it. They knew it "because it said what [they] expected to hear." It made a "neo-*Guevarista* guerrilla movement...led by non-Indians...look like an inevitable expression of indigenous needs."[45] Western scholars had been telling each other to "let the subaltern speak"—*subaltern* being code for indigenous populations excluded from power. But not just any subaltern. "By being selective about which Mayas they were listening to, they protected an ideal indigenous voice in dialogue with their own concerns," and they could "ignore Mayas who felt victimized by the guerrillas as well as by the Guatemalan army."[46]

Stoll had caught Menchú lying, but the university community did not respond by reproaching her. They responded by shooting the messenger. One writer asked how Stoll could have "an ethical compass whose point of orientation" was not the "monstrosities" of the Guatemalan army or the "corrupt complicity" of the United States, but instead whether Menchú was "present when the army killed her brother."[47] Others challenged the very concept of objective knowledge, invoking the Guatemalan tradition of the *testimonio*. This was not a tradition that "privileged" a "single 'objective' truth."[48] Instead, the *testimonio* "undermine[s] this hierarchy" of "lettered knowledge over narrated experience"—the oral testimony of marginalized speakers, in other words, trumps written records.[49] Henceforth, scholars would need to learn to understand "new voices" and "new ways" of recognizing "truth and responsibility," and to welcome other "positions and positionalities."[50]

In modern humanities circles, wrote Stoll, "legitimacy in scholarship" turned on "identifying with certain kinds of marginalized voices."[51] Not all marginalized voices, of course. The villagers in Menchú's hometown who rejected the guerrillas did not count. But Menchú herself had become inviolate. Her autobiography was a "semi-sacred... text."[52]

Just as not all marginalized voices were equally legitimate, neither did all scholars have equally legitimate access to the sources. As anthropologist Carol Smith put it, "men could not be trusted to represent women,... white women could not be trusted to represent black women,... [and] anthropologists from the imperial center could not be trusted to represent the 'natives....'"[53] Stoll observed that for himself—a white male—to "challeng[e] the reliability of *I, Rigoberta Menchú*" was to "cast...doubt on the entire project of bestowing authority on the voices of the oppressed—and on the authority that [the scholarly community] derive[d] from it."[54] Smith again: "Rigoberta exists as one (not the only) voice for 'all poor Guatemalans,'" but "Stoll exists to represent the illusory truth of 'objective' reportage."[55]

Few scholars anymore dispute Stoll's claim that Menchú failed to tell the truth. And Stoll himself survived the storm, but not before the anthropology and Latin American studies communities in North America had publicly disgraced themselves. Menchú had told them what they wanted to hear, and let them pretend to give voice to the oppressed. As a poor Mayan woman who had suffered under military rule and embraced the revolutionary cause, she had epitomized the favored moral status of subaltern victim. As such, she conferred moral authority on her North American patrons who protected her virtue (and assigned her book in their classes). She was lying, but no matter. By the very act of questioning her veracity, Stoll had jeopardized their own claim to moral authority.

We need—all of us need—to return to the lessons we learned in kindergarten: Do not lie. Because everyone—everyone—is capable of it.

> Men lie, women lie.
> Rich people lie, poor people lie.
> Caucasians lie, Mayans lie.
> Business executives lie, peasant farmers lie.
> Imperialists lie, subalterns lie.

And whenever any of these people lie, they violate norms that go to the very heart of what it means to live in a community. The respect for truth is not an artifact of the modern scientific West. People everywhere, now and in the distant past, have expected each other (as Horton put it) to say what they mean and mean what they say. If someone states that A happened when he knows it did not happen, people understand what that means: he lied. We all know this, because we learned it in kindergarten. No—we all know this because truth is our conscience's lodestar. *Testimonio* notwithstanding, Mayans know it, Americans know it, Japanese know it, and South Koreans know it. To expect less of anyone, anywhere is to treat the person as less than fully human. It is to indulge the quintessentially "Orientalist" bigotry of low expectations.

The parallels to the comfort women fiasco are so obvious that we spare readers the recitation. Note merely that:

> Americans lie, Japanese lie, Koreans lie.
> Professors lie, soldiers lie, prostitutes lie.

Lying happens. It is wrong. And it is the scholar's job to unravel lies.

Where does the party line come from?

In the standard comfort women account, we have a story (1) that is implausible, (2) for which there is no documentary evidence, (3) based on several entirely uncorroborated (and often labile) oral accounts, (4) some of which were told by women who were patently lying, (5) pushed aggressively by a North Korean–affiliated organization, (6) kept alive in an environment where prosecutors file criminal charges against professors who contest the account. Yet when scholars question the standard account—whether either of us, Lew Seok-choon, Younghoon Rhee, Park Yu-ha, Hata Ikuhiko, or Nishioka Tsutomu—U.S. professors summarily accuse them of "denialism."

The sex slave "narrative" obviously touches an American professorial nerve. More precisely, it seems to touch two nerves—it seems to confirm two beliefs held passionately within the academy: that we live in a world of deeply rooted, almost hardwired imperialist and capitalist instincts; and that men reflexively, almost primordially abuse women. When we understand society in these terms, the comfort women "narrative" generates a classic example of confirmation bias. To her Twitter friends, Stanley described her participation in the attacks on Ramseyer as part of her "feminist activism."[56] Megan Kate Nelson, author and podcast, radio and TV personality, wrote that Ramseyer's article illustrated the way that "every time a man acts badly, it takes a huge amount of energy and effort from a group of women to respond and call them to account for it." The Quintet's attack in response, she continued, "was masterful."[57]

The North Korean–allied Korean Council (and the South Korean Left more generally) tells a story about prewar East Asia in which an imperialist and capitalist Japan dictated the institutional structure of Korean society. Through that power, it created an order that exploited and marginalized Koreans. By the 1930s, it manipulated that institutional order to conscript teenage Korean girls into "sexual slavery" at bayonet-point.

Preposterous as it was, the story fit the account of primordial ethnic and sexual oppression by which too many of our humanities colleagues collectively (at least pretend to) imagine our world. "It's a 70-year-old fight and even though it happened in far away Asia, the abuse and rape that occurred happens in every country to women on a daily basis," proclaimed comfort women supporters in the U.S.[58] Half a century ago, we thought rape a serious crime—as we do today. But we recognized that men and women both lie. Men rape women, and lie to hide it. Women accuse men of rape to extort a variety of advantages, and lie about it. Because the act usually occurred (if it occurred) in an unobservable environment, we sometimes let the guilty but unconvictable rapist go free.

In the world of #MeToo and Obama-era "dear colleague" letters (the ones sent by the Department of Education forcing universities to adopt procedures in sexual assault cases that were severely biased against the accused), some scholars in the American professorial community have switched their instincts. Sometimes they tell us to "believe the victim" regardless of whether any evidence corroborates the claim of victimization. At the same time, some scholars retain a decidedly bourgeois (Victorian, actually) reluctance to accept that any woman anywhere, in any circumstances, would choose prostitution for the money.

For the comfort women dispute, the implication of the "dear colleague" letters and #MeToo is straightforward: believe the comfort women. For some academics, the fact that the claims turned solely on a woman's testimony was precisely the point. Return to the claims quoted in the introduction: "The oral status of [the] narrative," wrote one scholar, was "the very element that makes it radically transnational and feminist."[59] To even consider looking for verification, insisted another, would amount to "the trivialization of the women's testimony."[60]

The Korean Council told a story that was preposterous across a wide range of dimensions. We like to think that our colleagues would have responded with their usual skepticism if not for confirmation bias and the threat of ostracism. But the story confirmed modern (at least public) protestations about structural ethnic, imperialist, and capitalist oppression. It confirmed the modern (similarly public) creed about primordial male aggression. The loudest scholars called any of their colleagues who questioned the sex-slave narrative "deniers" and threatened to ostracize them. The rest of the university community tabled their critical sense and fell in line by the thousands. As in seventh grade, all too many of us would rather be wrong than alone.[61]

HOW IT ENDS AND WHERE ONE GOES

A year into Ramseyer's canceling, the attacks started to abate. Granted, the Quintet did not stop. As of early 2023, Chatani was still shouting into cyberspace about Ramseyer's "white supremacy" and "racist agenda."[62] Ambaras was declaring that Ramseyer's article had "been found to be worthless as historical scholarship and as theoretical work, and an insult to historians and economists alike."[63] Curtis was explaining that she "continue[d] to give talks about Ramseyer" because people were still "defending denialism, exploitation, and harassment."[64] Meanwhile, the Australian historian Tessa Morris-Suzuki was comparing him to Holocaust denialist David Irving.[65]

And Stanley was perfecting the art of "weaponized propriety." During an exchange with Shaun O'Dwyer of the Heterodox Academy, she tweeted, "I do feel like some of your Twitter invective toward me personally is really over the top in a way that poisons intellectual exchange."[66] Several months later, when another writer—quoting Stanley's own words—told her, "you do need to respond whether you behaved as a member of the 'cancel mob' on this issue," Stanley replied that this was "the kind of overheated language and name-calling I object to . . . so I will not respond."[67]

But as the attacks faded, Ramseyer realized what had not happened and what he had not lost: his law school colleagues had not ostracized him. They still talked to him. They joked with him at lunch. They met him for drinks after work. They welcomed him at workshops and listened to his comments. Several of them pointedly invited him to coffee to show that they cared about him. One member of the Reischauer Executive Committee suggested that he post a response to the Gordon-Eckert attack at her own independent website. His friends at home in Lexington remained friends as before.

Neither of us was abandoned. Through it all, many friends stood by us, and by doing so they saved us. We will never forget that they did. For without friends, a canceling is an endless nightmare. Only friends—close friends, friends willing to risk being canceled themselves—can keep one intact. To an ostracized victim, friendship is priceless. Oscar Wilde recalled being brought by two policemen from his jail cell to the court and finding a man who had waited for him "in the long dreary corridor" so that "he might gravely raise his hat to me, as, handcuffed and with bowed head, I passed him by." Wilde remarked, "Men have gone to heaven for smaller things than that."[68]

A year into the dispute, amidst the barrage of attacks and petitions, Ramseyer realized who had not signed. His colleagues at the law school had not signed the petitions. Many prominent American scholars in Japanese studies had not signed either. Some had, of course—Gordon most obviously. But others had not. To be sure, some may have been trekking the Himalayas and never noticed. God bless them. One could do worse than sit out the university wars in the Himalayas. But given the aggressive way in which the attackers solicited support, some at least must have flatly declined to sign.

As the hate email, the pit-bull articles, the petitions, the ad hoc meetings about dropping the offender from an academic board fade away—as all this comes to an end, a cancel victim faces a new question: how does he reboot the career—the life—that the mob tried so hard to destroy? "Academic assassin," one of Stanley's friends called her, and rightly so. The label does not exaggerate. Those who carry out the attacks inevitably try to minimize their significance, but there is nothing trivial about ostracism. Unlike ostracism among primates, a canceling does not kill physically, but it can indeed kill professionally. It kills academically, and it kills socially. The modern ostracism that is cancellation is about death.

For those who survive the ordeal, the puzzle is how to restart. Nicholas I sentenced Dostoevsky to die by firing squad, but stopped it at the last minute. Shimao Toshio's commanders had ordered him on "ready alert" for his "final mission" in his kamikaze squad when the emperor ended the war on August 15, 1945.[69] Dostoevsky and Shimao found themselves facing sure death, and somehow survived. Cancellation targets face professional, academic, and social death. The victims sometimes survive. Both of us survived. What now?

For a survivor, the mundane problems are legion. Where should he submit an article? Many editors will reject a cancellation survivor's submissions sight unseen. Many referees will trash them unread, and a survivor will need to guess which editors will turn to which referees. At some level, it may not even matter—the unsuccessful "assassins" will come back to finish the job. It wili not matter what the manuscript might say. Honesty never constrains attackers in an ostracism. It never constrained the villagers in the traditional exile, and it does not constrain the mob in the academic cancellation. Exhibit 1: Jim Sweet.

Beyond the mundane puzzles, the fundamental question from Ezekiel 33:10 will hit the survivor with a vengeance: how can we then live? As Hamlet put it: "What should such fellows as I do crawling between earth and heaven?" Readers who think this overly melodramatic miss the violent intensity of the attempted professional assassination that is the modern cancellation. Post-canceling, a survivor with 184 academic articles to his credit cannot just mail off his 185th. The lies told do not fade that fast or that easily. Iago knew what he was doing when he fanned Othello's jealousy. Lies live. They endure. They destroy.

A scholar may survive a cancellation, but he will not return to a world unchanged. He will need instead to try to fashion a life for himself afresh. As he does, the fundamental question will return dead center as never before: how then are we to live? And the hardest task may be to fight the bitterness and the hatred. The "first thing that I have got to do," wrote Oscar Wilde from prison, "is to free myself from any possible bitterness of feeling against the world.... The most terrible thing" about a prison sentence, he continued, was "not that it breaks one's heart—hearts are made to be broken—but that it turns one's heart to stone." For those with hearts of stone "cannot receive grace, to use the phrase of which the Church is so fond—so rightly fond, I dare say—for in life as in art the mood of rebellion closes up the channels of the soul, and shuts out the airs of heaven."[70]

At the University of Wisconsin where Morgan studied, the motto is "Sifting and Winnowing." Sifting and winnowing is just what scholars try to do. We try to look at questions from one angle after another. We turn hard problems over in our minds, day after day. This is often lonely work. It is often fruitless work. But this is the way the academy moves forward.

Unfortunately, this is not how the comfort women "narrative" was built. The story that began with Yoshida, was embroidered by the Korean Council, and then was imported into the United States through clueless professors (to put it most charitably) is a crusade. In this crusade, the personal has become political, and the political masquerades as scholarship. Disfavored questions are banned. The life of the mind stops, and only the ad hominem attacks, the Twitter mobs, the petitions, and the tendentious *New Yorker* articles remain. This is not scholarship. We could call it religion, except that it gives religion a bad name. At least in aspiration, religion is about truth and compassion and reconciliation. What we see in this crusade is merely hate and fear.

CHAPTER 8

ACADEMIC FREEDOM

When the mob turned on Ramseyer, they attacked a sixty-plus-year-old tenured professor. The attacks were brutal, but they left him a chance to fight back. Graduate students have no such leeway. Morgan's advisers disliked his politics—both about the comfort women and more generally—and decided to bar him from the academy. The "recommendation" letters from his adviser Sarah Thal ensured that he would not find a teaching position anywhere within the North American orb. Morgan happened to have a Japanese friend who knew of a job at Reitaku University. Absent that bit of dumb luck, Morgan would have been without a job.

If at one time universities took an absolutist approach to academic freedom, that time has long since passed. When our colleagues discuss the concept at seminars and meetings, even many self-described "liberal" scholars try to distinguish between deserving and undeserving academic work. "Of course we value academic freedom. We're a university," a well-meaning professor might say. Recall that the University of Wisconsin's dean, Susan Zaeske, responded with this kind of boilerplate to Morgan's complaints about the censorship of the news about his translation of Professor Hata's book on the comfort women. Jeannie Suk-Gersen claimed to "defend the rights of academics to express unpopular opinions with which

[she] strongly disagree[d]." But then come the buts: But we wouldn't protect a Holocaust denier. We wouldn't protect a racist either. And of course we don't protect fraudulent work. But really, we do prize academic freedom.

The well-meaning professor will insist that the qualifications impose no serious cost. After all, major research universities never hire Holocaust deniers to begin with. They do not knowingly hire racists either. If one of their hires faked his or her research, why should a university protect that person?

We confess: we were already academic-freedom absolutists before either of us ever heard of the comfort women. We are both libertarian by bent, with Morgan perhaps the more radical libertarian of us. We did not need to be convinced about the value of freedom. But our experiences illustrate starkly why the well-meaning conditional approach does not work. Even in universities, some people have no interest in letting others advance ideas they despise. When the intolerant person is a graduate adviser, a student has little recourse. When the intolerant person is a colleague, even a senior scholar can find himself in serious trouble.

And here lies the danger: in effect, the conditional approach to academic freedom provides a template for circumventing the principle itself. In so doing, it also offers incentives for hyperbole and defamation. Simply saying "I disagree" will not get an academic rival removed; ergo, those who wish to destroy a competitor or protect a narrative will up the ante. If the university does not protect racism, they will call their rivals "racists." If the university does not protect Holocaust denial, they will call their rivals "denialists." If the university does not protect fraudulent research, they will accuse their rivals of academic fraud. Whatever it takes. Or, as academic activists have become fond of saying (again) lately—quoting Frantz Fanon—"by any means necessary."

We examine the most commonly invoked "respectable" exceptions to academic freedom: "racism," "denialism," and "fraud." Then we look at other recent attacks on scholars who have expressed unpopular views, and finally we discuss the choice that each of us may someday need to make in the face of similar attacks.

Racism

Following the template to a tee, Western historians of Japan promptly accused Ramseyer of racism, even of "white supremacist views."[1] They routinely accuse Morgan of racism too. David Ambaras attributes the entire Heterodox Academy to racism. These attacks left us puzzled. If readers wonder what connection racism might have to a debate over whether Japanese soldiers conscripted Korean women, rest assured that we were just as confused. It made as much sense as calling Ramseyer's article an example of "anti-Asian hatred."

To us, the accusation of racism is as ridiculous as it is outrageous. But these days, saying "that's ridiculous" is not an acceptable response, as Donald McNeil learned. McNeil had been a science writer at the *New York Times* for over forty years when he was "up for a Pulitzer" in 2021. Then the *Daily Beast* published a story reporting that in 2019 he had uttered the N-word in the course of discussing the use of that word with a group of high school students. The predictable outrage erupted. McNeil asked his associate managing editor, "[W]hy are we even responding? You've heard all this before. You know it's mostly bullshit. Just ignore them." But the younger reporters called it racism and they were furious. He had "lost the newsroom," his supervisor told him. McNeil was fired.[2]

The reason to call someone a "racist" is to invoke an exception to academic freedom in its "nuanced" version. Call someone a "racist," and an attacker can deny the person a forum to speak. "Platforming racists and revisionists is bad and does harm," said one of Ramseyer's critics.[3] Later she explained at greater length why it was wrong to give "legitimacy" to what she characterized as "fundamentally invalid" views:

> When you platform racists, denialists, and other prejudiced speakers, harm is done by: 1) acknowledging fundamentally invalid & discriminatory ideas as valid and worthy of debate... 2) providing a venue to spread those ideas, no matter how small, you facilitate their dissemination 3) lending them credibility/conferring legitimacy from being hosted...4) fostering networking among those who share racist or denialist views, which strengthens their communities 5) generating visibility for individuals whose messaging denies identities, violent events, etc.[4]

Obviously, "racism" is an odd charge to lodge against scholars who argue that the Japanese were, and are, not as monstrous as the dominant narrative has it. But—as Forrest Gump almost put it—odd is as odd does. Odd as it may be, the accusation can effectively shut down debate all the same.

Denialism

"Denialists," they also call us. When we first heard the insult, it left us momentarily baffled: deny what? The Holocaust, they seemed to reply—usually implicitly, sometimes explicitly. The explanation puzzled us even more: what does the history of the comfort women have to do with the Holocaust?

Al Roth and Paul Milgrom, both Nobel laureates, tell the world that Ramseyer's article reminds them of Holocaust denial.[5] Tessa Morris-Suzuki compares Ramseyer to the infamous Holocaust denier David Irving.[6] "Comfort women denialism and anti-Semitism are related," Amy Stanley insists.[7] Ramseyer's article, she writes, resembles the claim "that Jews brought Kristallnacht on themselves because they cheated Germans in business."[8] Morgan has also been called a denialist repeatedly and likened to a Holocaust denier. The term for this is Godwin's Law: in online debates, someone (even a Nobel laureate) will eventually accuse his opponent of being just like Hitler. Or as Coleridge might have put it: Hitler, Hitler everywhere, and not a stop to think.

Yes, we deny some things. We deny that the Japanese army programmatically conscripted women into comfort station work. We also deny that the earth is flat, and that Elvis and Bigfoot are frozen cryogenically in a CIA bunker. Any proposition is a denial of its opposite. Gordon, the Quintet, Dudden, Jinhee Lee—all of them deny that Korean women chose to work at comfort stations for the high pay.

Everyone "denies" many things. Some denials make the speaker a "denialist" and others do not. At root, "denialism" means whatever the person using it wants it to mean. Attackers use it to shut down debate. "Denialism," as one of Ramseyer's critics put it, is equivalent to "mis/disinformation":

> This shouldn't have to be said, but apparently bears repeating: Platforming historical denialists lends them legitimacy and allows them to spread mis/disinformation. It's morally and intellectually irresponsible and undermines legitimate and ethically conducted academic work.[9]

Our critics make the "denialism" attack because so many university faculty believe that academic freedom does not protect it.

We deny some things, but we do not know anyone who denies that the comfort women existed, that they worked at comfort stations, or that they provided sex to Japanese troops. Morgan translated Hata Ikuhiko's landmark history of the comfort women. He read the sources that Hata quotes and cites. The picture that emerges is clear: the comfort women worked at brothels patronized by Japanese military clients. We know of no one who denies this. The sources also indicate that many of the women—probably most—worked there by choice. This, our critics fervently deny.

When our attackers call us "denialists," they seem to refer to some mix of other claims about the comfort women. Many Western writers have claimed that there were 200,000 comfort women. Peipei Qiu, a literature professor at Vassar, ramps up the number to 400,000.[10] Many writers characterize the women as "sex slaves." Many Western scholars assert that the Japanese army conscripted them at gunpoint. Some (like Michael Chwe) write that the army massacred most of them at the war's end.

We deny all of those claims (and discuss them at length in Chapters 2 through 6)—but which of these denials warrant calling us "denialists" our critics never say. Ironically, Morgan, apparently a profligate "denialist," has also been labeled (pejoratively) a "positivist" for doing documentary work on comfort women history. This makes it even less clear what he might be "denying" as a historian—perhaps the notion that one can just make things up about the past as one pleases?

In June 2022, one of Ramseyer's attackers referred to "the right-winger obsession of '200,000' victims and Yoshida Seiji testimonies," and then declared: "We are WAY beyond that."[11] We are glad to learn that she is "WAY beyond" the 200,000 claim. It was an egregious misstatement of history, and we hope her colleagues start to move beyond it as well. In the fourth edition of his Japanese history textbook, published in 2020, Gordon wrote that estimates of the numbers of comfort women "range from twenty thousand to over two hundred thousand."[12] Morris-Suzuki was still pushing the 200,000 line in April 2023.[13] As for "Yoshida Seiji testimonies," it was Yoshida who invented the story that the Japanese army dragooned Korean women at bayonet-point, and then admitted that it was a hoax. If one more scholar has moved "WAY beyond" Yoshida, we are delighted.

When we move beyond Yoshida, what remains to support the favored narrative are only the testimonials of those comfort women whom the North Korean–aligned leaders of the Korean Council allowed to speak publicly. For three decades now, the Council leaders have manipulated the memories of those women. They manipulated their memories toward political ends and for money. Often, they enforced their control by keeping the women under effective house arrest. At the outset of the controversy, the women had held wildly varying "memories" of the past. Those who decided to "remember" its preferred version of the past, the Korean Council allowed to speak. The others it prevented from appearing in public, and publicly shamed.

The only publicly available memories of the comfort women are the cruelly abused memories, the memories that have been filtered through a political screen. The women have been compelled to "remember" according to a script written and enforced by their handlers. No one misremembers the Holocaust. We know the names of those who remember it, and the names of those who died. And the memories of Holocaust survivors match point-for-point with documentary history. Holocaust survivors are not forced into "houses of sharing" and told what they can and cannot say. They speak freely, if they can bear it, of unspeakable horror and pain. They don't work, wittingly or unwittingly, on behalf of any government. And they don't need cue cards to remember that which haunts them.

Fraud

Colleagues taking a "nuanced" approach to academic freedom also invoke the caveat "but of course we would never protect fraudulent work." In Ramseyer's case, this caveat became the guide for gutting academic freedom. Within a week of the day that the summary of his article appeared in the *Sankei* newspaper, his Harvard colleague Andrew Gordon claimed to have checked his sources (though the library was closed for Covid). He charged that Ramseyer had no original contracts, despite knowing that Ramseyer never claimed to cite original contracts, and (probably) knowing that no original contracts survived the war. An abundance of secondary and tertiary sources document the nature of the contracts between the brothels and the comfort women (see appendix). But this is not Gordon's field. Perhaps he did not know that.

The Quintet (including two former students of Gordon) released their tendentious cite check shortly thereafter. The authors claimed over thirty pages of intentional errors. In fact, they identified only three substantive mistakes, none of consequence (discussed in Chapter 5).[14] Did they not realize how badly they missed the mark? Perhaps not. As they admitted to their friends (albeit only on Twitter and only in Japanese), they had no background in the subject. Once again, Hanlon's razor is usually a good guide: never attribute to malice that which is adequately explained by incompetence.

By claiming academic misconduct, the critics could invoke the fraud exception to the more nuanced versions of academic freedom. The university should not protect academic misconduct; ergo, they accuse Ramseyer of misconduct. End of discussion. "Our report is not 'our perspective.' It's a fact check. There is no room for debate," wrote one of the five.[15] According to another, "the core problem with R's article is failure to meet standards of *academic integrity.* That's the baseline, and it's not up for debate."[16]

Morris-Suzuki similarly claims a failure of academic integrity. In an essay for the Australian Academy of the Humanities, she asserts that Ramseyer's articles (take a deep breath) involve "a mass of factual mistakes, omissions of crucial information, misleading citation of source material... [and the] use of unscholarly and derogatory language."[17] Morris-Suzuki has herself written on some of the same subjects (e.g., crime rates among Japan-resident Koreans) that Ramseyer addresses in other articles, and by "factual mistakes" she apparently refers to interpretations with which she disagrees. Considering how wrong she is on so many topics, she and Ramseyer do indeed have many such disagreements. She does not specify quite what language she found "unscholarly and derogatory." Given that the articles appeared in law-and-economics journals, however, she may be taking issue with some economics terminology. She would not be the first. Even a friendly historian suggested that Ramseyer would do well to find another term when he described prostitution as involving "disamenities."

The Quintet similarly insist that Ramseyer misuses evidence. Obviously, that is not what drove them to do what they did. People do not write savage thirty-plus-page cite checks when they agree with an article's conclusion. Neither is it what prompted Gordon to make a public statement about what he did not find in Ramseyer's sources at a time when—rather obviously—he could not possibly have checked them. These were "academic assassins" coming in for the kill: men and women who, as Robert Duvall put it in *Apocalypse Now*, love the smell of napalm in the morning.

Ramseyer's critics attacked him because he suggested that many of the comfort women took the job for the money. Whether the women could think and act for themselves is the issue. We claim that, by and large, they could and did; our critics apparently disagree. The women were very poor. They were often badly educated. But they were human. They knew they faced a bad set of choices, but—as humans everywhere do—they chose as best they could. Our critics would deny that power to the comfort women.

Professional Exclusion—Heterodox Academy

Attackers levy these charges of racism or denialism or fraud to stop a target from explaining himself and his position. The Quintet rushed their embarrassment of a cite check into print in a frantic effort to force the *International Review of Law and Economics* to retract Ramseyer's article. The last thing they wanted was for someone to give him a forum to respond to their criticism.

In the spring of 2022 (as noted in Chapter 1), Joseph Yi and Shaun O'Dwyer, who coordinate the East Asian chapter of the Heterodox Academy, invited members of the Quintet to participate in their symposia. The two had also invited scholars like Ramseyer and Lew Seok-choon. To Yi's invitation, David Ambaras replied: he would not lend his "professional credibility" to a forum "that gives a platform to those who seek to obfuscate or deny Japanese military and state responsibility for the horrors of the Comfort Women system." He added: "The fact that you think your offer is reasonable speaks volumes about your own mentality, none of it good."[18]

When O'Dwyer reached out to the Quintet, they would not even give him the time of day. Infuriated by their refusal to treat him seriously, O'Dwyer tweeted on June 28, 2022:

> [You] Japan Studies scholars who've lately slurred me as a fellow traveler of Japanese rightists and historical denialists, perhaps you could do some homework and, like familiarize yourself with the scholarship I do.[19]

Ambaras did not lose a beat:

> If you actively host venues where denialists occupy center stage and treat their claims as legitimately worthy of debate, then it really doesn't matter what scholarship you do on your own time. And, like, you're more of a useful idiot than a fellow traveler.[20]

This tweet was duly "liked" by Paula Curtis and Hiromu Nagahara.

When Yi and O'Dwyer organized a Zoom workshop about the comfort women dispute in June 2023, none of the Quintet attended. Neither did their sidekick Paula Curtis. They could have participated in this discussion. They obviously cared about the topic. But they chose not to attend because, they explained, Yi and O'Dwyer should not have invited Ramseyer to speak.

Ramseyer was a fraud, they said, and scholars must not give frauds a platform. Quintet member Sayaka Chatani insisted to O'Dwyer, "We criticized Ramseyer NOT because the argument is disagreeable. It is because he committed academic misconduct. We have been explaining this to you for 2 years."[21]

The Quintet had appointed themselves both prosecutor and judge of academic misconduct. Once they published their cite check, they declared the case closed. They had proved Ramseyer's fraud and shown that he deserved no chance to say more. Curtis was more emphatic still:

> For the zillionth time THIS IS THE POINT. We have clearly stated that the issue with Ramseyer's article is academic integrity and the failure of the peer review process, which by all accounts should have rejected the article. That's regular academic practice! Not censorship.[22]

She exaggerates, of course. She did not post a "zillion" tweets. About the internet workshop that she deliberately chose not to attend, she posted only thirty-three tweets. As Dorothy Parker might have put it, the affair between Paula Curtis and Paula Curtis will go down in history as one of the prettiest love stories in all of literature.

And then, of course, there is Amy Stanley. After a long Twitter spat with O'Dwyer, she seems to have decided that he did not fully appreciate the stature of the person with whom he was debating. To rectify that problem, she posted a series of tweets:

> Post 1: "But here are two substantive points: first, on where I come from. I am a social historian and also a gender historian—that's true. So since this happened two (?) years ago, here's what I've been doing."

> Post 2: "I co-wrote, with four colleagues, a thorough critique of that article...."

> Post 3: "Hannah Shepherd...and I got interested in [comfort woman] Mun Ok Ju.... We got the rights, wrote a proposal, got it through review, and have the translation forthcoming with Columbia University Press."

> Post 4: "I taught a graduate seminar on the comfort women

> as history, and together with students from [Northwestern], Harvard, and Yale, we read and discussed primary and secondary sources...."
>
> Post 5: "I wrote a paper on the infamous POW Interrogation Report #49 [discussed in Chapter 7]...and presented it at Harvard and Columbia...."[23]

We can only imagine what O'Dwyer must have thought as Stanley unloaded this information he had never requested. He was probably remembering the tweet she had sent him a week earlier:

> I do not think you have produced any work on this issue "as history" and from what I've seen of your historical interpretations, I'm not optimistic. You may be a very good philosopher or intellectual historian, neither of which I can do. But you can't do this.[24]

And then Goshen College

You learn things about other people during an ostracism. You learn the darndest things. Note that Stanley managed to drop references to Harvard, Yale, and Columbia in her tweets to O'Dwyer. In the course of his comments at the Heterodox Academy workshop, Ramseyer had distinguished between research universities and small colleges as part of a larger point about how research and academic biases work in North America. To her thirty-three-tweet attack on Ramseyer, Curtis added: "P.S. Did you know he went to Goshen College."

Huh? Leave aside Stanley's name dropping. "Dr. Curtis," as Miss Manners might caution, "we are not in seventh grade anymore." And thank God for that.

Yes, Ramseyer attended Goshen College. It is a small, not-very-selective Mennonite college with virtually no endowment located in northern Indiana. It is run by good people. Ramseyer counts several of them as his friends. He is the son of Mennonite missionaries and went to a small Mennonite college. It is part of what it meant to be raised in the Mennonite Church during the second half of the twentieth century. It is who he is.

Morgan comes from similarly plebian roots. He remembers himself as a two-year straight-D-and-F student at the Chattanooga campus of the University of Tennessee. (Ramseyer suspects he exaggerates, but Morgan insists that he does not.) He had seriously considered attending the local community college, Chattanooga State. Yale? Princeton? He did not even know what states they were in.

And Morgan knows poor people. A lot of them, in fact. Some members of his extended family lived in a trailer, not even a double-wide, on a plot of land in the sticks outside Cleveland, Tennessee. He recalls going there as a child and loving it. BB guns and four-wheelers and hot dogs, and plenty of off-brand cola from the no-name grocery store a twenty-minute drive away, down mostly dirt roads.

Some of Morgan's friends in high school drove in from Soddy Daisy, which may be the redneck capital of the United States. (Morgan fit in beautifully, having been born not far from a swamp.) At his house, his mother fixed dinner every night, and it included vegetables. Some of his friends were not so lucky. One friend's mom left Little Debbies on the counter for supper. When paychecks came in, other friends had enough to go get Taco Bell. But a lot of their fathers' money went for Natural Light and cartons of Marlboros. It was not exactly Princeton and Yale country.

Dr. Curtis, this is relevant here. Your sneer illustrates nicely the nature of the pressures that faculty face. It shows the character of the sanctions a professor encounters should he or she refuse to conform. And it reflects the frankly cavernous social distance between the self-proclaimed academic elite and a wide swath of the American public.

Many Americans hate those of us who work in the academy. They have reason to hate us.

A Quiz and a Proposal

Ever the pedagogues, we pause for a pop quiz. First, consider another chapter in the modern history of cancellation. Bruce Gilley holds a PhD in politics from Princeton and taught political science at Portland State University. He had worked for a decade in Hong Kong, and he thought the British had done a remarkable job running the colony. In 2017, he published an article in *Third World Quarterly* called "The Case for Colonialism."[25] Imperialism was underrated, he wrote. Colonial powers did some awful things, but their replacements sometimes did things even worse. He suggested that his colleagues in "colonial" and "postcolonial studies" were letting ideology get in the way of thought.

Those colleagues responded by calling Gilley a "white nationalist" and his article "'morally tantamount' to Holocaust denial." They organized massive petitions calling for retraction. Nearly half of the *Third World Quarterly*'s editorial board resigned in protest over the decision to publish the article. Gilley had had a separate book accepted by a prominent publisher and it was scheduled to appear. In the face of charges that he was a "white nationalist," the publisher canceled the book.[26] What surprised us in looking at Gilley's case was how interchangeable the attacks on him were with those made against Ramseyer. In both cases, the critics used cookie-cutter attacks. Think Ramseyer, think Gilley.

Here is the quiz. In the list that follows, distinguish the attacks on Gilley from those on Ramseyer:[27]

A. "[D]espite [name's] complaints about being 'silenced,' the fact was that his thesis...was based on a misrepresentation of source material and egregious historical revisionism. More than one response to his retracted paper revealed the shoddiness of his research, demonstrating that he should not be taken as a scholarly expert in the area of [field]."

B. "We criticized [name] NOT because the argument is disagreeable. It is because he committed academic misconduct."
C. "His only published work in this area was retracted because it did not meet academic standards, because he misrepresented and misunderstood the work to which he was referring."
D. "We have clearly stated that the issue with [name's] article is academic integrity and the failure of the peer review process, which by all accounts should have rejected the article. That's regular academic practice! Not censorship."
E. "[His article] downplayed or overlooked [insert item], cherry-picked data, was full of historical inaccuracies and misrepresentations, poorly researched, and distorted truths." It was "hate speech" and it was "Holocaust denialism."
F. "[His article involved] a mass of factual mistakes, omissions of crucial information, misleading citation of source material...."
G. "Any direct engagement with this piece only amplifies and emboldens horrific ideologies and practices that persist in academia and beyond."
H. "This shouldn't have to be said, but apparently bears repeating: Platforming historical denialists lends them legitimacy and allows them to spread mis/disinformation. It's morally and intellectually irresponsible and undermines legitimate and ethically conducted academic work."

Correct answers: Gilley—A, C, E, G. Ramseyer—B, D, F, H.

We almost worry about plagiarism. We assume that someone, somewhere published a cookbook of mix-and-match attacks in order to make the work of the many "woke cancel mobs" more "easy and fun." What with Chat GPT, next year should be even more fun.

But "fun" fails to do justice to the gravity of the matters at stake. In particular, it ignores the time and energy that the many committed scholars devote to the task and the burden on the internet traffic that results, not to mention the cost in CO_2 emissions. We are all in luck, therefore, that the Chicago economist George Stigler suggested a partial solution a half century ago.[28] Stigler observed that his colleagues tended to "travel together a great deal" and attend the same conferences. They could, he suggested, economize on the discussion that followed the conference papers if they agreed on a list of standardized "comments, which [would then] cover a large share of the comments elicited in most conferences." The standard remarks by the designated commentators, for example, might include:

> B. The paper admirably solves the problem which it sets for itself; unfortunately, this was the wrong problem.

In turn, the complaints and suggestions from the audience would include:

> 3. The residuals are clearly nonnormal and the specification of the model is incorrect.
> 8. Have you tried two-stage least squares?
> 11. I proved the main results in a paper published years ago.

As Stigler explained it, after a paper presentation, the designated commentator could simply say "B." A member of the audience might complain "3," while another might ask "8." And of course, there will always be someone in the room who will stand up and insist "11."

For the Quintet and their friends, the obvious strategy would be to assemble a list of standard attacks. For example, they might start with:

1. He ignores the mass of careful scholarship that goes contrary to his biases.
2. He is cherry-picking data and misciting his critics, and all to legitimize horrific ideologies.
3. This paper epitomizes the domination by senior white men at elite institutions, a domination that has plagued this field for decades.
4. The conference organizers should never have lent their legitimacy to a historical denialist like this.

Many of their standard attacks could come in multiple forms. For example:

5. No one should provide a forum for a claim this obviously [insert a, b, c, or d].

The user could then insert: (a) "denialist," (b) "racist," (c) "fraudulent," or (d) "all of the above." "Misogynist" could remain unlisted, as a wild card.

As a variant on Stigler's number 11, the Quintet and their friends could include:

6. Professor [pick one: Dudden or Morris-Suzuki] proved that this is false in an article several years ago in [pick one: *Asia-Pacific Journal: Japan Focus* or *Critical Asian Studies*].

Should no plausible candidate for such a statement emerge despite thorough exploration, the user could try:

7. Professor [Dudden or Morris-Suzuki] will be proving this claim false in an article forthcoming next month in *Asia-Pacific Journal: Japan Focus.*

The user should follow this public statement with the appropriate private request to Professor [Dudden or Morris-Suzuki]. A week's advance notice should suffice. And scholars with a flair for the dramatic could try:[29]

8. Professor Dudden says that when she and three friends proved this statement false several years ago, those three friends—all scholars in Tokyo—found their offices firebombed.

Those users with a believability deficit should feel free to try strategies used by two of the Quintet members (whether to good effect, we do not know):

9. I don't know what it will take to convince the men of Twitter that women can have expertise in Japan, history, and/or World War II. There is no level of knowledge or accomplishment that seems sufficient to the task. (Amy Stanley)[30]

10. I am begging people: please stop explaining Japanese history to me. I have a PhD in this history. I teach this history. I write this history. (Hannah Shepherd)[31]

The list could go on *ad libitum*. Rather than post thirty-three tweets complaining about a Zoom conference, an attacker could simply write "2, 4, 11." A friend might respond, "13, but 6." And an especially verbose critic might write "1, 6, 13, except that 2, 8, which in turn requires 23. And 9. Especially 9!"

Chicago Principles

Our opponents insist on adding qualifiers to academic freedom. We call for an absolutist approach. To our minds, the University of Chicago put it best in its Report of the Committee on Freedom of Expression issued in 2014, commonly called the "Chicago Principles." According to the report,

> [T]he University's fundamental commitment is to the principle that debate or deliberation may not be suppressed because the ideas put forth are thought by some or even by most members of the University community to be offensive, unwise, immoral, or wrong-headed. It is for the individual members of the University community, not for the University as an institution, to make those judgments for themselves, and to act on those judgments not by seeking to suppress speech, but by openly and vigorously contesting the ideas that they oppose.... Although members of the University community are free to criticize and contest the views expressed on campus..., they may not obstruct or otherwise interfere with the freedom of others to express views they reject or even loathe.[32]

The report quotes Hanna Holborn Gray, a former University of Chicago president, making the point bluntly: "Education should not be intended to make people comfortable, it is meant to make them think."

The prose is nice, but the test lies in how a university enforces it. Or not. Princeton adopted the Chicago Principles too. A test came when Joshua Katz, a chaired professor in the Department of Classics, published an article criticizing a statement by his colleagues urging the school to adopt a variety of measures for the specific benefit of minority faculty.[33] Among those measures, Katz focused on this:

> Constitute a committee composed entirely of faculty that would oversee the investigation and discipline of racist behaviors, incidents, research, and publication on the part of faculty, following a protocol for grievance and appeal to be spelled out in Rules and Procedures of the Faculty. Guidelines on what counts as racist behavior, incidents, research, and publication will be authored by a faculty committee for incorporation into the same set of rules and procedures.[34]

Katz saw an invitation for abuse. He asked, "is there anyone who doesn't believe that this committee would be a star chamber with a low bar for cancellation, punishment, suspension, even dismissal?" He published his essay on July 8, 2020, in *Quillette*, an internet-based magazine out of Australia. It tends to focus on the academy, and its detractors (and some fans too) call it part of the "intellectual dark web."

Katz had been an academic star. As of May 23, 2022, he was out of a job. Princeton's president, Christopher Eisgruber, nominally fired him for hiding details in a Title IX proceeding.[35] Several years earlier, Katz had had a consensual affair with a twenty-one-year-old student. Princeton had held hearings and sentenced him to a year's unpaid leave.[36] Katz served the sentence and then returned to campus. By 2020, the Title IX issue was history. If you believe that Eisgruber fired Katz for the reason he claimed, we have a bridge to sell you.

Eric Rasmusen was a chaired professor in the business school at Indiana University (and a frequent co-author of Ramseyer's) when he ran up against the cancel mob. He is a social conservative and evangelical Christian. In 2019, he retweeted a post about women in science that made what was probably a bad joke about the issue. Students at the university noticed. Then they searched the web and found other tweets they did not like. No one claimed sexual assault, an affair, a proposition, or even a dirty joke. Rasmusen is a devout man and lives like it. But the university was vindictive, and seems to have been particularly upset with Rasmusen's conservative Christian faith. It swamped him in Title IX proceedings, and in 2021 he called it quits and retired.[37]

Laura Kipnis, a film professor at Northwestern (and a brilliant essayist), describes the university disciplinary scene with especial wit. She herself was charged twice with violating the Title IX sexual assault rules. The first time, it was after students complained about an article she had written regarding sex between professors and students—yes, you read that correctly: they complained about an article she wrote. The second time, it was after they complained about the book she wrote describing her first run-in with the Title IX patrol. Kipnis then posted an informal poll on the internet related to another book she was writing. As she explained in an essay in the *Chronicle of Higher Education*, she was "asking people how their relationships were faring, whether their ideas about love had changed during the pandemic, and other questions in this vein."[38] This time, someone complained to Northwestern's Internal Review Board (IRB) office claiming that Kipnis was conducting research on "human subjects" without having cleared the poll in advance.

Kipnis has enemies. Given her biting wit, it will not surprise anyone that she has enemies. Then again, she quotes an "old (possibly apocryphal) Algerian proverb: 'The man without enemies is a donkey.'" Everyone has enemies, and outspoken professors especially so. Academics have always had rivals. Envy is a common emotion, and it is a corrosive one. Othello had his Iago: "For that I do suspect the lusty Moor / Hath leap'd into my seat; the thought whereof / Doth, like a poisonous mineral, gnaw my inwards; / And nothing can or shall content my soul / Till I am even'd with him...."[39] Mortals far more ordinary than Othello find their lives sabotaged by their personal Iago.

As envy and rivalry are nothing new, Kipnis asks what has changed. Specifically, she asks what has changed in the modern university. Most obviously, universities have installed vast bureaucracies that take the policing of speech and thought crimes as almost their principal job description. "Want to muzzle your enemies?" asks Kipnis. "Accuse them of something. Title IX officers are standing by." She continues:

> Let us provisionally define snitching as turning someone in anonymously, for either minor or nonexistent offences, or pretextually. Also: using institutional mechanisms to kneecap rivals, harass enemies, settle scores and grudges, or advantage oneself.

Kipnis asks whether snitching has increased on modern campuses. "From everything I've heard and experienced, the answer is yes," she concludes. Universities have, "on the whole, become a hotbed of craven snitches."

> In higher ed's overfunded, secretive, and ever-expanding punishment infrastructure (hiring for which now vastly outstrips new faculty hires), glutted with vague regulations about everything from romance to comportment to humor, snitching has become a blood sport.

Free discussion is the first casualty. The snitches organize and join "online mobs to protest exercises of academic and intellectual freedom." Think scholarship by Twitter posts. Anyone "who's disliked by anyone is a sitting duck," and everyone is disliked by someone. For the young opportunist, a quick kill through a Twitter mob can bring—we estimate—notoriety worth ten article citations. A target may eventually be cleared, but so what? "The process itself is the punishment," writes Kipnis. All the while, the bureaucracies indulge in "mission creep," in "territory grabs," and in "encroachment on the intellectual life of the university."[40] Even the *Washington Post* noted that snitching incidents "often trigger lengthy and opaque investigations that can disrupt departments for years and turn students into witnesses against their professors."[41]

Raising the Stakes

Morris-Suzuki might as well have stepped straight out of a Kipnis essay. She would not stop with retracting Ramseyer's articles, she writes. Harvard should punish him besides. To Title IX and IRB investigations, she would add research integrity investigations.

According to Morris-Suzuki, Ramseyer's work involves the "falsification or fabrication of research findings." These are code words: these are the terms that university administrators use when reviewing misconduct claims in the experimental sciences. Traditionally, they did not use these terms in connection with most humanities research, for a very simple reason: the humanities generally involve public material. In the experimental sciences, if a scholar manipulates data (and no one in the laboratory discloses it), those outside his lab may never know. In the humanities, the original material is in the public domain. If someone thinks a scholar misdescribes the material, he can write an article pointing out the error.

Importing a test designed for the experimental sciences into the humanities would allow academics (like Morris-Suzuki) who disagree with someone else's (like Ramseyer's) interpretation to claim that he "falsified or fabricated" his research findings—and trigger an avalanche of disciplinary measures. Ramseyer heard that someone had gone over the head of one set of editors and filed "research misconduct" claims against him with the publisher's Committee on Publication Ethics. It is helpful to know that it was Morris-Suzuki.[42]

Morris-Suzuki writes that in the sciences, when a scholar's articles "are full of misinformation, flawed data, incorrect statements of fact, misleading citations, material taken from unverifiable sources etc.," the "outcome may be the sacking or resignation of the academic involved." Exactly—and Morris-Suzuki would apparently impose that "sacking" on Ramseyer. Generously, however, she adds that if a case were "[l]ess serious," a school might create "a supervisory system to oversee the academic's future research." If Harvard does not fire Ramseyer, perhaps Andrew Gordon could "supervis[e]" his "future research."

Morris-Suzuki complains that Ramseyer appended to one of his articles only "a very brief erratum which left nearly all of the identified problems in the article unaddressed while reporting factually incorrect information." Ramseyer knew that an undisclosed (to him) writer had harassed the editors of a journal with a long and tendentious list of purported mistakes. It is helpful to know that this too was Morris-Suzuki.[43] For her information, those were not mistakes. She is pushing the limits to Hanlon's razor here. She was flatly wrong, and Ramseyer gave her complaints all the attention they deserved.

That Morris-Suzuki can write as she does and expect a welcome reception signals how precarious the life of a scholar has become. Kipnis described the Title IX empires in the universities. Recall from Chapter 1 that the authors of a self-styled "feminist" petition urged people to file Title IX (sexual assault) claims against scholars like Ramseyer who write articles of which they disapprove. Recall as well that 1,500 people signed the petition, including two senior Harvard professors.

Kipnis also discussed the expanding IRB offices. Recall that Professor Pyong Gap Min (Queens College) argued that Harvard should have used its Internal Review Boards to stop Ramseyer's article. Now Morris-Suzuki urges Harvard to discipline Ramseyer for "falsifying and fabricating" his research.

Do step back and consider the context. A Japanese communist wrote a fake memoir. His claims were preposterous on their face. But a North Korean–affiliated group picked up those claims anyway and used them to stoke the anti-Japanese hatred that the South Korean Left needs in its effort to pull the country away from its alliances with Japan and the United States. Humanities scholars in North America then embraced the claims as evidence of "wartime violence against women." Never mind that the author himself essentially admitted that he had made up the entire memoir.

In effect, Morris-Suzuki, the self-styled "feminists," and Pyong Gap Min urge their colleagues to manipulate the university disciplinary process to prevent other scholars from publishing views they disfavor and to skirt academic quarrels they obviously would lose on the merits. Theirs are not empty threats. Universities blanket their disciplinary proceedings with stringent "gag rules" and threaten anyone who discloses what happened to him with sanctions that include firing. Notwithstanding, any scholar with an ear to the ground knows that universities are indeed abusing their disciplinary machinery to punish politically disfavored professors. Across the United States (and given Morris-Suzuki, probably across Australia and western Europe), hyperpartisan academics are exploiting university disciplinary processes to harass scholars with whom they disagree. The resulting self-censorship is palpable.

Self-Censorship

In mid-2020, several scholars asked the *Proceedings of the National Academies of Science* (*PNAS*) to retract an article they had published with the journal just a year earlier.[44] They had not faked their data. They had not cheated on their statistics. In fact, they had not made any mistakes in the article at all. Their critics claimed that they had described their results inaccurately in the "significance statement" that accompanied their article, and perhaps they had. But it was a close call, and the authors had already published a correction of that statement. Notwithstanding all that, they retracted their article altogether.

The authors had studied police shootings. More specifically, they had asked whether the odds of a black suspect being shot by the police rose if the police force included more white officers. They found that it did not. Heather Mac Donald of the Manhattan Institute noticed their research and played it up. During a long hot summer when Americans seemed obsessed with the risk that white police would shoot black suspects, the authors had found no racial bias. And a prominent conservative commentator had quoted them.

Initially, the scholars explained that they retracted the piece because Mac Donald had misused their study. In fact, she had "used" their study, but did not seem to mischaracterize it or misuse it. Shortly thereafter, the authors amended their explanation to deny that Mac Donald's articles had had anything to do with their decision to retract. But that, of course, made no sense at all.[45]

Several scholars had studied an important topic with high public visibility. They had designed and implemented an innovative study. They had (at most) briefly mischaracterized their work in a short summary, but had corrected that statement. When a conservative commentator noticed their study and captured public attention, students protested. Prominent scholars signed petitions urging them to retract their article. And the authors caved.

The authors had done nothing seriously wrong. They had simply reached a disfavored conclusion. What followed was a classic case of ostracism, and it had the desired result. Like Jim Sweet's groveling apology, the retraction is a disaster for social science research. As Mac Donald put it, the retraction "bodes ill for the development of knowledge. If scientists must disavow their findings because they challenge reigning orthodoxies, then those orthodoxies will prevail even when they are wrong."[46]

Do pause, however, before you judge. Yes, we would all like to believe that we would rise to the occasion and stare down the mob if it came after us. We can all pray that we would stare down the mob. We can memorize the lines we would repeat when the interrogation begins. But until it actually happens, we cannot know.

We do not know what the mob in this case did outside of the public view. We do not know what the universities that employed the scholars may have threatened. Bruce Gilley withdrew his article on colonialism when the journal's editor started to receive credible death threats. By the time the authors of the police study in *PNAS* retracted their article, the president of Michigan State University had fired his "vice president for research and innovation" for supporting the study.[47] Hordes of students and faculty had complained to the universities. The scholars faced mobs, and the scholars each had personal rivals too. Did any of these people (recall Kipnis's "snitches") file pretextual complaints? They could have asserted IRB violations, or found a graduate student willing to file a Title IX violation. They could have alleged research fraud.

Suppose a university told one of the authors: retract your article, or we will proceed with an investigation. We would like to think that the author would have refused to retract. But Vito Corleone could make offers that were hard to refuse, and the MSU president had already fired his vice president. The stars in the field who signed the petitions telling the authors to retract controlled the journals in the field. They controlled the research funding agencies. If a professor had decades to go in his or her career and supported a young family, how harshly should we judge that person for yielding to the pressure?

Do we have any evidence that one of the schools threatened disciplinary proceedings unless the authors retracted their article? No, none at all. But suppose it did happen. Would we have any evidence that it did? No, none at all. We know that scholars have enemies and rivals; we know that the modern mob polices its orthodoxies viciously; we know that university disciplinary offices typically share the mob's biases; and we know that these offices smother all of their disciplinary proceedings with gag orders.

Candor

Many of us have rivals who nurse a lifetime's worth of grudges, slights, and God knows what else. Perhaps most of us do. Claire Boothe Luce once complained that she didn't "have a warm personal enemy left. They've all died off." The two of us have not been so lucky. Envy is a powerful emotion, and it is universal. People in all communities, over all centuries have faced envious rivals determined to bring them down. Envy is debilitating. And it is toxic: per Proverbs 14:30, "A heart at peace gives life to the body, but envy rots the bones."

Rivalries have always been with us in the university, but the intolerant hit squads are new. Iagos trapped in their own malefic webs of envy: these we have ever had with us. The Duddens, the Chwes, the Morris-Suzukis, the Quintets screaming for a hanging: these are new.

Kipnis called the hit squads "craven snitches." In her ever-astonishing candor, Stanley called her Quintet a "woke cancel mob."

In Ramseyer's case, the two phenomena fed upon each other: An angry rival instigated the mob and fanned the outrage; the ugly mob, in turn, intimidated the brilliant but clueless into signing preposterous petitions. Call it Parker's Law: "Beauty is only skin deep, but ugly goes clear to the bone."

Faced with the mob, faced with the threat of the mob—how then are we to live? An action that is rational for the individual does not necessarily generate the society-wide optimum when everyone takes the same course. Reaching that optimum may require each of us to take actions that could exact a high individual cost. We can urge people to accept that risk for the greater good, but moral exhortation goes only so far. When the personal stakes are high, people tend to look out for themselves. This simple human tendency will all too often lead to a society-wide loss.

In the modern university, the individually rational choice for a scholar is almost always to skirt conflict. If the mob punishes scholars for stating A, then the individually rational scholar will not state it. If that scholar finds A to be the truth, he (or she) will either move on to a different research topic entirely, or temper his conclusions. Negotiate, befuddle, avoid, soften, prevaricate, and if necessary lie. Given the credible threat of a punitive sanction—remember that Michigan State vice president who was fired—a scholar who violates orthodox norms will individually suffer far more than he gains by holding firm.

We can tell our husbands or wives not to worry, that we have tenure and a steady income. We can assure them that we incur no risks. But aggressive rock climbers do the same thing. "We fool ourselves that what we are doing makes sense," writes one climber. "We go to funerals and tell each other our friend died doing what she loved," she continued. "We surround ourselves with climbers, call them 'our people,' because they understand us."[48] But free-soloing

El Capitan probably makes no sense to anyone who never dreams of making the attempt (even if someone has now managed to do it and survive). Neither does it make individually rational sense for a scholar to fight the mob and the campus bureaucracy.

Individually, we incur huge risks. The days are long gone when Title IX officers focused on date rape. DEI (Diversity, Equity, and Inclusion) officers take the elimination of thought and speech crimes as their very job description. And with people like Morris-Suzuki putting pretextual accusations of research fraud into play, the university "research integrity" officers may start to integrate their own meat-grinding machinery into the speech-crime industry as well.

Individually, it makes no sense for an ambitious scholar to buck this process. A talented academic can instead crank out Thomas Kuhn's "normal science" until kingdom-come. He (or she) can write it. Journals will accept it. Other specialists will cite it. And deans will reward it. Talented academics can do it in their sleep. They can go half-time, sail to the Galapagos, and take their grandchildren fishing besides.

Individually, a talented scholar earns nothing by trying to do more. We (let us make this personal) could demonstrate that the accounts repeated by the Duddens, the Suk-Gersens, the Chwes, or the Quintets are untrue. We could show that the summary of the comfort women in Gordon's history text is as ridiculous as it sounds. As we realize from time to time, however, there is no return on correcting these preposterous stories. There is no money in honesty. There are no honors to be had for it. We will put ourselves and our spouses through Dante's nine circles of hell, but we will earn no personal gain. We will have killed one politically convenient myth only to find it followed by another.

But perhaps we can hope. To be a scholar is—we say with unshaken optimism—to move beyond the individual. It is to work within and on behalf of a larger community of men and women trying to understand the universe in which we live. This community of scholars spans the globe. It reaches centuries back in time to Thucydides, Confucius, Sugawara no Michizane. It extends indefinitely into the future. To be a scholar is to become part of this transnational, transhistorical community of men and women working to understand.

Scholarship can entail risks. It entailed risks during the Counter-Reformation. It entailed risks under the Jacobins. It entailed risks under Mao and Stalin. Given those risks, it can be tempting to avoid the transnational, diachronic community of scholars. Involvement is not as safe as we might like. Telling the truth is the price of admission to the scholars' table, but it's much easier to fake it and call the faked material "scholarship" too. We can keep our heads down and count the number of times our safe, orthodox articles are cited by the herd of independent minds. Or we can say what is true, regardless, and watch the securities that others enjoy stripped away one by one. Delusions of grandeur? We wish. But we do have our pride, at the very least.

There's much more at stake than pride, of course. If we can overcome our short-term self-interest, if we can risk sacrifice, we can become part of that something that extends beyond ourselves. To join that community requires that we commit in advance to pursuing our leads and reporting them as we honestly perceive them. It requires commitment. In the amusingly redundant terminology of game theory, it requires precommitment. In this context, it means that we commit ourselves to searching honestly and reporting forthrightly: acknowledge errors, but never call a truth a mistake. We commit ourselves not to bend, not to negotiate, and not to apologize for being honest and forthright.

Fail to commit in advance, and we risk breaking at the crucial moment. That is what Jim Sweet did. He wrote a thoughtful essay. The mob attacked. And almost immediately he caved. The harm to the historical community, to the universities, to our own broader intellectual enterprise—the harm to our international and diachronic community—was enormous. To avoid this harm, we must commit to holding firm.

Odysseus tied himself to the mast.

Dr. Strangelove invented the Doomsday Machine.

Approaching the Death Star, Luke removed his targeting helmet and trusted to "the Force."

When we commit in advance, we try to make certain actions reflexive and inevitable. We try to transform ourselves into men and women who *must* act in certain ways. We try to make the choice now to remove any ambiguity in the future—because sometimes we can more surely make the right choice if we make it in advance. "Until one is committed, there is hesitancy, the chance to draw back, always ineffectiveness," wrote Goethe. But "the moment one definitely commits oneself, then Providence moves too."[49]

At stake is what one commentator calls "the moral center."[50] The universities need a moral center, a set of moral commitments by which we—scholars—agree to be bound. Yes, we are preaching, we realize—but as scholars we need (paraphrasing Yeats again) a center that holds. And toward that end, we must, each of us, ensure that it holds. Doing so will require that we take risks. Those risks may sometimes cost us more personally than we would ourselves ever gain. But this is what it means to take a stand.

This is about reestablishing a moral center in the university community. It is about returning to a classical focus on ideas. It is about a commitment to openness, inquiry, and simple honesty. It is about Lear's youngest daughter Cordelia. Reestablishing the moral center means putting an end to the fake claims of victimization—to fake attacks about denialism and racism and fake charges of academic fraud. The snitches know what they are doing, and it is profoundly dishonest. It is dishonest in a way that goes to the heart of the university. We—all of us—need Cordelia's candor and Yeats's famous "conviction," even, especially, when employing them would jeopardize our professional standing, our career, our peace. We need the candor to call a lie a lie, and the conviction to call it a lie publicly.

We can try to commit to Cordelia's honesty. Perhaps it is more than a bit sentimental, but we will be better scholars for it. And whatever metaphysics you choose, we will be better humans for it. We will have fought the good fight, finished the race, and kept the faith.

We are lucky ones. We may choose. By the 1990s, the surviving comfort women had lost their ability to choose—what academics like to call "agency." But they did not lose their agency to the Japanese military. They lost it to the very scholars and activists who purport to speak in their name and to work on their behalf. To rob people of their ability to make choices is to attack them at their very moral center as human beings. Cancellations come and go. We survived. The comfort women remain in captivity to a historical lie. We will not keep the lie going. We will fight it with everything we have in us.

EPILOGUE

As this book went into production, in February 2023, the Seoul Western District Court convicted Yoon Mee-hyang, longtime mastermind behind the comfort women crusade and head of the Korean Council (Chapter 6), of financial fraud and embezzlement. The court found that she and her husband had diverted contributions intended for the comfort women both to other pro–North Korean activities and to their private accounts.[1]

On March 1, 2023, South Korean author Kim Byungheon filed criminal charges against Jeannie Suk-Gersen's much-beloved "Grandma Lee" (Chapter 5). Kim and several other authors had detailed how the self-proclaimed former comfort woman Lee Yong-soo had lied repeatedly about her past. "Grandma Lee" reacted by filing criminal charges in an attempt to silence them. This strategy, explained Kim (quite plausibly in our mind), itself constituted the crime of malicious prosecution.[2]

The statement that many (probably most) comfort women took the job for the money is not the only historical claim banned in South Korea. In Chapter 5, we mentioned Ji Man-won, a management PhD who was sentenced to two years in prison for stating that North

Korean agents had played a part in the 1980 Gwangju riots against the conservative government. The Gwangju riots are apparently sacred, and suggesting North Korean involvement was a crime. In January 2023, the Supreme Court confirmed a two-year prison sentence for Ji, then eighty-one years old.

In February, leftist politicians (from former president Moon Jae-in's party, in power until 2022) announced that they were filing ethics charges against a legislator for yet another speech crime.[3] Tae Yong-ho is from North Korea. He had married into a family with close ties to the ruling Kim dynasty and had risen to a position near the top of the regime. He had been serving as the North Korean deputy ambassador to the United Kingdom when he defected with his wife and children in 2016, then moved to South Korea, where in 2022 he was elected to the National Assembly.

Tae's speech crime concerned an incident that occurred on the South Korean island of Jeju (the same island where Yoshida Seiji claimed to have led hunts for comfort women) on April 3, 1948. Communists on Jeju attacked police stations and killed several officers in what they saw as an insurrection—a campaign to "liberate" the island and join the North. Then-president Syngman Rhee sent in the South Korean military, and thousands died. In 2022, Tae stated that "the barbaric April 3 incident was obviously caused by the Kim family acting as they pleased." Kim Il-sung had "detonated the Jeju April 3 incident by command," he said. As "someone who played a part in the Kim regime," Tae continued, "I want to get down on my knees and beg forgiveness from the victims."

To the South Korean Left, suggesting that anyone other than Rhee might be responsible for the tragedy is apparently out of the question. For explaining that Kim Il-sung had started the Jeju killings, the Left declared it would file disciplinary charges against Tae.

The comfort women. The Gwangju riots. The April 3 incident. Where does all this censorship end? And what about the controversies more familiar in the West? May we safely study the recruitment of Korean men into Japanese factories and mines during the war? The number of Koreans who died in the 1923 Tokyo earthquake? The effect of the Japanese land surveys in Korea? The number of Koreans who volunteered to serve in the Japanese army? Crime rates among the Japan-resident Korean community? The domination of that community by the Japanese Communist Party?

In her *New Yorker* article on the comfort women dispute, Suk-Gersen—having contacted Chwe, Gordon, Stanley, Ambaras, Morris-Suzuki, and Dudden—repeats claims that Ramseyer "misused historical sources" in writing about several of these other topics as well. We assume that Suk-Gersen has not checked the records of the 1923 earthquake herself. She has made it clear that she will duly uphold the forced-conscription account of the comfort women mandated by the South Korean Left. Apparently, we are to understand that she will uphold the other mandated accounts as well. She may be on the Legal Advisory Council of the Academic Freedom Alliance, but that seems not to require standing up to what she called her "ethnic Korean" community. So be it. Everyone must choose. Those of us with an interest in Japanese and Korean history might have preferred a freer environment for our research, but we are now on notice.

And then: Hannah Shepherd decided to encourage her Twitter audience to pile on to an attempted cancellation of a young (untenured) assistant professor at the Harvard Law School. The assistant professor had co-authored a study that argued the need for additional police. Never mind whether any of the Quintet knew anything about law-enforcement policy in the U.S. or anywhere else. For an assistant professor to suggest that some communities might need stronger police protection was beyond the pale. Another writer on Twitter had already started the attack on the assistant professor's career. Shepherd pitched in by finding and posting the assistant professor's Harvard Law webpage. Paula Curtis, David Ambaras, Chelsea Szendi Schieder, and Sayaka Chatani all happily retweeted or "liked" the attacks.[4]

This is the group that forced *The Diplomat* to censor the Korean economist Lee Wooyoun; that joined the Red Guard–like assault on Jim Sweet, president of the American Historical Association; that reflexively dismisses the Heterodox Academy as "racist"; that refuses invitations to debate the comfort women issue. Tell us: are Ramseyer, Sweet, and this assistant professor the only scholars whose careers you've tried to end? Whose lives you've (effectively) tried to destroy? Whose families you've (effectively) tried to purge with them? No, we don't exaggerate. We mean exactly what we said: careers, lives, and families. Don't pretend you didn't realize that ostracism reaches so deeply into a person's core. Don't pretend you didn't know it threatens a victim's family too. Of course it does. This is how ostracism works. This is how it has always worked.

So: were these the only scholars you targeted? Or were there others in between, as Richard Blaine famously put it. Or aren't you the kind that tells?

We pause for a final brief quiz. For extra credit, identify the sender of this "anonymous" email.

> I have just come across the publication of your new garbage.... You describe the comfort women, the victims of the most serious human rights violations in the 20th century as "prostitutes."... Yes you both are selling your academic integrity (if any), humanity, and even your mental sanity to gain popularity and support from the equally sick people like both of you and to escape from the shame of admitting that Japan, the country you both dearly love, indeed committed the worst war crime

> in human history. Imagine your own mother, wife, and daughter—If you have any care for them—being dragged to the war zone as comfort women. . . .

The email arrived in both of our in-boxes in late May 2023. Sellers post announcements of forthcoming books several months before publication. That is what enabled the friends of Stanley's "woke cancel mob" to kill the publication of Ramseyer's book on discrimination. By the spring of 2023, the announcements of the book that you are just finishing were out, and the mob was beginning to learn of it.

So guess the sender, dear reader. Who would refer to "your own mother, wife, and daughter"? Who can muster this virulent a level of raw hatred toward Japan: "worst war crime in human history"? Really? Hitler? Stalin? Mao? The destruction of the planet Alderaan? More generally, who in these circles does the best Darth Vader imitation—release your anger, for anger leads to hatred, and hatred leads to the dark side of the Force? Luke, you have only begun to discover your power. Join me, and I will complete your training. And so forth and so on. Our cancellation taught us many things, and many things we did not want to learn. But one of those things—epitomized by this sender—was the Vaderesque level of anti-Japanese hatred on which North Korea and its allies in the South Korean Left depend, and how relentlessly they foment that hatred to their private and political (and professional) advantage.

Living through a canceling is a bit like waking up to find that the Sorting Hat has re-sorted your world into Slytherin. Given all this, a little sense of humor goes a long way—and for providing opportunities we once again thank Amy Stanley, "possibly the most prominent of R's *critics*" (her words, but why does she do this?).[5] In March 2023, she wrote that her "dream project is a Journal of Unintentionally Revealing Email where people submit examples of the genre and I publish them with light redactions and zero commentary."[6] Indeed—a lovely use of her talents. We look forward to subscribing (with Reischauer funds). In truth, of course, she and her Quintet colleagues have already, and ever-so-generously, enabled us to offer you a volume that perhaps we should have subtitled "The Book of Unintentionally Revealing Tweets."

Revealing, but also a bit confusing—sometimes even you-have-just-crossed-over-into-the-Twilight-Zone confusing. In early 2022, Stanley said to a reporter, "Scholars need to be on Twitter to promote their work and engage in scholarly discussions."[7] Well, yes, scholarly discussion—but as C3PO put it, "let the Wookie win." A year later, Stanley flatly declared an end to open discussion anyway. Henceforth, she declared, she would respond only to those who would not accuse her of being "woke" or of "calling out" Ramseyer. She explained: "I decided it wasn't worth talking to someone who doesn't understand that this isn't actually an issue of 'wokeness' or 'calling out.'"[8]

The early days of the anti-Ramseyer crusade seem to have been happier days for Stanley. Recall that back in early 2021 she had almost sounded euphoric (if a bit overwhelmed by the work). "I always thought joining a woke cancel mob would be easy and fun," she had mused.[9] And, "I did not think—when I decided to be a historian of early modern Japan—that it would be so thrilling and high-stakes and full of heart-pounding adrenaline and panic."[10] When a friend called her an "academic assassin," she returned a smiley face wearing dark glasses.[11]

A persistent theme in Stanley's Twitter-verse has been her shock upon finding that not everyone defers to her authority. One of her correspondents recalled an exchange with Stanley in the fall of 2021, by which time this person had taken to calling her "that woman again," and "the one who can't debate" with people.[12] The correspondent explained that when he (or she) referred to Stanley's happy tweet about "joining a woke cancel mob," she had insisted that "she was joking"—and insisted so adamantly (remember: let the Wookie win) that she "almost smashed my [i.e., the correspondent's] iPhone." And it was "an iPhone that I still owe money on."[13]

Well, we shall take a deep breath. The lady certainly doth protest quite a lot. Sounds almost like "denialism."

Play it, Stanley. We gather you'd like to think of yourself as Victor Laszlo leading the band in "La Marseillaise," but at least do a Woody Allen reprise. Borrow a trench coat, stand in the rain, and give the tarmac speech (again). Remember Marx as you recite it: history repeats itself, first as tragedy and second as farce—and we are solidly into Take Two.

Recall that months into coordinating a campaign to smother the journals with "polite requests to retract articles" (her words—no redactions or commentary from us),[14] Stanley announced that she would study the comfort women herself. In early 2023, she told her Twitter audience that she was enjoying her time at a cafe editing a draft of a new article.[15] Yes, very touching. And J.K. wrote her first book in a cafe too.

In the course of researching that article, she wrote, she found that at least some of the women involved in the system seem to have worked under contract. They had not been dragooned or conscripted. They had been recruited straightforwardly for "comfort service." And they had been paid large amounts upfront.[16]

Huh? Let us paraphrase Hannah Shepherd's exclamation from the early days of the dispute: "We don't really know where to start with this. A chaired professor of history at Northwestern is arguing that comfort women were prostitutes." Once upon a time, this chaired professor had declared:

> So I really couldn't care less whether the Japanese army kidnapped virgins at the point of a sword or whether they recruited women with promises of a job in a canteen. Or even whether

> they solicited volunteers. You don't bring women to a war zone and gang rape them. Period.[17]

And here is what Stanley had once declared beyond the pale:

> [Ramseyer] asserts that the Korean women confined in the Japanese military comfort stations were prostitutes held to standard contractual arrangements in which they were paid large sums of money upfront for their service.[18]

When Lee Wooyoun tried to make exactly these points in *The Diplomat,* Stanley called it "a good example of how fake history gets laundered into mainstream outlets." It was, she continued, "a good example of how epistemic injustice works. Women's testimony is not 'objective evidence' but the documents issued by a fascist state, read *extremely* generously and without any sort of context, are 'objective evidence.'"[19]

But she was misinformed, apparently. Or perhaps "uninformed." The five were upfront on Twitter (but not in their public attack) about the fact that they wrote their cite-check attack without having studied anything about the comfort women—without, in other words, learning "any sort of context."[20] This spared Stanley from having to choose which of Lee Yong-soo's twenty different testimonials (see Table 5.1) she wanted to anoint as the "objective evidence." Instead, when told early in the dispute that Lee had said that "Ramseyer was 'maybe actually a blessing in disguise,' because, thanks to him, there is suddenly more interest in the history of comfort women,'" Stanley replied, "I am actually in tears."[21]

Stanley now focused on the U.S. Army's POW Interrogation Report No. 49 (discussed in Chapter 7). This being an American document, it spared her from having to read "documents issued by a fascist state" (never mind the endless—to our knowledge, never settled—debates among professional historians in Japan about whether the country was ever properly "fascist"). This report, as we noted, is well known to anyone working on the history of the comfort women.

Stanley shared part of her draft article on Twitter in February 2023 (no, we don't know why she would do this either, but at this point who's asking?).[22] She writes that "the twenty 'comfort girls' apprehended in Myitkyina" had begun their "journey to Burma...in spring of 1942...." They had been recruited by a "Japanese couple, Kitamura Eibun and Tomiko," who "had previously owned a restaurant in Seoul...." Stanley continues:

> They were typical of the people the army recruited. By 1942, the domestic Korean economy, particularly the service economy, had been decimated by wartime austerity measures. People who operated restaurants, bars, and brothels, in particular, found their income drastically reduced.... On receiving their commission, the Kitamuras went out to recruit young women for jobs in "comfort service" in Singapore, an alluring modern city. They offered poor families between 300 and 1000 yen for their daughters. To parents, this sum...was between several months and two years [income—the rest of the sentence is missing].[23]

And no, she does not seem to have any actual contracts.

We hope Stanley realizes that the Kitamuras may have been Korean. At the time, Koreans sometimes went by Japanese names, and the Korean writer Bae Yeonhong concludes that Eibun was probably Korean.[24] We do wonder about Stanley's use of the term "commission." From our own reading of the historical materials, we are not aware that any recruiters held army "commissions." Stanley describes these "recruiters" as "subcontractors" to the army. Given that most comfort stations were privately owned, we wonder whether the term "subcontractor" might be inapposite. She identifies the "parents" as the actors. Read a bit more history and she might find that some of the young women sometimes took this money for themselves.

Stanley posted only one page of her draft. Perhaps in a later page she will disown all of this. We heard informally that she claimed at a workshop presentation that comfort women testimonials should trump contemporaneous written records. If this is true, then we look forward to learning *why*—why should retrospective oral accounts by people demanding financial compensation trump contemporaneous records? (Epistemic social justice?) We also look forward to learning *which*—which of Lee Yong-soo's twenty different testimonials are we to credit?

A few weeks later, in mid-March 2023, Stanley and Shepherd announced on Twitter that they had obtained a contract from Columbia University Press to translate Mun Ok-ju's memoir-biography. We wish them well. We hope they add detail that the Quintet kept out of their 2021 attack on Ramseyer: e.g., how Mun concluded her comfort station contract, obtained permission to return to Korea, bought a boat ticket, went to the harbor—and then decided to go back to the comfort station because (presumably) the money was so good. In 2021, the Quintet made much of the way that Mun claimed the Japanese army had forced her into the work. We trust that this time Stanley and Shepherd will also disclose that even their patron saint Yoshimi Yoshiaki does not believe this part of Mun's story.[25]

In any case, this is clearly an improvement. "Welcome back to the fight," per Victor Laszlo. Welcome back to the world of serious scholarship. Stanley will find it an ever-so-slightly different world, however, shaped in part by what she has done for the last two years. It is now a world in which a scholar takes serious risks if he or she decides that the comfort women worked under contracts paying them large amounts upfront.

Hang in there, Professor Stanley. Your Quintet's "thrilling" assassination, full of "heart-pounding adrenaline," helped unleash a massive number of Chewbacca wannabes with no inclination (and usually no ability) to do any serious scholarship on the subject. We doubt that your former professor Andrew Gordon will trouble you, though. You have no "actual contracts," but Gordon will pretend not to notice. Elsewhere, however, you will find that "an-enemy-of-Ramseyer-is-our-friend" will take you only so far. You would do well to keep your draft away from the Committee on Korean Studies of the Association for Asian Studies lest they blame you for the next murder of a Korean American. You could try running your article by Michael Chwe and Jeannie Suk-Gersen. For concluding that the comfort women took their jobs under contract for large upfront sums, perhaps Chwe could locate a few Nobel Prize winners willing to sign a petition in your honor. Who knows—Suk-Gersen might even profile you in the *New Yorker*. That would be fun to read.

Two years. It took two years to get this far. They were long years. She didn't count the days, said Ilsa Lund. But Richard Blaine did, and his description—melodramatic, to be sure—does a nice double of an academic canceling: A guy standing on a station platform in the rain with a comical look on his face, because his insides have been kicked out.

The "academic assassins" (no redactions from us) who canceled us found it "fun." We didn't. We would not wish our two years on anyone.

APPENDIX

INFORMATION ABOUT COMFORT WOMEN CONTRACTS

A. **"Naimu sho keiho kyoku, Shina toko fujo no toriatsukai ni kansuru ken" [Case Regarding the Treatment of the Passage of Women to China], February 18, 1938. In Suzuki Yuko et al., eds., *Nihon gun "ianfu" kankei shiryo shusei* [Collection of Documents Relating to the "Comfort Women" of the Japanese Military], vol. 1: 124–38. Tokyo: Akashi shoten, 2006.**

- Kobe brothel owner tries to recruit 500 women from Yamagata prefecture for north China comfort stations (part of a 2,500-women recruitment effort), ages 16–30, advances of 500–1,000 yen, maximum 2-year terms (p. 127).
- Kobe brothel owner tries to recruit 500 women from Gunma prefecture (part of a 3,000-women recruitment effort). First sample contract does not specify advance size or maximum term. Second sample contract specifies ages 16–30, advances of 500–1,000 yen, maximum 2-year terms (pp. 127–29).

- Miyagi governor reports Fukushima entrepreneur who recruited approximately 30 women to work at Shanghai comfort station, ages 20–35, advances of 600 yen, unspecified terms (p. 130).
- Ibaraki governor reports a Kobe brothel owner who recruited two women (already working as prostitutes) for Shanghai comfort station, one for an advance of 642 yen, and one for 691 yen. Sample contract (p. 131) included, but with maximum term and advance amount unspecified. A second sample contract (p. 132) also included, specifying ages 16–30, advances of 500–1,000 yen, and maximum 2-year terms (pp. 131–32).
- Wakayama governor reports recruitment effort involving 70 women for a Shanghai comfort station (part of a 3,000-women recruitment effort). Solicitation specified maximum advance of 800 yen. Additionally, the report discusses a 26-year-old who received 470 yen, and a 28-year-old who received 362 yen (pp. 134–35).
- With respect to all contracts for women from Japan, note the police order: All women traveling from Japan to north or central China to serve as prostitutes must bring their contract with them and apply in person at the police office for a permit. They must be told to return to Japan "upon the conclusion of their provisional contract" (p. 125). (Arima Tetsuo, a historian and specialist in government documents, explains that this directive would have applied to women traveling from Korea as well. Arima Tetsuo, *"Ianfu" ha mina goi keiyaku wo shiteita* [The "Comfort Women" Had All Agreed to Contracts] (Tokyo: WAC, 2021), chap. 11.)

B. SCAP. "Amenities in the Japanese Armed Forces," November 15, 1945. In Josei no tameno Ajia heiwa kokumin kikin, ed., *Seifu chosa: "Jugun ianfu" kankei shiryo shusei* [Government Investigation: Documents Relating to the "Military Comfort Women"], vol. 5: 137–66. Tokyo: Ryukei shosha, 1998.

- Report discusses a comfort station operator who "purchased 22 Korean girls, paying their families from 300 to 1,000 yen. . . ." The women were 19–31 years old and arrived in 1942 (p. 151).
- Report further notes: "Every 'comfort girl' was employed on the following contract conditions. She received 40 percent of her own gross takings and was provided with free passage, free food and free medical treatment" (p. 152).

C. U.S. Office of War Information, Japanese Prisoner of War Interrogation Report No. 49, October 1, 1944. In Josei no tameno Ajia heiwa kokumin kikin, ed., *Seifu chosa: "Jugun ianfu" kankei shiryo shusei* [Government Investigation: Documents Relating to the "Military Comfort Women"], vol. 5: 203–9. Tokyo: Ryukei shosha, 1998.

- This is an interrogation of 20 Korean comfort women found in Burma in 1944. The women had been recruited in 1942 through fraud, had received "an advance of a few hundred yen," and served maximum contractual terms of 6–12 months (p. 203). Yoshimi Yoshiaki (item H below, p. 95), states that they received advances of 300–1,000 yen.
- Report notes that about 800 women had been recruited through this effort (p. 204).
- Report notes that the army permitted "certain girls who had paid their debt" to return home (p. 205).

- Reports comfort-woman : comfort-station revenue split of 50:50 or 60:40, but also reports that comfort stations charged the women high prices for various goods (p. 205).

D. **"Fukuoka ken chiji, Shina tokosha ni taisuru mibun shomeisho hakkyu ni kansuru ken" [Case Regarding the Issuance of Identification Documents for People Traveling to China], December 15, 1937. In Josei no tameno Ajia heiwa kokumin kikin, ed., *Seifu chosa: "Jugun ianfu" kankei shiryo shusei* [Government Investigation: Documents Relating to the "Military Comfort Women"], vol. 1: 113–15. Tokyo: Ryukei shosha, 1997.**

- Document shows two prostitutes applying to travel in 1937 to a Shanghai comfort station—one for a 1-year term, and one for a 1¾-year term (p. 115).

E. **Park, Yu-ha. *Teikoku no ianfu* [Comfort Women of the Empire]. Tokyo: Asahi shimbun shuppan, 2014.**

- Park quotes a 1937 Korean newspaper article (p. 29): "Choi Jae-hyun (37) and his wife Lee Seong-Nyeo (24), from [address] conspired several days ago to entice Kim In-Sop's [address] second daughter Yohngoon (12) and sell her as a prostitute to a Chinese restaurant owner Chang Wookyeong at [address] for a 50-yen ransom [i.e., price]. He was caught by the police as he was drafting the contract, and is currently being stringently investigated."
- Park reproduces two 1944 Korean newspaper advertisements for comfort women (p. 33). One specifies women ages 18–30, with contractual details to be determined upon interview. The other specifies women ages 17–23, monthly income of at least 300 yen, and advances of up to 3,000 yen.

F. Senda, Kako. *Jugun ianfu* [Comfort Women of the Military]. Tokyo: Futaba sha, 1973.

- Reports being involved in the recruitment of over 100 women, both Korean and Japanese, for comfort women service from northern Kyushu (pp. 24–28). The advance was generally about 1,000 yen, and the women were free to leave when they had repaid the amount.
- Reports a recruiter from northern Kyushu who brought 20 women to serve as comfort women in Shanghai brothels in 1938 (pp. 60–62). The recruiter states (we find the claim implausible) that the women provided sexual services to the Japanese military personnel at the stations along the way, and by the time the train reached Shanghai they had repaid their 1,000-yen advance and were free.

G. Rhee, Younghoon. *Hannichi shuzoku shugi* [Anti-Japan Tribalism]. Tokyo: Bungei shunju, 2019.

- Reports a 22-year-old Korean woman sold by her father in 1937 to a Manchurian brothel for a 1,300-yen advance. She objected, and complained to the police (p. 251).
- The comfort women at a comfort station operated by a Korean in Burma in 1942 repaid their advances in 6 months (pp. 273–74).
- Reports a Rangoon comfort station from which 15 of the 20 comfort women completed their contractual obligations and went home to Korea in 1944. One of the comfort women had sent home 11,000 yen that year (pp. 275, 283, 320).

H. **Yoshimi, Yoshiaki. *Jugun ianfu* [Comfort Women of the Military]. Tokyo: Iwanami shoten, 1995.**

- Reports one Japanese woman who went to a Shanghai comfort station in early 1938 on an advance of 1,000 yen (pp. 88–89).
- Reports one Japanese woman who returned from prostitution in Saipan and Palau in 1939. She had repaid her advance, but then volunteered with several other women to go work in a Nanking comfort station (p. 89).
- Reports that a Japanese geisha went to work at a navy-operated comfort station in the Chuuk Islands in 1942 because the comfort station agreed to take on the nearly 4,000 yen she owed to her placement agency (*okiya*), on a 1½-year term (p. 89). See Hirota Kazuko (item Q below).

I. **Lee Wooyoun. "Chosenjin gyosha to keiyaku shi ianjo wo tenten to shita ianfu no shogen" [The Testimonial of a Comfort Woman Who Contracted with a Korean Member of the Industry and Moved from Comfort Station to Comfort Station]. *Yahoo News Japan*, March 7, 2021 (originally *JB Press*).**

- Sixteen-year-old Korean signs up for a 3-year term as a prostitute for an advance of 3,000 yen. Eventually, she consents to having her contract assigned to a comfort station. Date uncertain.

J. **Yamada, Seikichi. *Bukan heitan* [Wuhan Logistics]. Tokyo: Tosho shuppan, 1978.**

- Reports that Wuhan area comfort women (130 Japanese, 150 Koreans) in 1943–44 (by which time inflation was serious) had average advances of 6,000–7,000 yen, could repay 400–500 yen per month, and could repay their advances and return home after about 1½ years (pp. 77, 84).

- Revenue split for Wuhan area comfort stations was 60:40 comfort-station : comfort-woman for women with debt; it was 50:50 for those without debt.
- Reports one comfort woman from Osaka, age 20, with a 10,000-yen advance (p. 87).
- Reports a woman whose mother died when she was age 2 and whose father abandoned her, who then applied for work as a comfort woman and came to Wuhan (narrative notes that Korean recruiters often used other terms for the work), repaid the advance in 2 years, returned to Korea, and then signed up for another term in Wuhan (pp. 102–3).

K. **Nishino, Rumiko, et al. *"Ianfu" basshingu wo koete* [Beyond "Comfort Women" Bashing]. Tokyo: Otsuki shoten, 2013.**

- Reports accounts of Japanese prostitutes volunteering for comfort women service and repaying their advance in 1–2 years and then returning home (p. 37).
- Reports a Japanese 18-year-old who left to serve as a comfort woman in 1942; she returned in 1943, having repaid her 4,000-yen advance and saved an additional 10,000 yen (pp. 37, 53–54). Probably the same woman who went to the Chuuk Islands reported by Yoshimi (item H above), and also by Hirota (item Q below).
- Reports a Japanese geisha who received an advance of 2,300 yen to serve as a comfort woman on a 1-year contract (p. 37).
- Reports a Japanese prostitute who enlisted as a comfort woman for Shanghai on a 1,500-yen advance. She returned to Japan 2 years later and opened a restaurant

(pp. 37–38). She reports that the comfort women in Shanghai repaid their advances in 1–3 months.

L. **Soh, C. Sarah. *The Comfort Women: Sexual Violence and Postcolonial Memory in Korea and Japan.* Chicago: University of Chicago Press, 2008.**
   - Confirms that the "lived experience of some Korean comfort women" mirrors the contractual structure under which licensed Japanese prostitutes worked, including large upfront advances, maximum terms, and the ability to quit earlier by repaying the debt (p. 114).

M. **Hata, Ikuhiko. *Ianfu to senjo no sei* [Comfort Women and Sex in the Battle Zone]. Tokyo: Shincho sensho, 1999.**
   - Reports a Tokyo brothel owner who recruited 52 women in 1937 for Shanghai at the request of the army, at a total cost of 50,000 yen. The women repaid their loans in 1–3 months (p. 76).
   - Reports a woman who volunteered to work as a comfort woman on Chuuk Islands repaid her 4,000-yen advance in 2 years (p. 224). Possibly the same woman reported by Yoshimi (item H above).
   - Reports Korean owner of a comfort station in China noted that the women tended to repay their advances of 300–500 yen in 1–2 years; after they had saved additional money, they tended to marry or return home; hiring their replacements was one of his biggest problems (pp. 382–83).

N. **Hosoya, Kiyoshi. *Nihon gunjin ga shogen suru senjo no hana: Chosenjin ianfu* [The Flowers of War, Reported by Japanese Soldiers: Korean Comfort Women]. Tokyo: Haato shuppan, 2019.**

- Former Manchukuo police officer reports the comfort woman : comfort station revenue split as 40:60; reports claims that debt grew, and describes the role of the police as stopping such schemes; reports that all Korean comfort women had formerly worked as prostitutes in Korea (account concerns mostly Korean comfort women with some Japanese) (pp. 42–43).
- Former naval officer (1940s) reports that women were recruited on advances of 4,000–5,000 yen for a 1-year contractual term; most of the women were able to repay their advances in 6 months, but some within 3 months; further reports that women were able to save 5,000–10,000 yen (p. 140).
- Reports 50:50 split in Philippine comfort stations (p. 145).
- Reports 40:60 or 30:70 comfort woman : comfort station split (location unclear; p. 172).

O. Hasegawa, Shin. *Ikiteiru shosetsu* [A Living Novel]. 1958. Reprint, Tokyo: Chuo koron, 1990. (NB: notwithstanding the title, this is a memoir rather than a novel.)

- Account of a comfort station on an island off south China: reports one woman who caused so much trouble in the comfort station that the owner paid her additional money and sent her home to Taiwan (pp. 103–4); reports shipowner stating that the women who arrived at the island had been tricked (p. 106).
- Reports advances at the island comfort station (in 1938) ranging from 500–600 yen to 1,200–1,300 yen (women from Taiwan). Reports that women preferred dealing with nonofficers at 2 yen rather than with officers at 5 yen because the greater volume enabled them to earn more money.

- Reports a case where a physician discovered that a new recruit was a virgin; officers pooled their savings, repaid her advance, and negotiated her immediate return (pp. 107–9).

P. **Nakazawa, Ken'ichi. *Kanko ianjo* [The Hankou Comfort Stations]. Tokyo: Tosho shuppan sha, 1983.**

- Reports a revenue split for comfort women of 60:40 brothel : prostitute for women with loans, and 50:50 for women who had repaid their loans (p. 64).
- Reports one woman arriving from Korea in September 1944 who complained that she had been promised work other than prostitution. The military officer in charge of the area comfort stations ordered that she be given appropriate alternative work (p. 221).

Q. **Hirota, Kazuko. *Shogen kiroku: Jugun ianfu, kangofu* [Records of Testimonials: Military Comfort Women and Nurses]. Tokyo: Shin jinbutsu orai sha, 1975.**

- Reports Kikumaru at age 18, over the opposition of her father, signed on as a comfort woman for officers and went to Chuuk Islands in 1942. She had been a geisha, and the recruiter agreed to take on her 4,000-yen debt, for a 1½-year contract. Split of revenue was 60 to navy (this was a directly operated comfort station), 40 to her. When she returned home in 1943, she had repaid the 4,000 yen and saved another 10,000 yen (pp. 18–19, 24). After the war ended, Kikumaru invested her savings in her own unlicensed brothel and hired four women; she lost her money when the women she had hired ran away (pp. 89–90).
- Reports Suzuki Fumi, age 18, signed on as a comfort woman for the rank-and-file sailors and went to Chuuk

Islands in 1942. Like Kikumaru, she had been a geisha. She returned to Japan in 1943, having repaid her 2,300-yen advance, and (like Kikumaru) saved another 10,000 yen (pp. 42–43, 69).

- Reports that approximately 40 women came from Osaka and Kobe to work as comfort women in Chuuk Islands; they all repaid their debts quickly (p. 44).
- Reports a geisha from the Kansai area who came to Chuuk Islands to work as a comfort woman; she repaid her 500-yen advance in 3 months (p. 52).
- Reports that some women who came to Chuuk Islands were surprised by their job, but writes that they were sent home (p. 53).

BIBLIOGRAPHY

Ahn, J.H. 2017. "S. Korean Lawyers to Again Request Meeting with 12 Restaurant-worker Defectors." *NK News*, June 19, 2017. https://www.nknews.org/2017/06/s-korean-lawyers-to-again-request-meeting-with-12-restaurant-worker-defectors/.

Akaishi, Shin'ichiro. 2019. "Besuto seraa 'Hannichi shuzoku shugi' e no hanpatsu" [The Reaction to the Best-selling "Anti-Japanese Tribalism"]. *Bunshun online*, November 28, 2019. https://bunshun.jp/articles/-/15838.

Akaishi, Shin'ichiro. 2020a. "Firipin no ianfu mondai" [The Comfort Women Issue in the Philippines]. *Bunshun online*, June 29, 2020. https://bunshun.jp/articles/-/38632.

Akaishi, Shin'ichiro. 2020b. "Moto ianfu shien 30 nen" [The Thirty Years of Support for the Former Comfort Women]. *Bunshun online*, June 4, 2020. https://bunshun.jp/articles/-/38178.

Akaishi, Shin'ichiro. 2020c. "'Okane wo ageru kara ...'" ["We'll Pay You Money so ..."]. *Bunshun online*, June 16, 2020. https://bunshun.jp/articles/-/38366.

Amos, Timothy, Maren Ehlers, Anne McKnight, David Ambaras & Ian Neary. 2021. "Doing Violence to Buraku History: J. Mark Ramseyer's Dangerous Inventions," *Asia-Pacific Journal: Japan Focus* 19, no. 9 (May 1, 2021).

Ando, Yoshio. 1987. *Kindai Nihon keizai shi yoran* [Overview of Early Modern Japanese Economic History]. 2nd ed. Tokyo: University of Tokyo Press.

Arima, Tetsuo. 2017. *Koshite rekishi mondai ha netsuzo sareru* [This Is How Historical Problems Are Faked]. Tokyo: Shincho sha.

Arima, Tetsuo. 2021a. "Harvard dai 'Ianfu' ronbun wo hihan suru Kankokukei kyoju no rojikkuha goin deha naika" [The Logic of the Ethnic Korean Professor Criticizing the Harvard "Comfort Women" Article Is Forced]. *Daily shincho*, April 13, 2021 (parts 1 & 2).

Arima, Tetsuo. 2021b. *"Ianfu" ha mina goi keiyakuwo shiteita* [The "Comfort Women" Had All Agreed to Contracts]. Tokyo: WAC.

Arima, Tetsuo. 2021c. "Ramseyer kyoju 'ianfu ronbun' wo hihan suru Harvard daigaku kyoju ha bunken wo yomete inainodeha naika" [The Harvard Professors Criticizing Prof. Ramseyer's "Comfort Women Article" Seem Unable to Read the Documents]. *Daily shincho*, April 5, 2021 (part 1) and April 6, 2021 (part 2).

Arirang News Center. "Harvard Law Professor's 'Comfort Women' Article: Fellow Scholars Call It 'Fake News.'" February 16, 2021. https://www.youtube.com/watch?v=fxixpFncCeg.

"Asahi shimbun moto kisha" [Former Reporter for *Asahi shimbun*]. Zakzak, August 5, 2014.

Bak, Sunjong. 2023. "Comfort Women Agitators as Agents of the North." *JAPAN Forward*, February 17, 2023. https://japan-forward.com/comfort-women-agitators-as-agents-of-the-north/.

Bauerlein, Mark. 2022. "Why Is Princeton Silent?" *American Greatness*, June 6, 2022.

Burgis, Luke. "Why Everyone Wants the Same Things." *Common Sense with Bari Weiss*, November 28, 2022.

Bentley, Jerry H., & Herbert F. Ziegler. 2011. *Traditions and Encounters*. 5th ed. New York: McGraw-Hill.

Center for Korean Legal Studies, Columbia Law School. "Lawsuits brought against Japan by former Korean 'Comfort Women.'" n.d. https://kls.law.columbia.edu/content/lawsuits-brought-against-japan-former-korean-comfort-women.

Chatani, Sayaka. 2021. "Ramseyer ronbun ha naze 'jiken' to natta no ka" [Why Did the Ramseyer Article Turn Into an "Incident"?]. *Sekai*, May 2021.

Chatani, Sayaka. 2023. "How to Address the Racism at the Heart of Japan–South Korea Tensions." Sayaka Chatani blog, January 25, 2023. https://www.sayakachatani.com/post/how-to-address-the-racism-at-the-heart-of-japan-south-korea-tensions.

Choe, Kilsung, 2017. *Chosen shusshin no choba nin ga mita ianfu no jijitsu* [The Truth about Comfort Women, As Seen by a Korean Receptionist]. Tokyo: Haato shuppan.

Choe, Kilsung. 2021a. "'Ianjo nikki' kenkyusha ga akasu 'kyosei renko' to ha kakehanareta jittai" [Research of "Comfort Station Diary" Shows Reality Far Different from "Forced Conscription"]. *Daily shincho*, June 14, 2021.

Choe, Kilsung. 2021b. "Genshiryo ha watashino 'ianjo nikki' kenkyu" [The Original Source Was My Research on the "Comfort Station Diary"]. *Shukan shincho*, June 10, 2021.

Choe, Sang-Hun. 2015. "Japan and South Korea Settle Dispute Over Wartime 'Comfort Women.'" *New York Times*, December 28, 2015.

Choe, Sang-Hun. 2017. "Deal with Japan on Former Sex Slaves Failed Victims, South Korean Panel Says." *New York Times*, December 27, 2017.

Choe, Sang-Hun. 2018. "South Korean Court Orders Mitsubishi of Japan to Pay for Forced Wartime Labor." *New York Times*, November 29, 2018.

Choe, Sang-Hun. 2019. "Ex-Chief Justice of South Korea Is Arrested on Case-Rigging Charges." *New York Times*, January 23, 2019.

Choe, Sang-Hun, & Rick Gladstone. 2018. "How a World War II–Era Reparations Case Is Roiling Asia." *New York Times*, October 30, 2018.

"Chosen no josei, watashi mo renko" [I Too Dragooned Korean Women]. *Asahi shimbun*, September 2, 1982.

"Chosen no rodosha" [Korean workers], March 10, 1945. Reprinted in Suzuki Yuko et al., eds., *Nihon gun "ianfu" kankei shiryo shusei* [Collection of Documents Relating to the "Comfort Women" of the Japanese Military]. Tokyo: Akashi shoten, 2006, 2:563.

Chosen sotokufu tokei nempo. "Zaicho kanren gyosha" [Related Industry Parties in Korea], 1906–1942. Reprinted in Suzuki et al. (2006).

Chosen sotokufu [Governor-General of Korea]. 1935. *Chosen kokusei chosa hokoku* [Report of Korean Vital Statistics] (Chosen sotoku fu).

Chosen sotokufu [Governor-General of Korea]. 1944. "Kokumin choyo no kaisetsu" [Commentary on Citizen Mobilization], October 1944. Reprinted in Suzuki et al. (2006), 2:597.

Chuo shokugyo shokai jimukyoku. 1926. "Geishogi shakufu shokaigyo ni kansuru chosa" [An Investigation into the Placement Industry for Geisha, Prostitutes, and

Barmaids], 1926. Reprinted in Taniguchi Ken'ichi, ed., *Kindai minshu no kiroku* [A Report of the Modern Populace] (Shin jinbutsu orai sha), 3:412.

Chwe, Michael. 2021. Letter by Concerned Economists Regarding "Contracting for Sex in the Pacific War" in the International Review of Law and Economics. http://chwe.net/irle/letter/.

Comfort Women Justice Coalition. "Women's March, #MeToo and the 'Comfort Women'—All Fighting for Justice in 2018." January 22, 2018. https://remember-comfortwomen.org/womens-march-metoo-and-the-comfort-women-all-fighting-for-justice-in-2018/.

Coomaraswamy, Radhika. 1996. See UN Commission on Human Rights. 1996.

Coronel, Sheila, Steve Coll & Derek Kravitz. 2015. "Rolling Stone and UVA: The Columbia University Graduate School of Journalism Report." *Rolling Stone*, April 5, 2015.

Curtis, Paula R. 2021a. "Ramseyer and the Right-Wing Ecosystem Suffocating Japan." *Tokyo Review*, May 30, 2021.

Curtis, Paula R. 2021b. "Taking the Fight for Japan's History Online: The Ramseyer Controversy and Social Media." *Asia-Pacific Journal: Japan Focus* 22, no. 3 (December 1, 2021).

"Dappokusha ni kikoku susumeru ..." [Encouraging Refugees from the North to Return ...]. *Asahi shimbun*, May 23, 2020.

deBoer, Freddie. 2021. "That One Side Would Like to Utterly Destroy the Other Side Seems Significant, To Me." Freddie deBoer Substack, October 11, 2021. https://freddiedeboer.substack.com/p/that-one-side-would-like-to-utterly.

Devine, Maija Rhee. 2016. "Are Comfort Women Lying?" *Korea Times*, June 8, 2016. http://www.koreatimes.co.kr/www/news/opinon/2016/06/162_206538.html.

Digital Museum. The Comfort Women Issue and the Asian Women's Fund. n.d. http://www.awf.or.jp/e2/foundation.html.

Doke, Saiichiro. 1928. *Baishunfu ronko* [Studies in Prostitution]. Shishi shuppan. Reprinted in Suzuki et al. (2006), 1:786–820.

Dokuritsuzan hotei. "Jinchu nisshi" [Field Diary], April 1941. Reprinted in Josei no tameno Ajia heiwa kokumin kikin, ed., *Seifu chosa: "Jugun ianfu" kankei shiryo shusei* [Government Investigation: Documents Relating to the "Military Comfort Women"] (Tokyo: 1997–98), 4:377.

Dolgopol, Ustinia, & Snehal Paranjape. 1994. *Comfort Women: An Unfinished Ordeal*. Geneva: International Commission of Jurists.

Dudden, Alexis. 2008. Troubled Apologies Among Japan, Korea, and the United States. New York: Columbia University Press.

Dudden, Alexis, et al. 2015a. "Standing with Historians of Japan." *Perspectives on History*, March 1, 2015.

Dudden, Alexis, et al. 2015b. "Response to Naoko Kumagai (Sept. 2015)." *Perspectives on History*, December 1, 2015.

Dudden, Alexis. 2015c. "Learning from Past Best Way to Move Forward." *Japan Times*, December 26, 2015.

Dudden, Alexis. 2017. "Letter Campaigns, the Japanese Media, and the Effort to Censor History." In *Press Freedom in Contemporary Japan*, edited by Jeff Kingston. Oxon: Routledge, 2017.

Dudden, Alexis. 2019. "Japan's Rising Sun Flag Has a History of Horror. It Must Be Banned at the Tokyo Olympics." *Guardian*, November 1, 2019.

Dudden, Alexis. 2021. "The Abuse of History: A Brief Response to J. Mark Ramseyer's 'Contracting for Sex.'" *Asia-Pacific Journal: Japan Focus* 19, iss. 5, no. 15 (March 1, 2021).

Eckert, Carter J. 1996. "Total War, Industrialization, and Social Change in Late Colonial Korea." In *The Japanese Wartime Empire, 1931–1945*, edited by Peter Duus, Ramon H. Myers & Mark R. Peattie. Princeton: Princeton University Press.

Erdely, Sabrina Rubin. 2014. "A Rape on Campus: A Brutal Assault and Struggle for Justice at UVA." *Rolling Stone*, November 19, 2014. Archived at http://web.archive.org/web/20141119200349/http:/www.rollingstone.com/culture/features/a-rape-on-campus-20141119.

Fackler, Martin. 2007. "No Apology for Sex Slavery, Japan's Prime Minister Says." *New York Times*, March 6, 2007.

Fackler, Martin. 2014a. "Japan, Seeking Revision of Report on Wartime Brothels, Is Rebuffed." *New York Times*, October 16, 2014.

Fackler, Martin. 2014b. "Rewriting the War, Japanese Right Attacks a Newspaper." *New York Times*, December 2, 2014.

Fujinaga, Takeshi. 1998. "Nichiro senso to Nihon ni yoru 'Manshu' e no kosho seido ishoku" [The Russo-Japanese War and the Transplantation of the Licensed Prostitution System by Japan to "Manchuria"]. In *Kairaku to kisei* [Recreation and Regulation], edited by Katsurakawa Mitsumasa. (Osaka sangyo daigaku sangyo kenkyujo).

Fujinaga, Takeshi. 2000. "Chosen shokuminchi shihai to 'ianfu' seido no seiritsu katei" [Control over the Korean Colony and the Establishment Process of the "Comfort Women" System]. In *"Ianfu" senji seiboryoku no jittai*, I [The Reality of the "Comfort Women" and Sexual Violence in Wartime, I], edited by VAWW-NET (Ryokufu shuppan).

Fujinaga, Takeshi. 2001. "Shokuminchi Taiwan ni okeru Chosenjin sekkyakugyo to 'ianfu' no doin" [The Korean Entertainment Industry in Colonial Taiwan and the Mobilization of the "Comfort Women"]. In *Kindai shakai to baishun mondai* [Early Modern Society and the Prostitution Problem], edited by Katsurakawa Mitsumasa et al. (Osaka sangyo daigaku sangyo kenkyu jo).

Fujinaga, Takeshi. 2004. "Shokuminchi kosho seido to Chosenjin josei" [The Colonial Licensed Prostitution System and Korean Women]. In Niccho yuko sokushin, *Nihon to Chosen no kankei shi* [History of the Relations between Japan and Korea]. Agenda Project.

Fujioka, Nobukatsu. 2015. "Obei gakusha seimei ni igi: 'Mochiage' ha ianfu de shazai saseru wanaka" [Objection to the Declaration of Western Scholars: Is the "Raising [of the Issue]" a Trap to Induce an Apology over the Comfort Women]. Yukan Fuji, May 23, 2015. http://www.zakzak.co.jp/society/domestic/news/20150523/dms1505231530004-n1.htm.

Fukumi, Takao. 1928. *Teito ni okeru bai'in no kenkyu* [A Study of Prostitution in the Capital]. Tokyo: Hakubunkan.

Gluck, Carol. 2007. "Operations of Memory: 'Comfort Women' and the World." In *Ruptured Histories: War, Memory and the Post–Cold War in Asia*, edited by Sheila Miyoshi Jager & Rana Mitter. Cambridge, MA: Harvard University Press.

Gluck, Carol. 2021. "What the World Owes the Comfort Women." In *Mnemonic Solidarity: Global Interventions*. Entangled Memories in the Global South, edited by J. H. Lim & E. Rosenhaft. London: Palgrave Macmillan.

Gordon, Andrew. 2014. *A Modern History of Japan: From Tokugawa Times to the Present.* 3rd ed. New York: Oxford University Press.

Gordon, Andrew. 2020. *A Modern History of Japan: From Tokugawa Times to the Present.* 4th ed. New York: Oxford University Press.

Gordon, Andrew, & Carter Eckert. Statement, February 17, 2021. https://perma.cc/8ZHY-RD5C.

"Gun'ianjo jugyofuto boshu ni kansuru ken" [Regarding Military Comfort Women and Their Recruitment 1942.]. Army Ministry Infantry Bureau Proposal, to North and Middle China Forces, March 4, 1938. Riku shimitsu No. 745, vol. 10, 1938. Reprinted in Josei (1997), 2:5.

"Gunji hyoronka no Ji Man-won" [The Military Commentator Ji Man-won], September 29, 2013. https://s.webry.info/sp/92971510.at.webry.info/201309/article_88.html.

"Gunjin kyuyo" [Military Pay], 1945. http://tingin.jp/kyuyo_shi/gunjin-kyuyo.html.

Gunsei kanbu bisaya shibu [Military Administration Executive Staff, Visaya (Philippines) Outpost]. "Ianjo kitei sofu no ken" [Regarding Transmittal of Comfort Station Regulations], November 22, 1942. Reprinted in Josei (1997), 3:187.

"Hakken no gyosha gappei" [Eight Mergers of Firms]. *Keijo nippo,* November 30, 1943. Reprinted in Suzuki et al. (2006), 2:579.

"'Hannichi' no kamen wo kabutta moto ianfu shien dantai" [The Former Comfort Women Support Organization Wearing an "Anti-Japanese" Mask], March 22, 2014. http://blog.livedoor.jp/aryasarasvati/archives/37077764.html.

"Hanto no kinro doin taisei" [Labor Mobilization System on the Peninsula]. *Keijo nippo,* August 27, 1944. Reprinted in Suzuki et al. (2006), 2:595.

Hasegawa, Shin. 1958. *Ikiteiru shosetsu* [A Living Novel]. Reprint, Tokyo: Chuo koron, 1990.

Hata, Ikuhiko. 1992. "Showa shi no nazo wo tou" [Investigating the Puzzle of Showa History]. *Seiron,* June 1992.

Hata, Ikuhiko. 1999. *Ianfu to senjo no sei* [Comfort Women and Sex in the Battle Zone]. Tokyo: Shincho sensho.

Hata, Ikuhiko. 2018. *Comfort Women and Sex in the Battle Zone.* Translated by Jason Michael Morgan. Lanham, MD: Hamilton Books.

"Hatarakeru onna no hitoha hitori nokorazu hatarako" [Women Able to Work Should All Work]. *Mainichi shimpo,* September 23, 1943. Reprinted in Suzuki et al. (2006), 2:568.

Hicks, George. 1994. *The Comfort Women: Japan's Brutal Regime of Enforced Prostitution in the Second World War.* New York: Norton.

Hicks, George. 1996. The "Comfort Women." In *The Japanese Wartime Empire, 1931–1945,* edited by Peter Duus, Ramon H. Myers & Mark R. Peattie. Princeton: Princeton University Press.

Higuchi, Yuichi. 2005. "Soryokusen taisei to shokuminchi" [The Total War System and the Colonies]. In *Shokuminchi to senso sekinin* [The Colonies and War Responsibility], edited by Hayakawa Norio (Yoshikawa kobun kan).

Hirota, Kazuko. 1975. *Shogen kiroku: Jugun ianfu, kangofu* [Record of Testimonials: Military Comfort Women and Nurses]. Tokyo: Shin jinbutsu orai sha.

Hito gunsei kanbu. 1942. "Ianjo ... kitei sofu no ken" [Case Regarding the Transmittal of Comfort Station ... Rules], November 22, 1942. Reprinted in Suzuki et al. (2006), 1:383.

Hoang, Kimberly Kay. 2015. *Dealing in Desire: Asian Ascendancy, Western Decline, and the Hidden Currencies of Global Sex Work.* Oakland: University of California Press.

Horowitz, Mark, William Yaworsky & Kenneth Kickham. "Anthropology's Science Wars." *Current Anthropology* 60, no. 5 (October 2019).

Hosoya, Kiyoshi. 2019. *Nihon gunjin ga shogen suru senjo no hana: Chosenjin ianfu* [The Flowers of War, Reported by Japanese Soldiers: Korean Comfort Women]. Tokyo: Haato shuppan. (English translation at Mera & Hosoya, 2020.)

Howard, Keith, ed. 1995. *True Stories of the Korean Comfort Women.* London: Cassell.

"Ianfu ha jihatsuteki na baishun ga sekai no joshiki" [The Standard Wisdom Around the World Is That the Comfort Women Were Voluntary Prostitutes]. *Livedoor News,* March 24, 2018. http://news.livedoor.com/article/detail/14479996/.

"Ianfu hatsugen de monosawagi" [Trouble over Comfort Women Comments]. *Chosun online,* September 6, 2004. http://www.chosunonline.com/article/20040906000060.

"Ianfu mondai: Nikkan ayumi yori wo bogai suru ..." [The Comfort Women Problem: Blocking Rapprochement between S. Korea and Japan ...]. MSN Sankei Nyusu, September 23, 2012.

"Ianfu mondai wo meguru Nikkan kan no yaritori no keii" [The Course of the Exchanges between Japan and South Korea on the Comfort Women Problem]. *Asahi shimbun,* June 21, 2014.

"'Ianfu seidorei setsu' wo iidashita ..." [The First to Raise the "Comfort Women Were Sex Slaves Theory" ...]. *News Posuto,* August 15, 2012. https//www.news-postseven.com/archives/20120815_136788.html?DETAIL.

"Ianfu zo no seisakusha fufu ..." [The Couple Who Made the Comfort Women Statues ...]. *News Posuto Sebun,* March 7, 2017. https://www.news-postseven.com/archives/20170307_498048.html/2.

"Ianjo he no gun kanyo shimesu shiryo" [Documents Showing Military Involvement in the Comfort Stations]. *Asahi shimbun,* January 11, 1992.

"Ianjo jugyoin" [Comfort Station Workers]. *Mainichi shinbun,* August 7, 2013.

Ibaraki ken chiji [Governor of Ibaraki Prefecture]. 1938. "Shanhai haken gun nai rikugun ianjo ni okeru shakufu boshu ni kansuru ken" [Case Regarding the Recruitment of Barmaids for the Comfort Station Attached to the Army Stationed in Shanghai], February 14, 1938. Reprinted in Josei (1997), 1:47–52.

Ikeda, Nobuo. 2014. *Asahi shimbun: Seiki no dai goho* [The Asahi Newspaper: Fake News of the Century]. Tokyo: K.K. Asupekuto.

Imanishi, Hajime. 2017. "Kaihogo, Kankoku chishikijin no ayumi" [The Path of a South Korean Intellectual after Liberation] (Otaru shoka daigaku). *Shogaku token* 67 (2017): 244–45.

Ito, Hidekichi. 1931. *Kotoka no kanojo no seikatsu* [The Lives of Women under the Red Lights]. Tokyo: Jitsugyo no Nihon sha. Reprint, Tokyo: Funi shuppan, 1982.

Iwasaki, Tetsu. 2016. "Ianfu ni todomezu ..." [Not Stopping with the Comfort Women ...]. *Washington Times Japan,* January 11, 2016. https://vpoint.jp/media/all_media/58089.html.

"Ji Man-Won shi 'gi no ianfu'" [Mr. Ji Man-Won "Fraudulent Comfort Women"]. *Joong-Ang ilbo,* April 14, 2005. https://japanese.joins.com/article/j_article.php?aid=62513&sectcode=400&servcode=400.

"'Jitsuwa sono ki ga atte jugun shita'" ["They Followed the Army Because They Wanted To"]. *Joong-Ang ilbo,* September 18, 2018. https://japanese.joins.com/article/233/245233.htm.

"Jiyu ha ubawareta kyoseisei atta" [There Was Coercion in the Sense That Their Freedom Was Taken from Them]. *Asahi shimbun*, August 5, 2014.

Johnson, Jesse, & Magdalena Osumi. 2015. "Fifty Japanese Scholars Attack McGraw-Hill, U.S. Academics on 'Comfort Women' Issue." *Japan Times*, December 11, 2015.

Josei no tameno Ajia heiwa kokumin kikin, ed. *Seifu chosa: "Jugun ianfu" kankei shiryo shusei* [Government Investigation: Documents Relating to the "Military Comfort Women"]. 5 vols. Tokyo: Ryukei shosha, 1997–98.

"Kankoku ga Nihon no shinrai wo ushinatta ..." [South Korea Lost the Trust of Japan ...]. *Bunshun online*, May 14, 2022. https://www.jiji.com/jc/bunshun?id=54320.

"Kankoku gekishin ..." [Massive Shock in South Korea ...]. *Japan In-depth*, May 26, 2020.

"Kankoku, ianfu dantai ..." [South Korean Comfort Women Group ...]. *Daily shincho*, August 10, 2020. https://www.dailyshincho.jp/article/2020/08101145/?all=1.

"Kankoku no daigaku kyoju 'ianfu ha kyosei deha nai. Sono ki ga atta'" [Korean University Professor Says "Comfort Women Weren't Coerced. They Knew What They Were Doing"]. *Share News Japan*, November 16, 2018.

"Kankoku shakai ga wasureta saisho no ianfu shogensha" [Forgotten by South Korea, the First Comfort Woman to Give Testimonial]. *Hankyoreh Japan*, August 9, 2015. http://japan.hani.co.kr/arti/politics/21570.html.

Keijo [Seoul] nippo, June 12, 1918 (evening edition). Quoted in Fujinaga Takeshi, "Shokuminchi Chosen ni okeru kosho seido no kakuritsu katei" [The Establishment Process for the Licensed Prostitution System in Colonial Korea]. *Nijuseiki kenkyu*, December 2004.

Keishi cho. 2021. "Kitachosen ni yoru rachi yogi jian" [Cases with Suspicions of North Korean Abductions], September 21, 2021. https://www.keishicho.metro.tokyo.lg.jp/jiken_jiko/ichiran/ichiran_10/rachijian.html.

Keishi cho sokan kanbo bunsho ka. 1933. *Showa nana nen keishi cho tokei ichi ippan* [An Outline of Police Agency Statistics for 1932] (Sokan kanbo bunsho ka).

Kim, Ji-yu. 2020. "Pyonyan de hannichi wo sakenda ..." [Shouting Anti-Japanese in Pyongyang ...]. *Daily shincho*, June 23, 2020.

Kim, Pu-ja, & Yon Kim. 2018. *Shokuminchi yukaku* [Colonial Pleasure Quarters]. Tokyo: Yoshikawa kobunkan.

Kimura, Kan. 2014. *Nikkan rekishi ninshiki mondai toha nanika* [What Is the Japan-Korea Historical Awareness Problem?]. Tokyo: Mineruba shobo.

Kitashina haken jimukan [North China Outbound Affairs Office]. 1938. "Sainan yuki ryokaku no seigen" [The Limitation of Passengers Bound for Jinan], March 1, 1938. Reprinted in Suzuki et al. (2006), 1:143.

Kitashina homen gun shireibu [North China Area Military Command Post]. 1939. "Kyosanto to waga guntai ni taisuru ..." [Regarding the Communist Party and Our Military ...], April 5, 1939. Reprinted in Suzuki et al. (2006), 1:148.

Korea Institute of History. KIH 2016a. "'Comfort Women of the Empire' by Professor Park Yuha." April 30, 2016. http://scholarsinenglish.blogspot.com/2014/10/summary-of-professor-park-yuhas-book.html.

Korea Institute of History. KIH 2016b. "'Comfort Women of the Empire' Reviewed by Professor Jun Bong Gwan." April 21, 2016. http://scholarsinenglish.blogspot.com/2014/10/comfort-women-of-empire-reviewed-by.html.

Korea Institute of History. KIH 2016c. "Former Korean Comfort Woman Mun Okuchu's Memoir." April 20, 2016. http://scholarsinenglish.blogspot.com/2014/10/former-korean-comfort-woman-mun-oku.html.

Korea Institute of History. KIH 2016d. "Korean Comfort Station Manager's Diary," Analyzed by Professor Choe Kilsung. April 24, 2016. http://scholarsinenglish.blogspot.com/2016/04/korean-comfort-station-managers-diary.html.

Korea Institute of History. KIH 2016e. "'The Comfort Women' by Professor C. Sarah Soh." April 29, 2016. http://scholarsinenglish.blogspot.com/2014/10/the-comfort-women-by-chunghee-sarah-soh.html.

Kubota, Ruriko. 2020a. "Oshu de kita supai to renkei ..." [Collaboration with North (Korean) Spy in Western Europe ...]. *Sankei News*, May 30, 2020.

Kubota, Ruriko. 2020b. "Giwaku zokushutsu no Yoon Mee-hyang shi ..." [Doubts Grow over Yoon Mee-hyang ...]. *Sankei News*, May 23, 2020.

Kumagai, Naoko. 2015. "On 'Standing with Historians of Japan,'" *Perspectives on History*, September 1, 2015.

Kusama, Yasoo. 1930. *Jokyu to baishofu* [Waitresses and Prostitutes]. Tokyo: Hanjin sha.

Laney, James T., & Jason T. Shaplen. "How to Deal with North Korea." *Foreign Affairs* 82, no. 2 (March/April 2003): 16–30.

Lee, Dong-Jin. 2020. "Minzoku, chiiki, sekushuaritii: Manshukoku no Chosenjin 'seibaibai jujisha' wo chushin to shite" [Nation, Region, and Sexuality: The Case of Korean "Prostitution" in Manchukuo]. *Quadrante* 22 (2020): 39–62.

Lee, Tae-hee. 2018. "Professor Gets Prison for Insulting Comfort Women." *Korea Herald*, Novemer 15, 2018.

Lee, Wooyoun. 2021a. "Anti-Japan Tribalism on the Comfort Women Issue." *The Diplomat*, November 14, 2021. Censored under pressure from Ambaras, Stanley and Chatani. Archived at https://archive.ph/20211115071637/https://thediplomat.com/2021/11/anti-japan-tribalism-on-the-comfort-women-issue/#selection-1231.547-1231.1052.

Lee, Wooyoun. 2021b. "Chosenjin gyosha to keiyaku shi ianjo wo tenten to shita ianfu no shogen" [The Testimonial of a Comfort Woman Who Contracted with a Korean Member of the Industry and Moved from Comfort Station to Comfort Station]. *Yahoo News Japan*, March 7, 2021 (originally *JB Press*). Alternative translation: Lee Wooyoun. "Controversy over Harvard Article Can't Erase the Facts of Comfort Women Contracts." *JAPAN Forward*, April 3, 2021. https://japan-forward.com/bookmark-controversy-over-harvard-article-cant-erase-the-facts-of-comfort-women-contracts/.

Lee, Wooyoun. 2021c. "No Debate? The Diplomat's Cancellation of My Comfort Women Article." *JAPAN Forward*, December 4, 2021. https://japan-forward.com/no-debate-the-diplomats-cancellation-of-my-comfort-women-article/. Also archived at https://archive.ph/20211115071637/https://thediplomat.com/2021/11/anti-japan-tribalism-on-the-comfort-women-issue/.

Lee, Wooyoun. 2022. "Ramseyer's Paper, Criticism Against It, and Counter-Criticism For It." Naksungdae Institute of Economic Research, Working Paper 2022-02, January 2022. Published in *Japan Review*, Winter 2021: 37–54.

Lee, Yong-Shik, Natsu Taylor Saito & Jonathan Todres. 2021. "The Fallacy of Contract in Sexual Slavery: A Response to Ramseyer's 'Contracting for Sex in the Pacific War.'" *Michigan Journal of International Law* 42, no. 2 (2021): 291–319.

Lew, Seok-choon. 2022. "Hensen wo kasaneta 'Ianfu shogen' no uragawa" [What Lies behind the "Comfort Women Testimonials" That Have Changed Multiple Times]. *Shukan shincho*, June 2, 2022: 44–48.

Low, Morris. 2003. "The Emperor's Sons Go to War: Competing Masculinities in Modern Japan." In *Asian Masculinities: The Meaning and Practice of Manhood in China and Japan*, edited by Kam Louie & Morris Low. Oxon: RoutledgeCurzon.

Mainichi shimbun, February 26, 1944. Reprinted in Suzuki et al. (2006), 2:562.

Mandaree chutonchi shireibu [Mandalay Garrison Command Post]. 1943. "Chuteichi ianjo kitei" [Comfort Station Regulations in Occupied Areas], May 26, 1943. Reprinted in Josei (1997), 4:288.

Maree gunseikan [Malaysia Military Administration]. 1943. "Ianjo shisetsu" [Comfort Facilities], November 11, 1943. Reprinted in Suzuki et al. (2006), 1:433.

Martin, Timothy W., & Dasl Yoon. 2021. "Professor's 'Comfort-Women' Lecture Gets Him Indicted—And Sparks Debate on Academic Freedom." *Wall Street Journal*, August 21, 2021.

Mataconis, Doug. 2015. "Rolling Stone's Botched Rape Story: How Bad Journalism Happens." *Christian Science Monitor*, April 6, 2015. https://www.csmonitor.com/USA/Politics/Politics-Voices/2015/0406/Rolling-Stone-s-botched-rape-story-how-bad-journalism-happens.

Matsui, Yayori. 1984. "Hojin junsa ga kyosei renko" [Forcible Conscription by Japanese Patrolman]. *Asahi shimbun*, November 2, 1984.

Matsui, Yayori. 1991. "Chosenjin ianfu ni hikari wo" [Shining a Light on Korean Comfort Women]. *Asahi shimbun*, July 18, 1991.

McDougall, Gay J. 1998. See UN Sub-Commission on the Promotion and Protection of Human Rights. 1998.

McDougall, Gay J. 2000. See UN Sub-Commission on the Promotion and Protection of Human Rights. 2000.

McNeil, Donald G., Jr. "NYTimes Peru N-Word." 4 parts. March 1, 2021. https://donaldgmcneiljr1954.medium.com/nytimes-peru-n-word-part-one-introduction-57eb6a3e0d95.

Mera, Koichi, & Kiyoshi Hosoya. 2020. *American Soldiers Witnessed Korean Comfort Women—"Flowers of the War."* Privately published. (Translation of Hosoya 2019).

Military Intelligence Service Captured Personnel and Material Branch. Composite Report on Three Korean Navy Civilians. April 24, 1945. Reprinted in *Mainichi shimbun*, June 10, 2016.

Minami Shina hakengun [South China Expeditionary Force]. "Eisei shunpo" [Sanitation Dispatch], August 1939. Reprinted in Josei (1997), 2:79.

"Minbyun Efforts May Be More Harm Than Help for Defector Group." *Daily NK*, June 28, 2016. https://www.dailynk.com/minbyun-efforts-may-be-more-harm-t/.

Ministry of Foreign Affairs of Japan. Kita chosen [North Korea] website, March 28, 2022. https://www.mofa.go.jp/mofaj/a_o/na/kp/page1w_000081.html.

Ministry of Foreign Affairs of Japan. Statement by the Chief Cabinet Secretary [Kono], August 4, 1993. https://www.mofa.go.jp/a_o/rp/page25e_000343.html.

Miyamoto, Archie. 2017. *Wartime Military Records on Comfort Women*. 2nd ed. Privately published.

Miyamoto, Archie. 2021. "Some Uncomfortable Truths About Comfort Women for the International Mob." *JAPAN Forward*, February 22, 2021. https://japan-forward.com/some-uncomfortable-truths-about-comfort-women-for-the-international-mob.

Moon, Katherine H. S. 1997. *Sex Among Allies: Military Prostitution in U.S.-Korea Relations*. New York: Columbia University Press.

Morabito, Stella. 2022. *The Weaponization of Loneliness: How Tyrants Stoke Our Fear of Isolation to Silence, Divide, and Conquer*. New York: Bombardier Press.

Morgan, Jason. 2015a. "On 'Standing with Historians of Japan.'" *Perspectives on History*, July 1, 2015.

Morgan, Jason. 2015b. "U.S. Textbook Defender Lacks an Open Mind." *Japan Times*, December 18, 2015.

Morgan, Jason. 2018. "The History of the Unspeakable: Shimokawa Masaharu's The Forgotten History of Evacuation." *Inter-Asia Cultural Studies* 19, no. 4 (October 2018): 644–54.

Morgan, Jason. 2021a. "Waseda Professor Offers Evidence of Comfort Women Working Under Contract: Now Come the Attacks." *JAPAN Forward*, October 15, 2021. https://japan-forward.com/waseda-professor-offers-evidence-of-comfort-women-working-under-contract-now-come-the-attacks/.

Morgan, Jason. 2021b. "The Comfort Women Issue: Bashing the Factfinders and Policing the Party Line." *JAPAN Forward*, October 18, 2021. https://japan-forward.com/the-comfort-women-issue-bashing-the-factfinders-and-policing-the-party-line/.

Morgan, Jason. 2021c. "Conform or Get Attacked: Bigots Use Comfort Women Issue to Assault Free Speech in Japan." *JAPAN Forward*, October 20, 2021. https://japan-forward.com/conform-or-get-attacked-bigots-use-comfort-women-issue-to-assault-free-speech-in-japan/.

Morgan, Patrick M. 2006. "Deterrence and System Management: The Case of North Korea." *Conflict Management and Peace Science* 23, no. 2 (Summer 2006).

Morikawa butaicho [Morikawa detachment commander]. "Morikawa butai tokushu iangyomu ni kansuru kitei" [Morikawa Detachment Regulations Regarding Special Comfort Industry], November 14, 1939. Reprinted in Josei (1997), 2:327.

Morris-Suzuki, Tessa. 2022. "Research Integrity in the Age of 'Fake News': A Challenge to the Humanities." Australian Academy of the Humanities, July 2022.

Morris-Suzuki, Tessa. 2023. "Unwriting the Wrongs: History, Trauma and Memories of Violence in Germany and Japan." In *Routledge Handbook of Trauma in East Asia*, edited by Tina Burrett & Jeff Kingston. London: Routledge.

"Moto 'ianfu' e hosho wo" [Compensation for Former "Comfort Women"]. *Shimbun Akahata*, June 26, 2002.

"'Moto ianfu, hatsu no shogen' kiji ni jijitsu no nejimage nai" ["The First Testimonial of a Former Comfort Woman," Truth Not Twisted in Article]. *Asahi shimbun*, August 5, 2014.

"Moto ianfu Kim Hak Sun san" [Former Comfort Woman Kim Hak Sun]. *Asahi shimbun*, December 25, 1991.

"Moto ianfu 'zettai ni yurusenai'" [Former Comfort Woman "It's Absolutely Unforgivable"]. *Asahi shimbun*, May 26, 2020.

"Moto ianfu tachiga Kankoku Teishintai mondai ..." [Former Comfort Women on the CDH issue...]. *Bunshun online*, December 27, 2018.

Mun, Ok-ju. 1996. *Biruma sensen: Tateshidan no "Ianfu" datta watashi* [The Burmese Front: I Who Had Been a "Comfort Woman" for the Tate Division]. Translated by Morikawa Machiko. Tokyo: Nashi no kisha.

Murotani, Katsumi. 2020. "Kihonteki na daigimon ..." [A Basic, Major Doubt ...]. Zakzak (Yukan Fuji), June 11, 2020.

Naimusho. 1938. "Shina toko fujo ni kansuru kenshi" [Inquiry Regarding Passage of Women to China], February 18, 1938. Reprinted in Suzuki et al. (2006), 1:139.

Nihon Kirisuto kyo fujin kyofu kai [Japan Christian Women's Organization]. 1920. *Kaigai shugyofu mondai*, I [The Overseas Prostitution Problem, I] (Nihon kirisuto kyo, 1920). Reprint, Jobundo, 2010.

"Nihon no shokuminchi shihai to kokkateki kanri baishun" [Japan's Colonial Control and the Nationally Managed Prostitution]. *Chosenshi kenkyukai ronbun shu* 32 (1994).

Nihon yuran sha, ed. 1932. *Yukaku annai* [Guide to Pleasure Quarters] (Nihon yuran sha).

Nishino, Rumiko. 2018. "Forcible Mobilization: What Survivor Testimonies Tell Us." In *Denying the Comfort Women: The Japanese State's Assault on Historical Truth*, edited by Rumiko Nishino, Kim Puja & Akane Onozawa. London: Routledge.

Nishino, Rumiko, et al. 2013. *"Ianfu" basshingu wo koete* [Beyond "Comfort Women" Bashing]. Tokyo: Otsuki shoten.

Nishioka, Tsutomu. 2014. "Ianfu mondai no haikei ni ..." [In the Background of the Comfort Women Problem ...]. *Kin'yu fakushimirii shinbun*, November 17, 2014.

Nishioka, Tsutomu. 2017. "Why Korean Professor Believes Comfort Women Were Not Sex Slaves," *JAPAN Forward*, November 24, 2017. https://japan-forward.com/why-korean-professor-believes-comfort-women-were-not-sex-slaves/.

Nishioka, Tsutomu. 2020a. "Higaisha mo uso wo tsuku ..." [Victims Also Lie ...], part 3. August 9, 2020. https://salty-japan-net/2020/08/09/higaisyamo-usowotsuku-3_nishioka-tsutomu/.

Nishioka, Tsutomu. 2020b. "Kankoku no ianfu undo no 'naifun'" [The "Internal Dispute" of the Comfort Women Movement]. *Rekishi ninshiki mondai kenkyu* 7 (2020): 95–111.

Nishioka, Tsutomu. 2020c. "Saikin no Kankoku no anchihannichi no ugoki ni tsuite" [Regarding the Recent Anti-Anti-Japanese Movement in South Korea]. *Rekishi ninshiki mondai kenkyu* 8 (2020): 71–88.

Nishioka, Tsutomu. 2021. "Ianfu mondai wo kogi de furete ..." [Discussing the Comfort Women Problem in a Lecture ...], October 19, 2021. www.moralogy.jp/salon211019-1/.

Nishioka, Tsutomu. 2022. "Kankoku ni okeru gakumon no jiyu no kiki ni tsuite" [Regarding the Crisis in Academic Freedom in South Korea]. *Rekishi ninshiki mondai kenkyu* 10 (2022): 79–91.

Norma, Caroline. 2016. *The Japanese Comfort Women and Sexual Slavery during the China and Pacific Wars*. London: Bloomsbury.

O'Brian, Suzanne. 2000. Translator's Introduction to Yoshiaki Yoshimi, *Comfort Women: Sexual Slavery in the Japanese Military During World War II*. New York: Columbia University Press.

Odaka, Konosuke. 1975. "Nihon tochika ni okeru Chosen no rodo keizai" [Korean Labor Economy under Japanese Control]. *Keizai kenkyu* 26 (1975): 145.

Oh, Sonfa. 2021. *Kankoku "Han-nichi minzoku shugi" no naraku* [The Hell of Korean "Anti-Japan Tribalism"]. Tokyo: Bungei shunju.

Ohsato, Katsuma, ed. 1966. *Meiji iko honpo shuyo keizai tokei* [Principal Economic Statistics for Our Nation since the Meiji Period]. Bank of Japan.

Okubo, Hanayuki. 1906. *Kagai fuzoku shi* [A Record of the Customs of the Red-light District] (Ryubun kan, 1906). Reprint, Nihon tosho sentaa, 1983.

"Omoidasu to imamo namida" [Even Now, I Cry When I Remember]. *Asahi shimbun*, August 11, 1991.

Onuma, Yasuaki, Yokota Yozo & Wada Haruki. 2006. "Ajia josei kikin to watashi tachi" [The Asian Women's Fund and Us]. *Yobikake*, October 20, 2006.

Open Letter in Support of Historians in Japan. 2015. https://networks.h-net.org/system/files/contributed-files/japan-scholars-statement-2015.5.4-eng_0.pdf.

Park, Yu-ha. 2014. *Teikoku no ianfu* [Comfort Women of the Empire]. Tokyo: Asahi shimbun shuppan

Park, Yu-ha. 2022. *Rekishi to mukiau* [Facing History]. Tokyo: Mainichi shimbun shuppan.

Parker, Karen, & Jennifer F. Chew. 1994. "Compensation for Japan's World War II War-Rape Victims." *Hastings International and Comparative Law Review* 17 (1994): 497–549.

Phillips, Joe, Wondong Lee & Joseph Yi. 2019. "Future of South Korea–Japan Relations: Decoupling or Liberal Discourse." *Political Quarterly* 91, no. 2 (2019): 448–56.

Pratt, Mary Louise. 2001. "*I, Rigoberta Menchú* and the 'Culture Wars.'" In *The Rigoberta Menchú Controversy*, edited by Arturo Arias. Minneapolis: University of Minnesota Press.

Protecting the Human Rights of Comfort Women: Hearing before the Subcommittee on Asia, the Pacific, and the Global Environment of the Committee on Foreign Affairs, House of Representatives. 110th Cong., February 15, 2007.

Qiu, Peipei. 2014. *Chinese Comfort Women: Testimonies from Imperial Japan's Sex Slaves*. Oxford: Oxford University Press.

Ramseyer, J. Mark. 1991. "Indentured Prostitution in Imperial Japan: Credible Commitments in the Commercial Sex Industry." *Journal of Law, Economics, and Organization* 7, no. 1 (Spring 1991): 89–116.

Ramseyer, J. Mark. 1996. *Odd Markets in Japanese History: Law and Economic Growth*. Cambridge: Cambridge University Press.

Ramseyer, J. Mark. 2020. "Comfort Women: The Economics of the Contracts and the Politics of the Dispute." February 3, 2020. Available at SSRN: https://papers.ssrn.com/sol3/papers.cfm?abstract_id=3822439.

Ramseyer, J. Mark. 2021a. "Contracting for Sex in the Pacific War." *International Review of Law and Economics* 65 (March 2021).

Ramseyer, J. Mark. 2021b. "Recovering the Truth About the Comfort Women." *JAPAN Forward*, January 12, 2021. https://japan-forward.com/recovering-the-truth-about-the-comfort-women/.

Ramseyer, J. Mark. 2021c. "Social Capital and the Problem of Opportunistic Leadership: The Example of Koreans in Japan." *International Review of Law and Economics* Err. n.2 (2021).

Ramseyer, J. Mark. 2022. "Contracting for Sex in the Pacific War: A Response to My Critics." Harvard John M. Olin DP 1075. January 4, 2022. SSRN WP 400014. https://papers.ssrn.com/sol3/papers.cfm?abstract_id=4000145.

Redden, Elizabeth. 2021. "Harvard Prof Rejects Historical Consensus on 'Comfort Women.'" *Inside Higher Ed*, February 16, 2021.

Rhee, Younghoon. 2004. "Seoul dai kyoju 'jugun ianfu ha baishugyo'" [SNU Professor "Comfort Women Were Prostitutes"]. *Chosun online*, September 3, 2004. https://web.archive.org/web/20070517204644/http://www.chosunonline.com/article/20040903000051.

Rhee, Younghoon, ed. 2019. *Hannichi shuzoku shugi* [Anti-Japan Tribalism]. Tokyo: Bungei shunju.

Rhee, Younghoon, ed. 2020. *Hannichi shuzoku shugi to no toso* [The Fight against Anti-Japan Tribalism]. Tokyo: Bungei shunju.

Ri, Sotetsu. 2020. *Hannichi shuzoku no tabu* [The Taboos of Anti-Japan Tribalism]. Tokyo: Takarajima sha.

Rikugun sho. 1938. "Gun ianjo jugyofu to boshu ni kansuru ken" [Regarding the Solicitation of Employees, etc., for the Military Comfort Stations], March 4, 1938. Reprinted in Suzuki et al. (2006), 1:103.

Rohter, Larry. 1998. "Tarnished Laureate: A Special Report." *New York Times*, December 15, 1998.

"Romu kanri no kyoka e" [Toward Strengthening Labor Management]. *Keijo nippo*, September 23, 1943. Reprinted in Suzuki et al. (2006), 2:567.

Ruff-O'Herne, Jan. 2008. *Fifty Years of Silence*. North Sydney: William Heinemann.

"S. Korea Discloses Sensitive Documents." UPI, January 17, 2005. https://www.upi.com/Top_News/2005/01/17/SKorea-discloses-sensitive-documents/UPI-38131105952315/.

"'Saishuto de renko' shogen" ["Forcibly abducted in Jeju" Testimonial]. *Asahi shimbun*, August 5, 2014.

Sakurai Yoshiko shi kisha kaiken yoshi [Summary of Press Conference by Ms. Sakurai Yoshiko]. *Iza*, March 25, 2018. https://www.iza.ne.jp/article/20180325-FRV2772L-2JOJXBZJ2NG6XIKTLQ/.

"Sakurai Yoshiko vs Nishioka Tsutomu" ... , May 13, 2011. https://yoshiko-sakurai.jp/2021/05/13/9169.

Satia, Priya. 2022. "The Presentist Trap." *Perspectives on History*, September 7, 2022.

SCAP (Supreme Commander for the Allied Powers). 1945. "Amenities in the Japanese Armed Forces." November 15, 1945. Reprinted in Josei (1998), 5:137–66.

Senda, Kako. 1973. *Jugun ianfu* [Comfort Women of the Military]. Tokyo: Futaba sha.

"'Sengo 70 nen' zaigai Nihon kenkyusha seimei ..." ["70 Years after the War": Statement of Overseas Japan Researchers ...]. *Mainichi shimbun*, May 27, 2015.

"Senso he hanto romu wo gyoshu" [Focus Peninsular Labor on War]. *Keijo nippo*, October 9, 1943. Reprinted in Suzuki et al. (2006), 2:569.

"Seoul University Prof. Lee Yong-hoon [Younghoon Rhee] 'Comfort Women = Sex Slave' Is an Illusion." October 10, 2016. http://staff.texas-daddy.com/?eid=502.

Shakai jigyo kenkyujo [Social Conditions Research Institute], 1936. *Shuro shonen shojo rodo jijo chosa* [Survey of Working Conditions of Working Boys and Girls] (Chuo shakai jigyo kyokai).

Shaw, Meredith. 2022. "Godzilla vs Pulgasari: Anti-Japanism and Anti-Communism as Dueling Antagonisms in South Korean Politics." *Journal of East Asian Studies* 22, no. 2 (2022): 201–30.

Shigemura, Tomokazu. 2011. "Kita chosen no rachi, tero, kaku kaihatsu, yuji no kokusai kankei" [Internal Aspects of North Korea's Abductions, Terrorism, Nuclear Development, and Crises]. *Waseda daigaku shakai anzen seisaku kenkyujo kiyo* 3 (2011).

Shigemura, Tomokazu. 2016. "Kita chosen no tero, joho kosaku senso to Nihon no anzen" [Japan's Security and North Korea's Terrorism and Misinformation War]. *Waseda daigaku shakai anzen seisaku kenkyujo kiyo* 9 (2016).

Shina haken gun [China Expeditionary Army]. 1942. "Showa 17 nen 9 gatsu fukukankai doseki jo iken" [Opinions Expressed at the September 1942 Vice Officers Meeting], October 3, 1942. Reprinted in Josei (1997), 3:7.

"Shina toko fujo no toriatsukai ni kansuru ken" [Regarding the Handling of Women Bound for China], February 23, 1938. Home Ministry, Police Bureau, Hatsukei No. 5.

"Shinpan momoiro hakuku kyo". *Toa nippo*, March 7, 1939. Reprinted in Suzuki et al. (2006), 1:829.

"Shojo yuin dan kyukei" [Gang to Entrap Young Women Sentenced]. *Toa nippo*, November 5, 1937. Reprinted in Suzuki et al. (2006), 1:829.

Shorrock, Tim. 2019. "Welcome to the Monkey House: Confronting the Ugly Legacy of Military Prostitution in South Korea." *New Republic*, December 2, 2019.

Smith, Carol A. 2001. "Why Write an Expose of Rigoberta Menchú?" In *The Rigoberta Menchú Controversy*, edited by Arturo Arias. Minneapolis: University of Minnesota Press.

Soh, C. Sarah. 2008. *The Comfort Women: Sexual Violence and Postcolonial Memory in Korea and Japan*. Chicago: University of Chicago Press.

Sojo [Complaint], Park v. Nihon koku, December 6, 1991. https://www.awf.or.jp/pdf/195-k1.pdf.

Somaiya, Ravi. 2015. "Rolling Stone Article on Rape at University of Virginia Failed All Basics, Report Says." *New York Times*, April 5, 2015.

"South Korea Says It Will Dissolve Japan-Funded 'Comfort Women' Foundation." *Japan Times*, November 21, 2018. https://www.japantimes.co.jp/news/2018/11/21/national/politics-diplomacy/south-korea-says-will-dissolve-japan-funded-comfort-women-foundation/#.XHs-eLaZOB5.

"South Korean Academic Convicted of Defaming 'Comfort Women.'" *Straits Times*, October 27, 2017. https://www.straitstimes.com/asia/east-asia/south-korean-academic-convicted-of-defaming-comfort-women.

"South Korea's Former Chief Justice Yang Sung-tae Indicted in Abuse of Power Scandal." *South China Morning Post*, February 11, 2019.

Stanley, Amy. 2021. "On Contract." Amy Stanley blog, March 18, 2021. https://www.amy-stanley.com/blog-1/on-contract.

Stanley, Amy, Hannah Shepherd, Sayaka Chatani, David Ambaras & Chelsea Szendi Schieder. 2021. "'Contracting for Sex in the Pacific War': The Case for Retraction on Grounds of Academic Misconduct." *Asia-Pacific Journal: Japan Focus* 19, iss. 5, no. 13 (March 1, 2021). https://apjjf.org/2021/5/ConcernedScholars.html.

Stanton, Joshua. 2016. "Minbyun's Frivolous Lawfare Terrorizes 12 Young N. Korean Refugees & Endangers Lives." *Free Korea*, July 5, 2016. https://freekorea.us/2016/07/minbyuns-frivolous-lawfare-terrorizes-12-young-n-korean-refugees-endangers-lives/.

Stanton, Joshua. 2020. "The N.Y. Times, the Ningpo 12, Minbyun & Yoon Mee-hyang: The Story Behind the Story." *Free Korea*, June 8, 2020. https://freekorea.us/2020/06/the-n-y-times-the-ningpo-12-minbyun-yoon-mee-hyang-the-story-behind-the-story/.

Stoll, David. 1998. "Life Story as Mythopoesis." *Anthropology Newsletter*, April 1998.

Stoll, David. 2002. "Rigoberta Menchú." Letter to the Editor. *PMLA* 17, no. 1 (January 2002).

Stoll, David. 2008. *Rigoberta Menchú and the Story of All Poor Guatemalans*. Expanded edition. Boulder: Westview.

Stoll, David. n.d. "Moral Authority, Permission, and Deference in Latin American Studies." Unpublished.

Stone, Geoffrey R., et al. 2014. *Report of the Committee on Freedom of Expression*, University of Chicago. https://provost.uchicago.edu/sites/default/files/documents/reports/FOECommitteeReport.pdf.

Strauss, Robert. 1999. "Truth and Consequences." *Stanford Magazine*, May/June 1999.

Suk-Gersen, Jeannie. 2021. "Seeking the True Story of the Comfort Women." *New Yorker*, February 26, 2021.

Sweet, James H. 2022. "Is History History?" *Perspectives on History*, August 17, 2022.

Suzuki, Yuko, et al., eds. 2006. *Nihon gun "ianfu" kankei shiryo shusei* [Collection of Documents Relating to the "Comfort Women" of the Japanese Military]. 2 vols. Tokyo: Akashi shoten.

Taiwan sotokufu [Governor-General of Taiwan]. 1932. "Sekkyaku gyosha su" [Number of Entertainers], December 1932. Reprinted in Suzuki et al. (2006), 1:858.

Takei, Yoshimasa. 2012. "Nicchu senso ki Shanhai no chosenjin shakai ni tsuite" [Regarding the Korean Community in Shanghai during the (Second) Sino-Japanese War] (Nicchu senso shi kenkyukai). http://iccs.aichi-u.ac.jp/archives/010/201205/4fc4385498c26.pdf.

"Teitaikyo ha beigun kichi mondai ..." [The Korean Council Uses the U.S. Base Problem ...]. *News Posuto Sebun*, February 4, 2017. https://www.news-postseven.com/archives/20170204_490296.html/2.

"Teitaikyo ha beigun kichi mondai wo keiki ni ..." [Using the U.S. Base Dispute as an Opportunity, the Korean Council ...]. Zakzak, February 6, 2017. https://www.zakzak.co.jp/society/foreign/news/2017/02/06/frn1702061130005-n1.htm.

"Teitaikyo ni 'mono goi, aka' bogen ... Saibansho ga Ji Man-won shi ni yuzai hanketsu" [Court Convicts Ji Man-won for Disrespecting the CDH as "beggars, reds"]. *Hankyoreh*, November 10, 2018. http://japan.hani.co.kr/arti/politics/32072.html.

"Teitaikyo no shotai" [The Truth about the Korean Council]. May 2020. http://daishi100.cocolog-nifty.com/blog/2020/05/post-77ade9.html.

Thoma, Pamela. 2000. "Cultural Autobiography, Testimonial, and Asian American Transnational Feminist Coalition." *Frontiers: A Journal of Women Studies* 21, nos. 1/2 (Spring 2000): 29–54.

Togo, Kazuhiko. 2017. "Park Yuha and the Uncomfortable Realities of South Korean Democracy." *East Asia Forum*, November 22, 2017. http://www.eastasiaforum.org/2017/11/22/park-yuha-and-the-uncomfortable-realities-of-south-korean-democracy/.

"Tokyo bakuhatsubutsu tero jiken (Daden joshi ni yoru nisehata sakusen)" [Tokyo Terrorist Bombing Incident (Dudden's False Flag Strategy)]. https://dekabudou2.fc2.net/e/131.

Uemura, Yukitada. 1918. "Urare yuku onna" [Sold Women] (Daito kaku). Reprinted in *Kindai fujin mondai meichosaku shu zokuhen* [A Collection of Famous Works on Contemporary Women's Issues, Continued Series]. (Nihon tosho sentaa, 1982), 5:57.

Uemura, Yukitada. 1929. *Nihon yuri shi* [A History of the Japanese Pleasure Quarters] (Shun'yo do).

UN Commission on Human Rights. 1996. *Report on the mission to the Democratic People's Republic of Korea, the Republic of Korea and Japan on the issue of military sexual slavery in wartime. Report by Radhika Coomaraswamy, Special Rapporteur.* January 4, 1996. E/CN.4/1996/53/Add.1.

UN Sub-Commission on the Promotion and Protection of Human Rights. 1998. *Systematic rape, sexual slavery and slavery-like practices during armed conflict. Final report submitted by Gay J. McDougall, Special Rapporteur.* June 22, 1998. E/CN.4/Sub.2/1998/13.

UN Sub-Commission on the Promotion and Protection of Human Rights. 2000. *Systematic rape, sexual slavery and slavery-like practices during armed conflict. Update to the final report submitted by Gay J. McDougall, Special Rapporteur.* June 6, 2000. E/CN.4/Sub.2/2000/21.

"Uooru sutoriito jaaneru ni kansuru Lew kyoju to media uocchi no hanno" [The Reactions of Professor Lew and MediaWatch to the *Wall Street Journal*]. Rekishi ninshiki mondai kenkyu kai, August 23, 2021. Harc.tokyo/?p=2275.

U.S. House of Representatives. H.R. 121. 110th Congress, July 30, 2007.

U.S. Interrogation Report No. 573. January 23, 1945. Reprinted in Josei (1997), 5:107.

U.S. Office of War Information. 1944. Japanese Prisoner of War Interrogation Report No. 49. October 1, 1944. Reprinted in Josei (1998), 5:203–5.

Wakabayashi, Bob Tadashi. 2009. "Review of *Japan's Contested War Memories: The 'Memory Rifts' in Historical Consciousness of World War II*." *Journal of Japanese Studies* 35, no. 1 (Winter 2009): 181–85.

Watanabe, Manabu. 2014. "Dare ga heishi ni nattano ka" (1) [Who Became a Soldier? (1)]. *Shakai gakubu kiyo* 119 (2014): 1.

Williams, Mark. 2022. "From Out of the Depths: Shimao Toshio's Literary Response to Adversity." In *Handbook of Japanese Christian Writers*, edited by Mark Williams et al. Tokyo: MHM Ltd.

Winn, Patrick. 2017. "Why North Korean Peace Talks May Hinge on 12 Singing Waitresses." *The World*, September 15, 2017.

Yamada, Hiromichi & Hirama Sahashi. 1923. *Tokei yori mitaru karyubyo* [Venereal Diseases Seen through Statistics] (Nanzan do).

Yamada, Seikichi. 1978. *Bukan heitan* [Wuhan Logistics]. Tokyo: Tosho shuppan.

Yamamoto, Shun'ichi. 1983. *Nihon kosho shi* [A History of Licensed Prostitution in Japan]. Tokyo: Chuo hoki shuppan.

Yamaoka, Tetsuhide. 2021. "Ianfu harumoni ..." [The Comfort Women Grandmothers ...]. *Gekkan Hanada purasu*, May 26, 2020.

Yamashita, Yon'e. 2006. "Chosen ni okeru kosho seido no jisshi to sono tenkai" [The Realization and Development of the Licensed Prostitution System in Korea]. Reprinted in Suzuki et al. (2006), 2:675.

Yamazaki, Tomoko. 1972. *Sandakan hachiban shokan* [Sandakan Number 8 Brothel]. Tokyo: Chikuma shobo.

Yang, Hyunah. 1997. "Revisiting the Issue of Korean 'Military Comfort Women': The Question of Truth and Positionality." *Positions* 5, no. 1 (1997): 51–72.

Yasumura, Mitsutei. 1941. "Shisho no yurai oyobi genjo" [The Origins and Condition of Unlicensed Prostitution], February 1941. Reprinted in Suzuki et al. (2006), 1:272.

Yi, Joseph. 2018. "Confronting Korea's Censored Discourse on Comfort Women." *The Diplomat*, January 31, 2018.

Yi, Joseph. 2020. "Illiberal Means for Liberal Ends: Low-Road Challenge to Public Discourse and International Relations." APSA Preprints. https://preprints.apsanet.org/engage/apsa/article-details/5f52aa1a9277460012015626.

Yi, Joseph. 2021. "Debating Korea's Last Taboo: 'Comfort Women.'" *Asia Times*, March 3, 2021.

Yi, Joseph, & Joe Phillips. 2021. "On 'Comfort Women' and Academic Freedom." *The Diplomat*, February 18, 2021.

Yi, Joseph, Joe Phillips & Wondong Lee. 2019. "Manufacturing Contempt: State-Linked Populism in South Korea." *Society* 56, no. 5 (October 2019): 494–501.

Yoshida, Seiji. 1977. *Chosenjin ianfu to Nihon jin* [Korean Comfort Women and Japanese]. Tokyo: Shin jinbutsu orai sha.

Yoshida, Seiji. 1983. *Watashi no senso hanzai* [My War Crimes]. Tokyo: San'ichi shobo.

"'Yoshida shogen' yoyaku torikeshi ..." [At Last, the "Yoshida Testimonial" Withdrawn ...]. *Yomiuri shimbun*, August 6, 2014.

Yoshii, Riki. 2019. "'Hyogen no fujiyu' ko: 'Jugun ianfu ha dema' to iu dema, rekishigakusha, Yoshimi Yoshiaki shi ni kiku" [Thoughts on the "Lack of Freedom of Expression": Asking Historian Yoshimi Yoshiaki about the False Rumor That "Military Comfort Women Were a False Rumor"]. *Mainichi shimbun*, August 15, 2019.

Yoshimi, Yoshiaki. 1995. *Jugun ianfu* [Comfort Women of the Military]. Tokyo: Iwanami shoten.

Yoshimi, Yoshiaki. 2000. *Comfort Women: Sexual Slavery in the Japanese Military During World War II*. Translated by Suzanne O'Brien. New York: Columbia University Press.

Yoshimi, Yoshiaki. 2013. "'Kono danwa' wo do kangaeru ka" [How to Think about the Kono Statement]. In *"Ianfu" basshingu wo koete* [Beyond "Comfort Women" Bashing], edited by Nishino Rumiko et al. (Otsuki shoten).

Yoshimi, Yoshiaki. 2023. "Response to 'Contracting for Sex in the Pacific War,' by J. Mark Ramseyer." *International Review of Law and Economics*, August 9, 2023.

Young, Louise. 2022. "Past and Present in Japanese Historiography: Four Versions of Presentism." *Modern Intellectual History*, June 21, 2022. https://doi.org/10.1017/S1479244322000221.

Zai Shanhai soryo jikan [Shanghai Consulate]. 1937. "Zai Shanhai soryo jikan ni okeru tokko keisatsu jimu jokyo" [Official Circumstances of the Shanghai Consulate Special Police], December 1937. Reprinted in Suzuki et al. (2006), 1:74.

Zai Shanhai soryo jikan [Shanghai Consulate]. 1938. "Showa 13 nenju ni okeru zairyo hojin" [Resident Japanese in 1938], 1938. Reprinted in Suzuki et al. (2006), 1:118.

Zaisan oyobi seikyu ken ni kansuru mondai no kaiketsu narabi ni keizai kyoryoku ni kansuru Nihon koku to Dai kan minkoku to no aida no kyotei [Agreement between Japan and the Republic of Korea concerning the Economic Cooperation and the Resolution of Problems Involving Property and Claims]. Treaty No. 27, 1965.

NOTES

INTRODUCTION

1 Pamela Thoma, "Cultural Autobiography, Testimonial, and Asian American Transnational Feminist Coalition in the 'Comfort Women of World War II' Conference," *Frontiers* 21, nos. 1/2 (2000): 36.

2 Hyunah Yang, "Revisiting the Issue of Korean 'Military Comfort Women': The Question of Truth and Positionality," *Positions* 5, no. 1 (Spring 1997): 51–72.

3 Christopher Chabris, "IQ Since 'The Bell Curve,'" *Commentary*, August 1, 1998.

4 David Ambaras, Twitter, June 28, 2022.

5 Park Yu-ha, *Rekishi to mukiau* [Facing History] (Tokyo: Mainichi shimbun shuppan, 2022), 189.

CHAPTER 1—THE ANATOMY OF A CANCELING

1 J. Mark Ramseyer, "Contracting for Sex in the Pacific War," *International Review of Law and Economics* 65 (March 2021).

2 Hannah Shepherd, @hannahjshepherd, Twitter, February 1, 2021.

3 Daniel Martin, @DrDSM, Twitter, February 1, 2021.

4 Mark Ravina, @MarkRavina, Twitter, February 1, 2021.

5 Paul Kreitman, @Paul_Kreitman, Twitter, February 1, 2021.

6 Nick Kapur, @nick_kapur, Twitter, February 1, 2021.

7 Jeremy Yellen, @jeremyyellen, Twitter, February 1, 2021.

8 Gina Anne Tam, @DGTam86, Twitter, February 1, 2021.

9 Dr/Professor, @MarcyTanter, Twitter, February 1, 2021.

10 David Ambaras, Twitter, February 1, 2021.

11 Maren Ehlers, @MarenAnnika, Twitter, February 19, 2021.

12 Shepherd, Twitter, February 1, 2021.

13 Paula R. Curtis, @paularcurtis, Twitter, February 2, 2021.

14 Amy Stanley, @astanley711, Twitter, February 16, 2021.

15 Andrew Gordon & Carter Eckert, Statement, February 17, 2021, https://perma.cc/8ZHY-RD5C.

16 Jeannie Suk-Gersen, "Seeking the True Story of the Comfort Women," *New Yorker*, February 26, 2021.

17 Stanley, Twitter, February 2, 2021.

18 Rebecca Zorach, @rabbitrez, Twitter, February 12, 2021; Stanley, Twitter, February 12, 2021.

19 George Hicks, "The 'Comfort Women,'" in *The Japanese Wartime Empire, 1931–1945*, ed. Peter Duus, Ramon H. Myers & Mark R. Peattie (Princeton: Princeton University Press, 1996). See Andrew Gordon, *A Modern History of Japan: From Tokugawa Times to the Present*, 3rd ed. (New York: Oxford University Press, 2014).

20 Yoshida Seiji, *Watashi no senso hanzai* [My War Crimes] (Tokyo: Chikuma shobo, 1983).

21 Amy Stanley, Hannah Shepherd, Sayaka Chatani, David Ambaras & Chelsea Szendi Schieder, "'Contracting for Sex in the Pacific War': The Case for Retraction on Grounds of Academic Misconduct," *Asia-Pacific Journal: Japan Focus* 19, iss. 5, no. 13 (March 1, 2021), https://apjjf.org/2021/5/ConcernedScholars.html.

22 Sayaka Chatani, @SayakaChatani, Twitter, February 19, 2021.

23 Stanley, Twitter, February 21, 2021.

24 Stanley, Twitter, March 3, 2021.

25 Ethan Mark, Twitter, March 3, 2021.

26 Stanley, Twitter, March 3, 2021.

27 Ravina, Twitter, February 23, 2021; Stanley, Twitter, February 23, 2021.

28 Sachi Hirayama, @sachihirayama, Twitter, October 10, 2021.

29 Ambaras, Twitter, October 10, 2021.

30 Chatani, Twitter, October 10, 2021.

31 Ambaras, email to Joseph Yi, May 30, 2022.

32 Chatani, Twitter, August 14, 2023.

33 Ambaras, Twitter, June 14, 2022.

34 Ambaras, Twitter, November 4 & 8, 2022.

35 Ambaras, Twitter, June 6, 2022; Curtis, Twitter, June 6, 2022; Hiromu Nagahara, @HiromuNagahara, Twitter, June 6, 2022.

36 Ambaras, Twitter, April 17, 2022.

37 Stanley, Twitter, June 7, 2022.

38 Stanley, Twitter, February 7, 2021.

39 Stanley, Twitter, April 25, 2022.

40 Stanley, Twitter, April 25, 2022.

41 Stanley, Twitter, February 4, 2021.

42 Andrew Salmon, "Sparks Keep Flying Off Comfort Women Brouhaha," *Asia Times*, June 3, 2022.

43 Stanley, Twitter, June 4, 2022.

44 Stanley, Twitter, February 7, 2021.

45 Stanley, Twitter, June 16, 2021.

46 E.g., Chatani, Twitter, February 13 & 20, 2022; June 10, 2022.

47 Chelsea Szendi Schieder, "The History the Japanese Government Is Trying to Erase," *The Nation*, May 26, 2021.

48 Chelsea Szendi Schieder, @SzendiChelsea, Twitter, June 14, 2022.

49 Shepherd, Twitter, January 31, 2022.

50 Shepherd, Twitter, April 25, 2022.

51 Shepherd, Twitter, June 5, 2022.

52 Curtis, Twitter, June 2, 2022.

53 Statement by the Reischauer Institute of Japanese Studies, March 15, 2021, https://rijs.fas.harvard.edu/news/statement-reischauer-institute-japanese-studies-0. This is the second of the Reischauer statements; the first was issued in February.

54 Chatani, Twitter, February 19, 2021.

55 Stanley, Twitter, March 3, 2021.

56 Korea Institute of Harvard, Statement on Academic Integrity, February 19, 2021 (updated March 18, 2021), https://korea.fas.harvard.edu/news/statement.

57 Asia Center, Harvard University, "A Conversation with Professor Jeannie Suk Gersen About Her New Yorker Article: 'Seeking the True Story of the Comfort Women,'" Director's Conversations Series, Spring 2021, https://asiacenter.harvard.edu/conversation-professor-jeannie-suk-gersen-about-her-new-yorker-article-seeking-true-story-comfort. Suk-Gersen proudly advertised the video on her Twitter page: Jeannie Suk-Gersen, @JeannieSGersen, Twitter, March 8, 2021.

58 Ariel H. Kim and Simon J. Levien, "Grandson of Famous Korean Activist Withdraws Archival Donation Plans in Protest of Professor's 'Comfort Women' Paper," *Harvard Crimson*, February 18, 2021.

59 Committee on Korean Studies, Statement on Anti-Asian Racism and Historical Research, n.d., Northeast Asia Council, Association for Asian Studies, https://koreanstudies.org/cks-statement-on-anti-asian-racism-and-historical-research/.

60 Michael Chwe, @michael_chwe, Twitter, October 10, 2021; October 26, 2022; December 22, 2022.

61 Letter by Concerned Economists Regarding "Contracting for Sex in the Pacific War" in the International Review of Law and Economics (2021), http://chwe.net/irle/letter/.

62 Statement by Editors of the American Political Science Review, http://chwe.net/irle/apsr_editors.pdf.

63 Statement by Al Roth and Paul Milgrom, February 27, 2021, http://chwe.net/irle/roth_milgrom.pdf.

64 Statement by Roger G. Noll, February 27, 2021, http://chwe.net/irle/roger_noll.pdf.

65 Arirang News Center, "Harvard Law Professor's 'Comfort Women' Article: Fellow Scholars Call It 'Fake News,'" February 16, 2021, https://www.youtube.com/watch?v=fxixpFncCeg.

66 Alexis Dudden, March 10, 2021, https://news.v.daum.net/v/20210310213931702. Noted as well in "Tokyo bakuhatsubutsu tero jiken (Daden joshi ni yoru nisehata sakusen)" [Tokyo Terrorist Bombing Incident (Dudden's False Flag Strategy)], https://dekabudou2.fc2.net/e/131.

67 Suk-Gersen, "Seeking the True Story of the Comfort Women."

68 Shim Dal-yeon: "On one occasion, [a Japanese soldier] tied a woman naked, grabbed her by the breast, and slashed it with a sword. Blood and some white stuff gushed out. I fainted. It was done to show others the consequence of running away." See https://www.youtube.com/watch?v=VHTeogF281o&ab_channel=%EA%B3%BD%EC%9B%90%ED%9D%AC. We thank Mr. Kenji Yoshida for providing a translation.

69 Alexis Dudden, *Troubled Apologies Among Japan, Korea, and the United States* (New York: Columbia University Press, 2008), 93.

70 Claudia Junghyun Kim, "Transnational Advocacy, Norm Regress, and Foreign Compliance Constituencies: The Case of the 'Comfort Women' Redress Movement," *International Studies Quarterly* 66, iss. 3 (September 2022), https://doi.org/10.1093/isq/sqac059.

71 Komori Yoshihisa, "Doko ga kohei? Nihon tataki ni te wo kasu Kokuren tokubetsu hokokusha" [What is fair about this? UN special rapporteur reaches out to Japan-basher], *JB Press*, May 11, 2016, https://jbpress.ismedia.jp/articles/-/46808.

72 "Interesting historian who blocked Professor Ramseyer's Dissertation of the Korean Massacre," *Yonhap News*, February 21, 2021.

73 Jinhee Lee, email to G. Zanarone and Jens Prufer, March 26, 2021.

74 Jinhee Lee, email to Eric Helland, August 19, 2020 (FOIA request).

75 Suk-Gersen, "Seeking the True Story of the Comfort Women."

76 Arima Tetsuo, *"Ianfu" ha mina goi keiyakuwo shiteita* [The "Comfort Women" Had All Agreed to Contracts] (Tokyo: WAC, 2021), 119–20.

77 Ariel H. Kim, "Harvard Law Professor Ramseyer Responds to Critics, Sparking More Condemnation," *Harvard Crimson*, February 16, 2022.

78 Craig Freedman & Luke Nottage, "Revisiting Ramseyer: The Chicago School of Law and Economics Comes to Japan," *Arizona Journal of International and Comparative Law* 39, no. 2 (2022): 225–96.

79 Stanley, Twitter, May 11, 2021.

80 Chatani, Twitter, June 4, 2022. For the schedule of the Association of Asian Studies 2022 annual conference, see https://www.asianstudies.org/wp-content/uploads/AAS-AC-2022-Conference-Booklet-Web-FINAL-R1.pdf.

81 "Japan Anthropology in Difficult Times: The Ramseyer Controversy and Scholarly Responsibility," 2021 Annual Meeting of the American Anthropological Association, November 19, 2021.

82 Curtis, Twitter, April 22, 2022.

83 Pyong Gap Min, "My Response to Ramseyer's Effort to Deny the History of Japanese Military Sexual Slavery," *Journal of International Women's Studies* 24, iss. 9 (2022).

84 Laura Kipnis, "Why Are Scholars Such Snitches?" *Chronicle of Higher Education*, March 17, 2022.

85 Call for Papers, as posted by Pyong Gap Min in February 2022, at https://www.koreanamericandatabank.org/upcoming-events/244-call-for-papers-for-special-issue-responding-to-ramseyer-s-article-on-comfort-women.html.

86 Jinah Kim, "Why I Pulled My Rebuttal from the *International Review of Law and Economics*," Korea Policy Institute, February 24, 2021.

87 J. Mark Ramseyer, "Contracting for Sex in the Pacific War: A Response to My Critics," Harvard John M. Olin DP 1075, January 4, 2022, SSRN WP 4000145, https://papers.ssrn.com/sol3/papers.cfm?abstract_id=4000145.

88 Petition on Ramseyer: "Harvard Law School professor advocating war crimes of sexual slavery?" Change.org, posted February 3, 2021, https://www.change.org/p/harvard-law-school-professor-advocating-war-crimes-of-sexual-slavery; petition on Arima: "Online Petition Seeks Dismissal of Japanese Professor Who Denies Wartime Sexual Slavery," *TBS World*, October 7, 2021; petition on Helland: "CMC professors approve advocating war crimes of Korean comfort women during WWII," Change.org, posted February 28, 2021, https://www.change.org/p/claremont-mckenna-cmc-professors-approve-advocating-war-crimes-of-korean-comfort-women-during-wwii.

89 Teresa R. Manning, "Repeal Title IX," *First Things*, January 2023.

90 Feminist Open Letter Regarding Harvard Law School Mitsubishi Professor John Mark Ramseyer's Scholarship on Japanese Military "Comfort Women," February 17, 2021.

91 Paula R. Curtis, "Ramseyer and the Right-Wing Ecosystem Suffocating Japan," *Tokyo Review*, May 30, 2021.

92 Sonia Ryang, "Afterword: Transnational Asian Studies—Toward More Inclusive Theory and Practice," *Journal of Asian Studies* 80, iss. 4 (2021): 1034–35.

93 See generally SeongHan Kim, "An Open Letter to Mark Ramseyer," April 19, 2021, https://www.anabaptistwitness.org/2021/04/an-open-letter-to-mark-ramseyer/.

94 Paul de Vries, "A McGraw-Hill Textbook and the Search for Academic Honesty," *JAPAN Forward*, July 30, 2023, https://japan-forward.com/a-mcgraw-hill-textbook-and-the-search-for-academic-honesty/.

95 Komori Yoshihisa, "Bei rekishi kyokasho ianfu kijutsu e hihan, Bei gakkai ni 'shinpu,'" *Sankei shimbun*, May 2, 2015, https://www.sankei.com/article/20150502-UZAGH4GZGVPOPHBZ4SZNWW3EKU.

CHAPTER 2—THE COMFORT STATIONS

1 But see the 1960 CBS documentary *Harvest of Shame*, dir. Fred W. Friendly.

2 Kimberly Kay Hoang, *Dealing in Desire: Asian Ascendancy, Western Decline, and the Hidden Currencies of Global Sex Work* (Oakland: University of California Press, 2015), 17.

3 Ibid., 183.

4 Ibid., 17.

5 Ibid., 18.

6 Lee Wooyoun, "Anti-Japan Tribalism on the Comfort Women Issue," *The Diplomat*, November 14, 2021, https://archive.ph/20211115071637/https://thediplomat.com/2021/11/anti-japan-tribalism-on-the-comfort-women-issue/#selection-1231.547–1231.1052.

7 This passage follows J. Mark Ramseyer, "Indentured Prostitution in Imperial Japan: Credible Commitments in the Commercial Sex Industry," *Journal of Law, Economics, and Organization* 7, no. 1 (Spring 1991): 89–116.

8 See Fukumi Takao, *Teito ni okeru bai'in no kenkyu* [A Study of Prostitution in the Capital] (Tokyo: Hakubunkan, 1928), 26–28, 32, 50–56, 178.

9 See Chuo shokugyo shokai jimukyoku, "Geishogi shakufu shokaigyo ni kansuru chosa" [An Investigation into the Placement Industry for Geisha, Prostitutes, and Barmaids], 1926, reprinted in *Kindai minshu no kiroku* [A Report of the Modern Populace], ed. Ken'ichi Taniguchi (Shin jinbutsu orai sha), 381–82; Kusama Yasoo, *Jokyu to baishofu* [Waitresses and Prostitutes] (Tokyo: Hanjin sha, 1930), 27–30, 36.

10 See J. Mark Ramseyer, *Odd Markets in Japanese History: Law and Economic Growth* (Cambridge: Cambridge University Press, 1996), 116 & n.17; Keishi cho sokan kanbo bunsho ka, *Showa 7 nen keishi cho tokei ichi ippan* [An Outline of Police Agency Statistics for 1932] (Sokan kanbo bunsho ka, 1933), 143.

11 See Keishi cho sokan kanbo bunsho ka (1933), 143–144; Kusama, *Jokyu to baishofu* (1930), 288, 291; Fukumi, *Teito ni okeru bai'in no kenkyu* (1928), 93, 168–69; Chuo shokugyo shokai jimukyoku (1926), 433–35.

12 See Fukumi, *Teito ni okeru bai'in no kenkyu* (1928), 70.

13 See Chuo shokugyo shokai jimukyoku, 414–15; Kusama, *Jokyu to baishofu* (1930), 211.

14 See Ramseyer, "Indentured Prostitution" (1991), 95, table 1; Ramseyer, *Odd Markets* (1996), 115, table 6.2.

15 Ramseyer, "Indentured Prostitution" (1991).

16 Fukumi, *Teito ni okeru bai'in no kenkyu* (1928), 58–59.

17 Ito Hidekichi, *Kotoka no kanojo no seikatsu* [The Lives of Women under the Red Lights] (Tokyo: Jitsugyo no Nihon sha, 1931; reprint, Tokyo: Funi shuppan, 1982), 208–11; Kusama, *Jokyu to baishofu* (1930), 281.

18 See Yamamoto Shun'ichi, *Nihon kosho shi* [A History of Licensed Prostitution in Japan] (Tokyo: Chuo hoki shuppan, 1983), 388. Ito, *Kotoka no kanojo no seikatsu* (1931), 211–13, finds that 13,500 registered in one year and 11,000 deregistered. Note that Ito is less reliable because of the way he haphazardly combines data from several years. Ramseyer (1996) explicitly notes that data from Osaka indicated that "one-third of the new registrations were not genuinely new recruits but rather, inter

alia, prostitutes moving from one city to another or reenlisted with a new indenture contract." Accordingly, he continues, if one "assumes that one-third of Yamamoto's 18,800 registrants were not genuinely new registrants, then the annual industry turnover rate would be about one-fourth." Note, further, that "only about 1 percent of the licensed prostitutes quit their jobs with outstanding debt . . . ." Ramseyser, *Odd Markets* (1996), 124 n.45.

19 Keishi cho sokan kanbo bunsho ka (1933), 96–98; Kusama, *Jokyu to baishofu* (1930), 227–28.

20 Keishi cho sokan kanbo bunsho ka (1933), 96–98; Kusama, *Jokyu to baishofu* (1930), 213, 260–63.

21 Shakai jigyo kenkyujo [Social Conditions Research Institute], *Shuro shonen shojo rodo jijo chosa* [Survey of Working Conditions of Working Boys and Girls] (Chuo shakai jigyo kyokai, 1936), 53; Ohsato Katsuma, ed., *Meiji iko honpo shuyo keizai tokei* [Principal Economic Statistics for Our Nation since the Meiji Period] (Bank of Japan, 1966), 60, 68; Rodo sho fujin shonen kyoku, *Fujin rodo no jitsujo* [The Reality of Female Labor] (Tokyo: Rodosho, 1952), 14; Naikaku tokei kyoku, *Rodo tokei yoran* [Outline of Labor Statistics] (Tokyo: Tokyo tokei kyokai, 1930), 130; Ramseyer, "Indentured Prostitution" (1991), 95, table 1.

22 Keishi cho sokan kanbo bunsho ka (1933), 96; Kusama, *Jokyu to baishofu* (1930), 220–21; Uemura Yukitada, *Nihon yuri shi* [A History of the Japanese Pleasure Quarters] (Shun'yo do, 1929), 492–501.

23 Keishi cho sokan kanbo bunsho ka (1933), 96–98.

24 Fujinaga Takeshi, "Nichiro senso to Nihon ni yoru 'Manshu' e no kosho seido ishoku" [The Russo-Japanese War and the Transplantation of the Licensed Prostitution System by Japan to "Manchuria"], in *Kairaku to kci* [Recreation and Regulation], ed. Katsurakawa Mitsumasa (Osaka sangyo daigaku sangyo kenkyujo, 1998); Fujinaga Takeshi, "Shokuminchi kosho seido to Chosenjin josei" [The Colonial Licensed Prostitution System and Korean Women], in Niccho yuko sokushin, *Nihon to Chosen no kankei shi* [History of the Relations between Japan and Korea] (Agenda Project, 2004); Kim Pu-ja & Kim Yon, *Shokuminchi yukaku* [Colonial Pleasure Quarters] (Tokyo: Yoshikawa kobunkan, 2018), 18, 21.

25 Kim & Kim, *Shokuminchi yukaku* (2018), 18, 21; Fujinaga, "Shokuminchi kosho seido" (2004).

26 "Nihon no shokuminchi shihai to kokkateki kanri baishun" [Japan's Colonial Control and the National Management of Prostitution], *Chosenshi kenkyukai ronbun shu* 32 (1994): 58, 65, 76; Chosen sotokufu tokei nempo, "Zaicho kanren gyosha" [Related Industry Parties in Korea] (1906–1942), in Suzuki Yuko et al., eds., *Nihon gun "ianfu" kankei shiryo shusei* [Collection of Documents Relating to the "Comfort Women" of the Japanese Military] (Tokyo: Akashi shoten, 2006).

27 Odaka Konosuke, "Nihon tochika ni okeru Chosen no rodo keizai" [Korean Labor Economy under Japanese Control], *Keizai kenkyu* 26 (1975): 150, 153.

28 Kim & Kim, *Shokuminchi yukaku* (2018), 26, 89, 96; Nihon yuran sha, ed., *Yukaku annai* [Guide to Pleasure Quarters] (Nihon yuran sha, 1932), 461.

29 "Nihon no shokuminchi shihai to kokkateki kanri baishun" (1994).

30 Kim & Kim, *Shokuminchi yukaku* (2018), 96.

31 "Nihon no shokuminchi shihai to kokkateki kanri baishun" (1994), 63.

32 See Younghoon Rhee, ed., *Hannichi shuzoku shugi* [Anti-Japan Tribalism] (Tokyo: Bungei shunju, 2019), 284.

33 Kim & Kim, *Shokuminchi yukaku,* (2018), 97; see Ito, *Kotoka no kanojo no seikatsu* (1931), 172–94.

34 Doke Saiichiro, *Baishunfu ronko* [Studies in Prostitution] (Shishi shuppan, 1928), reprinted in Suzuki et al. (2006), 1:786–820.

35 See ibid.

36 See Lee Dong-Jin, "Minzoku, chiiki, sekushuaritii: Manshukoku no chosenjin 'seibaibai jujisha' wo chushin to shite" [Ethnicity, Region and Sexuality: The Case of Korean "Sex Workers" in Manchukuo], *Quadrante* 22 (2020): 47, table 5. Given the widespread use of *shakufu* to refer to prostitution, this would not have been misleading.

37 See Hata Ikuhiko, *Ianfu to senjo no sei* [Comfort Women and Sex in the Battle Zone] (Tokyo: Shincho sensho, 1999), 51.

38 The fact that the comfort station regime represented an overseas extension of the domestic licensing regime is a point made by multiple scholars. See, e.g., C. Sarah Soh, *The Comfort Women: Sexual Violence and Postcolonial Memory in Korea and Japan* (Chicago: University of Chicago Press, 2008), 117.

39 Jason Morgan, "The History of the Unspeakable: Shimokawa Masaharu's The Forgotten History of Evacuation," *Inter-Asia Cultural Studies* 19, no. 4 (October 2018): 644–54.

40 See Senda Kako, *Jugun ianfu* [Comfort Women of the Military] (Tokyo: Futaba sha, 1973), 16–17.

41 Gunsei kanbu bisaya shibu [Military Administration Executive Staff, Visaya (Philippines) Outpost], "Ianjo kitei sofu no ken" [Regarding Transmittal of Comfort Station Regulations], November 22, 1942, in Josei (1997), 3:187; Shina haken gun [China Expeditionary Army], "Showa 17 nen 9 gatsu fukukankai doseki jo iken" [Opinions Expressed at the September 1942 Vice Officers' Meeting], October 3, 1942, in Josei (1997), 3:7; SCAP, "Amenities in the Japanese Armed Forces," November 15, 1945, in Josei (1998), 5:139; Minami Shina hakengun [South China Expeditionary Force], "Eisei shunpo" [Sanitation Dispatch], August 1939, in Josei (1997), 2:79; Morikawa butaicho [Morikawa detachment commander], "Morikawa butai tokushu iangyomu ni kansuru kitei" [Morikawa Detachment Regulations Regarding Special Comfort Industry], November 14, 1939, in Josei (1997), 2:327; Mandaree chutonchi shireibu [Mandalay Garrison Command Post], "Chuteichi ianjo kitei" [Comfort Station Regulations in Occupied Areas], May 26, 1943, in Josei (1997), 4:288; Hito gunsei kanbu, "Ianjo ... kitei sofu no ken" [Case

Regarding the Transmittal of Comfort Station ... Rules], November 22, 1942, in Suzuki et al. (2006), 1:383.

42 Keisho cho sokan kanbo bunsho ka (1933), 93–98.

43 SCAP, "Amenities in the Japanese Armed Forces," 139.

44 See Hata, *Ianfu to senjo no sei* (1999), 394 (additional premia for combat pay possible).

45 The earlier figures for prostitute incomes in the domestic Tokyo market were from the 1920s. General price levels are stable until the late 1930s but then explode in the 1940s. The wholesale price index was 1.296 in 1921, 1.157 in 1926, 0.748 in 1931, and 1.036 in 1936. It hit 1.466 in 1939, 1.758 in 1941, and 2.046 in 1943. See Ando Yoshio, *Kindai Nihon keizai shi yoran* [Overview of Early Modern Japanese Economic History], 2nd ed. (Tokyo: University of Tokyo Press, 1987), 2–3. Over the course of these decades, the shadow wages for would-be prostitutes fell. These were women who would otherwise have worked in factories or on the farms. Factory wages for women were lower in the 1930s than they had been in the 1920s. A standard reference volume in economic history, Ando gives the daily female wage in manufacturing (in sen = 1/100 yen) as: 96 in 1920, 103 in 1925, 92 in 1930, 67 in 1935, 82 in 1939 (the table ends with 1939). Female wages in agriculture fluctuated more broadly: 94 in 1920, 131 in 1925, 86 in 1930, 70 in 1935, 131 in 1939. See Ando (1987), 12.

46 For an elaborate description of the accounting in English, see SCAP, "Amenities in the Japanese Armed Forces," 151–53.

47 See Rhee, *Hannichi shuzoku shugi* (2019), 261.

48 Ibid., 262.

49 See Hata, *Ianfu to senjo no sei* (1999), 392. This is a higher ratio than our own observations (detailed here) would suggest.

50 See Lee Wooyoun, "Anti-Japan Tribalism on the Comfort Women Issue."

51 Korea Institute of History (2016d), "Korean Comfort Station Manager's Diary," analyzed by Professor Choe Kilsung, April 24, 2016, http://scholarsinenglish.blogspot.com/2016/04/korean-comfort-station-managers-diary.html.

52 Park Yu-ha, *Teikoku no ianfu* [Comfort Women of the Empire] (Tokyo: Asahi shimbun shuppan, 2014), 111.

53 Korea Institute of History (2016c), "Former Korean Comfort Woman Mun Oku-chu's Memoir," April 20, 2016, http://scholarsinenglish.blogspot.com/2014/10/former-korean-comfort-woman-mun-oku.html.

54 On quitting by domestic licensed prostitutes, see Ramseyer, *Odd Markets* (1996), 122–26.

55 See Yamada Seikichi, *Bukan heitan* [Wuhan Logistics] (Tokyo: Tosho shuppan, 1978), 77, 84.

56 See Rhee, *Hannichi shuzoku shugi* (2019), 320.

57 Lee Wooyoun, "Ramseyer's Paper, Criticism Against It, and Counter-Criticism For It," Naksungdae Institute of Economic Research, Working Paper 2022-02 (January 2022), 8 (published at *Japan Review*, Winter 2021: 37–54).

58 Soh, *The Comfort Women* (2008), 114.
59 Ibid.
60 Park, *Teikoku no ianfu* (2014).
61 Ibid., 80.
62 Korea Institute of History, "Former Korean Comfort Woman Mun Okuchu's Memoir."
63 Park, *Teikoku no ianfu* (2014), 80.
64 Ibid., 86.
65 Ibid., 84–86.
66 Senda, *Jugun ianfu* (1973), 82.
67 Hirota Kazuko, *Shogen kiroku: Jugun ianfu, kangofu* [Statements and Records: Military Comfort Women and Nurses] (Tokyo: Shin jinbutsu orai sha, 1975), 39.
68 Ibid.
69 Ibid., 45.
70 Park, *Teikoku no ianfu* (2014), 84.
71 Ibid., 70–71.
72 Hirota, *Shogen kiroku* (1975), 38.
73 Archie Miyamoto, "Some Uncomfortable Truths about Comfort Women for the International Mob," *JAPAN Forward*, February 22, 2021, https://japan-forward.com/some-uncomfortable-truths-about-comfort-women-for-the-international-mob/.
74 Park, *Teikoku no ianfu* (2014), 83.
75 Ibid., 152.
76 Ibid., 15.
77 See UN Commission on Human Rights, *Report on the mission to the Democratic People's Republic of Korea, the Republic of Korea and Japan on the issue of military sexual slavery in wartime. Report by Radhika Coomaraswamy, Special Rapporteur*, January 4, 1996, E/CN.4/1996/53/Add.1, para. 69.
78 Tessa Morris-Suzuki, "Japan's 'Comfort Women': It's Time for the Truth (in the Ordinary, Everyday Sense of the Word)," *Asia-Pacific Journal: Japan Focus* 5, iss. 3 (March 1, 2007); Peipei Qiu, Su Zhiliang & Chen Lifei, *Chinese Comfort Women: Testimonies from Imperial Japan's Sex Slaves* (Vancouver: University of British Columbia Press, 2013).
79 See Hata, *Ianfu to senjo no sei* (1999), 402–6.
80 See ibid., 410.
81 See Yoshimi Yoshiaki, *Jugun ianfu* [Comfort Women of the Military] (Tokyo: Iwanami shoten, 1995), 78–80.
82 See Rhee, *Hannichi shuzoku shugi* (2019), 268–69.
83 See generally, "Nihon no shokuminchi shihai to kokkateki kanri baishun" (1994), 51; Yamashita Yon'e, "Chosen ni okeru kosho seido no jisshi to sono tenkai" [The Realization and Development of the Licensed

Prostitution System in Korea], in Suzuki et al. (2006), 2:675; *Keijo [Seoul] nippo*, June 12, 1918 (evening ed.), quoted in Fujinaga Takeshi, "Shokuminchi Chosen ni okeru kosho seido no kakuritsu katei" [The Establishment Process for the Licensed Prostitution System in Colonial Korea], *Nijuseiki kenkyu*, December 2004; Senda, *Jugun ianfu* (1973), 89; "Shojo yuin dan kyukei" [Gang to Entrap Young Women Sentenced], *Toa nippo*, November 5, 1937, in Suzuki et al. (2006), 1:829; "Shinpan momoiro hakuku kyo," *Toa nippo*, March 7, 1939, in Suzuki et al. (2006), 1:829.

84 See generally Arima Tetsuo, *"Ianfu" ha mina goi keiyaku wo shiteita* [The "Comfort Women" Had All Agreed to Contracts] (Tokyo: WAC, 2021), chap. 11.

85 See ibid.; Lee Wooyoun, "Ramseyer's Paper," 14; Tetsuo Arima, "Read the Endnotes! Comfort Women Paper Was Based on Wealth of Historical Facts," *JAPAN Forward*, July 2, 2022, https://japan-forward.com/read-the-endnotes-comfort-women-paper-was-based-on-wealth-of-historical-facts/; Tetsuo Arima, "What Happened to Comfort Women Recruitments: Facts, Not Conjectures," *JAPAN Forward*, July 3, 2022, https://japan-forward.com/what-happened-to-comfort-women-recruitments-facts-not-conjectures/; Naimusho, "Shina toko fujo ni kansuru kenshi" [Inquiry Regarding Passage of Women to China], February 18, 1938, in Suzuki et al. (2006), 1:124.

86 See Arima, *"Ianfu" ha mina goi keiyaku wo shiteita* (2021b), chap. 11; Lee Wooyoun, "Ramseyer's Paper," 14; Arima, "Read the Endnotes!"; Arima, "What Happened to Comfort Women Recruitments."

87 Park Yu-ha, *Rekishi to mukiau* [Facing History] (Tokyo: Mainichi shimbun shuppan 2022), 185–86.

CHAPTER 3—THE HOAX BUILDS

1 See Hata Ikuhiko, *Comfort Women and Sex in the Battle Zone*, trans. Jason Michael Morgan (Lanham, MD: Hamilton Books, 2018), 190.

2 See Yoshida Seiji, *Watashi no senso hanzai* [My War Crimes] (Tokyo: San'ichi shobo, 1983).

3 "Chosen no josei, watashi mo renko" [I Too Dragooned Korean Women], *Asahi shimbun*, September 2, 1982.

4 See Yoshida, *Watashi no senso hanzai* (1983), 108.

5 Hata, *Comfort Women* (2018), 183.

6 See "'Yoshida shogen' yoyaku torikeshi ..." [At Last, the "Yoshida Testimony" Withdrawn ...], *Yomiuri shimbun*, August 6, 2014; Hata, *Comfort Women* (2018); Ikeda Nobuo, *Asahi shimbun: Seiki no dai goho* [The Asahi Newspaper: Fake News of the Century] (Tokyo: K.K. Asupekuto, 2014).

7 "Chosen no josei" (1982).

8 "Watashi wa moto ianfu" [I Am a Former Comfort Woman], *Asahi shimbun*, November 2, 1984; C. Sarah Soh, *The Comfort Women: Sexual Violence and Postcolonial Memory in Korea and Japan* (Chicago:

University of Chicago Press, 2008), 166–67; Arima Tetsuo, *Koshite rekishi mondai ha netsuzo sareru* [This Is How Historical Problems Are Faked] (Tokyo: Shincho sha, 2017), 104–11.

9 Park Yu-ha, *Rekishi to mukiau* [Facing History] (Tokyo: Mainichi shimbun shuppan, 2022), 169.

10 "Chosenjin jugun ianfu ni hikari wo" [A Light on the Korean Military Comfort Women], *Asahi shimbun*, July 18, 1991.

11 See Nishioka Tsutomu, "Ianfu mondai no haikei ni ..." [In the Background of the Comfort Women Problem ...], *Kin'yu fakushimirii shinbun*, November 17, 2014.

12 "Omoidasuto imamo namida" [When I Remember It, I Still Cry], *Asahi shimbun*, August 11, 1991.

13 "Chosen no josei" (1982).

14 Sakurai Yoshiko shi kisha kaiken yoshi [Summary of Press Conference by Sakurai Yoshiko], *Iza*, March 25, 2018, https://www.iza.ne.jp/article/20180325-FRV2772L2JOJXBZJ2NG6XIKTLQ/.

15 "Sakurai Yoshiko vs Nishioka Tsutomu," May 13, 2011, https://yoshiko-sakurai.jp/2021/05/13/9169.

16 "'Moto ianfu, hatsu no shogen' kiji ni jijitsu no nejimage nai" ["The First Testimonial of a Former Comfort Woman," Truth Not Twisted in Article], *Asahi shimbun*, August 5, 2014.

17 See generally Ikeda, *Asahi shimbun: Seiki no dai goho* (2014), 48–52. Regarding the Uemura dispute, see [No names given], 1479 Hanrei taimuzu 217 (Tokyo D. Ct. June 26, 2019), aff'd, (Tokyo High Ct. Mar. 3, 2020), aff'd, (Sup. Ct. Mar. 11, 2021); [No names given], 1477 Hanrei taimuzu 57 (Sapporo D. Ct. Nov. 9, 2018), aff'd, 1477 Hanrei taimuzu 48 (Sapporo High Ct. Feb. 6, 2000), aff'd, (Sup. Ct. Nov. 18, 2020).

18 [No names given] v. Koku, 1879 Hanrei jiho 58 (Sup. Ct. Nov. 29, 2004). At least two other cases were also filed, but these were dismissed by the Supreme Court as well. See Zaisan oyobi seikyu ken ni kansuru mondai no kaiketsu narabi ni keizai kyoryoku ni kansuru Nihon koku to Dai kan minkoku to no aida no kyotei [Agreement between Japan and the Republic of Korea Concerning the Economic Cooperation and the Resolution of Problems Involving Property and Claims], Treaty No. 27, 1965.

19 "Moto ianfu Kim Hak Sun san" [Former Comfort Woman Kim Hak Sun], *Asahi shimbun*, December 25, 1991.

20 Ikeda, *Asahi shmbun: Seiki no dai goho* (2014), 25, 51.

21 Lew Seok-choon, "Hensen wo kasaneta 'Ianfu shogen' no uragawa" [What Lies behind the "Comfort Women Testimonies" That Have Changed Multiple Times], *Shukan shincho*, June 2, 2022, at 45.

22 "'Moto ianfu, hatsu no shogen' kiji ni jijitsu no nejimage nai" (2014).

23 Quoted in [No names given], 1479 Hanrei taimuzu 217 (Tokyo D. Ct. June 26, 2019), aff'd, (Tokyo High Ct. Mar. 3, 2020), aff'd, (Sup. Ct. Mar. 11, 2021).

24 Arima, *Koshite rekishi mondai ha netsuzo sareru* (2017), 106; Ikeda, *Asahi shmbun: Seiki no dai goho* (2014), 25.

25 Sojo [Complaint], Park v. Nihon koku, December 6, 1991, at 51–52, https://www.awf.or.jp/pdf/195-k1.pdf.

26 Yoshimi's document is "Gun ianjo jugyofu to boshu ni kansuru ken" [Regarding the Solicitation of Employees, etc., for the Military Comfort Stations], Rikugun sho, March 4, 1938, Riku shimitsu No. 745, vol. 10, 1938, reprinted in Suzuki et al. (2006), 1:103, and in Josei (1997), 2:5.

27 Ibid.

28 Bob Tadashi Wakabayashi, "Review of *Japan's Contested War Memories: The 'Memory Rifts' in Historical Consciousness of World War II*," *Journal of Japanese Studies* 35, no. 1 (Winter 2009): 184.

29 Yoshimi's attack appears as Yoshiaki Yoshimi, "Response to 'Contracting for Sex in the Pacific War,' by J. Mark Ramseyer," *International Review of Law and Economics*, August 9, 2023. Ramseyer's reply to Yoshimi appears in "Contracting for Sex in the Pacific War: A Response to My Critics," Harvard John M. Olin DP 1075, January 4, 2022, SSRN WP 4000145, https://papers.ssrn.com/sol3/papers.cfm?abstract_id=4000145.

30 Hata, *Comfort Women* (2018), chap. 8; Hata Ikuhiko, *Ianfu to senjo no sei* [Comfort Women and Sex in the Battle Zone] (Tokyo: Shincho sensho, 1999), chap. 8.

31 See Hata, *Comfort Women* (2018), 201; Hata, *Ianfu to senjo no sei* (1999), 252.

32 See generally ibid.

33 Statement by Chief Cabinet Secretary, August 4, 1993, Ministry of Foreign Affairs of Japan, https://www.mofa.go.jp/a_o/rp/page25e_000343.html.

34 Other discussions of the changes in stories told by the comfort women appear in, e.g., Park, *Rekishi to mukiau* (2022), 127–31.

35 "Nihon no shokuminchi shihai to kokkateki kanri baishun" [Japan's Colonial Control and the National Management of Prostitution], *Chosenshi kenkyukai ronbun shu*, 32 (1994): 37, 51; Yamashita Yon'e, "Chosen ni okeru kosho seido no jisshi to sono tenkai" [The Realization and Development of the Licensed Prostitution System in Korea], in Suzuki et al. (2006), 2:675.

36 *Keijo [Seoul] nippo*, June 12, 1918 (evening ed.), quoted in Fujinaga Takeshi, "Shokuminchi Chosen ni okeru kosho seido no kakuritsu katei" [The Establishment Process for the Licensed Prostitution System in Colonial Korea], *Nijuseiki kenkyu*, December 2004; Senda Kako, *Jugun ianfu* [Comfort Women of the Military] (Tokyo: Futaba sha, 1973), 89.

37 "Shojo yuin dan kyukei" [Gang to Entrap Young Women Sentenced], *Toa nippo*, November 5, 1937, reprinted in Suzuki et al. (2006), 1:829.

38 Ibid.; Yamashita, "Chosen ni okeru kosho seido no jisshi to sono tenkai" (2006), 675.

39 "Shina toko fujo no toriatsukai ni kansuru ken" [Regarding the Handling of Women Bound for China], February 23, 1938, Home Ministry, Police Bureau, Hatsukei No. 5.

40 Digital Museum, The Asian Women's Fund, various materials available at http://www.awf.or.jp/e2/foundation.html, http://www.awf.or.jp/e3/Korea.html.

41 UN Commission on Human Rights, *Report on the mission to the Democratic People's Republic of Korea, the Republic of Korea and Japan on the issue of military sexual slavery in wartime. Report by Radhika Coomaraswamy, Special Rapporteur*, January 4, 1996, E/CN.4/1996/53/Add.I.

42 See George Hicks, *The Comfort Women: Japan's Brutal Regime of Enforced Prostitution* (New York: Norton, 1994).

43 Ustinia Dolgopol & Snehal Paranjape, *Comfort Women: An Unfinished Ordeal* (Geneva: International Commission of Jurists, 1994).

44 See, e.g., Hicks, *The Comfort Women* (1994), Acknowledgements.

45 Soh, *The Comfort Women* (2008), 154.

46 See UN Coomaraswamy Report (1996), para. 55.

47 See ibid., para. 56.

48 See J. Mark Ramseyer, "Social Capital and the Problem of Opportunistic Leadership: The Example of Koreans in Japan," *European Review of Law and Economics*, Err. n.2 (2021).

49 UN Coomaraswamy Report (1996), para. 54; see Yong-Shik Lee, Natsu Taylor Saito & Jonathan Todres, "The Fallacy of Contract in Sexual Slavery: A Response to Ramseyer's 'Contracting for Sex in the Pacific War,'" *Michigan Journal of International Law* 42 (2021): 308; Michael Chwe, Letter by Concerned Economists Regarding "Contracting for Sex in the Pacific War" in the International Review of Law and Economics (2021), http://chwe.net/irle/letter/.

50 See Hata, *Ianfu to senjo no sei* (1999), 273.

51 Ibid., 326–27; UN Coomaraswamy Report (1996), para. 2, 47, 66.

52 Park, *Rekishi to mukiau* (2022), 143, 180.

53 UN Sub-Commission on the Promotion and Protection of Human Rights, *Systematic rape, sexual slavery and slavery-like practices during armed conflict. Final report submitted by Gay J. McDougall, Special Rapporteur*, June 22, 1998, E/CN.4/Sub.2/1998/13, para. 7.

54 Ibid., para. 7.

55 Thomas M. McDonnell, announcement of AALS award, email, January 1, 2023.

56 Karen Parker & Jennifer F. Chew, "Compensation for Japan's World War II War-Rape 1Victims," *Hastings International and Comparative Law Review* 17 (1994): 497–549.

57 Ibid., 498–99.

58 Hwang v. Japan, 172 F. Supp. 2d 52 (D.D.C. 2001), aff'd, 332 F.3d 679 (D.D.Cir. 2003), remanded, 413 F.3d 45 (D.C. Cir. 2005), cert. den'd, 2006 U.S. Lexis 1691 (2006). See *Protecting the Human Rights of Comfort Women: Hearing before the Subcommittee on Asia, the Pacific, and the*

Global Environment, of the Committee of Foreign Affairs, U.S. House of Representatives, 110th Cong., February 15, 2007.

59 See Carol Gluck, "What the World Owes the Comfort Women," in *Mnemonic Solidarity: Global Interventions*, Entangled Memories in the Global South, ed. J. H. Lim and E. Rosenhaft (London: Palgrave Macmillan, 2021), 80.

60 Lee, Saito & Todres, "The Fallacy of Contract in Sexual Slavery," 294 n.11.

61 Rumiko Nishino, "Forcible Mobilization: What Survivor Testimonies Tell Us," in *Denying the Comfort Women: The Japanese State's Assault on Historical Truth*, ed. Rumiko Nishino, Kim Puja & Akane Onozawa (London: Routledge, 2018), 40, 43–44. Timothy Webster seems to make the same mistake as Y.S. Lee and Carol Gluck when he asserts that the district court in the Tokyo case made "factual findings that reflect Yoshimi's view." Immediately before the passage that Webster quotes, the district court explicitly noted that these facts were uncontested. See Timothy Webster, "The Minds Behind the Movement: The Role of Academics in East Asia's War Reparations Litigation," *Case Western Reserve Journal of International Law* 54 (2022): 14.

62 See Kuni v. [Unnamed parties], 1642 Hanrei jiho 24 (Shimonoseki Br. Off. Apr. 27, 1998), rev'd, 1759 Hanrei jiho 42 (Hiroshima High Ct. Mar. 29, 2001), [aff'd], (Sup. Ct. Mar. 25, 2013).

63 See [No names given] v. Kuni, (Tokyo D.Ct., Mar. 26, 2001), aff'd, 1843 Hanrei jiho 32 (Tokyo High Ct. July 22, 2003), aff'd, (Sup. Ct. Nov. 29, 2004); Song v. Kuni, 1741 Hanrei jiho 40 (Tokyo D. Ct. Oct. 1, 1999) (appendix), aff'd, 1741 Hanrei jiho 40 (Tokyo High Ct. Nov. 30, 2000), aff'd, (Sup. Ct. Mar. 28, 2003).

64 UN Sub-Commission on the Promotion and Protection of Human Rights, *Systematic rape, sexual slavery and slavery-like practices during armed conflict. Update to the final report submitted by Gay J. McDougall, Special Rapporteur*, June 6, 2000, E/CN.4/Sub.2/2000/21, para. 75.

65 Alexis Dudden, "'We Came to Tell the Truth': Reflections on the Tokyo Women's Tribunal," *Critical Asian Studies* 33, no. 4 (2001): 591 602.

66 Norma Field, "The Courts, Japan's 'Military Comfort Women,' and the Conscience of Humanity: The Ruling in VAWW-Net Japan v. NHK," *Asia-Pacific Journal: Japan Focus* 5, iss. 2 (February 2, 2007): 2.

67 Hata, *Comfort Women* (2018), 220.

68 The Women's International War Crimes Tribunal for the Trial of Japan's Military Sexual Slavery, January 31, 2002, para. 124, 189, https://archives.wam-peace.org/wt/wp-content/uploads/2020/03/Cover-Page_Judgement.pdf.

69 Ibid., para. 167.

70 Christine M. Chinkin, "Women's International Tribunal on Japanese Military Sexual Slavery," *American Journal of International Law* 95, no. 2 (2001): 336.

71 Amnesty International, *Still Waiting after 60 Years: Justice for Survivors of Japan's Military Sexual Slavery System*, ASA 22;012;2005 (October 2005), 1.

72 Ibid., 6.

73 Ibid., 8.

74 Ibid., 9.

75 Jerry H. Bentley and Herbert F. Ziegler, *Traditions and Encounters*, 5th ed. (New York: McGraw-Hill, 2011), 853.

76 Alexis Dudden et al., "Standing with Historians of Japan," *Perspectives on History*, March 1, 2015.

77 Jesse Johnson and Magdalena Osumi, "Fifty Japanese Scholars Attack McGraw-Hill, U.S. Academics on 'Comfort Women' Issue," *Japan Times*, December 11, 2015.

78 Ibid.

79 Ibid.

80 Alexis Dudden, "Letter Campaigns, the Japanese Media, and the Effort to Censor History," in *Press Freedom in Contemporary Japan*, ed. Jeff Kingston (Oxon: Routledge, 2017), 157.

81 Jason Morgan, "U.S. Textbook Defender Lacks an Open Mind," *Japan Times*, December 18, 2015; Alexis Dudden, "Learning from Past Best Way to Move Forward," *Japan Times*, December 26, 2015.

82 "'Sengo 70 nen' zaigai Nihon kenkyusha seimei ..." ["70 Years after the War": Statement of Overseas Japan Researchers ...], *Mainichi shimbun*, May 27, 2015.

83 Naoko Kumagai, "On 'Standing with Historians of Japan,'" *Perspectives on History*, September 1, 2015.

84 Alexis Dudden et al., "Response to Naoko Kumagai (Sept. 2015)," *Perspectives on History*, December 1, 2015.

CHAPTER 4—THE HOAX COLLAPSES

1 Hata Ikuhiko, *Comfort Women and Sex in the Battle Zone*, trans. Jason Michael Morgan (Lanham, MD: Hamilton Books, 2018), 185; see "'Ianfu seidorei setsu' wo iidashita" ... [The First to Raise the "Comfort Women Were Sex Slaves Theory" ...], *News Posuto*, August 15, 2012, https//www.news-postseven.com/archives/20120815_136788.html?DETAIL.

2 Yoshida Seiji, *Chosenjin ianfu to Nihon jin* [Korean Comfort Women and Japanese] (Tokyo: Shin jinbutsu orai sha, 1977), chap. 15.

3 Hata, *Comfort Women* (2018), 182–84.

4 Ibid., 186.

5 Ibid., 191–92.

6 Ibid., 192.

7 Ibid.

8 Ibid.

9 Ibid., 186.

10 Archie Miyamoto, "Some Uncomfortable Truths about Comfort Women for the International Mob," *JAPAN Forward*, February 22, 2021, https://japan-forward.com/some-uncomfortable-truths-about-comfort-women-for-the-international-mob.

11 Hata, *Comfort Women* (2018), 189; "'Saishuto de renko' shogen" ["Forcibly abducted in Jeju" Testimonial], *Asahi shimbun*, August 5, 2014.

12 Yoshii Riki, "'Hyogen no fujiyu' ko: 'Jugun ianfu ha dema' to iu dema, rekishigakusha, Yoshimi Yoshiaki shi ni kiku" [Thoughts on the "Lack of Freedom of Expression": Asking Historian Mr. Yoshimi Yoshiaki about the False Rumor That "Military Comfort Women Were a False Rumor"], *Mainichi shimbun*, August 15, 2019.

13 See generally [No names given], 1479 Hanrei taimuzu 217 (Tokyo D. Ct. June 26, 2019), aff'd, (Tokyo High Ct. Mar. 3, 2020), aff'd, (Sup. Ct. Mar. 11, 2021); [No names given], 1477 Hanrei taimuzu 57 (Sapporo D. Ct. Nov. 9, 2018), aff'd, 1477 Hanrei taimuzu 48 (Sapporo High Ct. Feb. 6, 2000), aff'd, (Sup. Ct. Nov. 18, 2020). For an excellent background, see Arima Tetsuo, *Koshite rekishi mondai ha netsuzo sareru* [This Is How Historical Problems Are Faked] (Tokyo: Shincho sha, 2017), 108–9.

14 [No names given], 1479 Hanrei taimuzu 217 (Tokyo D. Ct. June 26, 2019).

15 "Sakurai Yoshiko vs Nishioka Tsutomu" ..., May 13, 2011, https://yoshiko-sakurai.jp/2021/05/13/9169.

16 [No names given], 1479 Hanrei taimuzu 217 (Tokyo D. Ct. June 26, 2019).

17 H. Res. 121, 110th Congress, July 30, 2007.

18 Office of Congressional Ethics, U.S. House of Representatives, Report: Review No. 15-2070, https://ethics.house.gov/sites/ethics.house.gov/files/Rep.%20Honda%20OCE%20Report%20and%20Findings.pdf.

19 Bethany Allen-Ebrahimian, "Exclusive: Chinese Spy Targeted California Politicians," *Axios*, updated December 8, 2020, https://www.axios.com/2020/12/08/china-spy-california-politicians.

20 Peter Hasson, "All Signs Point to One Man as Chinese Spy in Feinstein's Staff, and He Wasn't a Driver," *Daily Caller*, August 6, 2018, https://dailycaller.com/2018/08/06/feinstein-chinese-spy/.

21 Trevor Loudon, "Feinstein's Spy: Russell Lowe and San Francisco's Pro-China Left," *Epoch Times*, August 20, 2018.

22 Mike Gonzalez, "Yes, a Pro-China Group in America Supports a Black Lives Matter Founder," The Heritage Foundation, October 21, 2020, https://www.heritage.org/progressivism/commentary/yes-pro-china-group-america-supports-black-lives-matter-founder.

23 Eric Mar, San Francisco State University faculty profile, https://aas.sfsu.edu/eric-mar, accessed August 4, 2023.

24 "Jugun ianfu: kesenai jijitsu" [Military Comfort Women: The Reality That Cannot Be Dismissed], *Asahi shimbun*, March 31, 1997.

25 "'Yoshida shogen' yoyaku torikeshi ..." [At Last, the "Yoshida Testimony" Withdrawn ...], *Yomiuri shimbun*, August 6, 2014; "Jiyu wa ubawareta kyoseisei atta" [There Was Coercion in the Sense That Their Freedom

Was Taken from Them], *Asahi shimbun*, August 5, 2014; "'Saishuto de renko' shogen" ["Forcibly Abducted in Jeju" Testimony], *Asah shimbun*, August 5, 2014; "Asahi shimbun moto kisha" [Former Reporter for *Asahi shimbun*], Zakzak, August 5, 2014.

26 "'Saishuto de renko' shogen" (2014).

27 Martin Fackler (2014a), "Japan, Seeking Revision of Report on Wartime Brothels, Is Rebuffed," *New York Times*, October 16, 2014.

28 Martin Fackler (2014b), "Rewriting the War, Japanese Right Attacks a Newspaper," *New York Times*, December 2, 2014.

29 Fackler (2014a), "Japan, Seeking Revision of Report…"

30 The report of its investigation (the source for the material in the text) appears at "Ianfu mondai wo meguru Nikkan kan no yaritori no keii" [The Course of the Exchanges between Japan and South Korea on the Comfort Women Problem], *Asahi shimbun*, June 21, 2014.

31 Ibid.

32 Ibid.

33 Ibid.

34 See C. Sarah Soh, *The Comfort Women: Sexual Violence and Postcolonial Memory in Korea and Japan* (Chicago: University of Chicago Press, 2008), 159–69.

35 Ibid., 159.

36 Ibid., 160.

37 Ibid.

38 Senda Kako, *Jugun ianfu* [Comfort Women of the Military] (Tokyo: Futaba sha, 1973).

39 Soh, *The Comfort Women* (2008), 161.

40 Ibid., 166.

41 Ibid., 166–67.

42 See generally Arima, *Koshite rekishi mondai ha netsuzo sareru* (2017), 104–11. There was no corroborating evidence or testimony in support of the woman's account. Matsui Yayori (discussed in the text) was the reporter on this story.

43 See Hata Ikuhiko, *Ianfu to senjo no sei* [Comfort Women and Sex in the Battle Zone] (Tokyo: Shincho sensho, 1999), 366–76.

44 See Soh, *The Comfort Women* (2008), 162.

45 See generally Josei no tameno Ajia heiwa kokumin kikin, "'Ianfu' mondai to Ajia josei shikin" [The "Comfort Women" Issue and the Asian Women's Fund] (2003), 10–12, https://www.awf.or.jp/pdf/0169.pdf. See also Onuma Yasuaki, Yokota Yozo & Wada Haruki, "Ajia josei kikin to watashi tachi" [The Asian Women's Fund and Us], *Yobikake*, October 20, 2006, 23.

46 Park Yu-ha, *Teikoku no ianfu* [Comfort Women of the Empire] (Tokyo: Asahi shimbun shuppan, 2014). 128.

CHAPTER 5—THE ATTACKS REDUX

1 An attack by Yoshimi, written in 2021, was published in the IRLE in 2023. See Yoshiaki Yoshimi, "Response to 'Contracting for Sex in the Pacific War,' by J. Mark Ramseyer", *International Review of Law and Economics*, August 9, 2023. Ramseyer's reply to Yoshimi appears in "Contracting for Sex in the Pacific War: A Response to My Critics," Harvard John M. Olin DP 1075, January 4, 2022, SSRN WP 4000145, https://papers.ssrn.com/sol3/papers.cfm?abstract_id=4000145.

2 Andrew Gordon, private email to J. Mark Ramseyer, February 7, 2021.

3 Jeannie Suk-Gersen, "Seeking the True Story of the Comfort Women," *New Yorker*, February 26, 2021.

4 Arirang News, March 1, 2021, https://www.youtube.com/watch?v=JXFzdV8YRGQ&t=20s.

5 Andrew Gordon, *A Modern History of Japan: From Tokugawa Times to the Present*, 3rd ed. (New York: Oxford University Press, 2014), 222–23. Gordon revised this passage in his 4th edition (2020).

6 For a detailed response to the attack, please see Ramseyer, "Contracting for Sex in the Pacific War: A Response to My Critics."

7 See Yoshimi, "Response to 'Contracting for Sex in the Pacific War,' by J. Mark Ramseyer"; and Ramseyer, "Contracting for Sex in the Pacific War: A Response to My Critics," Appendix II.

8 Ibid.

9 Sayaka Chatani, @SayakaChatani, Twitter, February 19, 2021.

10 Amy Stanley, @astanley711, Twitter, June 16, 2021.

11 Paula R. Curtis, "Taking the Fight for Japan's History Online: The Ramseyer Controversy and Social Media," *Asia-Pacific Journal: Japan Focus* 19, iss. 22, no. 3 (December 1, 2021).

12 Yoshimi Yoshiaki, *Jugun ianfu* [Comfort Women of the Military] (Tokyo: Iwanami shoten, 1995), 98.

13 Younghoon Rhee, ed., *Hannichi shuzoku shugi* [Anti-Japan Tribalism] (Tokyo: Bungei shunju, 2019), 279–80; Mun Ok-ju, *Biruma sensen: Tateshidan no "Ianfu" datta watashi* [The Burmese Front: I Who Had Been a "Comfort Woman" for the Tate Division], trans. Morikawa Machiko (Tokyo: Nashi no kisha, 1996), 114–22.

14 Mun, *Biruma sensen* (1996), 122.

15 Hata, *Comfort Women* (2018), 234.

16 Yamazaki Tomoko, *Sandakan hachiban shokan* [Sandakan Number 8 Brothel] (Tokyo: Chikuma shobo, 1972), 104–8.

17 Ibid.

18 Amy Stanley, "On Contract," Amy Stanley blog, March 18, 2021, https://www.amy-stanley.com/blog-1/on-contract.

19 Stanley, Twitter, March 19, 2021.

20 Jan Ruff-O'Herne, *Fifty Years of Silence* (North Sydney: William Heinemann, 2008).

21 David Ambaras, Twitter.

22 David Horowitz Freedom Center, https://www.horowitzfreedomcenter.org.

23 Jason Morgan, "'Nyu Refuto' no enkaku to Beikoku no 'hanNichi' shiso no seiritsu" [The Evolution of the New Left and the Rise of Anti-Japan Thinking in the United States], *Rekishi ninshiki mondai kenkyu* 9 (2021), http://harc.tokyo/wp/wp-content/uploads/2021/09/3598c3539a13c25ebd44a0702b5f1527.pdf.

24 Jason Morgan, "Waseda Professor Offers Evidence of Comfort Women Working Under Contract," *JAPAN Forward*, October 15, 2021, https://japan-forward.com/waseda-professor-offers-evidence-of-comfort-women-working-under-contract-now-come-the-attacks/; Jason Morgan, "The Comfort Women Issue: Bashing the Factfinders and Policing the Party Line," *JAPAN Forward*, October 18, 2021, https://japan-forward.com/the-comfort-women-issue-bashing-the-factfinders-and-policing-the-party-line/; Jason Morgan, "Conform or Get Attacked: Bigots Use Comfort Women Issue to Assault Free Speech in Japan," *JAPAN Forward*, October 20, 2021, https://japan-forward.com/conform-or-get-attacked-bigots-use-comfort-women-issue-to-assault-free-speech-in-japan/.

25 Paula R. Curtis, "Ramseyer and the Right-Wing Ecosystem Suffocating Japan," *Tokyo Review*, May 30, 2021.

26 See Lee Wooyoun, "Anti-Japan Tribalism on the Comfort Women Issue," *The Diplomat*, November 14, 2021, archived at https://archive.ph/20211115071637/https://thediplomat.com/2021/11/anti-japan-tribalism-on-the-comfort-women-issue/#selection-1231.547-1231.1052.

27 Ambaras, Twitter, November 14, 2021.

28 Mitch Shin, @MitchShin5, Twitter, November 15, 2021.

29 Ambaras, Twitter, November 15, 2021.

30 Ibid.

31 A@AResFin, Twitter, November 15, 2021.

32 Ethan Mark, Twitter, November 15, 2021.

33 Ambaras, Twitter, November 15, 2021.

34 Shin, Twitter, November 15, 2021.

35 Ambaras, Twitter, November 15, 2021. Readers interested in the article that Ambaras, Stanley, and Chatani harassed *The Diplomat* into censoring will find it at Lee Wooyoun, "No Debate? The Diplomat's Cancellation of My Comfort Women Article," *JAPAN Forward*, December 4, 2021, https://japan-forward.com/no-debate-the-diplomats-cancellation-of-my-comfort-women-article/; and also archived at https://archive.ph/20211115071637/https://thediplomat.com/2021/11/anti-japan-tribalism-on-the-comfort-women-issue/.

36 Chizuko Allen, *The Making of Korea in East Asia* (Colano Beach, CA: Cognella, 2021), 105.

37 Jinhee Lee, email to Angela Schultz, Cognella, April 30, 2021 (FOIA request).

38 Jinhee Lee, email to David Miano, Cognella, May 10, 2021 (FOIA request).

39 Jinhee Lee, email to David Miano, Cognella, August 17, 2021 (FOIA request).

40 Arirang News Center, "Harvard Law Professor's 'Comfort Women' Article: Fellow Scholars Call It 'Fake News,'" February 16, 2021, https://www.youtube.com/watch?v=fxixpFncCeg.

41 Alexis Dudden, "The Abuse of History: A Brief Response to J. Mark Ramseyer's 'Contracting for Sex,'" *Asia-Pacific Journal: Japan Focus* 19, iss. 5, no. 15 (March 1, 2021). Italics in the original.

42 Jeannie Suk-Gersen, "Seeking the True Story of the Comfort Women," *New Yorker*, February 26, 2021.

43 E.g., Chelsea Szendi Schieder, @SzendiChelsea, Twitter, https://twitter.com/SzendiChelsea/status/1379969613631393794.

44 Soh, *The Comfort Women* (2008), 12–13, 98–100; Keith Howard, ed., *True Stories of the Korean Comfort Women* (London: Cassell, 1995), 89; Joseph Yi, "Confronting Korea's Censored Discourse on Comfort Women," *The Diplomat*, January 31, 2018; Joseph Yi, "Illiberal Means for Liberal Ends: Low-Road Challenge to Public Discourse and International Relations," APSA Preprints, 2020, https://preprints.apsanet.org/engage/apsa/article-details/5f52aa1a9277460012015626.

45 "Moto 'ianfu' e hosho wo" [Compensation for Former "Comfort Women"], *Akahata*, June 26, 2002.

46 Martin Fackler, "No Apology for Sex Slavery, Japan's Prime Minister Says," *New York Times*, March 6, 2007.

47 Nishioka Tsutomu (2020c), "Saikin no Kankoku no anchihannichi no ugoki ni tsuite" [Regarding the Recent Anti-Anti-Japanese Developments in South Korea], *Rekishi ninshiki mondai kenkyu* 8 (2020): 83; private email from Hwang Uiwon, August 6, 2023.

48 Nishioka Tsutomu (2020b),, "Kankoku no ianfu undo no 'naifun'" [The "Internal Dispute" of the Comfort Women Movement], *Rekishi ninshiki mondai kenkyu* 7 (2020): 103–5.

49 Ibid., 103–5; Personal correspondence with Hwang Uiwon, February 27, 2022.

50 See Park Yu-ha, *Teikoku no ianfu* [Comfort Women of the Empire] (Tokyo: Asahi shimbun shuppan, 2014). To the same effect, Park Yu-ha, *Rekishi to mukiau* [Facing History] (Tokyo: Mainichi shimbun shuppan, 2022), 125.

51 See Park, *Teikoku no ianfu* (2014), 28.

52 Ibid., 143.

53 Korea Institute of History, "Comfort Women of the Empire" Reviewed by Professor Jun Bong Gwan, April 21, 2016, http://scholarsinenglish.blogspot.com/2014/10/comfort-women-of-empire-reviewed-by.html.

54 Joe Phillips, Wondong Lee & Joseph Yi, "Future of South Korea–Japan Relations: Decoupling or Liberal Discourse," *Political Quarterly* 91 (2019): 452–53.

55 Nishioka Tsutomu, "Kankoku ni okeru gakumon no jiyu no kiki ni tsuite" [Regarding the Crisis in Academic Freedom in South Korea], *Rekishi ninshiki mondai kenkyu* 10 (2022): 79–91.

56 Ibid.

57 See Tsutomu Nishioka, "Why Korean Professor Believes Comfort Women Were Not Sex Slaves," *JAPAN Forward*, November 24, 2017, https://japan-forward.com/why-korean-professor-believes-comfort-women-were-not-sex-slaves/; "Seoul University Prof. Lee Yong-hoon 'Comfort women = Sex slave' is an illusion," October 10, 2016, http://staff.texas-daddy.com/?eid=502.

58 See "Rhee Younghoon Seoul dai kyoju 'jugun ianfu ha baishugyo'" [SNU Professor Younghoon Rhee, "Comfort Women Were Prostitutes"], *Chosun online*, September 3, 2004, https://web.archive.org/web/20070517204644/http://www.chosunonline.com/article/20040903000051; "Ianfu hatsugen de monosawagi" [Trouble over Comfort Women Comments], *Chosun online*, September 6, 2004, http://www.chosunonline.com/article/20040906000060.

59 See Younghoon Rhee, ed., *Hannichi shuzoku shugi* [Anti-Japan Tribalism] (Tokyo: Bungei shunju, 2019); Younghoon Rhee, ed., *Hannichi shuzoku shugi to no toso* [The Fight against Anti-Japan Tribalism] (Tokyo: Bungei shunju, 2020).

60 See Akaishi Shin'ichiro, "Besuto seraa 'Hannichi shuzoku shugi' e no hanpatsu" [The Reaction to the Best-selling "Anti-Japan Tribalism"], *Bunshun online*, November 28, 2019.

61 See ibid.

62 Meredith Shaw, "Godzilla vs Pulgasari: Anti-Japanism and Anti-Communism as Dueling Antagonisms in South Korean Politics," *Journal of East Asian Studies* 22, no. 2 (July 2022): 224; see Akaishi, "Besuto seraa 'Hannichi shuzoku shugi' e no hanpatsu" (2019).

63 See Timothy W. Martin & Dasl Yoon, "Professor's 'Comfort-Women' Lecture Gets Him Indicted—And Sparks Debate on Academic Freedom," *Wall Street Journal*, August 21, 2021. A transcript of Lew's remarks in class appears in Nishioka, "Kankoku ni okeru gakumon no jiyu no kiki ni tsuite" (2022).

64 See "Uooru sutoriito jaaneru ni kansuru Ryu kyoju to media uocchi no hanno" [The Reactions of Professor Lew and MediaWatch to the Wall Street Journal], *Rekishi ninshiki mondai kenkyu kai*, August 23, 2021, harc.tokyo/?p=2275.

65 Email available upon request.

66 Email available upon request.

67 Nishioka, "Kankoku ni okeru gakumon no jiyu no kiki ni tsuite" (2022), 79.

68 Ibid.

69 Private email from Hwang Uiwon, MediaWatch, February 22, 2022, and August 6, 2023. More generally, see "'Hannichi' no kamen wo kabutta moto ianfu shien dantai" [The Support Organization for Former Comfort Women Wearing an "Anti-Japanese" Mask], March 22, 2014, http://blog.livedoor.jp/aryasarasvati/archives/37077764.html; "'Ianfu ha jihatsuteki na baishun ga sekai no joshiki'" ["The Standard Wisdom around the World Is That the Comfort Women Were Voluntary Prostitutes"], *Livedoor News*, March 24, 2018, available at http://news.livedoor.com/article/detail/14479996; "'Jitsuwa sono ki ga atte jugun shita'" ["They Followed the Army Because They Wanted To"], *Joong-Ang ilbo*, September 18, 2018, https://japanese.joins.com/article/233/245233.htm; "Kankoku no daigaku kyoju 'ianfu ha kyosei deha nai. Sono ki ga atta'" [Korean University Professor says "Comfort Women Weren't Coerced. They Knew What They Were Doing"], *Share News Japan*, November 16, 2018, https://snjpn.net/archives/7863.

70 See "Ji Man-Won shi 'nise no ianfu' ..." [Mr. Ji Man-Won "Fraudulent Comfort Women"...], *Joong-Ang ilbo*, April 14, 2005, https://japanese.joins.com/article/j_article.php?aid=62513&sectcode=400&servcode=400; "Gunji hyoronka no Ji Man-won ..." [The Military Commentator Ji Man-won ...], September 29, 2013, https://s.webry.info/sp/92971510.at.webry.info/201309/article_88.html.

71 Shin Min-jung, "Supreme Court Confirms 2-Year Sentence to Conservative Commentator for Defamatory Comments on Gwangju Uprising," *Hankyoreh*, January 13, 2023.

72 See Lee Tae-hee, "Professor Gets Prison for Insulting Comfort Women," *Korea Herald*, November 15, 2018; private email from Kenji Yoshida, MediaWatch, February 17, 2022, and from Hwang Uiwon, MediaWatch, February 22, 2022.

73 Lew Seok-choon, "Hensen wo kasaneta 'Ianfu shogen' no uragawa" [What Lies behind the "Comfort Women Testimonies" That Have Changed Multiple Times], *Shukan shincho*, June 2, 2022, at 44–48.

74 Ibid., 44.

CHAPTER 6—THE KOREAN COUNCIL

1 Shigemura Tomokazu, "Kita chosen no rachi, tero, kaku kaihatsu, yuji no kokusai kankei" [International Aspects of North Korea's Abductions, Terrorism, Nuclear Development, and Crises], *Waseda daigaku shakai anzen seisaku kenkyujo kiyo* 3 (2011): 181; Patrick M. Morgan, "Deterrence and System Management: The Case of North Korea," *Conflict Management and Peace Science* 23, no. 2 (Summer 2006): 123.

2 Shigemura Tomokazu, "Kita chosen no tero, joho kosaku senso to Nihon no anzen" [Japan's Security and North Korea's Terrorism and Misinformation War], *Waseda daigaku shakai anzen seisaku kenkyujo kiyo* 9 (2016); James T. Laney & Jason T. Shaplen, "How to Deal with North Korea," *Foreign Affairs* 82, no. 2 (March/April 2003): 16–30; see

generally Keishi cho, "Kitachosen ni yoru rachi yogi jian" [Cases with Suspicions of North Korean Abductions], September 21, 2021, https://www.keishicho.metro.tokyo.lg.jp/jiken_jiko/ichiran/ichiran_10/rachijian.html.

3 Ministry of Foreign Affairs of Japan, Kita chosen [North Korea] website, March 28, 2022, https://www.mofa.go.jp/mofaj/a_o/na/kp/page1w_000081.html.

4 Bak Sunjong, "Comfort Women Agitators as Agents of the North," *JAPAN Forward*, February 17, 2023, https://japan-forward.com/comfort-women-agitators-as-agents-of-the-north/.

5 Park Yu-ha, *Rekishi to mukiau* [Facing History] (Tokyo: Mainichi shimbun shuppan, 2022), 169.

6 Ibid., 169–70.

7 Meredith Shaw, "Godzilla vs Pulgasari: Anti-Japanism and Anti-Communism as Dueling Antagonisms in South Korean Politics," *Journal of East Asian Studies* 22, no. 2 (July 2022): 212.

8 Ibid., 213.

9 See Korea Institute of History (2016a), "'Comfort Women of the Empire' by Professor Park Yuha," April 30, 2016, http://scholarsinenglish.blogspot.com/2014/10/summary-of-professor-park-yuhas-book.html. This is from a website that summarized and translated Park Yu-ha's views in English.

10 Joseph Yi, "Confronting Korea's Censored Discourse on Comfort Women," *The Diplomat*, January 31, 2018.

11 See Korea Institute of History (2016a), "'Comfort Women of the Empire' by Professor Park Yuha."

12 See ibid.

13 See "Moto ianfu tachiga Kankoku Teishintai mondai…" [Former Comfort Women on the CDH issue…] *Bunshun online*, December 27, 2018.

14 Imanishi Hajime, "Kaihogo, Kankoku chishikijin no ayumi" [The Path of a South Korean Intellectual after Liberation] (Otaru shoka daigaku), *Shogaku token* 67 (2017): 244–45.

15 Akaishi Shin'ichiro (2020a), "Firipin no ianfu mondai…" [The Comfort Women Issue in the Philippines…], *Bunshun online*, June 29, 2020, https://bunshun.jp/articles/-/38632.

16 Akaishi Shin'ichiro (2020c), "'Okane wo ageru kara…'" ["We'll Pay You Money so ..."], *Bunshun online*, June 16, 2020, https://bunshun.jp/articles/-/38366.

17 See Korea Institute of History (2016a), "'Comfort Women of the Empire' by Professor Park Yuha." This is 61 out of 236 registered comfort women. See Nishioka Tsutomu (2020a), "Higaisha mo uso wo tsuku ..." [Victims Also Lie ...], part 3 (August 9, 2020), 96, https://salty-japan-net/2020/08/09/higaisyamo-usowotsuku-3_nishioka-tsutomu/; see also Akaishi (2020a, 2020c).

18 Akaishi (2020a).

19 Korea Institute of History (2016a), "'Comfort Women of the Empire' by Professor Park Yuha."

20 Akaishi (2020a).

21 See C. Sarah Soh, *The Comfort Women: Sexual Violence and Postcolonial Memory in Korea and Japan* (Chicago: University of Chicago Press, 2008), 101.

22 See Choe Sang-Hun, "Japan and South Korea Settle Dispute over Wartime 'Comfort Women,'" *New York Times*, December 28, 2015.

23 "Ianfu zo no seisakusha fufu ..." [The Couple Who Made the Comfort Women Statues ...]. *News Posuto Sebun*, March 7, 2017, https://www.news-postseven.com/archives/20170307_498048.html/2.

24 See Choe Kilsung, *Chosen shusshin no choba nin ga mita ianfu no shinjitsu* [The Truth about Comfort Women, as Seen by a Korean Receptionist] (Tokyo: Haato shuppan, 2017).

25 "Kankoku ga Nihon no shinrai wo ushinatta ..." [South Korea Lost the Trust of Japan ...], *Bunshun online*, May 14, 2022, https://www.jiji.com/jc/bunshun?id=54320; Park Yu-ha *Rekishi to mukiau* (2022), 157, notes that in 2015 alone, the Japanese Foreign Ministry contacted the comfort women and their associations about 15 times.

26 See Nishioka Tsutomu (2021), "Ianfu mondai wo kogi de furete ..." [Discussing the Comfort Women Problem in a Lecture ...], October 19, 2021, www.moralogy.jp/salon211019-1/.

27 See Korea Institute of History (2016a), "'Comfort Women of the Empire' by Professor Park Yuha."

28 See "Kankoku gekishin ..." [Massive Shock in South Korea ...], *Japan In-depth*, May 26, 2020.

29 "Teitaikyo no shotai" [The Truth about the Korean Council], May 2020, http://daishi100.cocolog-nifty.com/blog/2020/05/post-77ade9.html.

30 See "Kankoku gekishin ..." (2020).

31 See "Ianfu mondai: Nikkan ayumi yori wo bogai suru ..." [The Comfort Women Problem: Blocking Rapprochement between S. Korea and Japan ...], *MSN Sankei Nyusu*, September 23, 2012; "Kankoku gekishin ..." (2020).

32 See Kim Ji-yu, "Pyonyan de hannichi wo sakenda ..." [Shouting Anti-Japanese in Pyongyang ...], *Daily shincho*, June 23, 2020; Kubota Ruriko (2020a), "Oshu de kita supai to renkei ..." [Collaboration with North (Korean) Spy in Western Europe ...], *Sankei News*, May 30, 2020.

33 See Kubota Ruriko (2020b), "Giwaku zokushutsu no Yoon Mee-hyang shi ..." [Doubts Grow over Yoon Mee-hyang ...], *Sankei News*, May 23, 2020; Kim Ji-yu, "Pyonyan de hannichi wo sakenda ..." (2020); Ri Sotetsu, *Hannichi shuzoku no tabu* [The Taboos of Anti-Japan Tribalism] (Tokyo: Takarajima sha, 2020), 53.

34 Private correspondence from Hwang Uiwon, MediaWatch, January 25, 2022.

35 See Ri, *Hannichi* (2020), 112–13.

36 See Kubota (2020a); Ri, *Hannichi* (2020), 53.

37 Shaw, "Godzilla vs Pulgasari," 11.

38 Joshua Stanton, "The N.Y. Times, the Ningpo 12, Minbyun & Yoon Mee-hyang: The Story Behind the Story," *Free Korea*, June 8, 2020, https://freekorea.us/2020/06/the-n-y-times-the-ningpo-12-minbyun-yoon-mee-hyang-the-story-behind-the-story/.

39 See Nishioka (2021); Kubota (2020a); Ri, *Hannichi* (2020), 53–56.

40 Nishioka (2022).

41 Patrick Winn, "Why North Korean Peace Talks May Hinge on 12 Singing Waitresses," *The World*, September 15, 2017.

42 Ibid.; Joshua Stanton, "Minbyun's Frivolous Lawfare Terrorizes 12 Young N. Korean Refugees and Endangers Lives," *Free Korea*, July 5, 2016, https://freekorea.us/2016/07/minbyuns-frivolous-lawfare-terrorizes-12-young-n-korean-refugees-endangers-lives/; Stanton, "The N.Y. Times, the Ningpo 12 …."

43 Winn, "Why North Korean Peace Talks May Hinge on 12 Singing Waitresses."

44 Ibid.; Stanton, "The N.Y. Times, the Ningpo 12 …."

45 Stanton, "Minbyun's Frivolous Lawfare."

46 Ibid.

47 Stanton, "The N.Y. Times, the Ningpo 12 …."

48 Stanton, "Minbyun's Frivolous Lawfare"; Stanton, "The N.Y. Times, the Ningpo 12 …"; "Minbyun Efforts May Be More Harm than Help for Defector Group," *Daily NK*, June 28, 2016, https://www.dailynk.com/minbyun-efforts-may-be-more-harm-t/; J.H. Ahn, "S. Korean Lawyers to Again Request Meeting with 12 Restaurant-worker Defectors," *NK News*, June 19, 2017, https://www.nknews.org/2017/06/s-korean-lawyers-to-again-request-meeting-with-12-restaurant-worker-defectors/.

49 Stanton, "Minbyun's Frivolous Lawfare."

50 Stanton, "The N.Y. Times, the Ningpo 12 …."

51 See "Dappokusha ni kikoku susumeru ..." [Encouraging Refugees from the North to Return ...], *Asahi shimbun*, May 23, 2020; Ri, *Hannichi* (2020), 113–15.

52 Nishioka (2020a).

53 Nishioka Tsutomu (2020b), "Kankoku no ianfu undo no 'naifun'" [The "Internal Dispute" in the Comfort Women Movement], *Rekishi ninshiki mondai kenkyu* 7 (2020), 107. The revolutionary anthem was probably this: https://www.youtube.com/watch?v=Usi-YZH5gWw.

54 Nishioka (2020b), 107. See "Dappokusha ni kikoku susumeru ..." [Encouraging Refugees from the North to Return ...], *Asahi shimbun*, May 23, 2020; Ri, *Hannichi* (2020), 113–15; Stanton, "Minbyun's Frivolous Lawfare"; Stanton, "The N.Y. Times, the Ningpo 12 …."

55 Nishioka (2020a); "Kankoku gekishin …" (2020).

56 See Soh, *The Comfort Women* (2008), 12–13, 98–100; Keith Howard, ed., *True Stories of the Korean Comfort Women* (London: Cassell, 1995), 89; Joseph Yi, "Confronting Korea's Censored Discourse on Comfort Women," *The Diplomat*, January 31, 2018; Joseph Yi, "Illiberal Means for Liberal Ends: Low-Road Challenge to Public Discourse and International

Relations," APSA Preprints, 2020, https://preprints.apsanet.org/engage/apsa/article-details/5f52aa1a9277460012015626; Ikuhiko Hata, *Comfort Women and Sex in the Battle Zone*, trans. Jason Michael Morgan (Lanham, MD: Hamilton Books, 2018), 235.

57 See "Moto 'ianfu' e hosho wo" [Compensation for Former "Comfort Women"], *Akahata*, June 26, 2002; Hata, *Comfort Women* (2018), 235.

58 Martin Fackler, "No Apology for Sex Slavery, Japan's Prime Minister Says," *New York Times*, March 6, 2007; see Soh, *The Comfort Women*, 100–101; *Protecting the Human Rights of Comfort Women: Hearing before the Subcommittee on Asia, the Pacific, and the Global Environment, of the Committee of Foreign Affairs, U.S. House of Representatives*, 110th Cong., February 15, 2007, at 17; Hata, *Comfort Women* (2018), 236.

59 See Ri, *Hannichi* (2020), 88–103 (Kitamura, author).

60 Ibid., 122–26 (Kitamura).

61 For the financial data, see Nishioka (2020b), 98.

62 Ibid., 98–102.

63 See Ri, *Hannichi* (2020), 99; Nishioka (2020b), 101–2.

64 See Yamaoka Tetsuhide, "Ianfu harumoni ..." [The Comfort Women Grandmothers ...], *Gekkan Hanada purasu*, May 26, 2020; Murotani Katsumi, "Kihonteki na daigimon" [A Basic, Major Doubt], Zakzak (Yukan Fuji), June 11, 2020. Lee herself explained that she began the conversation by stating that she was calling on behalf of her "friend" because she hesitated to describe herself as a comfort woman at the outset in a conversation with someone she had not met. Nishioka (2020a), 109 n.2, otherwise a strong critic of Lee, finds this credible.

65 "Moto ianfu 'zettai ni yurusenai'" [Former Comfort Woman "It's Absolutely Unforgivable"], *Asahi shimbun*, May 26, 2020, at 11.

66 Nishioka (2020b), 102–6.

67 Nishioka Tsutomu (2020c), "Saikin no Kankoku no anchihannichi no ugoki ni tsuite" [Regarding the Recent Anti-Anti-Japanese Movement in South Korea], *Rekishi ninshiki mondai kenkyu* (2020): 83.

68 Nishioka (2020b), 103–5.

69 Ibid., 105. Hwang contacted Suk-Gersen at the time she was writing her *New Yorker* (2021) article purporting to be "seeking the true story of the comfort women." He warned her that Lee did not tell the truth. Suk-Gersen chose to dismiss his warning as coming from what she described in her article as "a small far-right fringe group." For purposes of her Harvard Law School talk, Lee apparently claimed to have been "conscripted as a comfort woman at fifteen." Personal correspondence with Hwang Uiwon, February 27, 2022.

70 Nishioka (2020b), 103.

CHAPTER 7—MAKING SENSE OF THE CANCELING

1 Adapted (not directly quoted) from Daphne du Maurier, *Rebecca* (1938).

2 Paula R. Curtis, @paularcurtis, Twitter, June 1, 2022.

3 David Ambaras, Twitter, August 2, 2022.

4 Dante Alighieri, *The Divine Comedy*, trans. A. S. Kline (2000), *Purgatorio*, Canto XXIII:81 (Forese Donati).

5 J. Mark Ramseyer, "Recovering the Truth About the Comfort Women," *JAPAN Forward*, January 12, 2021, https://japan-forward.com/recovering-the-truth-about-the-comfort-women/.

6 "Harvard Law School professor advocating war crimes of sexual slavery?" Change.org, https://www.change.org/p/harvard-law-school-professor-advocating-war-crimes-of-sexual-slavery.

7 Zaisan oyobi seikyu ken ni kansuru mondai no kaiketsu narabi ni keizai kyoryoku ni kansuru Nihon koku to Dai kan minkoku to no aida no kyotei [Agreement between Japan and the Republic of Korea concerning the Economic Cooperation and the Resolution of Problems Involving Property and Claims], Treaty No. 27, 1965.

8 J. Mark Ramseyer, "Comfort Women: The Economics of the Contracts and the Politics of the Dispute," February 3, 2020, https://papers.ssrn.com/sol3/papers.cfm?abstract_id=3822439.

9 Amy Stanley, @astanley711, Twitter, June 16, 2021.

10 Stanley, Twitter, June 7, 2022.

11 Stanley, Twitter, June 29, 2022.

12 Stanley, Twitter, November 7, 2022.

13 Jesus Falcis, @jesusfalcis, Twitter, July 30, 2022.

14 Stanley, Twitter, August 15, 2022.

15 U.S. Office of War Information, Japanese Prisoner of War Interrogation Report No. 49, October 1, 1944, in Josei no tameno Ajia heiwa kokumin kikin, ed., *Seifu chosa: "Jugun ianfu" kankei shiryo shusei* [Government Investigation: Documents Relating to the "Military Comfort Women"] (Tokyo: Ryukei shosha, 1998), 5:203–5.

16 Louise Young, "Past and Present in Japanese Historiography: Four Versions of Presentism," *Modern Intellectual History*, June 21, 2022, https://www.cambridge.org/core/journals/modern-intellectual-history/article/past-and-present-in-japanese-historiography-four-versions-of-presentism/A29E2199354BDD896F1EAB42B60B9AC1.

17 Arirang News Center, "Harvard Law Professor's 'Comfort Women' Article: Fellow Scholars Call It 'Fake News,'" February 16, 2021, https://www.youtube.com/watch?v=fxixpFncCeg.

18 Hiromu Nagahara, @HiromuNagahara, Twitter, July 1, 2022.

19 Sayaka Chatani, @SayakaChatani, Twitter, July 1, 2022.

20 Curtis, Twitter, July 1, 2022.

21 Timothy Amos, Maren Ehlers, Anne McKnight, David Ambaras & Ian Neary, "Doing Violence to Buraku History: J. Mark Ramseyer's Dangerous Inventions," *Asia-Pacific Journal: Japan Focus* 19, iss. 9, no. 9 (May 1, 2021) (quoting Freedman & Nottage).

22 Ambaras, Twitter, July 1, 2022.

23 Curtis, Twitter, July 1, 2022.

24 Priya Chand, Twitter, July 1, 2022.

25 Sharon Domier, @SharonDomier, Twitter, July 1, 2022 (italics added).

26 James H. Sweet, "Is History History?" *Perspectives on History*, August 17, 2022.

27 Geoffrey R. Stone et al., *Report of the Committee on Freedom of Expression*, University of Chicago, 2014, https://provost.uchicago.edu/sites/default/files/documents/reports/FOECommitteeReport.pdf.

28 Priya Satia, "The Presentist Trap," *Perspectives on History*, September 7, 2022.

29 Katherine H. S. Moon, *Sex Among Allies: Military Prostitution in U.S.-Korea Relations* (New York: Columbia University Press, 1997), chap. 2; Tim Shorrock, "Welcome to the Monkey House: Confronting the Ugly Legacy of Military Prostitution in South Korea," *New Republic*, December 2, 2019.

30 Luke Burgis, "Why Everyone Wants the Same Things," *Common Sense with Bari Weiss*, November 28, 2022.

31 Mark Bauerlein, "Why Is Princeton Silent?" *American Greatness*, June 6, 2022. Emphasis in the original.

32 Sabrina Rubin Erdely, "A Rape on Campus: A Brutal Assault and Struggle for Justice at UVA," *Rolling Stone*, November 19, 2014, archived at http://web.archive.org/web/20141119200349/http:/www.rollingstone.com/culture/features/a-rape-on-campus- 20141119.

33 Doug Mataconis, "Rolling Stone's Botched Rape Story: How Bad Journalism Happens," *Christian Science Monitor*, April 6, 2015, https://www.csmonitor.com/USA/Politics/Politics-Voices/2015/0406/Rolling-Stone-s-botched-rape-story-how-bad-journalism-happens.

34 Ibid.

35 Sheila Coronel, Steve Coll & Derek Kravitz, "Rolling Stone and UVA: The Columbia University Graduate School of Journalism Report," *Rolling Stone*, April 5, 2015.

36 Ravi Somaiya, "Rolling Stone Article on Rape at University of Virginia Failed All Basics, Report Says," *New York Times*, April 5, 2015.

37 Freddie deBoer, "That One Side Would Like to Utterly Destroy the Other Side Seems Significant, To Me," Freddie deBoer Substack, October 11, 2021, https://freddiedeboer.substack.com/p/that-one-side-would-like-to-utterly.

38 Larry Rohter, "Tarnished Laureate: A Special Report," *New York Times*, December 15, 1998.

39 Ibid.

40 Ibid.

41 Ibid.

42 David Stoll, "Life Story as Mythopoesis," *Anthropology Newsletter*, April 1998, 9.

43 Robert Strauss, "Truth and Consequences," *Stanford Magazine*, May/June 1999.

44 David Stoll, *Rigoberta Menchú and the Story of All Poor Guatemalans*, expanded ed. (Boulder: Westview, 2008).

45 David Stoll, "Rigoberta Menchú," Letter to the Editor, *PMLA* 117, no. 1 (January 2002), 125.

46 Ibid., 124.

47 Mary Louise Pratt, "*I, Rigoberta Menchú* and the 'Culture Wars,'" in *The Rigoberta Menchú Controversy*, ed. Arturo Arias (Minneapolis: University of Minnesota Press, 2001), 29, 45–46.

48 Quoted in Mark Horowitz, William Yaworsky & Kenneth Kickham, "Anthropology's Science Wars," *Current Anthropology* 60, no. 5 (October 2019): 676.

49 Pratt, "*I, Rigoberta Menchú* and the 'Culture Wars,'" 41.

50 Carol A. Smith, "Why Write an Expose of Rigoberta Menchú?" in *The Rigoberta Menchú Controversy*, ed. Arias, 151–52.

51 Stoll, *Rigoberta Menchú and the Story of All Poor Guatemalans*, chap. 1.

52 David Stoll, "Moral Authority, Permission, and Deference in Latin American Studies," unpublished (n.d.), 2.

53 Smith, "Why Write an Expose of Rigoberta Menchú?" 151.

54 Stoll, "Moral Authority, Permission, and Deference in Latin American Studies."

55 Smith, "Why Write an Expose of Rigoberta Menchú?" 152.

56 Stanley, Twitter, February 16, 2021.

57 Megan Kate Nelson, Twitter, February 23, 2021.

58 Comfort Women Justice Coalition, "Women's March, #MeToo and the 'Comfort Women'—All Fighting for Justice in 2018," January 22, 2018, https://remembercomfortwomen.org/womens-march-metoo-and-the-comfort-women-all-fighting-for-justice-in-2018/.

59 Pamela Thoma, "Cultural Autobiography, Testimonial, and Asian American Transnational Feminist Coalition in the 'Comfort Women of World War II' Conference," *Frontiers* 21, nos. 1/2 (2000): 36.

60 Hyunah Yang, "Revisiting the Issue of Korean 'Military Comfort Women': The Question of Truth and Positionality," *Positions* 5, no. 1 (Spring 1997): 51–72.

61 See Stella Morabito, *The Weaponization of Loneliness: How Tyrants Stoke Our Fear of Isolation to Silence, Divide, and Conquer* (New York: Bombardier Press, 2022).

62 Sayaka Chatani, "How to Address the Racism at the Heart of Japan–South Korea Tensions," Sayaka Chatani blog, January 25, 2023, https://www.sayakachatani.com/post/how-to-address-the-racism-at-the-heart-of-japan-south-korea-tensions.

63 David Ambaras, @dambaras@mastodon.online, Mastodon, January 18, 2023.

64 Curtis, Twitter, April 15, 2023.

65 Tessa Morris-Suzuki, "Unwriting the Wrongs: History, Trauma and Memories of Violence in Germany and Japan," in *Routledge Handbook*

of Trauma in East Asia, ed. Tina Burrett & Jeff Kingston (London: Routledge, 2023), 49–61.

66 Stanley, Twitter, September 14, 2022.

67 Stanley, Twitter, February 12, 2023.

68 Oscar Wilde, "De Profundis," https://www.online-literature.com/wilde/1306/.

69 Mark Williams, "From Out of the Depths: Shimao Toshio's Literary Response to Adversity," in *Handbook of Japanese Christian Writers*, ed Mark Williams et al. (Tokyo: MHM Ltd., 2022), 170.

70 Wilde, "De Profundis."

CHAPTER 8—ACADEMIC FREEDOM

1 Chelsea Szendi Schieder, @SzendiChelsea, Twitter, April 7, 2021.

2 Donald G. McNeil, Jr., "NYTimes Peru N-Word," 4 parts, March 1, 2021, https://donaldgmcneiljr1954.medium.com/nytimes-peru-n-word-part-one-introduction-57eb6a3e0d95.

3 Paula R. Curtis, @paularcurtis, Twitter, April 22, 2022.

4 Curtis, Twitter, June 2, 2022.

5 Statement by Al Roth and Paul Milgrom, February 27, 2021, http://chwe.net/irle/roth_milgrom.pdf.

6 Tessa Morris-Suzuki, "Research Integrity in the Age of 'Fake News': A Challenge to the Humanities," Australian Academy of the Humanities, July 2022.

7 Amy Stanley, @astanley711, Twitter, August 14, 2022.

8 Stanley, Twitter, February 20, 2021.

9 Curtis, Twitter, April 2, 2022.

10 Peipei Qiu, *Chinese Comfort Women: Testimonies from Imperial Japan's Sex Slaves* (Oxford: Oxford University Press, 2014).

11 Sayaka Chatani, @SayakaChatani, Twitter, June 4, 2022.

12 Andrew Gordon, *A Modern History of Japan*, 4th ed. (Oxford: Oxford University Press, 2020), 231.

13 Tessa Morris-Suzuki, "Unwriting the Wrongs: History, Trauma and Memories of Violence in Germany and Japan," in *Routledge Handbook of Trauma in East Asia*, ed. Tina Burrett & Jeff Kingston (London: Routledge, 2023), 49–61.

14 For a line-by-line examination of the Quintet's claims, see J. Mark Ramseyer, "Contracting for Sex in the Pacific War: A Response to My Critics," Harvard John M. Olin DP 1075, January 4, 2022, SSRN WP 4000145, https://papers.ssrn.com/sol3/papers.cfm?abstract_id=4000145.

15 Chatani, Twitter, October 10, 2021.

16 David Ambaras, Twitter, October 10, 2021.

17 Morris-Suzuki, "Research Integrity in the Age of 'Fake News.'"

18 David Ambaras, email to Joseph Yi, May 30, 2022.

19 Shaun O'Dwyer, @shaunodwyer, Twitter, June 28, 2022.

20 Ambaras, Twitter, June 28, 2022.

21 Chatani, Twitter, June 3, 2023.

22 Curtis, Twitter, June 6, 2023.

23 Stanley, Twitter, June 10, 2023.

24 Stanley, Twitter, June 3, 2023.

25 Bruce Gilley, "The Case for Colonialism," republished in *Academic Questions* 31 (Summer 2018): 167–85.

26 Bruce Gilley, *The Last Imperialist: Sir Alan Burns' Epic Defense of the British Empire* (Washington: Regnery Gateway, 2021); Bruce Gilley, "The Case for Colonialism: A Response to My Critics," *Academic Questions* 35 (Spring 2022): 89–126; Bruce Gilley, "Taking Power in the Academy," *First Things*, March 2020; Helen Andrews, "Rule, Britannia!" *Claremont Review of Books*, Winter 2021/22; Stephen Kershnar, "British Imperialism, the Better Alternative," *Academic Questions* 35 (Spring 2022): 155–58; Colleen Flaherty, "Is Retraction the New Rebuttal?" *Inside Higher Ed*, September 18, 2017; Joshua Moufawad-Paul, "Against Bruce Gilley's Colonial Apologetics," Change.org, September 27, 2020, https://www.change.org/p/academics-against-bruce-gilley-s-colonial-apologetics.

27 The attacks on Ramseyer appear elsewhere in this book; the attacks on Gilley appear in the sources cited above.

28 George J. Stigler, "The Conference Handbook," *Journal of Political Economy* 85, no. 2 (1977): 441–43.

29 Alexis Dudden, March 10, 2021, https://news.v.daum.net/v/20210310213931702. Noted as well in "Tokyo bakuhatsubutsu tero jiken (Daden joshi ni yoru nisehata sakusen)" [Tokyo Terrorist Bombing Incident (Dudden's Fake Flag Strategy], https://dekabudou2.fc2.net/e/131.

30 Stanley, Twitter, April 25, 2022.

31 Hannah Shepherd, @hannahjshepherd, Twitter, April 25, 2022.

32 Geoffrey R. Stone et al., *Report of the Committee on Freedom of Expression*, University of Chicago, 2014, https://provost.uchicago.edu/sites/default/files/documents/reports/FOECommitteeReport.pdf.

33 Joshua T. Katz, "A Declaration of Independence by a Princeton Professor," *Quillette*, July 8, 2020.

34 Princeton Faculty Letter to President Eisgruber, Provost Prentice, Deans Kulkarni and Dolan, Vice President for Campus Life Calhoun, and members of the Princeton Cabinet, July 4, 2020, https://docs.google.com/forms/d/e/1FAIpQLSfPmfeDKBi25_7rUTKkhZ3cyMICQicp05ReVaeBpEdYUCkyIA/viewform?ref=quillette.com.

35 Quillette Editorial Board, "The Disgraceful Firing of Joshua T. Katz," *Quillette*, May 26, 2022.

36 For Katz's statement about this, see Joshua T. Katz, "My Confessions," *First Things*, October 2021.

37 See generally Eric Rasmusen Twitter Cancelling Page, May 19, 2023, https://www.rasmusen.org/special/2019kerfuffle/.

38 Laura Kipnis, "Why Are Scholars Such Snitches?" *Chronicle of Higher Education*, March 17, 2022.

39 Shakespeare, *Othello*, 2.1.315–19.

40 Kipnis, "Why Are Scholars Such Snitches?"

41 Jack Stripling, "The Professor Is Canceled. Now What?" *Washington Post*, June 21, 2023.

42 Explicitly confirmed by Morris-Suzuki herself in "Unwriting the Wrongs."

43 Confirmed by Morris-Suzuki herself in "Unwriting the Wrongs."

44 Retraction for Johnson et al., "Officer Characteristics and Racial Disparities in Fatal Officer-Involved Shootings," *PNAS* 117 (2020): 18130. See D. J. Johnson, T. Tress, N. Burkel, C. Taylor & J. Cesario, "Officer Characteristics and Racial Disparities in Fatal Officer-Involved Shootings," *PNAS*, 116 (2019): 15877–15882.

45 "Retraction of Paper on Police Killings and Race Not Due to '"Mob" Pressure' or 'Distaste for the Political Views of People Citing the Work Approvingly,' Say Authors," *Retraction Watch*, July 8, 2020; Jillian Kay Melchior, "A Twitter Mob Takes Down an Administrator at Michigan State," *Wall Steet Journal*, June 25, 2020.

46 Heather Mac Donald, "I Cited Their Study, So They Disavowed It," *Wall Street Journal*, July 8, 2020.

47 Melchior, "A Twitter Mob Takes Down an Administrator at Michigan State."

48 Majka Burhardt, "How Do We Manage Fear When Our Friends Keep On Dying?" *Climbing*, June 12, 2023, https://www.climbing.com/people/guide-on-fear-and-death-in-climbing/.

49 Johann Wolfgang von Goethe, "On Commitment," https://medium.com/market-force/goethe-on-commitment-d94eb8be4651.

50 David French, "The Moral Center Is Fighting Back on Elite College Campuses," *New York Times*, April 16, 2023.

EPILOGUE

1 Hyonhee Shin, "South Korea Court Convicts 'Comfort Women' Activist of Embezzling Donations," *Japan Today*, February 11, 2023. In September 2023, Yoon's conviction was upheld.

2 Kim Byungheon, "Nise ianfu ..." [Fake Comfort Woman ...], Nadeshiko Action, March 2, 2023.

3 "Moto chuei kita chosen koshi no Tae Yon-ho ..." [Former North Korean Diplomat to the U.K. Tae Yong-ho ...], *Chosun online*, February 15, 2023.

4 Hannah Shepherd, @hannahjshepherd, Twitter, November 3, 2022; Alec Karakatsanis, @equalityAlec, Twitter, November 3, 2022.

5 Amy Stanley, @astanley711, Twitter, June 7, 2022.

6 Stanley, Twitter, March 24, 2023.

7 Alexandra F. Levy, "Trolling History: Social Media Harassment from Abroad," *Perspectives on History*, February 14, 2022 (quoting Stanley).

8 Stanley, Twitter, February 20, 2023.

9 Stanley, Twitter, March 3, 2021.

10 Stanley, Twitter, February 21, 2021.

11 Mark Ravina, @MarkRavina, Twitter, February 23, 2021; Stanley, Twitter, February 23, 2021.

12 Ahmet Stuhrmann Strong Type, @wae2eub, Twitter, November 15, 2021.

13 Ahmet Stuhrmann Strong Type, Twitter, November 16, 2021.

14 Amy Stanley, "Nazi Tactics," October 16, 2021, https://www.amy-stanley.com/blog-1.

15 Stanley, Twitter, February 23, 2023.

16 Ibid.

17 Stanley, Twitter, date unclear, reproduced at https://together.com/li/2109659?page=3.

18 Amy Stanley, "On Contract," March 18, 2021, https://www.amy-stanley.com/blog-1/on-contract.

19 Stanley, Twitter, November 14, 2021.

20 Sayaka Chatani, @SayakaChatani, Twitter, February 19, 2021.

21 Chelsea Szendi Schieder, @SzendiChelsea, Twitter, February 25, 2021; Stanley, Twitter, February 25, 2021.

22 Stanley, Twitter, February 23, 2023.

23 Ibid.

24 Bae Yeonhong, "Jugun ianfu mondai no genten (jo)" [The Source of the Military Comfort Women Problem (I)], https://beh3.hatenablog.com/entry/2021/10/26/163853. Bae discusses both the murder of some comfort women by the Japanese army at the end of the war, and the camaraderie between the soldiers and the comfort women.

25 Yoshimi Yoshiaki, *Jugun ianfu* [Comfort Women of the Military] (Tokyo: Iwanami shoten, 1995), 98. Neither does Younghoon Rhee believe Mun's account. See Younghoon Rhee, ed., *Hannichi shuzoku shugi* [Anti-Japan Tribalism] (Tokyo: Bungei shunju, 2019), 277; Younghoon Rhee, ed., *Hannichi shuzoku shugi to no toso* [The Fight against Anti-Japan Tribalism] (Tokyo: Bungei shunju, 2020), 43.

INDEX